MW01252569

HEALT]

IN AUSTRALIA

AND

NEW ZEALAND

ABBY L. BLOOM

OXFORD
UNIVERSITY PRESS

OXFORD

UNIVERSITY PRESS

253 Normanby Road, South Melbourne, Australia

Oxford University Press is a department of the University of Oxford. It furthers
the University's objective of excellence in research, scholarship, and education
by publishing worldwide in

Oxford New York

Athens Auckland Bangkok Bogotá Buenos Aires Calcutta Cape Town Chennai
Dar es Salaam Delhi Florence Hong Kong Istanbul Karachi Kuala Lumpur
Madrid Melbourne Mexico City Mumbai Nairobi Paris Port Moresby São Paulo
Singapore Taipei Tokyo Toronto Warsaw

with associated companies in Berlin Ibadan

OXFORD is a trade mark of Oxford University Press
in the UK and in certain other countries

National Library of Australia
Cataloguing-in-Publication data:

Health reform in Australia and New Zealand.

Bibliography.
Includes index.
ISBN 0 19 550860 2.

1. Health care reform—Australia. 2. Health care reform—New Zealand.
3. Medical policy—Australia. 4. Medical policy—New Zealand. I. Bloom, Abby L.

362.10993

Edited by Venetia Somerset
Text designed by Derrick I. Stone Design
Cover designed by Modern Art Production Group
Typeset by Solo Typesetting, South Australia
Printed through Bookpac Production Services, Singapore

Contents

Part IV   The New Wave of Health Sector Reform

Contributors

Jennifer Alexander is currently CEO and member of the board of directors of the Australian and New Zealand Health Management Network (ANZHMN), which is an initiative of the Australian Health Ministers' Advisory Council (AHMAC) and the New Zealand Ministry for Health. Dr Alexander has extensive experience in health management, and management and organisational development, with experience in Australia, New Zealand, Asia, the UK, Europe and the USA. Her qualifications include degrees in medicine, health planning and commerce. She holds a fellowship in public health medicine. She was president of the Royal Australasian College of Medical Administrators, and a member of the NSW Medical Board for 10 years.

Abby Bloom, MPH, PhD, is a specialist in health policy and health reform. She has spent the past fifteen years in Australia as an executive and adviser in the health industry, the most recent eight as managing director of a specialist consulting firm, Health Innovations International in Sydney. Dr Bloom has worked on health programs in twenty countries for private industry, governments, and international organisations, including the World Bank. Between 1975 and 1984 she managed primary health and population projects and was senior health policy adviser with the US Agency for International Development. Dr Bloom has been a lecturer at Yale and Sydney universities, and is currently a fellow of the Australian International Health Institute of the University of Melbourne.

Simon Corden is assistant commissioner, Productivity Commission. Currently he is manager of the Secretariat of the Review of Commonwealth/State Service Provision which has published: *Report on Government Services*, 1999 (containing information on the performance across Australia of twelve key government services, including health, aged care and disability services); *Implementing Reforms in Government Services*, 1998; and *Reforms in Government Service Delivery*, 1997, (which included case studies on implementing competitive tendering and contracting for public hospital services, offering direct consumer funding and client choice in disability services, and casemix funding for public hospitals).

Philip Davies is deputy director-general (policy) in New Zealand's Ministry of Health. He heads a team of eighty staff which is responsible for providing advice on the overall policy direction and priorities for health. This includes advice on funding levels, the regulatory framework for health and disability services, and intersectoral initiatives for improved health and independence. Prior to taking up his present position Philip worked for more than fourteen years as a management consultant specialising in health care policy, management and finance. In that capacity he was involved in health reforms in both the UK and New Zealand. He also worked for a variety of health sector clients in developed and developing countries. Philip holds degrees in mathematics and operational research. He has also written and spoken widely on aspects of health policy and health reform.

Stephen Duckett is professor of health policy and dean of the faculty of health sciences at La Trobe University, Bundoora. From 1994 to March 1996 he was secretary of the Commonwealth Department of Human Services and Health. From 1983 to 1993, Professor Duckett held various operational and policy positions in the Victorian Department of Health and Community Services and its predecessors, including that of regional director of the Western Metropolitan Region and director of acute health services.

Mary Foley is a senior executive in Mayne Nickless Limited, which is the largest private health care organisation in Australia through its health care group, Health Care of Australia. Mary's background includes sixteen years in public policy at federal and state government level. Mary has held positions as deputy head of the New South Wales Department of Health and as head of the Office of Policy before joining the private sector in 1992. Mary is also a member of the board of the University of Western Sydney and chairman of the University's finance committee.

Michael Frommer MB BS, D ObstRCOG, MPH, FAFPHM, FAFOM is currently deputy director of the Australian Centre for Effective Healthcare, a new unit in the University of Sydney's department of public health and community medicine dedicated to the implementation of research-based knowledge in all aspects of health care. Before joining the Centre, he was director of research and development in the New South Wales Health Department, with responsibility for R & D policy and funding in the NSW health system. He also served as chief executive officer of the NSW Cancer Council. His background is in medical epidemiology, public health medicine, and occupational health and safety.

Rhonda Galbally is managing director of the University of Melbourne's Australian International Health Institute (AIHI). The AIHI offers training modules, consultancy and advisory services to governments, development banks and corporations for strategic planning, the development of organisational infrastructure, financing models and program planning for health sector development and reform, and partnering countries such as Thailand, Indonesia and South Africa for health development. Rhonda is the founding CEO of VicHealth and is a trustee of the Lance Reichstein Charitable Foundation. Rhonda is a member of the WHO Working Groups on Tobacco and Health and Environmental Factors in Disablement.

Philip Hagan is an economist/policy adviser who has worked Australian governments at both the Commonwealth and state levels. During his career, he has been involved in microeconomic reform initiatives across most sectors of the Australian economy, as well as working on individual projects (e.g. the proposed Alice Springs to Darwin railway). More recently, his focus has been on reforms to the health care system. He has bachelor degrees in science and economics, and a masters degree in business admin-istration. His current academic appointments include adjunct associate pro-fessor at the University of the Northern Territory, and adjunct research fellow at Flinders University.

Jane Hall is the founding director of the Centre for Health Economics Research and Evaluation, and a medical foundation fellow and associate professor in the department of public health and community medicine at the University of Sydney. Her research includes economic evaluation studies in many areas of health services and public health and she has published extensively on methods of economics evaluation. Jane is involved in health policy and planning issues and has served on numerous advisory committees and working parties. She is a member of the NSW Health Economics Reform Advisory Committee and has recently been appointed to the Australian Medical Workforce Advisory Committee. She is a member of the Co-ordinating Committee for the Commonwealth Fund International Program in Health Policy.

Don Hindle is visiting professor in the School of Health Services Manage-ment at the University of New South Wales. He is an applied math-ematician by background, but has spent most of his working life in the health sector. This included periods in the United States, Europe, and Australia, and over a decade in the third world.

Cathy King is a trained social worker and has worked with children, young people, and families in the non-government welfare sector in rural Victoria and in the United Kingdom. She also worked as a social policy researcher and adviser under the Keating Labor government and as a policy adviser for the Australian New Zealand Food Authority. Cathy has a masters degree in public policy, and is currently working within the Commonwealth Department of Health and Aged Care.

Helen Lapsley is an economist in the school of health services management at the University of New South Wales. She teaches postgraduate courses in health economics and quality assurance. She has been a member and a chairperson of a number of Commonwealth and state government committees, reviews and task forces, and of committees of the National Health and Medical Research Council. Helen is an author and co-author of books, papers and reports addressing issues relating to health services cost, quality and health economics, and has undertaken consultancies on these topics in Australia and internationally.

Vivian Lin has worked in public health policy and planning in New South Wales and Victoria as well as at the National Occupational Health and Safety Commission in Australia, and in the United States. She has a bachelor of arts degree in biology and political science from Yale University and a masters degree and a doctorate in public health from the University of California, Berkeley. She has undertaken research in Singapore and Malaysia and maintains an international interest through consultancy for the World Bank in China. Vivian is presently executive officer of the National Public Health Partnership and holds adjunct appointments at LaTrobe University and Deakin University.

Jenny Luxmoore is an assistant director in the social infrastructure branch of the Productivity Commission. This branch of the Commission is the Secretariat for the Steering Committee for the Review of Commonwealth/State Service Provision—a cooperative Australian government exercise that aims to facilitate well-informed judgements and sound public policy by developing and publishing comparable data on the performance of government services. Jenny is the secretariat member for the health working group and has oversight for the 'Health' section of the Report on Government Services (health delivery mechanisms and health management issues). She has a bachelor of economics (honours) degree from the University of Queensland.

Keith Lyon FCPA FAIM is deputy president of the Defense Housing Authority of Australia. One of Keith's roles has been to oversee the divestment of the Repatriation Commission's health institutions (acute, sub-acute and psychiatric hospitals, and artificial-limb manufacturing facilities), and the development of a strong, holistic health-purchasing organisation. Other roles have included strategic overseeing of the modernisation of the Department of Veterans' Affairs' compensation business, and the outsourcing of a range of corporate activities, including all IT infrastructure. Before going to the Veterans' Affairs' portfolio, Keith was a deputy secretary in the Territories' portfolio (primarily responsible for developing the financial and administrative arrangements for a self-governing Canberra).

John McCallum BEcon Hons Psych (UofQ), MPhil, DPhil (Oxon) is dean, faculty of health, University of Western Sydney, Macarthur. He has authored numerous books and papers on ageing and health services. He has validated in Australia a range of self-report outcome measures including the SF-36, the CESD, and the enablement index and undertaken research in the USA, the UK, Japan, China, and ASEAN countries. Currently he directs the Australia–Japan Study of Community Care for Older People and, with Associate Professor Simons, the Dubbo Study of the Health of the Elderly. He is an active consultant to governments in Australia.

Laurence Malcolm is professor emeritus of the University of Otago and consultant in health services in Aotearoa Health, a private consultancy company working with a range of agencies in New Zealand. For ten years until 1995 he was professor of community health at the Wellington school of medicine. From 1957 to 1974 he worked in a variety of clinical and management positions in Papua New Guinea. He has been closely involved in a variety of roles with WHO including being chairman of the Western Pacific Advisory Committee and a member of the Global Advisory Committee on Health Research.

Nigel D. Millar, MB., BS, MRCP, FRACP, qualified at Newcastle-upon-Tyne, UK, in 1980. He trained in general medicine and geriatrics in Sunderland, Bristol and Exeter in the UK. Dr Millar is currently clinical director of older persons' health, and geriatrician at the Princess Margaret Hospital, and general physician at Christchurch Hospital.

Rod Perkins is a senior lecturer in health management at the University of Auckland. Until 1993 he was a manager in the New Zealand health system. He graduated BDS before going to graduate school in the USA. He is currently enrolled in the UNSW PhD program.

Andrew Podger is the secretary of the Commonwealth Department of Health and Family Services of Australia. His responsibilities include the management of Australia's health financing system; Medicare; public health and medical research; primary health care for Aboriginal and Torres Strait Islander people; and services for the aged. He has previously worked in a range of other Commonwealth departments, working on various areas of social policy and financial management. He is also president of the ACT Division of the Institute of Public Administration of Australia, and a former chairman of the OECD Working Party on Social Policy.

Karen Poutasi is director-general and chief executive of the Ministry of Health, New Zealand. She is a medical graduate of Otago University, New Zealand. Her area of specialisation is public health medicine and she holds both Otago and Harvard management qualifications. Karen has worked for nearly twenty years in health care management, holding positions throughout New Zealand.

George Rubin MB,BS, FRACP, FACE, FACPM is foundation director of the Australian Centre for Effective Health Care, and professor of public health and community medicine in the University of Sydney at Westmead Hospital. The centre is a new unit dedicated to the implementation of research-based knowledge in all aspects of health care. He was chief health officer of New South Wales from 1994 to 1997 and, before that, director of epidemiology in the NSW Health Department. He is a medical epidemiologist with extensive international experience, including nine years at the United States Center for Disease Control and Prevention, and service with the Ford Foundation in Bangladesh.

Anne Somjen is the senior economic analyst of the Inner and Eastern Health Care Network in Victoria, Australia. The network is directly responsible for the management of ten public hospitals within the inner and eastern precincts of metropolitan Melbourne, and is the largest provider of health care services in Australia. Anne previously worked at a number of major Melbourne public health institutions including the Department of Human Services. Anne has a bachelor of arts degree from the University of Melbourne with honours in economics. She commenced her MBA at Stanford University in September 1999.

Johannes Stoelwinder is a member of the Private Health Insurance Administration Council and a health services consultant. For seventeen years he was chief executive officer of the Southern Health Care Network and its antecedent hospitals, Monash Medical Centre and Queen Victoria Medical Centre in Melbourne, Victoria. He has held academic appointments in the business school and medical faculty at Monash University, and a number of international organisations including the King's Fund, London.

Rosalie Viney is deputy director of the Centre for Health Economics Research and Evaluation and a lecturer in health economics at the University of Sydney. Her research interests include health financing and delivery arrangements, resource allocation and priority setting, the interface between research and policy and decision-making under uncertainty in health. Prior to joining CHERE, she was a senior policy analyst in the NSW Department of Health, where she principally worked on Commonwealth–state relations.

Tables

Figures

Boxes

Foreword

The word 'reform' leads one to think of something that needs to be fixed and afterwards left alone. During the 1980s and 1990s, however, health care reforms became almost a permanent fixture in health policy in developed and developing nations alike. During that time, if any trend was evident, it was the growth in the magnitude and frequency of attempts to reform health systems. Not reforming was seen as clinging to an outmoded past, or as an unwillingness to face the challenges of the future.

Unfortunately, despite the rapid accumulation of experience with health care reforms, most of the big questions are left unanswered. How can a system best be organised to deliver the three central goals of equity, efficiency and quality? How can we balance the high-powered incentives associated with consumer choice, markets, and competition with our commitment to public policies that secure universal access and clinical quality in service delivery?

Against this background, policy-makers in many countries, including the many client countries of the World Bank, are reviewing their health systems and seeking to prepare for the challenges ahead. In most, if not all cases, governments are revisiting the role of the state in health service delivery and financing to improve the performance of their system.

In countries that have traditionally relied on markets, attempts are being made to broaden coverage through public or publicly mandated financing or to improve the use of regulation and planning to ensure equity and access in service delivery. In other settings, countries that have relied in the past on centralised planning and a state monopoly are introducing financial incentives and market or market-like pressures in an attempt to make the system more responsive to consumer demand and expectations, and to improve the efficiency and quality of care.

Because health systems exhibit such a variety of structures and because they are inherently so complex, policy-makers often struggle to find guidance on how to proceed. Typically they look abroad to gain usable insights and lessons from other countries' reforms. For these to be applicable, however, one wishes very much for context and depth. That is what this book provides.

Policy-makers will find useful insights from the rich reform experiences of Australia and New Zealand outlined in this book. Both countries have well-performing health care systems. Both have a long history of securing universal access to a comprehensive range of health services and protection against the impoverishing effects of illness. New Zealand started their reforms with an NHS-style integrated model of finance and service delivery. Australia has a mixed system, with national health insurance for primary-care services, and an integrated system for acute and tertiary services. Both have recently undertaken reforms to enhance market pressures in the context of maintaining universal access.

For example, New Zealand experienced a first wave of reforms in the 1980s, introducing area health boards, which integrated many health services under a common geographic structure. In a second phase, in the 1990s, it created a purchaser/provider split. This subsequently evolved into a funder/provider arrangement after the 1996 elections, with the partial corporatisation of publicly owned health enterprises. Australia is experimenting with performance-based hospital financing and competition between public and private hospitals. Both are attempting to expand and improve the functioning of existing markets in health care.

The alert reader may wish to contemplate the responses of policy-makers in New Zealand and Australia to the following challenges frequently encountered in health reform.

- By their nature, reforms to increase efficiency and responsiveness often appear to threaten the key objectives of equity and cost control. It is the rare reform indeed that can deliver all objectives in one tidy package. How have policy-makers in Australia and New Zealand met this challenge? Have they established a balance?
- It can be argued that health systems are interconnected and require coherent and consistent reforms. Yet most reforms in the health sector are incremental, and often piecemeal. Incremental reforms risk being disjointed, incurring costs greater than the problems they were designed to address. Comprehensive reforms can overreach the willingness of both stakeholders and the general public to accept change. The New Zealand and Australian experiences give some evidence of both risks.
- Reforms that focus on improving the use of resources and efficiency often require rationing to be made more explicit, a move that is universally unpopular. How has this been approached—or avoided—in Australia and New Zealand?
- Many elements of health reform are unpopular with medical staff. Because these professionals have a dominant influence over public opinion on health systems and health reforms, changes that they oppose are politically very costly.

Health reforms as planned often bear only passing resemblance to the actual changes implemented. Fortunately, many of the contributors to this book have experience on the front line in implementation and are thus able to give revealing details about how the reforms evolved, including planned and unplanned variations. As such, the book offers an invaluable guide for both policy-makers and scholars to a rich array of health reform experiences that are not widely known but that generate substantial insights into reforms that are being considered and implemented in other parts of the world.

As a former New Zealand Director-General of Health (1992–95) and, as a consequence, a member of the Australian Health Ministers Advisory Council, I confess to a particular fascination with the similarities, and perhaps more importantly, the richness of the differences taken in health reform in these two fascinating cross-Tasman neighbours. Add to this the increasingly different approaches taken by the Australian states and you have a set of valuable case studies for the policy analyst and policy-maker to consider.

Happy reading.

Christopher Lovelace
Director, Health, Nutrition, and Population
World Bank
Formerly Director-General, New Zealand Health

Acknowledgments

The inspiration for a book on health reform came from my colleagues and from my experience in Australia and internationally. I am particularly grateful to my colleague and friend April Harding at the World Bank, who has channelled limitless enthusiasm and energy into health reform. She convinced me that what was happening in Australia and New Zealand was worth documenting, and constantly prodded me, 'No one has written this down! You've got to write it down!' She also reminded me why this book had to have a very practical as well as a conceptual thrust. Additional support came from Alex Preker, whose dynamism and intellectual leadership in health economics are inspiring. I am also grateful for the support provided by Dr Karen Poutasi and Mr Philip Davies and their staff in the New Zealand Ministry of Health; their contribution was essential in making the book reflect both the New Zealand and Australian experience in health reform.

My other main sources of inspiration are the senior health experts from government and the private sector with whom I have worked on the design and implementation of health reform internationally. All sought to understand the alternatives available to them, as well as their risks and dangers. Theory and generalisations are abundant, they challenged, but what was the *real* experience of health reform? I am particularly grateful to my colleagues in Slovenia, Mongolia, and Australia, all pioneers in health reform, all of whom prodded me to synthesise our health reform experience so they could adapt and apply that knowledge locally.

An edited collection is the product of a team. The team involved in health reform in Australia and New Zealand is very special indeed. The pressure of time and responsibility usually means that those most intimately involved as architects of reform are least likely to write about it. Thus valuable experience and insight is lost. The contributors to this volume were deliberately chosen because of their seminal involvement in the decision-making and implementation of health reform in the two nations. Some are full-time scholars and teachers, but few have the luxury of time or academic milieu to reflect on and write about the process of reform. I am deeply indebted to them for agreeing to contribute to this book and for their cooperation along the way. I am also grateful to individuals who, for various reasons, were unable to contribute to the book but who supported it in other ways.

Inspiration and eloquence are inadequate without the skills and persistence to manage and coax a book through to its conclusion. The swift completion of this book owes much to the project management skills of Kylie Rylands in its early stage. But the book could not have come together so professionally without the professional and editorial expertise of Dr Evelyn Sharman. Working with Evelyn has been a very special privilege.

I am particularly indebted to Jill Henry, my publisher at OUP, for her immediate and unwavering confidence in the proposal, and her quiet, gentle and learned support throughout. I am also grateful to Chris Lovelace for agreeing to write the book's foreword and for highlighting its global as well as regional significance.

Finally, I appreciate the tolerance and support of my family, who are the answer to the question, 'Where did you find the time to edit a book?' They helped me clear the time and understood that I had to see the project through to its conclusion. I promised for years that I would dedicate my next book to my younger daughter. Chloe, this one's for you.

Abby Bloom

Abbreviations

ABS	Australian Bureau of Statistics
ACC	Accident Compensation Commission (also known as ARCI)
ACD	advanced-care directive
ACHS	Australian Council on Hospital Standards (now Australian Council on Healthcare Standards)
ACT	Australian Capital Territory
ACTU	Australian Council of Trade Unions
ADL	activity of daily living
AGPS	Australian Government Publishing Service
AHCA	Australian Health Care Agreement
AHMAC	Australian Health Ministers' Advisory Council
AHS	area health service
AIDS	acquired immune deficiency syndrome
AIHI	Australian International Health Institute
AIHW	Australian Institute of Health and Welfare
ALP	Australian Labor Party
AMA	Australian Medical Association
AN-DRG	Australian national diagnostic-related groups
APEC	Asia Pacific Economic Co-operation
AQoL	Australian quality of life
ARCI	Accident Rehabilitation and Compensation Insurance Corporation (also known as ACC)
ATSI	Aboriginal and Torres Strait Islander
BMA	British Medical Association
BOOT	build-own-operate-transfer
CEO	chief executive officer
CHD	coronary heart disease
CHE	Crown health enterprise
CME	continuing medical education
COAG	Council of Australian Governments
COPD	chronic obstructive pulmonary disease
CQI	continuous quality improvement
CSC	community services card
DHCS	Department of Health and Community Services
DOF	Department of Finance
DRG	diagnosis-related group
DVA	Department of Veterans' Affairs

EPAC	Economic Planning and Advisory Council
EPR	electronic patient record
GDP	gross domestic product
GMS	general medical services
GP	general practitioner
GST	goods and services tax
HFA	health funding agency/authority
HHS/H+HS	hospital and health services
HIC	Health Insurance Commission
HIV	human immunodeficiency virus
HSA	health/hospital services agreement
IEC	Information, Education and Communication
IPA	independent practice association (now independent practitioner association)
ISO	international standards organisation
JCAH	Joint Commission on Accreditation of Hospitals
JCAHO	Joint Commission on Accreditation of Health Care Organisations
LMO	local medical officer
MBF	Medical Benefits Fund
MBS	Medical Benefits Scheme Schedule
MHPB	Metropolitan Hospitals Planning Board
MOH	Ministry of Health
MPC	multi-purpose centre
MPS	multi-purpose service
MRI	magnetic resonance imaging
MSAC	Medical Services Advisory Committee
NGC	National Guideline Clearinghouse
NGO	non-government organisation
NH&MRC	National Health and Medical Research Council
NHI	National Health Index
NHS	National Health Service (UK)
NPHP	National Public Health Partnership
NSW	New South Wales
NT	Northern Territory
NZ	New Zealand
OECD	Organisation for Economic Cooperation and Development
PBS	Pharmaceutical Benefits Scheme
PET	positive electron tomography
PHC	Public Health Commission
PHIAC	Private Health Insurance Advisory Council

PHOFA	Public Health Outcome Funding Agreement
PRRC	peer review resource centre
QC	quality circles
QI	quality improvement
RACMA	Royal Australian College of Medical Administrators
RAF	resource allocation formula
RDF	resource distribution formula
RFP	request for proposal
RHA	regional health authority
RIM	retirement income modelling
RPPS	Repatriation Private Patient Scheme
RSL	Returned and Services League
SCRCSSP	Steering Committee for the Review of Commonwealth/State Service Provision
SOE	state-owned enterprise
SPP	specific-purpose payment
SRCSSP	Secretariat for the Review of Commonwealth/State Service Provision
TQM	total quality management
UK	United Kingdom
UN	United Nations
USA	United States of America
WA	Western Australia
WIES	weighted inlier equivalent separations
WHO	World Health Organisation

General Introduction

Abby Bloom

This book is about the major theme facing health systems today, health reform. The book examines health reform in two specific contexts, Australia and New Zealand. Its purpose is threefold: to provide a conceptual and practical introduction to health sector reform; to analyse systematically the process of reform by reviewing and comparing the experience of two nations highly regarded for both their health systems and their progress in health reform; and to consider the lessons learnt from health reform in Australia and New Zealand that are applicable to other settings. The material is presented in a way that is intended to provide insight into the issues precipitating health reform, the forces that drive the process, and the impact that theory, politics, history, culture, and contemporary concepts of health care delivery typically have on reform and its outcomes. In the more detailed case studies, authors describe in very specific detail how reforms were implemented, and the crucial success factors and lessons learned from the experience. Part V places reform in the two countries within the broader context of the reform experience of Western Europe and the USA. It then considers where health reform in Australia and New Zealand is likely to head next.

The book is intended to fill a gap in the literature of health reform. To date published materials comparing health reform in different countries have been brief—usually chapters in larger volumes—and often have not captured the richness of the reform process. In addition, the experts documenting and assessing reform have logically tended to be drawn largely from academia and rather less often from other realms. This volume deliberately expands on that range. Those who have participated in the process directly (as architects rather than advisers or scholars) are infrequently represented in the literature on health reform. This is an important omission, because health reform has tended to be management of change on a massive, rapid scale, often undocumented. Precisely what occurred, how, and why is sparsely documented, and is best known to those who took part in the process.

The process of health reform is a long-running saga, yet few national experiences have been documented systematically and in detail. Without a detailed, cohesive understanding of the process, decision-makers cannot know what relevance one nation's experience might have for another. Emulating other countries' health reform strategies thus carries a high risk.

In-depth comparisons of two or more countries tend either to be general or to focus on a restricted aspect of reform, such as finance, the public–private balance, competitive contracting, or a particular level of care (e.g. primary care or hospital treatment). It is left to the reader to piece together a cohesive picture of the reform process.

This volume originated in the editor's participation in health reform in numerous countries in recent years, countries as diverse as Australia and Mongolia, Slovenia and Indonesia. Through discussions with government officials, clinicians, managers, and politicians, it became clear that there are neither road maps nor case studies to guide decision-makers through reform. Whereas preferred approaches, models, and mechanisms for reform are eagerly promoted, the real life experience, especially the reasons behind success or failure, are not widely known or shared.

The contributors to the book have been selected to reflect a range of perspectives and experiences in health reform. All have written about the reforms in which they have been the architects, drivers, leaders, and champions. Some of the authors are university-based; all have played a pivotal role in the implementation of health reform in Australia or New Zealand. They have generously and candidly documented their experience and extracted lessons learned as a guide for others. The book does provide the theoretical background necessary to understand health reform, but it is not a theoretical analysis of reform. Rather, it provides an insider's understanding of the process of reform—not merely what was intended, but what actually happened and why—something that has been sorely lacking.

Why Australia and New Zealand?

One of the more fascinating features of health reform globally is its many variations. Australia and New Zealand are only two among dozens of countries that are undergoing reform, but they are of particular significance for several reasons. First, they had more continuous experience in health reform in the 1990s than most countries. Second, they generated instructive models and many valuable lessons in reform. Next, looking at the two countries comparatively provides an opportunity to examine how reform affected two nations that have evolved from similar social and cultural systems and whose health reform processes both borrowed heavily from the same sources.

Neither country is promoted as a health reform success story. Nor is either touted as the ideal health system or 'best workable model' (Hsiao 1998: 13–14). Nevertheless, their experience does provide valuable insight and guidance.

The Theme of Reform

Language is often hijacked in the field of health, and in the process devalued. As Ham (1997b: 25) and Reinhardt (1999: 92) observe, there is an evolving vocabulary of health reform that includes such terms as 'purchaser', 'provider', 'service agreement', 'contract', and, more recently, 'managed competition'. But their definitions are usually coloured by local politics, and the symbolic import of the language of health reform should not be underestimated. This has certainly been observed in Australia.

For example, in the early 1980s 'rationalise' became synonymous with 'close down hospitals' and had to be deleted from the health lexicon in Australia. 'Managed care', synonymous in Australia with 'American-style medicine', is a repugnant term, and has been replaced with 'managed competition', in a very specific, Australian interpretation. For some stakeholders in health and social services in Australia and New Zealand, even the word 'reform' has an unfortunate negative connotation. They observe that for proponents of the private sector, reform is synonymous with 'market-based reform', which means privatisation (*Economist*, 8 May 1999: 37–8).

In this book 'health reform' means reconfiguration of the major structural features of a health system—finance, provision, and regulation—on a national or statewide basis. The rationale for health reform and its main objectives vary by setting. Improvements in technical efficiency and quality are usually the two major aims, though reform may be prompted by other, underlying objectives or ideologies. In Australia and New Zealand technical and allocative efficiency—specifically equity—is high on the reform agenda, as it is in Central European countries, for example. This is quite a different motivation from the many settings in which the catalyst for reform is a system that has irretrievably broken down, or has never reliably delivered health care of reasonable quality to a large proportion of the population.

Health reform may include a shift in the respective roles of public and private sectors, but it does not necessarily imply a larger or more powerful role for the private sector. It may or may not entail a restructuring of whole systems of finance, and it may or may not encourage new providers or mechanisms for competition. What is common to health reform globally is that governments are holding up to scrutiny long-accepted beliefs about health systems. The questions are similar, and the alternatives few. This is why it is valuable to study the health reform experience of other nations.

Forces Driving Reform in Australia and New Zealand

The forces driving reform in Australia and New Zealand in the 1980s and 1990s were similar to those affecting most Western economies: an increased demand for health care, and constraints on the amount of finance governments are prepared to allocate to health. The factors contributing to increased demand for health services in Australia and New Zealand during the 1990s are also common to most Western nations, and will soon be operative globally: a perception that ageing populations were consuming unsustainably increasing quantities of health services; increased consumer knowledge and expectations for health care; advances in technology; and higher expectations of the health outcomes.

Compared with other Western nations, Australia and New Zealand do not currently spend an excessive proportion of GDP on their health systems. Most health experts would agree that the approximately 8 per cent of GDP spent on health in Australia and New Zealand, and the absolute amount per capita allocated in each country, are both adequate and reasonable. Moreover, the standard of health care provided in both countries is impressively high. Yet behind the push for health reform in both countries has been the fear of increasing costs and the determination to preserve and even increase equity in health and in access to health care. A dearth of investment capital for infrastructure development, increasing technical efficiency, and improving quality were equally powerful forces behind reform. The history of reform in the antipodes epitomises Ham's second and third phases of reform, in which the themes of micro-efficiency and responsiveness to users dominate but where public health, primary care, evidence-based medicine, and managed care (competition) are beginning to take root (Ham 1997b).

Models and Phases of Reform

Ham (1997a, 1977b), Hsiao (1992), and others (World Bank 1997) describe different approaches to reform and phases in the reform process. Australia and New Zealand are clearly examples of the 'supply-side approach' (Hsiao 1992: 617) to health reform. This approach maintains that health is different, and that these differences justify government intervention in the market in order to ensure that all people have reasonable access to health care regardless of ability to pay (Hsiao 1992: 617). What is interesting is how each of the two nations has developed a distinctive supply-side approach.

Australia and New Zealand have also emerged from the first decade of reform as examples of 'incremental reform', despite what looked initially to be a radical approach in New Zealand. One of the lessons of health reform in the two countries is that, however earnest and passionate the original intent, neither the politics of health care nor the pragmatics of implementing change permit the emergence of radical ideas. The phasing of reform in most Western nations, too, has come face to face with reality, and the fact that it is unnecessary and ill advised to move too swiftly and change everything at once; the risk and cost of political backlash are too great. As the case studies in this book illustrate, it takes many years to introduce sustained, micro-level change of the degree and complexity entailed in health system reform.

Lessons from Health Reform in Australia and New Zealand

Of the many lessons conveyed in this volume, the following stand out:

- Health reform will almost inevitably be incremental rather than radical. This is the approach that sits most comfortably in Western democratic societies. Health and health care are so politicised and so fraught with tensions among numerous powerful stakeholders that radical reform is impractical and unlikely.
- Health reform is a lengthy process, and is likely to take more than a decade, potentially two, from start to finish.
- The direction and features of health reform are determined by politics—by political structures, political interests, and the political process. Even though the forces driving reform transcend politics, the prescription will vary according to the politics of the day.
- Finally, health reform is inevitably anchored in local values and history, making each nation's experience of health reform unique.

Thus while reform processes will share similar dimensions and features, another nation's experience is useful only when adapted to the local situation.

How to Use This Book

The book is organised in five parts. It is suggested that readers familiarise themselves as needed with the context and framework for reform in Part I, where three chapters summarise the basic features of Australia and New Zealand and their health systems, and define fundamental concepts and theories in health reform.

Parts II to IV examine in detail the different dimensions, models, and current issues being addressed in reform in Australia and New Zealand, all of which are relevant to other nations.

Chapter 3 provides the reader with a summary comparison of the reform experience of the two countries, preparing readers for the more detailed analysis to come.

Part II considers key dimensions of the reform process in the two countries: health care finance, the evolving role of government, the role and transition of doctors through the reform process, and how the introduction of casemix (the mix of types of patients treated; see Eager and Hindle 1996) provided a 'level playing field', a means of accounting for and comparing value for money in health care delivery.

Part III explores the introduction of new models at different levels within the health care system, including those most often addressed in reform—primary care and hospital treatment. It then compares and contrasts the process of reform within Australia's two largest states in order to highlight how differences in politics, economic policy, and government departments can generate very different responses to the same reform drivers. Two chapters in Part III are devoted to two aspects of health most notable for their absence in health reform, public health, and health promotion and illness prevention, and provide models for their inclusion in reform.

Part IV looks towards the future and considers how the issues dominating the current phase of reform are being addressed in the two countries: improving and measuring quality, implementation of evidence-based health care, strengthening government's performance management capacity, and meeting the health care challenges of an ageing society.

The Conclusion summarises the experience and lessons learned so far in health reform in Australia and New Zealand, and attempts to predict how health reform will unfold in the future.

THE CONTEXT AND FRAMEWORK OF HEALTH SECTOR REFORM IN AUSTRALIA AND NEW ZEALAND

Introduction

Abby Bloom

Part I of this book establishes the conceptual and situational environment for health reform in Australia and New Zealand. Many readers will not be familiar with the focus of health reform: the finance, structure, and regulatory features of health systems. The three chapters in this part are designed to prepare readers for the detailed description and analysis of the reform process in each setting. There are several scholarly approaches to analysing health care and health policy. The main perspectives are economic, political, sociological, and that of public health and epidemiology (Palmer and Short 1994).

To date most of the comparative studies of health reform have been undertaken from an economic perspective. Such a perspective is largely concerned with the finance and organisation of health systems, and with the incentives that foster particular funding and structural approaches (Palmer and Short 1994: 39–42; Hsiao 1992: 619). Although this approach has been dominant in health care reform, it does not by any means account for the full scope of health care systems, nor does it claim to.

A political perspective concentrates on how health, access to health care, and power and influence in the health care system differ among groups according to their socio-economic status and professional affiliations (e.g. medical associations and the professional colleges of doctors, nurses and others) (Palmer and Short 1994: 42–5). A number of the authors in the book (see in particular Stoelwinder and Viney in Chapter 11) refer to the seminal work of Alford (1975) to explain the interplay of ideas and interest groups in health reform. Health care systems have always been characterised by strong political interests. As Hall and Viney note in

Chapter 2, the politics of health is, after all, about the power to determine 'who shall live'. International experts consider that the politics of health in Australia is particularly fraught, noting that in few other nations undergoing reform will the newspapers almost daily carry stories calling into question some aspect of the health system (April Harding, pers. comm., May 1999).

The next approach to the analysis of health care systems is the sociological perspective. This approach has tended to focus on the dominant influence of medicine as a profession on the structure and function of health systems (Palmer and Short 1994: 47–9). A recurring theme in this book is the pivotal role of doctors in determining the direction of health systems because of their ability to foster demand as well as to control supply of important health services and goods. Thus Chapter 9 focuses specifically on the role of doctors in the reform process. This is not to suggest that other professions, particularly nursing, are not important in health care and health reform. In both Australia and New Zealand, however, particular attention and resources have been directed at changing doctors' organisational and clinical behaviour and at engaging them in the process of reform both in the community and in hospitals.

Reform in both Australia and New Zealand has been 'top-down' (see Introduction to Part II). The public, including patients, have been little involved in precipitating or influencing the direction of reform, even when reforms have been introduced in their name. An anthropological approach might have examined the experience and impact of reform from an ethnological perspective, that is, from the point of view of indigenous minorities in each country. Unfortunately, this analysis will have to await a second volume.

The fourth major approach to the analysis of health care systems and health is the public health and epidemiological approach. The book includes two chapters on this, one examining organisational approaches to public health and their reform (Chapter 14), the other a case study of an important health promotion model (Chapter 15). Both demonstrate how these perspectives can be integrated into the reform process. A third chapter (Chapter 18) considers evidence-based health care and how it has fostered the integration of research-based clinical decision-making.

A deliberate effort has been made in this book to provide a well-rounded perspective on health reform. Thus, in addition to examining each context over time and comparing the two countries (as well as making an internal comparison of two different states within Australia), the book includes all of the major theoretical perspectives on health care and health policy.

The major features of each nation's health system are set out in Chapter 1. Bloom outlines the geographic, social, cultural, and political backdrop of reform in each country, and then summarises the important antecedents of reform in each setting. The two countries are geographically close, share similar histories as former British colonies, have the same historical links with British medical training and practice, and even appear to have similar health care systems. This is deceptive: although their health systems have evolved in parallel, they have made significantly different choices along the way.

Thus, for example, both Australia and New Zealand enacted crucial social security legislation, but the turning point and the decision taken differed markedly. The passage of New Zealand's *Social Security Act 1938* marked the introduction of a comprehensive health system guided by government policy, legislation, finance, and provision in that country. The Act provided universal entitlement and access to a tax-financed, comprehensive system of health care.

The comparable turning point in Australia's history was the establishment first of Medibank, and its evolution into Medicare (1984), Australia's first compulsory and universal health insurance scheme, designed to ensure universal access to basic hospital and medical care. Enacted in 1975, Medibank was promptly subjected to several modifications. Although it failed to give a cohesive response to the pressures of providing health finance and services, and within a decade was replaced by Australia's current system of universal health insurance, Medicare, it established an important precedent: universal and compulsory, taxation-based health insurance. It is Medicare—and the excellent access and quality it affords—that makes Australia's health system the envy of many other nations.

Thus an understanding of the factual points of difference between the two nations is a key to understanding how and why each has taken a different path in health reform. For example, several authors will subsequently emphasise the influence of Australia's federal system of government on health reform. Because responsibilities for health funding and provision are split largely between the Commonwealth and the states (with local communities playing a part in public and environmental health), each influences the structure, financing, and priorities of the health system. Because different political parties can rule at the same time at federal and state levels, a dynamic tension often exists within the health system.

Another distinguishing feature of Australia's health system is the constitutional requirement that doctors may not be compelled to work as employees of the government, a position upheld by the courts on the ground that it would imply conscription. This has meant that Australia has a national, compulsory, taxation-based health-financing system, coupled with private health insurance. But it has not been able to opt for a National Health Service (provision) model as in the United Kingdom. Rather, all doctors in general practice remain employed in the private sector, whereas doctors employed by government hospitals have a range of options.

In Chapter 2, Hall and Viney place health care reform in a framework of political economy. The basic economic concepts and assumptions presented by the authors will be familiar to many, but perhaps not to all. One of the features of the process of health reform internationally is the diversity of stakeholders and their backgrounds. This has meant that the 'debate' over health reform sometimes occurs between protagonists who may not agree on, or even share, the same conceptual frameworks. The aim of this chapter is to map that terrain, and identify for readers the main conceptual features of the landscape in which health reform occurs.

Hall and Viney believe that the fundamental values of societies and individuals will colour their positions on health policy and health reform. They themselves adhere to the dominant view that traditional theories about 'markets' and their operation are not apt for health. This is the 'supply-side approach' (Ham 1997b). Health, they argue, is fundamentally different, and, like other authors in this volume (Hindle and Perkins, Poutasi), they emphasise the need for government intervention in health.

One of the distinguishing features of health reform is that experts are not in agreement about how, and to what degree health is 'different'. Thus, as later chapters by Foley (Chapter 5) and Bloom (Chapter 13) will show, the dominance of 'supply-side' theory in health reform in Australia and New Zealand has not excluded growth of private sector involvement in health. What is interesting is the degree to which both private sector financing and provision have expanded further in Australia than in New Zealand.

Building on the historical and conceptual background of the first two chapters, Somjen (Chapter 3) prepares readers for the differences they should expect to find in the health reform experiences of Australia and New Zealand. She first summarises the distinguishing features of reform in the two countries. Hall and Viney have cited the significance of political leadership in influencing the course of health reform. Somjen emphasises on precisely how those differences come into play to influence the focus and outcome of reform. She observes that both nations are struggling with the same issues: how best to contain costs, how to enlist the private sector's resources, how best to stimulate competition, and how to improve the health of the indigenous populations. The chapter concludes by highlighting the strengths and weaknesses of each system at this juncture in the continuing saga of health reform.

By the end of Part I, readers previously unfamiliar with the two nations should have a comprehensive understanding of each setting and of the social, political, and historical backdrop of reform. Subsequent parts look, in increasingly greater depth, at the experience of reform.

1

Context and Lead-up to Health Reform

Abby Bloom

This chapter provides a summary description of the health systems of Australia and New Zealand and chronicles the main developments leading up to health reform in the late 1980s and 1990s. Each profile comprises a brief description of the country, salient health statistics, a succinct history of its health system, and the essential features of its current health system focusing on four dimensions: structure, finance, provision, and regulation and quality.

Tables 1.1 (p. 14), 1.2 (p. 15), 1.3 (p. 16), and Figure 1.1 (p. 17) compare basic health data for Australia and New Zealand with that of other OECD nations. They depict salient features of health and health care funding in the two nations: a health profile that is equal to, or better than that in most OECD nations. The percentage of GDP expended on health in Australia and New Zealand compares favourably with other, largely publicly financed health systems, leading to the conclusion that both Australia and New Zealand provide a relatively high level of access at a comparatively reasonable cost.

Australia

Country profile

Australia, an island continent of 18.7 million people, is located south of the equator between the Indian and Pacific Oceans, and to the west of New Zealand. Its land area of 7 680 000 square kilometres is slightly smaller than the continental USA. Like New Zealand, Australia has a

Table 1.1   Total health expenditures in OECD countries as a percentage of GDP, selected years, 1975–95

Country	1975	1980	1985	1990	1991	1992	1993	1994	1995
Australia	7.5	7.3	7.7	8.2	8.2	8.6	8.6	8.5	8.4
Austria	7.3	7.9	6.7	7.1	7.2	7.6	7.9	7.8	7.9
Belgium	5.9	6.6	7.4	7.6	8.0	8.2	8.2	8.1	8.0
Canada	7.2	7.3	8.4	9.2	9.9	10.2	10.2	9.9	9.7
Denmark	6.5	6.8	6.3	6.5	6.5	6.6	6.8	6.6	6.4
Finland	6.4	6.5	7.3	8.0	9.1	9.3	8.4	7.9	7.5
France	7.0	7.6	8.5	8.9	9.1	9.4	9.8	9.7	9.9
Germany	8.0	8.1	8.5	8.2	9.6	10.2	10.1	10.3	10.5
Greece	3.4	3.6	4.0	4.2	4.2	4.5	5.0	5.5	5.8
Iceland	5.8	6.2	7.3	8.0	8.1	8.2	8.3	8.1	8.2
Ireland	7.7	8.8	7.8	6.6	6.8	7.1	7.0	7.4	7.1
Italy	6.2	7.0	7.1	8.1	8.4	8.5	8.6	8.4	7.7
Japan	5.5	6.4	6.7	6.0	6.0	6.3	6.6	6.9	7.2
Luxembourg	5.1	6.2	6.1	6.6	6.5	6.6	6.7	6.5	7.0
Netherlands	7.5	7.9	7.9	8.3	8.6	8.8	8.9	8.8	8.8
New Zealand	6.7	6.0	5.3	7.0	7.5	7.6	7.3	7.1	7.1
Norway	6.1	7.0	6.6	7.8	8.1	8.2	8.1	8.0	8.0
Portugal	5.6	5.8	6.3	6.5	7.2	7.4	7.7	7.8	8.2
Spain	4.9	5.7	5.7	6.9	7.1	7.2	7.3	7.3	7.6
Sweden	7.9	9.4	9.0	8.8	8.7	7.8	7.9	7.6	7.2
Switzerland	7.0	7.3	8.1	8.4	9.0	9.4	9.5	9.5	9.8
Turkey	2.7	3.3	2.2	2.5	3.2	2.7	2.5	5.2	–
UK	5.5	5.6	5.9	6.0	6.5	6.9	6.9	6.9	6.9
USA	8.2	9.1	10.7	12.7	13.5	14.1	14.3	14.1	14.2
OECD average (excluding Turkey)	6.5	7.0	7.2	7.6	8.0	8.2	8.2	8.3	8.2

Source: OECD 1997

democratically elected government. In contrast to its near neighbour, however, Australia has a three-tiered system of government: the federal (Commonwealth) level, six states and two territories, and local government.

Australia's population is concentrated along two coastal regions, one stretching from Queensland in the north to Victoria in the southeast, and the other along a smaller coastal zone in the southwest of Western Australia. Smaller regional centres and towns are scattered throughout the country, but most of the continent is uninhabited. Australia is highly urbanised; about 70 per cent of its population lives in its ten largest cities. The current GDP per capita (March quarter 1999, trend figure) is $7730 (ABS 1999).

Australia is a multicultural society. The nation's indigenous inhabitants, Aboriginal and Torres Strait Islander (ATSI) people, totalled 386 049 in 1996 (AIHW 1998a: 241), and comprise nearly 1.5 per cent of the

Table 1.2 Life expectancy, OECD member countries

	Male life expectancy at birth		Female life expectancy at birth	
Country	1960	1995	1960	1995
Australia	67.9	75	73.9	80.9
Austria	65.4	73.5	71.9	80.1
Belgium	67.7	73.3	73.5	80.0
Canada[a]	68.4	75.3	74.3	81.3
Denmark	72.3	72.5	74.1	77.8
Finland	64.9	72.8	71.6	80.2
France	67.0	73.9	73.6	81.9
Germany	66.9	73.0	72.4	79.5
Greece	67.5	75.1	70.7	80.3
Iceland	70.7	76.5	75.0	80.6
Ireland	68.5	72.9	71.8	78.5
Italy[a]	67.2	74.4	72.3	80.8
Japan	65.3	76.4	70.2	82.8
Luxembourg	66.1	72.5	71.9	79.5
Netherlands	71.6	74.6	75.5	80.4
New Zealand	68.7	73.8	73.9	79.2
Norway	71.3	74.8	75.8	80.8
Portugal	61.7	71.5	67.2	78.6
Spain	67.4	73.2	72.2	81.2
Sweden	71.2	76.2	74.9	81.5
Switzerland	68.7	75.3	74.1	81.7
Turkey[b]	46.5	65.4	49.7	70.0
UK	68.3	74.3	74.2	79.7
USA	66.6	72.5	73.1	79.2
OECD average (excluding Turkey)	67.9	74.1	73.0	80.3

a Male and female life-expectancy data for Canada and Italy are for 1961.
b Male and female life-expectancy data for Turkey are for 1994.

Source: OECD 1997

population. Two-thirds of indigenous people live in towns and cities. Immigration has always been a major factor in Australia's population growth and change. Today 40 per cent of Australians are themselves immigrants, or children of immigrants, and half are from non-English-speaking backgrounds. People of Anglo-Celtic extraction have dominated Australia's ethnic mix, but are declining as a proportion of the population. The 'White Australia Policy' restricted migration until 1945. Since then successive waves of immigrants have come from southern Europe (Italy, Greece, Turkey, and the Baltic), and more recently from Asia (including Vietnam and China). In 1991/92 East Asia contributed 41 per cent of settler arrivals. New Zealanders and South Pacific Islanders comprise a significant proportion of Australia's immigrants.

Table 1.3 Public health expenditure as a percentage of total health expenditure for 24 OECD countries, 1980–95

Country	1980	1985	1990	1991	1992	1993	1994	1995
Australia	62.9	71.7	68.1	67.8	67.8	67.9	68.5	66.7
Austria	68.8	77.6	75.0	74.9	75.1	75.7	76.0	75.6
Belgium	83.4	81.8	88.9	88.1	88.9	88.9	87.9	87.8
Canada	75.7	75.7	74.6	74.6	74.1	73.0	71.8	71.4
Denmark	85.2	84.4	82.3	83.3	83.6	83.1	83.4	82.7
Finland	79.0	78.6	80.9	81.1	79.6	76.3	74.8	74.7
France	78.8	76.9	74.5	74.7	74.6	74.2	78.4	80.6
Germany	79.2	77.9	76.8	78.6	78.9	78.5	78.4	78.4
Greece	82.2	81.0	82.3	80.2	76.1	76.2	76.2	75.8
Iceland	88.2	87.0	86.6	86.9	85.1	83.7	84.0	84.2
Ireland	82.2	77.4	74.7	77.2	7.8	88.2	80.7	80.8
Italy	80.5	77.2	78.1	78.4	76.3	72.9	70.6	69.6
Japan	71.3	70.7	77.6	78.3	78.1	79.3	76.8	78.4
Luxembourg	92.8	89.2	93.1	93.0	92.8	92.9	91.8	92.8
Netherlands	74.7	75.1	72.7	74.1	77.7	78.6	77.7	77.1
New Zealand	88.0	85.0	82.4	82.2	79.0	76.6	76.8	76.4
Norway	85.1	85.8	83.3	83.5	85.1	83.3	83.0	82.8
Portugal	64.3	54.6	65.5	62.8	59.6	63.0	63.4	60.5
Spain	79.9	81.1	78.7	78.9	78.8	78.6	78.6	78.2
Sweden	92.5	90.4	89.9	88.2	85.4	83.9	83.0	81.6
Switzerland	67.5	66.1	68.4	68.6	70.1	71.8	71.9	71.9
Turkey	27.3	50.2	40.0	50.0	33.3	60.0	50.0	–
UK	89.4	85.8	84.1	83.7	84.5	84.8	84.1	84.3
USA	42.4	40.7	40.8	42.0	42.6	42.3	44.8	46.2
OECD average (excluding Turkey)	78.0	77.0	77.4	77.4	74.0	77.1	76.6	76.5

Source: OECD 1997

The health picture

Life expectancy for Australians as a whole is high by world standards: 75.4 years for men and 81.1 years for women (AIHW 1998a: 11). Infant mortality is 5.7 per 1000 live births for the nation as a whole (AIHW 1998a: 251), with continuing declines in recent years (AIHW 1998a: 56).

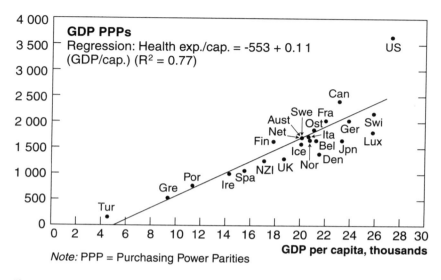

Figure 1.1   Per capita health expenditure as a percentage of per capita GDP, OECD member countries, 1992

Source: OECD (1995).

Commonwealth of Australia copyright reproduced by permission.

Patterns of morbidity and mortality in Australia reflect trends in other Western countries. Between 1987 and 1996, the four major causes of death in Australia were ischaemic heart disease, cerebrovascular disease (stroke), chronic obstructive pulmonary disease (COPD), and colorectal cancer (AIHW 1998a: 7–9). In recent years, however, there has been a steady decline in deaths due to ischaemic heart disease (declining at the rate of 3.6 per cent per annum for males and 3.5 per cent for females) and cerebrovascular disease (declining at a rate of 2.8 per cent per annum for males and 3.0 per cent for females) (AIHW 1998: 8–9; see also analysis in Chapter 19).

The health of Australia's indigenous population is significantly worse than the average: 'Babies born to Aboriginal and Torres Strait Islander mothers are 2–4 times more likely to be stillborn or die within the first twenty-eight days of life than babies born to other Australian mothers'(AIHW 1998a: 34). In 1995–96 the crude hospitalisation rate of indigenous Australians was more than 50 per cent higher than the Australian population as a whole (AIHW 1998a: 32). Australia's indigenous population also has the world's highest prevalence of Type 2 diabetes (AIHW 1998a: 112). Not surprisingly, life expectancy among Aborigines and Torres Straits Islanders is between fourteen and twenty years less than the Australian average (AIHW 1998a: 28).

The lead-up to reform

Western medicine and health care in Australia began with the colonial medical service shortly after European settlement in 1788 and the founding of the colony's first general hospital. Government was the source of providing both funds and health care in the colony's early days. Over time, personal health services became available either directly from doctors in private practice (on a private fee-for-service basis), or from a growing number of 'friendly societies' set up to provide social benefits that included health care. Public hospitals were little used for two reasons: fear of hospitalisation (deservedly so, as hospital mortality was high, conditions were 'appalling', and hospitals were full of convicts, ex-convict paupers, the insane, and people with infections who were forcibly detained) and the stigma of being considered impoverished (Sax 1984: 3–7). Yet public hospitals proliferated in the second half of the nineteenth century. Some of this expansion was funded in part by each colony, but much of it came from public subscriptions.

The state began to play a major role in provision of health care between the two World Wars as demand for health services escalated. Though still seen primarily as a source of charitable health care for the indigent, public hospitals multiplied. In response, state governments established separate public (state-subsidised) and private (paid directly by the patient) wards in hospitals.

The colonies on the Australian continent became a federated nation in 1901. But a Commonwealth Department of Health was not established until 1921 (AIHW 1998a: 159). Commonwealth government involvement in health care, initially for the purpose of controlling communicable disease, was carried along on a wave of social reform in the next decade. Australia's first health insurance legislation was introduced in the late 1930s; most notable was the short-lived *National Health and Pensions Act 1938*. Whereas the main responsibility of the Commonwealth Department of Health in the years after its establishment had been quarantine, an amendment to Australia's Constitution in 1946 granted specific powers to the Commonwealth to legislate on the provision of health care services. These powers were later extended to the states through special-purpose grants under Section 96 of the Constitution (AIHW 1998a: 158).

This legislation was pivotal in determining the direction of Australia's future health system. It provided the legal basis for Commonwealth as well as state involvement in funding and regulation of doctors' services, prescription medications, and nursing homes. Thus the Commonwealth has, since 1946, had both the authority and the leverage to influence health policies and their implementation by the individual states. In fact without Commonwealth funding the states cannot discharge their responsibilities for providing health care, a situation termed 'vertical fiscal imbalance' (Mooney and Scotton 1998: 35–6).

Through the 1940s repeated attempts were made to legislate a national health insurance and pharmaceutical benefits scheme. Doctors' resistance (through the then British Medical Association) to a compulsory national health scheme was both fierce and effective. But as a result of a High Court decision in the 1940s, Australian doctors have substantial independence and cannot be compelled by government to participate in any national health scheme.

Since the late 1940s, Australian governments have supported a national health scheme with four components: the Pharmaceutical Benefits Scheme (PBS, which first became law in the late 1940s and has been in existence since then in various forms); the hospital benefits scheme (through which the Commonwealth government became involved in the funding of hospitals owned and operated by the states from 1952); the Medical Benefits Scheme (MBS, initially enacted in 1953, a voluntary insurance scheme relying on not-for-profit organisations); and the pensioner medical service (enacted in 1951 for all aged and invalid persons, including persons on welfare pensions and their dependants—later a means-tested benefit). These four pillars were enshrined in the *National Health Act 1952*. Actuarial-based private health insurance schemes were first introduced on a large scale in Australia in the 1950s. The artificial subsidy of hospital costs by government meant that their very modest premiums hardly reflected the actual cost of care.

Between 1959 and the early 1970s, as the costs and utilisation of government-provided health and hospital care increased, so too did the debate over the funding and provision of health care. The first turning point in reform came with the introduction of Medibank, mandatory, universal, public health insurance, in 1975. For the first time in Australia, health insurance was legislated as an entitlement. The scheme was enacted after a lengthy struggle among political and medical stakeholders. Medibank was intended to provide access to free hospital and medical care for all Australians. It was designed as a public, non-contributory, tax-based scheme—a national health insurance system with a dominant (but not exclusive) insurer, the Health Insurance Commission (HIC).

By then, public funding for health care was being negotiated periodically in formal agreements between the Commonwealth and state governments on sharing the costs of health care. This has been called the 'elephant dance of Commonwealth/State relations' (Duckett 1998: 22). The principle of paying 85 per cent of a scheduled (government-approved) fee was introduced, as was the concept of 'bulk-billing' (doctors billing government directly, and accepting 85 per cent of the scheduled fee from government as payment). Prescription pharmaceuticals were subsidised through the Pharmaceutical Benefits Scheme (PBS). Voluntary private health insurance continued as an optional supplement to Medibank, and the health system was mainly funded by government (nearly 78 per cent in 1974/75) (Peabody et al. 1996: 58).

Medibank went through continuing revisions virtually from its inception: variations in Schedule fee, subsidies, doctors' billing procedures, payment arrangement, entitlement to free hospital care, tax deductibility of private health insurance premiums—all part of government's budget strategy (Sax 1984: 127–62). By 1982/83 the private sector financed approximately 40 per cent of health expenditure, the public sector 60 per cent (Peabody et al. 1996: 57). Yet between 10 and 15 per cent of Australians had no hospital cover, and despite government subsidies, private insurance premiums were regressive. After six major policy changes over the course of a decade, it was clear that a new approach was needed (OECD 1994: 15).

The major turning point in the recent history of the Australian health care system occurred in 1984, with the legislative introduction of Medicare, which is now the fulcrum of Australia's health system. Medicare is a national, universal health-financing scheme. It provides access to public hospitals at no charge, subsidised access to medical practitioners (through the MBS), and access to subsidised pharmaceuticals, mainly prescription medications. Medicare differed from its predecessor in that it was substantially self-funded through a levy on personal taxable income (initially 1 per cent, now 1.5 per cent), and a redistribution of pre-existing health insurance subsidies (Sax 1984: 175). Additional, earmarked sources of funding have since been added. Within a few years after the introduction of Medicare, government funding had increased to approximately 70 per cent of total health financing. Tax relief on private health insurance was terminated. Insurance was not permitted to cover the 'gap' between the benefit and the Schedule fee of a service.

Lead-up to the current reforms

The current wave of health reforms in Australia started in the second half of the 1980s, not through any central initiative but as a result of several factors. First, the states were becoming apprehensive about their ability to fund the rising costs and increasing demand for hospital care over the long term. For its part, the Commonwealth government initiated an ongoing series of measures to increase cost-effectiveness and efficiency in the sector. Finally, initiatives by the private sector to establish a more attractive alternative to government-funded hospitals (see Chapters 5 and 13) resulted in still further changes.

In 1990 the Commonwealth government launched the National Health Strategy (for details see Macklin 1990), which examined more than a dozen components of Australia's health system and issued recommendations for reforms in financing and service provision. The National Health Strategy proposed a series of reforms, including:

- national goals and targets to guide resource allocation;
- improvements in access to services, and in their quality and coordination;
- incentives to encourage efficiency and effectiveness of services;
- improved responsiveness to consumers; and
- increased accountability.

The Commonwealth was at the same time encouraging and financing activities typical of health reform, notably the development of a casemix system for Australian conditions and measures to increase service efficiency. The development of Australian national diagnostic-related groups (AN-DRGs, see Chapter 6) and the training and capacity-building activities the Commonwealth funded, produced a system that individual states could now implement to improve the cost-effectiveness of hospitals and related services.

The Commonwealth, responsible for the funding of medical services under the MBS, also began to implement a series of measures designed to make general practitioners (GPs) more efficient as 'gatekeepers':

- fostering and funding the development of local GP networks nationally (see Chapter 8);
- accreditation of GPs;
- developing standards of general practice; and
- commissioning and funding research projects aimed at strengthening general practice.

Meanwhile, in the states and territories the issue of financing rising demand, coupled with the increased costs of adopting new technology, was putting unremitting pressure on budgets. Capital infrastructure surveys confirmed that sources of capital investment would have to be forthcoming either from state treasuries or from other, private, sources.

Decentralisation, or devolution, was gradually adopted by the major states, and most introduced new area or regional structures. Funding, purchasing, and provision remained fused, as distinct from the funder/

purchaser/provider split that would be introduced in New Zealand. Health reform was now on the agenda nationally and by the 1990s had begun in earnest within every state and territory, though in varying forms.

At the state level, the restructuring of the 1980s was then followed in most states by a sharp focus on technical efficiency. The 1990s saw the introduction of competitive processes and mechanisms aimed at increasing the cost-effectiveness of health care delivery, and at encouraging innovation in service delivery. The same three reform approaches have been adopted in most of the Australian states, though to differing degrees (see especially Chapter 11):

1. the introduction of managerial reform (often promoted in the interest of 'contestability' and 'greater transparency') in the public health care bureaucracies, parallel with the reforms introduced elsewhere in OECD nations;
2. increasing reliance on the private sector, particularly for capital infrastructure development, and for growth in service delivery; and
3. adoption of casemix as a means of increasing accountability and, in some instances, allocation of funds.

Unlike New Zealand, the current wave of health reform was never launched in Australia as what Ham (1997b: 1844) calls a carefully designed and comprehensive 'big bang' approach. Moreover, all reform initiatives have assumed that the very popular Medicare will be retained. Reform efforts have therefore tended to concentrate on increasing technical efficiency, and on other aspects of micro-economic reform. Australia's approach to reform has also assumed that the mixed public–private, and multi-tiered (federal/state/local) division of responsibilities will remain. In short, Australia's approach to health reform in the late 1980s and the 1990s can best be characterised as incremental and syncretic, consisting of a range of independent but interactive measures in different parts of the system.

The current Australian health system

Structure

Australia's health care system has three levels within the public sphere: Commonwealth, state, and local (Figure 1.2, p. 23). The extent to which responsibilities for health are divided among the different levels of government, and between the public and private sectors, is a distinguishing feature of the Australian health system (AIHW 1998a: 157). In general the Commonwealth government is responsible for the funding of health services. The states have principal responsibility for the direct provision of services, and the health responsibilities of local government (which vary from state to state) lie mainly in environmental control measures and a broad range of community-based and home-care services (Palmer and Short 1994: 10–12). The private sector is involved at all levels in funding (insurance and out-of-pocket, personal payments) and provision (general practice, medical specialities, diagnostics, hospitals, and aged care).

Financing

Australia spends approximately 8.4 per cent of GDP on health care annually, a figure that has held fairly constant over the past two decades (AIHW 1998a: 164, 1999: 1). Government spending on health is equivalent to 5.6 per cent of GDP; the balance being derived from private sources (Figure 1.3, p. 25). In 1995/96 total spending on health in Australia was A$7267 billion or an average of $2536 per person (AIHW 1998a). This figure includes medical services of doctors and specialists; hospital treatment; pharmaceuticals; dental, physiotherapy and other allied health services; community and public health services; and nursing-home care. Of total health care funding, 37 per cent was allocated to acute-care hospitals, 20.2 per cent to medical services, and 12 per cent to pharmaceuticals (AIHW

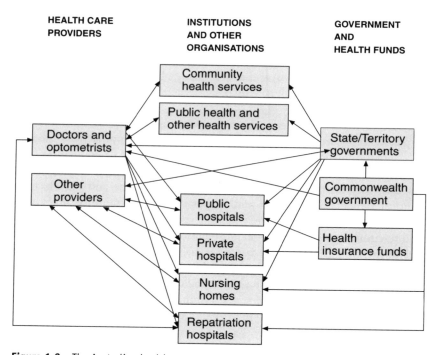

Figure 1.2 The Australian health care system

Source: Palmer and Short 1994

1998a: 163–7). Of this amount nearly 18 per cent was funded through benefits paid by private health insurance funds (AIHW 1998a: 175).

Health care is funded by a combination of general taxation and hypothecated (i.e. earmarked) taxes, much of which is channelled through a compulsory insurance scheme managed by a single insurer (Medicare). Some of the revenue is allocated directly by the Commonwealth on health services (notably aged care); the balance is allocated as block grants directly to the states. Additional sources of funding are voluntary private health insurance and direct payment by individuals. Health care funding in Australia is dominated by the public sector, which accounts for approximately 69.1 per cent of all funding (AIHW 1998a: 1). Of this the Commonwealth accounts for 45.5 per cent and the states for 23.6 per cent. Private sources (including not-for-profit organisations, private health insurance, and self-funding) account for about 31.3 per cent of all health expenditure, representing a gradually increasing share of health funding over the preceding decade (AIHW 1998a: 163). The source of public funding is general revenue raised through taxation. Since 1984 a slowly increasing Medicare levy, initially 1 per cent of taxable income, now 1.5 per cent, is earmarked for health. A Medicare levy surcharge was introduced in 1997 for single individuals with taxable incomes in excess of A$50 000 and couples and families with combined taxable incomes in excess of A$100 000 who do not have private hospital cover through private health insurance. As of 1 January 1999, however, a 30 per cent tax rebate was available for the cost of private health insurance premiums, and a later change linked private health insurance premiums to the age at which the beneficiary commences coverage ('age–adjusted' rates).

The complicated mechanisms for funding health in Australia are depicted in Figure 1.3 (p. 25). Australia's complex approach to funding incorporates virtually every method in the entire range of popular funding methods described by Ham (1998: 5). The Commonwealth takes primary responsibility for funding the Medical Benefits Scheme and the Pharmaceutical Benefits Scheme (35 and 12 per cent of Commonwealth health spending respectively), and for residential aged care. It shares with the states and territories the costs of public hospitals (31 per cent of Commonwealth health spending), community-based services, and public health. The states and territories fund public hospitals, public health, mental health, disability support, and aspects of community, rehabilitation, and residential aged–care services. Nearly two-thirds of states' funding (64.5 per cent) supports the public hospital system (AIHW 1997; Commonwealth Department of Health and Aged Care, n.d.).

Individuals purchase private health insurance to supplement the services provided through Medicare, and make direct payments for dental

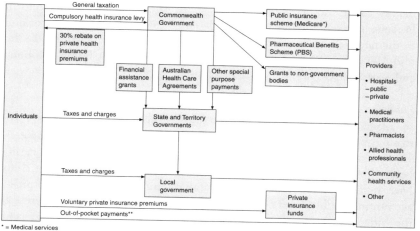

* = Medical services
** Includes mandatory copayment on PBS items

Figure 1.3 Australia: Financing of health care, 1999

Source: 'The Reform of Health Care Systems: A Review of Seventeen OECD Countries', Health Policy Studies, no. 5,
courtesy of Australian Commonwealth Department of Health and Aged Care

services, allied health services (e.g. physiotherapy), and nursing care at home and in the community. Private health insurance enrolment has declined steadily since 1984, from 50 per cent in June 1984 to 31.6 per cent in December 1997 (AIHW 1998a: 176), and is continuing to decline. Of private expenditure for health care, 35 per cent is sourced from private insurers and 54 per cent from out-of-pocket payments, including pharmaceuticals.

Medicare covers all Australians for medical services outside hospitals (at 85 per cent of the fee schedule set by Medicare), and for the cost of in-hospital treatment and accommodation when treated in public hospitals as public patients. Private patients treated in public or private hospitals are entitled to 75 per cent of the Medicare Schedule for doctors' services. The balance, 25 per cent, is reimbursed by private insurance. Geographical coverage by hospitals, medical practitioners and other providers is excellent in urban areas and larger regional centres but is poorer in rural and isolated areas, where few doctors choose to practise and it is not considered economically viable to support more than basic hospital and clinic treatment.

The Commonwealth maintains most responsibility for funding of aged care, whereas provision (in the form of nursing homes and hostels, and the increasing 'packages' of support for older people remaining at home) is mainly a state and private responsibility. An Aged Care Structural Reform Package, implemented in 1997, was designed to provide funding according to the needs of the individual older person, not aged-care facilities. In the mid-1990s over 83 per cent of older Australians lived at home (Mooney and Scotton 1998: 34).

Provision of services

In Australia's mixed public–private health system, medical services are mainly provided privately, since most of the medical workforce is engaged in private employment. However, most hospitals have historically been publicly owned and funded. Since the 1980s three important shifts have influenced the number, size, and casemix of Australian hospitals, accounting for an 11 per cent reduction in available public beds, whereas at the same time the number of private acute beds has increased by 5 per cent (AIHW 1998a: 188). A trend towards fewer, larger facilities, and substantial reductions in lengths of stay have reduced the total number of hospitals, which now have a more acute casemix. Next, an emphasis on assisting people with mental illness to remain in the community, or, when they need hospital treatment, to get it in general public hospitals rather than psychiatric hospitals, has meant the closure of many large psychiatric hospitals. Finally, a policy to assist older people with lower dependency to remain at home or in assisted living environments (e.g. hostels), has meant a slight decline in nursing-home accommodation in spite of significant growth in the number of older people (AIHW 1998a: 190).

Of the more than 85 000 acute hospital beds in Australia, a ratio of 4.5 beds per 1000 population (AIHW 1998a: 191), 70 per cent are located in public hospitals and slightly less than a quarter in private facilities. Private hospitals may be not-for-profit, charitable facilities, or for-profit institutions. Hospitals in each category are rapidly affiliating into corporate groups (see Chapter 5). Nearly all public hospitals are owned and managed by the states and territories, some of which have devolved management responsibility, if not ownership, to local areas or networks (for detailed and current data on the health and health system of Australia, see AIHW 1998a).

Australians must seek treatment first from their general practitioner, the 'gatekeeper' with the authority to refer them for specialist treatment if this is required. GPs, all privately employed, have historically been in one- or two-person practices. Only recently have they been offered government financial incentives to affiliate into larger groups, but the large, comprehensive medical centres that include GPs, common in the USA and elsewhere, have not proved popular in Australia, though a number did spring up during the 1980s. Pharmacies, privately owned and operated, are in the throes of amalgamation into larger chains, within the constraints imposed by national competition and regulatory guidelines.

For certain health and health-related conditions, people may turn first to their local publicly funded community health centre. These have integrated primary-care facilities that generally do not provide medical treatment but do have 'well-baby' clinics, psychological and other mental health services, adolescent health services, and drug and alcohol treatment.

Regulation and quality

Responsibility for regulation and control of quality in the Australian health system is shared by the Commonwealth and state governments, and by professional boards and associations. The Australian Council on Health Care Standards (ACHS), established in 1974 (see Chapter 16), provides accreditation and quality assurance for hospitals and health-related facilities, though accreditation is not mandatory. Licences for hospital beds are granted by state departments of health. Other sources of quality assurance for facilities are private quality-assurance accrediting firms that certify compliance with the ISO and other standards.

Medical and health care professionals are registered by professional colleges and boards in the states and territories. The colleges (e.g. Royal Australasian College of Surgeons, Royal College of Nursing, Australia) provide another form of quality assurance through their training programs and certification. Consumers tend to be active in organisations that focus on research, prevention, and treatment of particular diseases (the Stroke, Heart, and Diabetes Foundations, and volunteer groups for the aged, disabled, and homebound). Consumer advocacy organisations specialising in health policy and advocacy (e.g. the Consumers' Health Forum) are comparatively few, but have direct and effective access to government.

New Zealand

Country profile

New Zealand, one of Australia's closest neighbours, consists of two main islands and a number of lesser islands. Compared with Australia, it is much smaller in size (270 000 square kilometres) and in population (3.7 million people at 1996). New Zealand's North Island contains approximately two-thirds of the country's population.

New Zealand is also highly urbanised: roughly 80 per cent of the population lives in urban areas, with just over 50 per cent concentrated in the five main cities (Auckland, with 1.1 million residents; Wellington, 350 000;

Christchurch, 340 000; Hamilton, 165 000; Dunedin, 113 000). The balance of the population is distributed among smaller urban centres, towns, and rural communities. Like Australia, New Zealand has a sizeable number of isolated settlements. The majority (approximately 80 per cent) of the country's population is of European descent, predominantly British or Irish. Māori comprise 15 per cent of the population.

In 1996 New Zealand's GDP was NZ$95 816 million, the equivalent of US$17 433 per capita, placing it twentieth among OECD countries. Like Australia, New Zealand's economy traditionally relied heavily on the export of raw agricultural produce, mainly to Britain. As these trade opportunities declined, New Zealand began to export a much wider range of goods and services to more diverse markets. In recent years, the country's trade focus has shifted from the United Kingdom and Europe to the Asia–Pacific region. This trend is mirrored in New Zealand's recent immigration patterns: newer migrants are more likely to be of Asian than of European background.

New Zealand has a unique ethnic composition: 14.5 per cent of its population identify as Māori and 5.6 per cent is of Pacific Islander origin. Like Australia, the country's age structure is typical of a developed Western economy. The proportion of people aged 65 and older (estimated to be 11.6 per cent in 1998) is similar to Australia, but lower than in many Western European countries. The structure of New Zealand's population will change rapidly over the next twenty-five years. Whereas the European population is ageing as the 'baby boomers' born in the 1950s approach retirement age, around 60 per cent of New Zealand's Māori and Pacific Island population is under 25 years of age. This demographic transition will generate a different pattern of health needs and has significant implications for the future planning and delivery of health services.

The health picture

The health status of New Zealanders is similar to the profile observed in Australia: Average life expectancy at birth is high, currently 76.9 years overall—79.6 for females and 74.2 for males, placing New Zealand about fifteenth for males and twentieth for females among OECD countries. Infant mortality is 6.54 per 1000 live births (Statistics New Zealand 1998).

However, these figures belie significant differences in health indicators among New Zealanders. While life expectancy for non-Māori New Zealanders is 75.3 years for men and 80.6 years for women, Māori life expectancy at birth is only 67.2 years for men and 71.6 years for women (Statistics New Zealand 1998). The Māori infant mortality rate (13.8 per

1000 live births) is more than twice the non-Māori rate (6.8 per 1000 live births) (NZ Health Information Service n.d.). Rates of hospitalisation for such conditions as influenza, pneumonia and stroke may be as much as four times higher among Māori residents (NZ Health Information Service, unpublished morbidity data).

The lead-up to reform

Both Australia and New Zealand have experienced milestones in health reform in the late 1980s and the 1990s. For Australia, the defining date was 1984 and the introduction of Medicare, though the recent wave of reform dates from the late 1980s. In New Zealand, 1993 saw the culmination of a reform process that had gathered pace throughout the 1980s and early 1990s.

As in Australia, the involvement of the NZ government in health and health care was prompted by concern about communicable diseases. Until the end of the nineteenth century, the health sector comprised individual practitioners, nearly fifty hospitals (subsidised by the Office of the Colonial Secretary), and eight lunatic asylums (Dow 1995: 244).

Formal government involvement in the management and provision of health care began with passage of the first Public Health Act in 1872. The establishment of the NZ Ministry of Health in 1900, which preceded its counterpart in Britain by nineteen years, led to creation of a State Department of Health under a Minister of the Crown (Heggie 1958: 32–3). The public health responsibilities of government evolved, and, after the 1918 influenza epidemic, the Board of Health was created under the Health Bill of 1920. Public hospitals proliferated in ensuing years (Heggie 1958: 35).

The *Social Security Act 1938* included provision for medical, hospital, and other health-related benefits, placed under the responsibility of the Minister of Health. Its intent was to legislate universal access to a comprehensive health care system. In practice the system that emerged was a much more complex pattern of public and private funding and provision.

However, the New Zealand government never assumed responsibility for either the provision or the financing of all health services. Health service delivery remained in the private sector at the primary level (GPs), whereas an admixture of large and small voluntary (not-for-profit) providers, some reliant on government funding, provided essential ambulance, child health, and other services. As early as 1938, government recognised that without appropriate intervention, rationing and inequity in health services was inevitable as increasing demand and capacity to provide treatment exceeded the financial means of significant numbers of New

Zealanders. The structure of New Zealand's health care system at the beginning of the 1980s is depicted in Figure 1.4 (p. 33).

The New Zealand economy had been subjected to limited micro-economic reforms during the 1970s. For a protracted period starting in the mid-1980s (1986–92), New Zealand's economy experienced no overall GDP growth. In response to this situation, government embarked on a wide-ranging economic reform agenda. To dramatic fiscal measures, and the introduction of a goods and services tax (GST), government added other mechanisms designed to create a more efficient and market-oriented economy. This included deregulation of the labour market, imposition of tight inflation targets, and budgetary constraints in social sectors, notably education and health.

The early reforms of the 1980s were characterised by corporatisation— the establishment of state-owned enterprises (SOEs) and other initiatives at the central and local levels—all aimed at improving technical efficiency (OECD 1994). During the late 1980s and the 1990s the government of New Zealand, like many other countries, had been observing the health system reforms implemented in Britain. Of particular interest was the move towards devolution of responsibility and accountability. The initial result was the establishment of New Zealand's fourteen area health boards. Their purpose was to better calibrate services with need, and to improve resource allocation by devolving substantial responsibility from central government to more local agencies.

The *Area Health Boards Act 1983* established the first area boards by merging the previous hospital boards and health development units (the latter reporting to the Department of Health). As in New South Wales in Australia, the process began with a series of pilots. By 1989 fourteen area health boards, covering populations ranging from 35 000 to 900 000, encompassed all of New Zealand. The boards were charged with planning and delivering health services and protecting the health of their stipulated populations. The funding of the boards, initially pegged to the historical cost of services, was replaced by a population-based funding formula. Area health boards were given responsibility for capital expenditures in 1991. At the primary level, GPs continued to operate independently, on a government-subsidised fee-for-service basis. Government also met the costs of pharmaceuticals, in whole or in part.

The formation of area health boards obviously changed the role and functions of the Department of Health. For example, whereas services were previously centrally planned, by 1989 they were planned at the area level, within parameters stipulated by the Minister of Health and agreed by the area boards in annual contracts.

However, as was the case in New South Wales, regionalisation through area health boards did not address most of the issues driving reform. First, the boards, as planners, purchasers, and providers of health services, were seen as insufficiently motivated to disturb entrenched patterns of health service delivery, and in some cases, (ironically for regionally based entities) not responsive enough to the needs of local consumers, including Māori. Second, the services controlled by the area health boards and those delivered by independent practitioners (notably in the primary-care arena) were still funded by separate funding streams. This meant that no single agency had a strong incentive to change the discontinuity of services involving different levels of care (notably between primary and secondary care), or among aspects of care (clinical procedures, pharmaceuticals, continuing care).

Restructuring had little impact on overall costs or efficiency and did not diminish financial risk to government, as key elements of the health care system remained essentially based on fee for service (Davies 1998).

The reform process in New Zealand (1993–99)

The 1993 reforms
By the early 1990s New Zealand's economy was emerging from its long period of economic decline. Costs had increased in the health sector, but the availability and quality of services had not improved commensurately. In fact there was a general perception that access and coverage were deteriorating, enough to suggest that a crisis was imminent. Meanwhile, reforms had begun in other sectors of New Zealand's economy. Government's next step was to initiate further reform of the health sector.

In 1991 the government that had been elected in late 1990 proposed a radical reform of New Zealand's health sector. The focus of the reform was allocative and technical efficiency, 'value for money' (Ashton 1997: 16). The aims of the system-wide reform were:

- to improve access to effective and affordable health care;
- to promote flexibility and innovation in delivery of health care;
- to provide greater choice to consumers, and improve their access to quality health care;
- to support public health; and
- to increase the flexibility of the health care system and its capacity to respond to changing needs (Ashton 1997: 16).

The proposals, outlined in *Your Health and the Public Health*, came into effect on 1 July 1993 when the government introduced a coherent model that separated the roles of funding, purchasing, and provision of health services. To achieve this, the previous network of area health boards was removed. The health system was restructured along lines similar to reforms in other sectors (Figure 1.5, p. 33). The intended features of the reform were the following:

1. Funding for all personal health services in a region was integrated within a single agency so that resources could be shifted according to priority health needs.
2. All residents were to be provided with services of appropriate quality and level, with individuals able to exercise a greater degree of choice in service provider.
3. Separation of purchaser and provider was introduced to enable purchasers to acquire services from the most appropriate and cost-effective providers.
4. Competition among providers was encouraged.
5. 'Contestability' was introduced to publicly owned hospitals, which were restructured as business units and required to compete with private providers in the interest of increasing efficiency and effectiveness.
6. Contracts between purchasers and providers, previously implicit, became more explicit: accountability structures were sharpened and outputs in terms of efficiency and health gains were better quantified and embedded in new contracts.
7. Health services came under scrutiny for their capacity to achieve improvements in the health status of New Zealanders.
8. Public and personal health services were financed separately to better protect investments in health protection and promotion from the incessant funding pressures of acute health services.
9. While the state would retain the primary role for health funding, private finance would continue, the system of user charges was formalised, and individuals were encouraged to assume greater responsibility for their own health.
10. 'Core health services'—the focus of government health funding— would be explicitly defined.

In practice, the intended reforms were achieved to a varying degree. For example, competition was minimal, and attempts at introducing contestability progressed haltingly. Defining 'core health services' was a vexed process, and the segregation of health promotion funding was soon abandoned.

Figures 1.4 (p. 33) to 1.7 (p. 34) depict the organisation of New Zealand's health sector before reform (Figure 1.4), immediately after the 1993 reforms (Figure 1.5), in 1996 (Figure 1.6), and in 1999 after the amalgamation of the four regional health authorities into a single Health Funding Authority (Figure 1.7).

Restructuring for reform

The main features of the restructure were four regional purchasers, distinct providers, and a continuation of user charges pegged to family income.

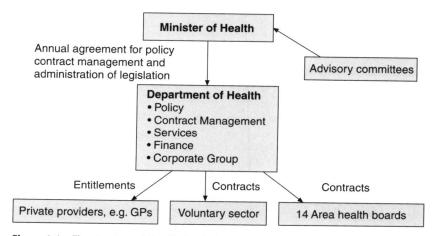

Figure 1.4 The structure of New Zealand's health system before 1993

Source: Courtesy of Ministry of Health, New Zealand

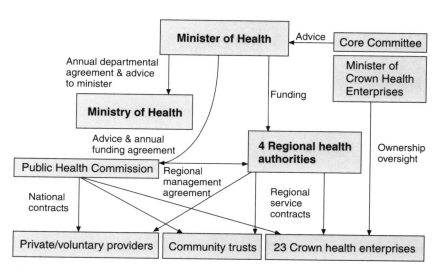

Figure 1.5 The structure of New Zealand's health system after enactment of 1993 reforms

Source: Courtesy of Ministry of Health, New Zealand

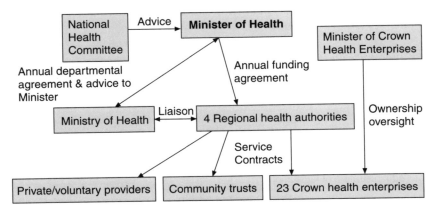

Figure 1.6   The structure of New Zealand's health system, 1996

Source: Courtesy of Ministry of Health, New Zealand

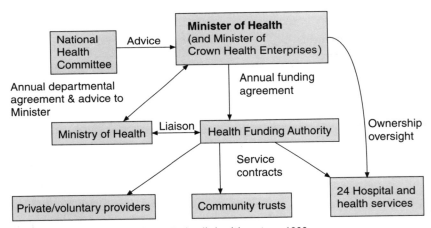

Figure 1.7   The structure of New Zealand's health system, 1999

Source: Courtesy of Ministry of Health, New Zealand

The reformed health system included a Minister of Health (the 'purchasing Minister'); the Minister of Crown Health Enterprises (the 'providing minister'); the Minister of the ACC (which has a role in funding treatment for injuries sustained in accidents); and a series of formally constituted advisory bodies (Ashton 1998: 16).

To implement the reforms, four regional health authorities were established as purchasers of health care. Each RHA had responsibility for funding the health care of a population. These ranged in size from 750 000 to 1 million. Twenty-three Crown health enterprises (CHEs) were established as government-owned providers of health services.

As purchasers, RHAs were responsible for monitoring the health needs of their populations and identifying the appropriate sources of health and disability services. With their capped budgets, they purchased health care, entering into and monitoring contracts with providers. Services purchased included primary, secondary, and specialist, as well as continuing care. They purchased from government as well as private (including not-for-profit) service providers.

The RHAs' goals were both health-related and operational: to purchase care that contributed most cost-effectively as well as efficiently to health outcomes. This meant shifting greater resources to primary care (where the shift could be shown to be beneficial) and providing incentives for greater technical efficiency. The pooling of most health funding under the aegis of a single funder was intended to reduce, if not eliminate, cost-shifting among different agencies and service levels.

The government-owned providers, the CHEs, were defined as 'state-owned enterprises', consistent with a corporatisation model. Each CHE had two shareholders, the Minister for Crown Health Enterprises (a newly established portfolio) and the Minister of Finance. They were permitted to raise capital, enter into local employment contracts with staff, and operate independently under the Companies Act as companies with limited liability. The new structure was introduced all at once on 1 July 1993. However, as is common in reform of social sectors, some allowances were made in the detailed implementation to soften the blow of the reforms, particularly the introduction of payments to CHEs.

Other significant structural reforms saw the establishment of a Public Health Commission (PHC), a Crown agency independent of the Ministry of Health (MOH), responsible for public health policy, monitoring of health indicators, and purchase of public health services, among other responsibilities. The PHC entered into contracts with CHEs and other service providers for provision of services considered to be 'investments' in public health. The MOH continued to regulate public health.

The Department of Health was restructured as a Ministry of Health. It remained the government's principal adviser on strategic health policy, health financing, the regulatory framework, and monitoring of health outcomes. Perhaps its most important role in the reformed health system was monitoring of health sector performance in general and the performance of RHAs against their funding contracts in particular. A separate body, the Crown Companies Monitoring Advisory Unit, was given the task of representing the government's interests as shareholder of the new CHEs.

The current New Zealand health system

Structure

During the early years of the new system a number of fine-tuning changes were made (Figure 1.7, p. 34). The PHC and the Public Health Agency were eliminated. Public health was to be protected not by a separate administration but by 'ring-fencing' of its funds (Davies 1998). User charges that had originally been introduced for selected hospital services were removed, plans to allow the establishment of 'alternative health care plans', mooted in the government's original proposals, were dropped and, as Hindle and Perkins describe in Chapter 4, efforts to agree on 'core health services' were abandoned.

Publicly funded health care is now purchased by a single national purchaser (the Health Funding Authority, or HFA). It decides whether to buy services through contracts with Hospitals and Health Services (H&HSs, formerly CHEs), community trusts, or for-profit and not-for-profit (voluntary) providers.

The direction of the reforms changed further with the election of a new, coalition government in 1996. In 1996 it appeared to some that reform had 'halted in its tracks'. This was perhaps true for some aspects of the health system, but it was not so not for others, and from a distance it may even appear that important progress has been made.

Financing

Health services in New Zealand are financed through taxation at the national level. Funds are obtained from general revenue and New Zealanders are subject neither to payroll taxes nor to any dedicated health tax (as in Australia). Health expenditure trends over the period 1970/71 to 1996/97 show that the average annual increase in both public and private expenditure on health in New Zealand was approximately 3.5 per cent per annum. Total health expenditure over the same period increased from 5.2 per cent of GDP to 7.6 per cent.

In 1996/97 about 77 per cent of total health expenditure was financed from general taxation (Ministry of Health 1998). The government has recently adopted a process of establishing a three-year 'indicative' funding path for health in order to aid longer-term planning in the sector. Actual allocations are, however, still confirmed as part of the annual budget round.

Secondary and tertiary hospital services are available free at the point of use for all New Zealanders, but payment of all or some of the cost of primary care (including pharmaceuticals) and long-term residential services is commonly required. Residents with low incomes, or whose medical conditions require very frequent use of services, can be exempted from co-payments.

About 37 per cent of the population is estimated to be covered by private health insurance (compared with just over 30 per cent of Australians). But the policies are more limited in coverage, typically covering the costs of elective surgery and, in some cases, reimbursement of charges levied in respect of GP visits, pharmaceuticals, and other items. From the policy-holders' point of view, the main attraction of private insurance is more timely access to elective surgery, choice of surgeon, and certainty as to where and when surgery will take place (as is the case in Australia).

Provision
The four RHAs were merged into a single, national purchaser, the Health Funding Authority, designed to lower administration costs and eliminate unjustifiable geographic variations in service access. CHEs have been renamed 'hospitals and health services' (HHSs) and are no longer required to earn profits. A twenty-fourth HHS has been established to manage blood services nationally (the first HHS with a specifically national focus). The position of Minister for Crown Health Enterprises disappeared, and HHSs are accountable to the Ministers for Health and Finance.

As noted above, primary medical services are provided largely by private medical practitioners. Over recent years, individual practitioners have tended to affiliate in independent practitioner associations (IPAs), described and analysed at length in Chapter 10. Whereas hospitals are predominantly public in ownership and management, with a number operated by not-for-profit organisations, private participation in other forms is growing.

Regulation and quality
As in Australia, the regulation and monitoring of health care is carried out by a combination of professional bodies, a non-government organisation that accredits health care facilities, government-funded 'watchdogs', and consumer organisations.

Professional colleges supervise and monitor medical and nursing professionals' qualifications and accreditation in New Zealand. Doctors are licensed by the NZ Medical Council (advised by the medical colleges), and nurses by the NZ Nursing Council, both of which establish the minimum educational and practical standards and act as the disciplinary bodies for registered practitioners.

Quality Health, formerly the NZ Council on Healthcare Standards, was established in 1993 with seed funding from government. A not-for-profit organisation like its counterpart the Australian Council for Healthcare Standards, it accredits hospitals for a stipulated period, applying a formal process. Sixty per cent of public hospitals and 43 per cent of private hospitals in New Zealand are accredited or preparing for accreditation through Quality Health.

Current developments

The health system of New Zealand is continuing to evolve. The main focus has once again returned to the key issue of improving performance in the sector. Recent initiatives include the establishment of integrated-care organisations, implementation of 'booking systems' as an alternative to waiting lists for elective surgery, promulgation of clinical guidelines to enhance the effectiveness of services, and introduction of more explicit prioritisation criteria for clinical services.

Conclusion

The salient features of the Australian health care system are first, the division of responsibility for health care between three levels of government—Commonwealth, state, and local—and second, its financing through Medicare, a universal funding scheme based on tax revenue, which provides universal access to medical, hospital and pharmaceutical benefits. Both finance and provision are dominated by the public sectors, and public and private currently coexist in 'dynamic tension' (Peabody et al. 1996). However, strains on the public system, further deregulation of the industry, and promotion of the principles of competition across government as a whole, including the health sector, are the backdrop for recent incremental reforms. Australia had no 'big bang'. Nor was reform the result of any coherent, unified process, but instead the cumulative result of many independent initiatives responding to the same drivers.

Although there are some parallels in the historical development of the health systems of New Zealand and Australia, they differ in some fundamental respects. First, New Zealand's central government has responsibility for funding and provision of most publicly financed health care. As we shall see, this greatly influenced the likelihood of more sweeping and homogeneous reform. When health reform came to New Zealand, however, it was radical, on a national scale, much earlier than in Australia, and has since evolved through several metamorphoses. Health reform in each nation was influenced by the concept of market reform as an antidote to similar cost and demand pressures. Yet New Zealand has never developed the same degree of private as well as public provision of health care, particularly in its hospital system.

Throughout this book comparisons and distinctions will be drawn between the two health care systems in order to illustrate the influence of crucial factors on the pace, direction, and sustainability of health reform.

2

The Political Economy of Health Sector Reform

Jane Hall and Rosalie Viney

Health care expenditure comprises between 6 per cent and 10 per cent of the gross domestic product (GDP) of most developed nations (and even more in the USA) (AIHW 1998a). In all developed countries governments play a large part in financing and regulating the health system, and in some countries they are the main providers of health services. Governments have historically stepped in to play this role because of the interplay of several factors, among them the problem that unregulated markets for health care do not work efficiently, and social concerns about the distribution of health care. Further, health is highly valued because it is fundamental to the definition of how we live. Health care is perceived to underpin an individual's health, and it is therefore virtually impossible to separate health care from issues of life, death, and quality of life. So, for example, Victor Fuchs (1974) aptly named his classic book about resource allocation in the health system, *Who Shall Live?*.

The high and growing costs of health care mean that the sector provides employment for many health professionals and others. (Health services require clerical workers, accountants, maintenance staff, cooks, gardeners, and so on.) The health industry is a major client for many suppliers of specialised (e.g. intensive-care equipment) and non-specialised (e.g. computers, refrigerators, food) goods and services. The health industry involves numerous suppliers in a range of sectors as well as trained health workers and ancillary staff. Since expenditure on health therefore translates into income for a wide range of individuals and businesses, reductions in such expenditure will affect their livelihood and well-being.

All of these factors together make issues of health care as much part of the political agenda as they are matters of economics. Even in those countries where government does not provide services directly, health care is still a large item of government expenditure. Questions about the efficiency and effectiveness of government spending on health therefore touch on the role of government itself. Political discourse in the last decade has focused on reducing the role of government, minimising its intervention, and reducing government expenditure, yet, through the actions of government, ensuring the efficacy of markets and competitive forces. Predictably, similar ideas have been advanced in the interest of reforming health care systems.

This chapter gives a conceptual framework for understanding the context and drivers of health reform. First it analyses health care as a commodity and shows that there is a number of reasons for competitive markets not existing for health care. It then considers the social and political context of health care. The special features of health systems lead to certain predictable institutional responses in the health care market, as discussed in the third section. The fourth section outlines the problems of health insurance costs for certain groups, particularly the elderly and those with chronic illness. The distribution of health care costs as determined by actuarial methods often does not accord with the socially desirable distribution of those costs. That leads to a discussion of the objectives of health care systems, and of their opposed, underlying values. Finally, an overview of health care reform against this background is presented.

Health Care as an Economic Commodity

Economics is about how societies and individuals decide to use resources, what to produce, and how to distribute the goods and services produced. In a command economy, the state determines the allocation of resources. The Soviet economies were command economies; their breakdown has shown that these systems were inflexible and inefficient at organising production and distribution (though whether that would apply to all command economies is another issue). Nonetheless, the collapse of the former Soviet economies has had major political and economic consequences, including a growing acceptance that market economies work better.

In market economies, the allocation of resources is determined by the interaction of demand and supply, in markets mediated by price signals. Consumers' demand for a good or service is an expression of their willingness to pay for that good or service—that is, their willingness to devote their resources to it rather than to other goods and services. Consumer demand is determined by consumer preferences, what consumers want or value. The resultant resource allocation is responsive to consumers, hence the idea of consumer sovereignty. Consumer demand is also responsive to price: the higher the price the more value consumers expect from something. In general, demand will fall as price increases. Suppliers produce goods and services for sale. They want to make a profit above their costs of manufacture or acquisition. Suppliers' readiness to produce is determined by their costs of production. The higher the price, relative to cost, the more attractive that market. In general, supply will increase as price increases.

Thus price is the mechanism through which information about consumer preferences (demand) and production costs (supply) is conveyed. A market functioning effectively is able to adjust quantity supplied to equate with quantity demanded. Economists use the term 'the invisible hand' to describe how the market 'signals' and responds in this way. Under the conditions of perfectly competitive markets, there is no other allocation of resources and distribution of commodities that could make someone better off without making someone else worse off. Perfectly competitive markets maximise the well-being of consumers. In market economies the 'invisible hand' is allowed to determine the allocation of resources for most commodities most of the time, even though few real markets meet the conditions of perfect competition. (A good introduction to the 'invisible hand' is given in Donaldson and Gerard 1993: ch. 2.)

Health care, however, has a number of features that make it quite different from the typical commodity conceptualised in the market model. Much of health economics is concerned with the extent and significance of those differences, and therefore the question arises whether resource allocation for health care can be left to the imperfect market like other commodities, or whether it should be treated differently.

What makes health care different? (This is covered in more depth in many introductory health economics texts, including Donaldson and Gerard 1993.) First, the demand for health care can be thought of as a 'derived demand'. That means that consuming health care is not valued in itself but as a way of producing health. So consumer demand is not just a matter of tastes and prices but will vary with the consumer's state of health. Second, the typical consumer does not have the necessary expertise to act as a rational and informed consumer. To decide how much health care to buy, the consumer needs to understand how health care will affect his or her health status. Yet to be able to diagnose a health problem and to prescribe the appropriate treatment requires highly complex knowledge, the result of years of specialist training. Third, health care is characterised by a high degree of uncertainty. Even with the right diagnosis and the best treatment, the health outcome is not predictable with total confidence. There is a further degree of uncertainty for the consumer: the individual does not know when he or she will become ill and so health care purchases cannot be planned. Fourth, consumption of health care by one person may affect the health and/or well-being of another. This is obvious in cases such as immunisation or treatment for communicable diseases, where the interest in another's health and health care consumption is enlightened self-interest. Health is also different in its altruistic effects: most people genuinely desire that others not suffer when suffering can be averted or remedied by health care. And they are willing to acquiesce to priorities and funding that enact these altruistic principles.

When these characteristics exist, economists say that markets fail; that is, they fall short of achieving the socially optimal allocation of resources one would expect in a perfectly competitive market. Some of the characteristics of health care also occur, to a greater or lesser extent, in other commodities. In these instances markets can respond to these sources of market failure without the large-scale intervention of governments that characterises health care.

For instance, where there is a problem of information (i.e. where consumers lack the detailed information to judge the performance of the product), better-informed technical advisers may be sought. Consumers who rely on suppliers for their technical advice may be sold more commodities, at higher prices, since it is in the seller's interest to maximise sales. Consumers usually recognise this and act accordingly. For example, consumers of stereo equipment or new motor vehicles rarely understand the technical workings of the product and rely on advice from manufacturers, retailers, and consumer reports. Consumers tend to be wary of used-car salespersons. In health care, 'the technical adviser' is most often the doctor, who is also a seller of health care. To address this potential risk, doctors have a professional code of ethics that outlaws using their patients for profit rather than treating for the patients' good. But there is an important difference between the consumer of stereo equipment and the consumer of health care. The stereo buyer can judge what is wanted from the equipment in terms of quality of sound production, remote control, tapes and compact discs and so on. But the consumer of health care is rarely able to assess what treatment is needed (e.g. should a headache be treated with aspirin or investigated as a brain tumour?), though the consumer can judge how personal well-being would be improved by elimination of the headache. The imbalance in information between consumer and adviser, patient and doctor is called asymmetry of information.

Another characteristic not unique to health is the problem of uncertainty. Uncertainty about the need for future consumption, where the potential financial cost is large, has led markets to develop mechanisms to protect against that risk. A common mechanism is insurance. Insurance allows consumers to trade an uncertain but possibly large loss, for a certain but much smaller cost—in insurance terminology, the continuous small payments called 'premiums'. Insurance arises in many markets where the probability of loss is uncertain for the individual and the potential loss is large, such as house fires and motor vehicle accidents.

The problem of one person's consumption having an effect on another's well-being is also not unique to health care. But government action can avert or neutralise this. Specifically, consumers can collectively subsidise the cost of others' consumption of goods or services (e.g. health care) where it is agreed that access to those goods or services is beneficial to others or to society as a whole. In some cases these external benefits may be so great that the government will provide the commodity free of charge to the user. Examples of commodities seen to have high 'externalities' are free compulsory education and universal immunisation against communicable diseases.

Health Care as a Social Issue

The economics framework is often criticised for ignoring various social aspects of communities, including power relationships, social influences, and social goals. In the market model, power relationships may be ignored because, where there are many sellers and many buyers, no one has more power than any other. In real markets, some sellers/buyers are stronger than others, so there are uneven power relationships. In the market model, consumers have tastes (or preferences); they not only know what they want but they are also unaffected by others' preferences. In the real world, individuals' choices are influenced by advertising, by popular culture, and by peer-group pressure. In the market model, consumers pursue their own self-interest; the socially efficient outcome is the maximisation of the well-being of consumers in total. In the real world, people have social goals as well as selfish goals. Social goals might include pride in one's country and caring about protection of the environment.

Further, the market model has nothing to say about the distribution of income, wealth, or talent. Given a particular distribution of these characteristics, the perfectly competitive market results in allocation of resources such that no reallocation can make someone better off (as defined) without making someone else worse off. This is defined as an efficient allocation of resources. Given another starting distribution, the resultant allocation will be different—but still no reallocation can make someone better off without making someone else worse off. There is a number of possible efficient solutions, and which of them is best in a social sense, or is fairer, cannot be addressed within the neo-classical economics framework.

This analytical approach is the traditional approach in economics (described as the neo-classical school; see Rice 1998 for a good critique of the application of neo-classical analysis to health care). These criticisms apply to the analysis of all commodities including health. In spite of these, the production and distribution of most commodities is left to the market. But health care, as already mentioned, has features that distinguish it from other commodities and make it a special case. These differences, which are quite important, can be summarised as vulnerability, altruism, professional-isation, rights, and entitlements.

The health care consumer is more vulnerable than consumers in other markets. Emergency health care can be a matter of life or death. Even a delay in the provision of the appropriate care can be life-threatening. Not all health care is for potentially fatal conditions. Nonetheless, the conventional approach to hospital treatment of patients is, as many sociologists have noted, designed to emphasise their vulnerability: their familiar clothes, sleep patterns and meals are taken from them and replaced by unpredictable demands and unexplained routines. Even outside the hospital setting, patients cannot be unaware of their vulnerability (Morgan et al. 1991). Consuming health care involves, at best, waiting, discomfort, and anxiety; at worst, it is undignified, painful, and frightening.

Altruism is a stronger concern in health care than in many other aspects of life. The strength of altruism in health has been explained as a form of self-interest. For example, apparently altruistic support for measures that reduce infection may, ultimately, be a matter of self-interest in reducing one's risk of infection from others. But infectious disease is a small component of the workload of the health care system in developed countries, and quarantine is an effective and cheaper form of control than providing universal health care. The unpredictability of illness may give individuals an interest in supporting a health system that ensures at least some treatment irrespective of ability to pay. But even this is not enough to explain the widespread altruistic motivation underlying health care. It seems there is something in health and/or health care that engenders caring (Evans 1984). Many religious traditions advocate caring for the sick as an expression of religious commitment. Thus those who care for the sick are considered virtuous.

The delivery of health care is marked by strong professional groupings. This is a response to market failure; the existence of professionalisation and an ethical code gives an assurance that the uninformed consumer can trust the supplier's advice to be in the interests of the patient's health, not the supplier's income. But the role of the professional confers a degree of authority, since the professional is the keeper of a body of specialised knowledge. This entrenches an unequal power relationship between buyer and seller: 'doctor knows best' rather than 'the customer is always right'. Interestingly, this deference to professional authority is transferred to other areas in which doctors are involved but do not necessarily have expertise, such as advice on how to organise the health care system.

Health care is also discussed in terms of rights and entitlements. Perhaps because health is a precondition for many other capacities and function-ings, good health is fundamental to the exercise of liberties and choices. The United Nations includes among its basic freedoms, the freedom from disease. But society cannot guarantee 'good health for all'. What it can do is determine access to health care services. Thus health care itself can be seen in terms of a basic human right.

Institutional Responses

The widespread existence of market failure, and the particular social context of health care, mean that the health care market will give rise to institutions to deal with these economic and political problems. Government involvement in markets is a typical response, and an almost universal response to the failure of markets in health care, as in other sectors.

One form of government involvement in health care is the licensing of the professions, so as to protect poorly informed consumers from 'quacks' or persons without the necessary expertise. This type of accreditation, based on requirements of education and experience, is backed up with the force of law. Although enforcing these licensing arrangements involves government as regulator, the level of technical expertise in setting licensing standards is sophisticated enough to require the advice of the professions themselves.

These professional groups, however, will be influenced by the interests of their members. Their advice will be based both on the technical expertise to which they have access and on protecting and advancing the position of the group. Hence although government may encourage them to develop organised groups to coordinate advice, this may inadvertently further weaken the operation of markets. Thus experts may act to protect the incomes of their members, by restricting entry to the group (restricting the number of suppliers will reduce competition), raising prices, and acting to ensure that health care bills are paid. In health care, examples of this type of group include professional associations (e.g. medical associations, nursing associations), or organisations (e.g. hospital associations).

The development of insurance creates 'third-party payers'. In addition to the consumer and the provider, a 'third party', the insurer, enters the transaction. Government can also act as a third-party payer. Insurance is designed to protect the consumer from catastrophic financial losses should an uncertain event occur, so when the good or service is needed, the third party pays on behalf of the consumer. This introduces another organisational group which, as well as acting in the interests of consumers (their customers), will act in its own interests.

The other effect of insurance is to reduce or eliminate the price mechanism. As the consumer no longer pays the full price of the commodity, its cost does not influence or constrain consumers' demand. Under insurance, consumers are likely to use more than if they paid the full price at the point of consumption. This applies to all commodities, including health care. It is what economists call 'moral hazard', though it denotes rational self-interested behaviour, not an offence against some moral standard (Donaldson and Gerard 1993).

In the health care market, providers can be expected to favour insurance. It reduces or eliminates their bad debt problems. But the problem of moral hazard has a further complication since consumers rely on health care professionals' advice, particularly doctors' advice, to know when they require health care and which services they need. Doctors, as advisers to health care consumers, do not have to consider patients' capacity to pay. Equally, they do not have to consider patients' willingness to pay and so they may be encouraged to advise the use of more health care than patients, as informed consumers with other demands on their incomes, would purchase. Thus moral hazard affects doctors as well as patients.

Insurance provides consumers with the security that they will be able to pay for costly health care in the future. Government involvement is required to ensure the viability of insurance companies so that they will exist to pay future claims, and again in a regulatory capacity to ensure the fair and ethical operation of insurers. In many countries governments signal a belief in the special nature of health care through their attitudes towards insurance; they may, for example, mandate a specified minimum package that health insurance must cover.

The viability of any particular insurance scheme depends on the ability of the insurer to set premium prices so that they cover what has to be paid out. That, in turn, depends on the insurer having accurate information on the likely claims of each customer (where premiums are set for different groups according to the risk of that group, which is known as risk rating).

Determining risk with accuracy and defining groups with the same risk is more difficult in health care insurance than in many other forms of insurance. Further, the unpredictability of events requiring different forms of treatment and the high costs of treatment for severe, protracted illness mean that a cluster of major claims could be a financial catastrophe for an insurance firm. Insurers themselves seek arrangements that limit this risk of costly health care claims, often in the form of reinsurance, which entails sharing the major risks across numerous insurers. Government intervention is also required to support these arrangements.

Thus the health insurance market typically involves a high government intervention and highly organised suppliers. It should not be surprising that health insurers seek to bolster their financial viability by turning to government for direct support, through subsidies and/or tax relief.

Health care insurance can be provided by for-profit firms or by friendly or mutual societies. The not-for-profit insurer is more commonly found in settings where health care is seen as something 'different', where consumers are suspicious of for-profit organisations' involvement in providing health care and where there is a history of mutual support organisations successfully assisting families and communities to cope with illness and accident.

For much of their existence health insurers have acted largely as passive conduits, channelling payments to health care providers. They have not managed claims as aggressively as insurers of other risks (e.g. automobiles, property). An explanation for this can be found in the special nature of health care: it is difficult effectively to deny someone health care when it is needed. In many cases, health care is needed immediately and urgently if it is to be effective at all. Patients cannot be kept waiting (as motor vehicles can be kept waiting for repair) while insurance assessors determine the extent of the claim. And there is social opprobrium in denying health care to the sick.

In summary, the institutional nature of the health care market involves strong government participation in the regulation of suppliers. Both health care providers and insurers form strong organisations with considerable political and economic power.

Difficulties in Insurance Markets

A market for insurance develops when there is uncertainty. For some groups of people, however, there is little uncertainty about their future consumption of health care. Those with chronic conditions, ongoing disease, and handicap will certainly be large users of health care and therefore very costly to insure. Any group with a very high probability of using high-cost services will be uninsurable in a normal market (the premiums will cost the same as the cost of their health care). In addition, there are those whose predicted use is so great, based on other risk factors including their previous illness, that they will not normally be able to afford actuarially determined premiums. The exclusion of any large group of the population from the health care market because of their high probability of illness and/or poverty is unacceptable in most developed countries. Governments therefore intervene in the health care market to some extent to protect equitable access to health care.

Further government intervention is also typically needed to meet social and political objectives. In addition to pre-existing conditions, the main predictors of health care use are age and sex. On strictly actuarial grounds, premiums should increase with age and be higher for women. While this may be actuarially fair, it may not be regarded as socially fair, as age and sex are characteristics the individual can do little to change. Further, in societies with significant and politically powerful ageing populations, the actuarially fair distribution of the costs of health care may simply be politically unacceptable.

Although there is a wide range of government responses to address the equity problems in health insurance, these can be categorised into three major approaches. First, government may, in effect, override the insurance market by publicly financing health care through taxation. This is often referred to as the Beveridge model (after the British academic who laid the blueprint for the welfare state and the National Health Service; see Ham 1997a, particularly chapter 1). Government may also take on the direct provision of health care, funding and operating hospitals and employing health care workers. Or it may act as an insurer, reimbursing fees for private providers in what has been summarised as 'private practice, publicly supported'.

Second, government may become the insurer by raising public finance through compulsory social insurance. This is known as the Bismarck model (after the German chancellor who developed it; again see Ham 1997a: ch. 1). This may be funded through one national insurer or several competing insurance schemes. Most European countries have adopted either the Beveridge or the Bismarck model. The third approach is the USA style of voluntary, private finance with publicly financed benefits for some population groups.

Experience with health care financing has shown there are substantial problems with voluntary private insurance. In addition to the problems described above, there are serious problems in achieving universal coverage and ensuring equitable access to health care. Multiple insurers generate high administrative costs. Further, those countries that have been most successful at controlling overall health care expenditure have been more likely to rely on public finance.

A Strife of Ideologies

The health care market is thus characterised by multiple sources of market failure, extensive government intervention, organised special-interest groups, and highly emotive subject matter. No wonder it has been described as 'a strife of interests' (Sax 1984). The tension among different stakeholder groups goes beyond protecting their own positions. Under-lying these positions are conflicting stakeholder values—a strife of ideologies (Williams 1988 gives a clear exposition).

Thus on the one hand there is the value position that health care is pre-dominantly a social good; on the other that it is essentially an individual good. The latter view was expressed most eloquently by the founder of the National Health Service (NHS) in the United Kingdom, Aneurin Bevan (quoted in Whitehead 1994):

> Society becomes more wholesome, more serene and spiritually healthier, if it knows that its citizens have at the back of their consciousness the knowledge that not only themselves, but all their fellows have access to the best health care that society can provide.

In this view of the world, the financing, organisation, and delivery of health care must be oriented to the collective good. Health care systems organised for this reason can be described as egalitarian. They are likely to be organised as public systems, in which economic standing does not buy better access or better-quality health care. Government's role is to ensure that social objectives are pursued.

The opposing world-view is that health care is a commodity like any other, access to which is part of the reward system of the market economy. Those able and willing to pay more should be able to purchase what they want. Health care systems organised according to this view emphasise libertarian principles, including the right of individuals to choose for themselves. They are likely to be organised as private systems. Govern-ment's role is to look after those disadvantaged who are otherwise excluded from health care.

In reality, no health care system is purely egalitarian or purely liber-tarian. Even the strongest libertarians admit the pervasiveness of market failure in health and endorse some government intervention in order to achieve equity objectives. Differences in the values of societies will drive quite different approaches to health care organisation and reform, even though value positions are rarely stated explicitly as part of any health care reform debate. In Australia and New Zealand, health care is financed primarily by general taxation. In Australia there is a relatively large reliance on private finance that accounts for around 30 per cent of total health care expenditure, about 30 per cent of which is raised through private health insurance; in New Zealand, private finance accounts for around 20 per cent of total expenditure, a figure much closer to most European countries (Human Development Report 1998). Health care is provided largely privately, except in the hospital sector where public ownership and operation predominate. In both countries, the system can be described as 'private provision, publicly supported'.

The debate about health care reform is, then, essentially a debate at two levels. At the first level, the debate is about the market functioning: the extent of market failure, the degree to which government should intervene, how much it can correct market failure and how it should go about doing so. Most of the health policy debate is explicitly at this level. At the second level, it is about the objectives of the health care system and whether they are to satisfy individual preferences or social goals.

Health Care Reform

Health care reform is in fashion. In fact it has never really been out of fashion; change and restructuring of health systems has occurred continuously. But health care reform itself is subject to fashion, in that broader ideas in political economy influence the direction of reform. Many of these broader ideas and ideologies are international, and consequently movements in health reform tend to converge around similar themes (Ham 1997a; Saltman and Figueras 1998).

The 1960s were in general a time of economic prosperity. Increasing government revenues allowed governments to tackle broad and ambitious programs, such as anti-poverty programs, ambitious preschool and other programs designed to expand educational opportunity, and investment in science and technology. Societies had confidence in the combination of political will and new technology to deliver major advances, such as putting a man on the moon. This optimism and prosperity affected views about health care, encouraging increasing government expenditure on health care. Behind these buoyant views lay the assumption that advances in health technology delivered across the population would succeed in ameliorating the problem of ill health; and that better lifestyles, prevention, and effective treatment would reduce the burden of illness and thence the cost of providing health care.

By the late 1970s and the 1980s, this optimism and confidence in the ability of governments to act for the common good had paled. Society's emphasis had switched from collective goals and advances ('a giant step for mankind') to individual gain. The concept that government's proper function was to ensure that peoples' basic needs were met was criticised for sapping individual responsibility and initiative. It was rejected, and the welfare state was dubbed the 'Nanny State'. Analysts of government programs of the time pointed to sources of government failure, including the tendency for the bureaucracy to serve the interests of the regulated. Government programs were criticised for rigidity and failure to serve the customer's interests, as well as for their cost.

In health care, the 1970s was a period of significant increase in health care expenditure (OECD 1994). This spending was not accompanied by significant improvements in health status, at least as indicated by traditional measures such as mortality. Further, cross-country comparisons showed that higher levels of spending were not associated with better population health. There seemed to be no natural limit to health care spending, and it appeared that demand could increase infinitely. Studies of variations in medical practice began to appear in the literature at the time, showing significant variability in how doctors treated the same conditions. Critics of modern medicine demonstrated the level of iatrogenic illness and injury. All in all these trends served to shake confidence in the view that there was a simple and scientifically determined relationship between medical need and use of services, that doctors knew best and did so on the basis of science, and that governments throwing resources at a problem would solve it (Evans et al. 1994).

The rise of economic rationalism was a phenomenon of the late 1980s and the 1990s. Economic rationalism is built on the idea that deregulated markets are the most efficient means of resource allocation. It promotes the use of competition, advocates consumer choice linked to user payments, rejects the use of government provision of services, and would eliminate welfare payments. In this school of thinking, the role of government is to foster competitive markets. Where markets do not naturally provide essential services, such as help for the unemployed, government's role is to create a market for such services (e.g. becoming a 'purchaser' rather than a 'provider' and administering contracts for service provision).

By the 1990s most developed countries had managed to control the total level of health care expenditure (Ham 1997a; Saltman and Figueras 1998). Yet a number of pressures suggest that cost control may not be as readily sustained. These include the ageing of the population, changing patterns of disease in which chronic disease and disability have become more important, and new means of prevention, screening, and treatment made possible by emerging technologies. In addition, public expectations of health care availability, and level of sophistication, have increased markedly in recent years. At the community level, at least in Australia, the electorate expects access to all that medical science has to offer. At the individual level, there has been an increase in advocacy on behalf of patients/consumers, public expressions of patients' rights in the form of charters and customer contracts, and pervasive demand for more patient-centred services.

The influence of economic rationalism on health care reform is readily discernible. The separation of the role of purchasing or commissioning health services from their delivery has been seen as a mechanism for establishing markets and introducing competition. This has required new developments in contracting and performance management, as services are required to compete on both price and quality. At the same time, the position of the consumer has been strengthened. Community values, rather than the wisdom of central planners, are now held as the touchstone for resource allocation decisions (though there remain difficulties in identifying and using these values in decision-making).

But it is still possible to discern different underlying values in spite of similar directions in reform strategies. In those countries that endorse health care as a social good, governments act as the purchasers of health care on behalf of the community. The role of the consumer is to facilitate the emergence of community values that purchasers can use in their decision-making. In those countries that see health care as an expression of individual consumer sovereignty, the role of the consumer is to make informed insurance purchasing decisions which, through the operation of a market, will ensure efficiency is achieved.

Conclusion

The nature of health care—that is, the existence of market failure, the social and cultural meaning of health, altruistic concerns for access to health care, the extent of professionalisation and the economic interests of stakeholders—means that there is a much more interventionist role for government in the health sector than in many other sectors of economic activity. The consequence of government involvement is that the organisation and financing of health care is a political issue. It also means that the role of government in health care will be part of a broader debate on the appropriate role of government in the macro-economy and in society as a whole. These are conditions that predispose the health sector to notions of reform. New ideas about the role of governments as purchasers and regulators, about the need to demonstrate accountability and value for money, and about responsiveness to consumers are likely to emerge within the health policy debate.

While these conditions are necessary, they are perhaps not enough to explain what has come to be a fixation on reform in health care. Perhaps the most fundamental precondition for reform is a sense that the existing system cannot cope, either currently or with emerging trends. The problems of rising health care expenditure, increasing community and individual expectations about what health care can deliver, new technologies, new diseases, and the growing prevalence of chronic diseases and disability, are problems faced by all health care systems. Hence reform is reinforced by the idea that something needs to be changed.

But a broad consensus on the need for change is not the same as an agreed direction for change. Indeed, the lesson from the failed Clinton attempts to reform health care in the USA is that it is not enough to have widespread public support for change. There are strong vested interests in health care that will resist any attempt to lessen their political and economic power. This makes it difficult to gather a constituency for any particular direction of change.

So why have some countries embarked on radical reforms whereas others have implemented slow incremental change? Radical reform has been achieved by new governments, with a new political agenda and a strong majority. Thus radical reform was possible in New Zealand, under a new right-wing government. The New Zealand parliament is unicameral, thus enabling strong action by one government. In contrast, Australia, like the USA, has a bicameral federal parliament; in recent years there has been a different balance of power between the two houses. In addition, health is also the responsibility of the various state and territory governments. This makes it unlikely that there will be a political consensus on the direction of reform. And as a result reform can be advanced only through incremental change.

Finally, and in spite of the similarity of the themes of reform across countries, the way to reform is strongly influenced by the underlying values of society. Thus the implementation of market reforms in the United Kingdom has been set within a commitment to a Beveridge model of taxation finance and a universal system. In the United Kingdom, health care is essentially seen as separate from other marketable goods and services. In contrast, in the USA, similar ideas of competitive markets have been applied in a culture in which access to health care is like other rewards.

3

Distinguishing Features of Reform in Australia and New Zealand

Anne Somjen

During the 1990s, governments of most of the twenty-four countries of the OECD, in keeping with their role in health care, were either planning or implementing reforms. The motivation for these reforms was financial, cultural, and political. Their main aims were to control costs, to improve access, and to maintain the quality of health care (Franks et al. 1993; Grant et al. 1997). Although most were responding to common drivers and objectives, no universal formula emerged, and each nation was carving its own path through the forest of obstacles. This chapter considers the reasoning behind the different directions of reform chosen by Australia and New Zealand and examines the success and failure of each. The framework is based loosely on the observations of Gray (1998) comparing the Canadian and Australian health systems. Gray identifies three areas most influential in shaping health policy directions during the 1990s:

1. attitudes, values and public opinion (cultural factors);
2. budgets (financial factors); and
3. the federal division of power (political and governmental factors).

Importantly, New Zealand has the advantage of a single, federal governmental structure. Australia's diverse political landscape, by contrast, is reflected in differing models of health care delivery. This and other differences mean that the 'lessons learned' through comparative analysis are frustratingly generic.

Reform in the health care context is sometimes used to mean change in a pure sense. There is often heated debate about whether reform is in fact for the better. Moreover, there is no expert consensus on how best to measure the outcomes of health reform. For pragmatic reasons, health reform has never been appraised in a controlled situation. Consequently arguments about the merits and benefits of health reform are often based on opinion rather than fact.

The reform processes instigated in Australia and New Zealand have differed markedly in structure and efficacy. This chapter examines how and why in the context of the demographic, social, cultural and political features of each country.

The Geographic and Cultural Environment

The Australian context

Like other OECD nations, Australia has an ageing population. This trend, in parallel with a declining birthrate, is expected to continue well into the next century, with the effect that the older population is increasing at a higher rate than the population as a whole, and will comprise a growing proportion of Australia's total population. Between 1995 and 2025 the population of Australians 65 years of age and older is expected to increase from 11.6 per cent to 17.2 per cent of the total population (AIHW 1998).

The New Zealand context

The structure of New Zealand's population is expected to change rapidly over the next 25 years. It is projected that 21 per cent of New Zealand's population will be aged over 65 years by 2031, compared with only 12 per cent in 1994. New Zealand's European population is ageing more rapidly than its Māori and Pacific Island population. Māori and Pacific Islanders, who comprise approximately 13 per cent of the nation's total population, constitute a younger group: 60 per cent is younger than 25 years of age. The two groups will obviously have very different health care needs well into the next century.

Global positioning

The economies of both Australia and New Zealand historically relied heavily on the export of agricultural products to Britain. Today exports comprise a much wider range of goods and services and are distributed to a larger number of international markets. The trade focus of both nations has shifted in recent years from Europe to the Asia–Pacific region.

Immigration patterns of the two countries mirror this shift: an increasingly higher proportion of migrants from Asian countries rather than the countries of Europe.

These trade and immigration shifts have had, and will continue to have, a significant impact on national income, and hence on the funds each country has available to dedicate to health care. The Asia Pacific Economic Co-operation (APEC) free trade agreements will reduce tariff protection for industry and affect the global competitiveness of the two nations, whose industries previously enjoyed substantial protection through tariffs (MAPA Highlights, APEC). This will affect export revenue, and hence national income. The 'Asian crisis', the significant downturn in the economies of East Asia in the late 1990s, will also affect the competitiveness of the two nations' economies.

Evolution of the Health Care System

Australia and New Zealand have taken very different paths to their present health care systems. Both countries have a taxation-based system, with universal coverage. Beyond this the two differ substantially. Although resources for health are allocated by government in both countries, allocation occurs at different levels of government and according to different principles. The pace of change in health reform has also differed markedly.

The Australian health care system

Australia's health care system has evolved in a relatively slow, incremental and lumbering way over the past century. Between the 1920s and 1940s government made several attempts to introduce a system of national health insurance and a pharmaceutical benefits scheme. Compulsory, universal health insurance in the form of Medibank was finally introduced in 1975 (Palmer and Short 1994: 56). This system was progressively modified over the next six years until the introduction of Medicare, the current taxation-based system of universal health coverage and pharmaceutical benefits, in February 1984. Since this date there have been four different Medicare (later Australian Health Care) agreements. The fundamental principles have been preserved: free access to acute services for all residents has been the cornerstone of the Australian health care system for nearly two decades. In addition to Medicare a smaller, privately financed system, operating on a user-pays basis, is described by Foley in Chapter 5.

The health status of Australians has improved under Medicare. An international comparison readily demonstrates that Australians enjoy good health and relatively good access to services at a reasonable cost (WHO 1993; Johnston and Stanford 1996: 1986). Mortality and morbidity rates have fallen, deaths from cardiovascular disease have declined, and predicted life-expectancy at birth has risen significantly.

Medicare has historically been very strongly supported by the Australian people, though there is some degree of dissatisfaction with its operation in practice (Hall 1999: 13). Since the introduction of Medicare, Australians have increasingly chosen to rely on publicly financed health care, resulting in an almost uninterrupted decline in private health insurance enrolment. Many Australians consider private health insurance superfluous. The visibility of the Medicare levy as a component of income tax is a further deterrent. As private health insurance premiums have risen, the proportion of Australians privately insured has declined. Whereas 68 per cent of the population had private health coverage in 1982, enrolment had ebbed to a mere 30.5 per cent in 1998, and was continuing to fall. As a result the proportion of total health care financed by government has increased commensurately. Although Medicare has been an issue in the elections of 1996 and 1998 (especially in 1996), its popularity has caused government to focus on incremental changes to the existing system rather than devising new models to solve old problems.

The New Zealand health care system

The recent history of New Zealand's health care system contrasts sharply with Australia's experience. New Zealand's system has been subjected to significant and rapid change, especially during the 1980s and 1990s. New Zealand was the first nation to introduce a universal system of free hospital in-patient treatment, as part of a post-depression welfare state (Hornblow 1997: 1892). By 1947 New Zealand had established a predominantly taxation-funded system (Scott 1996: 32). Until the mid-1980s this system was seen to provide a reasonable level of service, and its cost per capita was one of the lowest in the world. However, as New Zealand began to feel the economic pinch in the 1980s, health care funding was not increased in parallel with continued growth in demand (Beuzenberg 1997).

In the mid-1980s the government of New Zealand began to implement a program of substantial economic and social reform. As in other countries undergoing similar processes, the reforms were characterised by an increasing reliance on market forces. Major initiatives included the removal of industrial and export subsidies and the deregulation of industry, restructuring government departments, reduction of welfare benefits, and corporatisation or privatisation of state trading departments. Increased emphasis on market-based provision also led in the early 1990s to restructuring of some government-funded services, for example housing, education, and health care (Ashton 1996: 270). Government introduced a market-influenced model as an alternative to the previous centralised, interventionist approach. The underlying assumption was that if the private sector could operate more efficiently than the public sector in providing these services, and maintain sufficient profitability, its knowledge and practices should be transferable to the public arena (Gauld 1997: 68). Managerial autonomy would be fostered as a means of encouraging creative thinking and innovation in resource use. The key element in this transformation to a more competitive structure was clarification of the components and roles in service provision, specifically the separation of the roles of funder, purchaser and provider of health care.

Despite the fact that there is relatively low 'customer' satisfaction with the health care system in New Zealand (Hall 1998–9: 13), people are not supplementing their public health entitlement with additional private insurance. In fact Statistics New Zealand estimates a small but steady decline in the proportion of the population covered by private health insurance, from around 41 per cent in 1994/95 to 37 per cent in 1996/97.

The Influence and Impact of Financing Constraints and Policy

Financing: principles of allocation

The health systems of both Australia and New Zealand are financed largely through funds raised by general taxation. In both countries the private health care markets are small in relation to the public system, though in both countries primary care (general practice) is mostly provided by physicians in private practice. This means that the role of determining the allocatively efficient level of resources for health care rests largely with central government in both Australia and New Zealand. The term 'allocatively efficient' recognises that scarce resources have alternative uses and that there is a cost associated with the application of resources to the production of one good rather than another. Spending more on health care, for example, diminishes the funding that governments have available to devote to education, defence, road maintenance, etc. Governments in Australia and New Zealand and comparable democracies distribute resources so as to maximise the overall benefit to society.

Governments make decisions about the allocation of resources to health care services for two main reasons. First, since health care is not a 'normal good' (see below), the free market fails to provide the appropriate level and range of services to meet society's needs. Second, as Hall and Viney, and Hindle and Perkins explain in this volume, medical and health care services can be seen as quasi-public goods, the benefits of which are passed on to all citizens, irrespective of who pays. Humans usually have a desire to live in, and derive benefit from, a healthy society. Thus, as Poutasi elaborates in Chapter 7, government plays an important role when it redistributes health care resources to achieve a more equitable allocation of resources, services, and products, and hence obtains greater marginal benefit for society.

It is worth reiterating the crucial differences between health care services and 'normal' commodities. In health care,

- there is no generic product;
- it is very difficult, sometimes impossible, to measure outcome or success;
- services are not exchangeable or refundable, and they cannot be passed on to others;
- there is a need to maintain unprofitable product lines; and
- consumers rely exclusively on advocate purchasing (the recommendations of doctors and others who interpret 'need' and recommend that consumers 'purchase' health care), made necessary because of the information asymmetry between consumers and providers about the (health care) product or service.

Perfect health for all is an unattainable goal, so value judgments must be made about priorities in health care and, indeed, about the allocation of funds for health as against other 'goods.' Yet because it is very difficult to get agreement on what should and should not be provided, in what quantities, and for whom, and because there is no precise formula for calculating health expenditure, most governments determine that a given share of GDP is an appropriate level of expenditure for health care.

The role of public expectations

Public expectations also have a considerable influence on the total amount that any society allocates to health care, for what goods and services, and how. As a general rule society's expectations of health care services are increasing. As people lead longer and healthier lives their experience of ill health is reduced and disease and disability become increasingly unacceptable. Expectations placed on the health system to prevent mortality and morbidity rise. Similarly, as medical information has become more freely available to the general public through the media, including television, magazines and the Internet, the asymmetry of knowledge between patient and physician has begun to diminish, further raising consumers' expectations.

Further, it is politically difficult for governments to implement any change that leaves some better off at the expense of others. Democratically elected governments strive to maintain social balance, and the perception that the social balance (social solidarity) is or may be disturbed usually leads to a public outcry. Thus governments are constrained in the degree of change they may practically introduce. For example, in December 1991 the Australian Commonwealth government attempted to introduce a co-payment of $2.50 for Medicare-rebatable GP services that were previously 'free of charge'. The co-payment was dropped in March 1992, a mere three months later. During 1997/98 the government tried to introduce what were effectively compulsory payments for nursing-home care. Facing vocal opposition, the government subsequently made significant changes to its aged care and nursing-home policy. By contrast, in New Zealand, where user charges have long been a part of the primary-care system, there is no expectation that these services should be free of charge. But public expectations did play a major role in the NZ government's redesign of initial attempts to prioritise or ration treatment.

The impact of rising costs

Both Australia and New Zealand, like all other nations, face rising health care costs driven primarily by:

- the increasing costs of new technologies, such as diagnostic procedures and pharmaceuticals; and
- increases in the numbers of treatable conditions and improvements in the management of chronic diseases, as well as extended life spans in which people manage multiple conditions.

A third, less influential factor, is the ageing of the population in both countries. Both nations are focusing on cost containment. Although Australia's average per capita health expenditure is a full point higher than New Zealand's as a percentage of GDP, the amount spent annually in each country has stabilised in recent years.

The Influence and Impact of Systems of Government

In contrast to the issues associated with financing a health care system, which are universal, the solutions, or reforms, to address them are not. The main differences in the reforms undertaken in Australia and New Zealand are attributable in large part to the two nations' different systems of government and to the degree to which responsibility for health care finance and provision are devolved to funders, providers, and purchasers of health care. In Australia, responsibility for the funding, provision, and planning of health care is split among three tiers of government, with some private sector involvement. In New Zealand there are no intermediary levels of government between the central government and the (government and other) agencies that provide health services.

In New Zealand the major political parties, whose solutions for the health system differ starkly, alternated rule in the 1990s. In contrast, relative stability in health system policies has characterised Australia's recent history, despite occasional calls for a complete overhaul of Medicare.

The influences of the Australian system of government

As noted previously, responsibility for ensuring access to health care services in Australia is split among Commonwealth, state and local governments. Most medical and dental services, and some other professional services, are provided by private practitioners. The non-government sector accounts for just under a third of total health care expenditure.

State and territory governments are accountable for providing public hospital services. Funding of these services is mainly provided to the states by the Commonwealth in accordance with periodic federal–state Medicare agreements (now called Australian Health Care Agreements). Funds are transferred to the states because constitutionally the states do not have the power, which is vested in the federal government, to raise funds through taxation to finance the hospital system. The obligations of local government vary from state to state, but generally concern public health and environmental control activities such as rubbish collection, recycling, and the management of local home-care services such as meals on wheels.

The mixture of responsibility for funding and provision of health care services in Australia is a restrictive historical remnant, a reminder that Australia was originally settled as independent colonies that did not coalesce into a single nation until Federation in 1901. In fact there was no Commonwealth Department of Health until 1921. The Commonwealth government gained increasingly wider influence over health policy as a result of a constitutional amendment passed in 1946, which increased the scope of its authority to include pharmaceuticals, sickness and hospital benefits, and medical and dental benefits. The Constitution also allows the Commonwealth to provide funding to the states for specific-purpose grants. This mechanism enables the Commonwealth to fund the states according to specific terms and conditions, such as those outlined in the

Australian Health Care Agreement Grants. The Commonwealth thereby exerts additional, albeit indirect, influence over the delivery of health services. The federal/state dichotomy of funding and responsibility for planning and design of health care has led inevitably to cost-shifting between the two.

The Australian Health Care Agreements require that the states ensure reasonable access for all Australians to health services provided free of charge in public hospitals. Commonwealth government funding for hospital treatment is capped at the levels negotiated within the current agreement. The states have the power to meet the terms and conditions of the agreement through whatever methods they consider most efficient, equitable and appropriate to local circumstances. This process results in variation in acute and elective hospital treatment, as each state juggles its resources in a different way. Elective surgery waiting lists typically lengthen when shortages of funding for acute treatment are supplemented by drawing down on funds allocated for elective surgery.

Medical and pharmaceutical services outside hospitals are funded on a fee-for-service basis directly by the Commonwealth government. Unlike grants to the states for the provision of hospital services, the medical services and pharmaceuticals budgets are uncapped. Indeed, whereas hospital budgets were tightly controlled, the total cost of pharmaceuticals benefits increased by 99 per cent in dollar terms over the period 1991–97 (AIHW 1998: 286), a period of minimal inflation. This uncapped growth has been criticised by the OECD as inimical to cost containment.

The apparently unlimited pool of funds for medical services and pharmaceuticals may also provide false incentives to medical practitioners. Australia's ratio of GPs to population is high enough by OECD standards to provide an adequate service for the population as a whole, yet one of the intractable problems of Australia's health care system today is the paucity of primary-care services available to rural populations. If Australia has enough GPs to satisfy national demand, yet too few practitioners in rural areas, by deduction residents of metropolitan areas are receiving more than their fair share of services. Incentives are required to redistribute GPs more equitably across rural and urban areas.

The split of funding between federal and state governments in Australia also encourages the states and hospitals to shift costs out of hospital budgets and into the federal budget. One commonly used approach is to privatise hospital out-patient departments, which removes the costs of providing these services from the hospital's (state) budget, and places it within the federal budget. Patient consultations in these departments are billed to the federal government by (private) attending physicians as out-of-hospital services. Australia's federal/state funding split, an artefact of its system of government, absorbs considerable effort on the part of administrators in 'gaming', which might more productively be used improving service access, quality and range.

The devolution of considerable—but only partial— responsibility for health care has predictable results. Because various state and territory governments differ in their political affiliations, aims and ideologies, and because each confronts different geographic and demographic situations, it is no surprise that health reform has taken a different course in each state. Two major approaches have emerged: a focus on integrated, regional health care through a centralised purchaser and provider (as in New South Wales and Queensland), and the more market-oriented approach adopted by other states (notably Victoria and South Australia), characterised by a purchaser/provider split and output-based funding.

The sharing of power between the Commonwealth and states, which has produced such major differences among the states' health systems, complicates and impedes cohesive reform. Two recent initiatives outside the health sector have, however, provided strong incentives for more homogeneous reform. The National Competition Policy has encouraged the application of best-practice models and mechanisms nationally. The Council of Australian Governments (COAG) has begun reform of the complex array of state and Commonwealth funding arrangements for health. It has redefined health care, and by extension its funding, into three streams of care: primary care, acute care and coordinated care (for those with chronic conditions). COAG's reform objective is 'to minimise overlap and duplication and encourage each level of government to contribute appropriately to health care funding'. This would be achieved by linking a portion of the more than sixty government services available for people with chronic conditions and ensuring that people received the mix of coordinated care best suited to their needs. Large pilot Coordinated Care Trials with comprehensive evaluative research components are being conducted to identify the most cost-effective, appropriate approach to coordinated care. Each involves a single fund-holder for all patients irrespective of their health needs (Johnston et al. 1996: 1986). The results of these trials are eagerly awaited by policy-makers at all levels of government.

Other recent initiatives with the potential to reduce the inefficiencies in Australia's system of government health funding of health care are the development of casemix information systems and changes to the Residential Aged Care Structural Reform Package. None of these measures, however, has been powerful enough to overcome the entropy caused by Australia's historically entrenched division of powers between the states and the Commonwealth.

The influences of the New Zealand system of government

While New Zealand's government structure lacks the complexity of Australia's, health care reform has been challenged by a rapid succession of three different governments, each of which has attempted to overhaul the entire system. Most of the reform and restructuring has been driven by financial imperatives.

Between 1984 and 1990 New Zealand's fourth Labor government attempted to restructure the health care system consistent with its objectives of restraining overall government expenditure, improving efficiency and effectiveness, and increasing accountability. Fourteen regionally based, largely elected, boards were established with a mandate to integrate population health with hospital and related community-based services. Each board received a capitated budget for its defined population (Barnett and Malcolm 1997: 93). After six years of major change, the electorate voted the Labor government out of office in 1990. The new National government, at least as radical as its predecessor, further deregulated the labour market and reduced government involvement in social services. It did not believe the 1989 restructuring capable of ensuring access or efficiency, pointing to cost-shifting, provider capture, and lack of management competence. It viewed New Zealand's high level of social expenditure as a significant factor contributing to the nation's debt burden, encouraging welfare dependency and undermining prospects for economic growth (Scott 1996: 35). With a parliamentary majority, the new government quickly pushed through commercially driven changes in the health system, starting in 1993 (Ham 1997b: 1844). New Zealand's previously regulated health care system was transformed dramatically into one characterised by a high degree of market-oriented competition.

The government encountered hostility and resistance to its new 'business-like' health agenda. However, policy-makers in New Zealand had gained considerable experience in the implementation of unpopular policies under the previous, reform-oriented Labor government. They thus proposed a transitional period of two years, during which detailed structures and implementation arrangements were developed. The National Interim Provider Board was established to plan and manage the transition, and the government undertook an extensive and determined communications campaign involving advertising agencies and well-known journalists.

The imposition of a market-driven health care system in 1993 challenged existing values, practices, and widely held assumptions within the community. Although the government was reasonably successful in overcoming opposition to the new system, its approach to implementation led to a fragmented system (Gauld 1997: 77) and polarisation of clinical and commercial cultures (Hornblow 1997: 1892). Lack of prior health management experience among new senior managers recruited from the private sector resulted in a clash of cultures, particularly between management and specialist medical staff. None of the CEOs from outside the health sector appointed in 1993 still holds her or his position (Malcolm 1998b: 147).

Between 1993 and 1997 new problems emerged and opposition to the reforms intensified. Although the government had promised reduced waiting times, waiting lists in fact increased by 50 per cent in three years (Coney 1996: 1825). Networks and coalitions were forged among a wide range of health stakeholder groups and public organisations. Their effective use of the media undermined government's promotion and defence of its reforms. (Hornblow 1997: 1894). Whereas reforms and restructuring in other sectors proceeded, in the health sector government retreated from some of the more radical reform proposals in reaction to opposition from industry (Barnett and Malcolm 1997: 89), and in the face of political reprisals for pursuing an increasingly unpopular policy agenda.

The next coalition government (comprising the National and New Zealand First parties), quickly abandoned competition in favour of collaboration. The reforms introduced by the Labor government might have worked as intended over a longer period (Crown Company Monitoring Advisory Unit 1996). The coalition document *Policy Area: Health*, released 9 December 1996, envisaged a health sector in which 'principles of public service replace commercial profit objectives' with 'co-operation and collaboration rather than competition between services'.

With the general direction of policy set, the government announced that planned changes would be introduced gradually in order to minimise disruption. The 'big bang' approach gave way to incrementalism, reflecting concern over the 'reorganisation fatigue' reported by health service staff, as well as a paradigm shift in government planning (Ham 1997b: 1845). The four RHAs were replaced by a central funding body, the HFA (see page 33 above), though the basic principle of separating purchasing from provision remained. Pricing of services across geographical boundaries is now more consistent. In the absence of a national needs analysis, however, despite population-based allocation of health and disability funding, there are still significant discrepancies among geographic areas, especially in access to elective surgery. The competitive model persists in the continuing belief that a more commercial focus will foster more efficient delivery of health care services. Hence most service planning is undertaken by providing agencies rather than by government. However, a system of deficit-sharing still provides inappropriate incentives to public hospitals. Those that remain within their funding and achieve or exceed service delivery targets are not rewarded; those that do not meet their budgets are not punished.

The Successes and Failures of the Two Systems

Any analysis of the reforms implemented in Australia and New Zealand during the 1980s and 1990s immediately highlights the overriding influence of politics, political reaction, and political conservatism. Neither nation has developed a clear, detailed blueprint for the health care system of the twenty-first century. The many reform measures thus remain piecemeal approaches that together do not constitute a systematic, strategic approach. Sophisticated purchasing approaches have stalled, and involvement of the private sector has been limited in coverage and unevaluated. In both countries political pragmatism has retarded reform. Another all too apparent impediment is the lack of any real competition in market-based reform.

Both nations have experienced continuing improvements in overall health status in the wake of reforms. Australia has achieved and maintained a higher ranking among OECD nations, and the proportion of the population that believes that the health care system works well is larger in Australia than in New Zealand (Hall 1998–9: 13). New Zealand has achieved better health outcomes for its indigenous population than Australia, but in both countries the unequal health status of indigenous people remains a serious problem. Each nation has used the same pressure valves in response to similar health system constraints: in particular, elective surgery waiting lists have grown and government capital investment in health has contracted under increasingly tight fiscal pressures.

In the 1990s New Zealand attempted to impose a framework for rationing health care. As expected, given experience elsewhere, it was unsuccessful. In both nations the alternative to overt, systematic rationing has taken the form of rationing through delay. Patients with private health insurance or other means can avoid public hospital waiting lists by financing their own care and obtaining it elsewhere. In New Zealand elective surgery waiting lists have grown to the point where a points system has been introduced to triage the waiting lists. In Australia the acute elective waiting lists in public hospitals have grown with the decline in private insurance as the overall acute public hospital workload has expanded.

Hospital buildings and other health care infrastructure in both countries require levels of funding for capital renewal and redevelopment well beyond what government has been willing or able to provide. Both countries have addressed the deficit through increased involvement of the private sector in financing and provision of health care. The proportion of non-government expenditure on health has risen in both countries over the past decade, though at 20 and 30 per cent of total health spending in New Zealand and Australia respectively, it remains very much the lesser component of health funding.

New Zealand's competitive model, in which purchasing and provision of health care are separated, was expected to bring the private sector into direct competition with the public sector in the provision of public services. In practice the private sector has tended to limit its range of services to niche markets. In Australia the competitive model being promoted in the National Competition Policy has been designed to reduce barriers to private sector entry into the health arena; to date, private sector involvement has been limited to certain parts of the market, and certain services. This pattern may prove to be another obstacle to a congruent national health policy.

Finally, both countries face declining levels of private health insurance, which places a greater strain on their public health care systems. It remains to be seen whether the tax rebates on private health insurance introduced in Australia in 1999 will stem the exodus or place a further drain on limited national resources available for health.

Conclusion

The Australian and New Zealand health care systems, with their distinct contexts and structures, have evolved along different paths resulting in significantly different systems. The problems they face and the drivers of change—costs, demand, expectations, and politics—are common to both. Despite differences in population size, political systems, and health care models, both nations face the same fundamental problems: how to contain costs in an environment of increasing demand; how to increase the involvement of the private sector in health and engender further competition; how to leverage additional resources into the public health care market; and how to improve the health status of indigenous populations.

Both countries seem to be struggling with health reform. New Zealand has been comparatively successful in constraining health care costs, but elective surgery waiting lists have surged. Australia has been quite successful in implementing and maintaining a system that satisfies its citizens, yet, as in New Zealand, an increasing proportion of the population sees room for major improvements (Hall 1998–9: 13).

New Zealand's unified governance structure places it in an advantageous position, enabling sweeping national reforms. Yet the health sector has become both weary and wary of change. Corporatisation and commercialisation have not proved an adequate package for solving the ills of the sector, and have tended to deflect long-term sector planning. Australia's federal system of government has thwarted congruent and consistent health reform on a national scale, and has also impeded implementation of long-term planning.

In conclusion, whereas both countries are admired for the cost and quality of their health care systems compared with other OECD nations, neither has introduced a comprehensive reform model capable of guiding it into the future. For very different reasons, reform initiatives introduced in each country have proved to be temporary measures. The pressures on both systems and the drivers for reform persist. Success has been piecemeal and more likely to endure in the form of incremental improvements at the operational level. The chapters that follow provide further illustration of what can be considered to be partial success in meeting the challenge of health reform.

KEY DIMENSIONS OF THE REFORM PROCESS

Introduction

Philip Davies

The chapters in Part II describe various aspects of the reform processes that have taken place in Australia and New Zealand. Collectively, they offer a number of valuable, and potentially generalisable, insights into both the 'what' and the 'how' of health-sector reform.

The term 'reform' is generally seen to signify large-scale change that has sector-wide impacts. It has been noted, however, that 'there is no consistent and universally accepted definition of what constitutes health sector reform' (WHO 1997: 2).

One of the 'key elements' of reform identified by WHO (1997: 3) is that it is a 'political top-down process led by national, regional or local governments'. Recent experience in Australia and New Zealand supports that view. Indeed, it is remarkable how, with a few notable recent exceptions (such as the emergence of 'integrated care' in New Zealand), there is little evidence of pressures for change emerging 'bottom up' from health professionals or consumers in either country. This is in marked contrast to the incremental changes in clinical practice, consumer expectations, and medical technology that have been an accepted feature of the health sector since time immemorial.

Health sector reform is thus markedly different in both its scale and its origins from changes in health-service delivery. It can be argued, however, that the ability of health services to offer better and more effective services (and the fact that citizens expect to receive such services) is a factor that has led so many developed countries to embark on sector-wide programs of reform.

As Podger and Hagan explain in Chapter 6, governments the world over have an interest, and hence an involvement, in health. The USA is often cited as typifying a free-market approach to health care in which the private sector dominates and government plays only a minor role. It is indeed true that much health care in the USA is delivered by private (or not-for-profit) enterprises; but government meets almost half the costs of health services in the USA and is massively involved at both federal and state level in regulating the health care market and those who are active in it. It is not surprising then that the following discussion of recent health reforms in both Australia and New Zealand centres largely on changes to the part government plays in the sector or, as Poutasi (Chapter 7) describes it, how governments intervene to 'achieve their interests' in the sector.

Despite the differing perspectives adopted by the contributors in Part II, it is clear that the recent reforms in both Australia and New Zealand have, at their heart, efforts to enhance either allocative or technical efficiency in the sector. Thus issues of how and by whom decisions on health spending are made, coupled with efforts to improve the performance of those who deliver services, have featured prominently in both countries' reform programs.

The significance of allocative efficiency stems from the way in which health services are funded. Of all the social changes that took place in the developed world during the twentieth century, perhaps one of the most far-reaching was the shift from individual to collective funding of health care. The last hundred years have seen, to differing degrees in different countries, the emergence of commercial markets for health insurance, the development of social insurance schemes (the 'Bismarck' model, which is applied in many European countries), and the establishment of tax-financed, 'single-funder' systems (e.g. in Scandinavia, the United Kingdom and many other English-speaking nations; see page 48 above). Despite their widely differing origins and objectives, these changes have all sought to bring about a pooling of risks and resources in health.

In any health system the move from individual to collective funding also requires that the individual consumer/payer must surrender to a third party a degree of decision-making responsibility as to what services should be provided to whom. This may be limited in the case of simple indemnity insurance (it still exists in the form of exclusions and reliance on 'gate-keepers' in many policies) but is more apparent when the third party concerned is either the government itself or a government agency (area health service in Australia or Health Funding Authority in the New Zealand system).

Efforts to make such decision-making more rational and explicit have underpinned many components of recent Australian and New Zealand reforms. This is the vexed but (as Hindle and Perkins clearly state in

Chapter 4) unavoidable territory of rationing—or 'priority-setting' to the more up-beat. It is an issue that is exercising the minds of politicians and health-policy experts the world over, regardless of the specific characteristics of the systems in which they operate and the levels of funding available to them.

Several of the contributions in Part II indicate how, until fairly recently, a combination of fee-for-service payments in primary care and bulk funding of hospitals (typically on the basis of historical spending patterns) effectively prevented any planned resource allocation decisions in Australia and New Zealand. Such decisions were typically the domain of doctors and other health care professionals.

It is undoubtedly right and proper that informed providers should have a say in how and to whom they deliver services. It is also inevitable that their focus should mainly be on the individual in their care rather than on broader societal needs and priorities. The legacy of relying on such a *laissez-faire* approach (which might be termed covert rationing) over a period of years became clear in New Zealand in 1992 with publication of the first report of the National Advisory Committee on Core Health and Disability Support Services (1992). In the case of publicly funded cataract surgery, to cite just one example, the committee found that age-adjusted discharge rates in 1991 ranged from 76 per 100 000 population in the Auckland area to 228 per 100 000 in the adjacent Northland area—almost a 300 per cent variation. (The nationwide variation diminished to 200 per cent if privately funded procedures were included with the highest and lowest rates being, respectively, 310 and 155 discharges per 100 000 population.) These and similar figures for other procedures led the committee to conclude that, in the case of surgical intervention rates, 'there is a great deal of variation that does not seem to be explained by differences in need' (National Advisory Committee on Core Health and Disability Support Services 1992: 35). Coupled with similar findings on other services, those variations pointed to a highly inequitable historical allocation of resources.

In recent years, as the chapters in Part II make clear, Australia and New Zealand have both sought to address this issue as part of their respective reform programs. The approach adopted has been to introduce more explicit processes for deciding how best to spend health dollars on behalf of citizens and to ensure that, with due deference to clinical judgment, those decisions are implemented. Thus Australia has pursued the casemix funding approach (described by Duckett in Chapter 8) whereas New Zealand has added the further structural variant of a formal purchaser/provider split.

Such moves have undoubtedly done much to 'change the focus from producers to consumers of health care' (Podger and Hagan in Chapter 6) and to contain supplier-induced demand (see Hindle and Perkins in

Chapter 4). At the same time, however, they have revealed a number of significant practical difficulties that arise as a result of attempts to contract for health services on a transactional basis. Podger and Hagan cite Light (1997: 299), who has argued that products in the health care setting often cannot clearly be defined. A rigid contractual environment may also create perverse incentives for providers to limit the scope of the services they deliver, to manipulate patient classifications, to engage in adverse selection (i.e. seek to avoid taking on potentially costly cases), or to shift costs to other providers. Poutasi, in her critique of 'contractual theory' in Chapter 7, highlights such risks.

Over time, improvements to information systems and the emergence of more sophisticated contracting processes will doubtless help to overcome some of these problems. It is noteworthy, however, that both countries are also exploring 'integrated' care arrangements (in the guise of coordinated care trials in Australia). These initiatives seek to encourage closer collaboration, better communication, and more effective coordination among the various health professionals and agencies responsible for an individual's care. In doing so they shift the emphasis in contracts away from one-off transactions between consumers and health professionals and instead encourage providers to take a broader view of their patients' needs, which might extend over time and across many different components of care.

In some cases the move to integrated care also seeks once again to move resource allocation decisions closer to providers. Unlike earlier fee-for-service arrangements, however, they do so within an overall capitated budget.

In relation to allocating resources, therefore, recent reforms in Australia and New Zealand may be viewed as having had a common goal of making decisions on resource allocation and prioritisation more transparent. The approaches used vary, and in some areas they are still evolving, but the underlying imperative is to ensure a fairer balance between individual and societal needs and preferences.

Of course, much hinges on what a 'fairer balance' in fact is. As Reinhardt (1998) has argued, the concept of 'efficiency' in health is often value-laden and, depending on the definition used, a more efficient allocation of resources might not be regarded universally as a 'better' allocation of resources. Despite the significance of allocative efficiency issues to the reforms in both Australia and New Zealand, it is, then, perhaps surprising that the concept has not been spelt out more clearly. What, in other words, is the objective function defining allocative efficiency that the health systems of the two countries are seeking to maximise?

Clearly, many of the changes described above have sought to bring this issue into sharper focus. Some ambiguities remain, however. For example, is New Zealand's failure successfully to apply user charges in the hospital setting, while maintaining such charges for many primary-care services delivered in the community, 'efficient'? And is the NSW Health Department's (1998b) stated goal that 'health care is provided by NSW Health according to patient or client need and not financial status' truly consistent with a system that uses tax incentives to encourage people whose financial status is high to take out private health insurance?

Among the various achievements and initiatives described in the chapters that follow, New Zealand's move to develop booking systems for elective surgery (Chapter 7) stands out as one of the most ambitious attempts to make the basis for allocating resources explicit. The systems are based on 'clinical priority assessment criteria' that reflect individuals' ability to benefit from treatment. As such, they represent a significant move beyond the simple concept of 'need' that has previously underpinned many prioritisation processes.

Alongside efforts to improve allocative efficiency, a great deal of attention has also been paid to matters of technical efficiency, especially in those health care facilities and services that are owned or delivered by public sector bodies.

As the chapters in this part make apparent, the history of publicly owned hospitals extends back over at least fifty years in both Australia and New Zealand. In contrast, neither country has succeeded in establishing (or has even sought to establish) a wholly salaried medical profession. Indeed the continued role of direct payments by patients for primary medical services is a key feature that distinguishes the Australian and New Zealand health systems from the British NHS. The fact that GPs can use patient charges to supplement or replace government subsidies is an important but sometimes overlooked constraint on the importation of UK-based models that rely on the fact that GPs receive all their remuneration from government.

It is notable that, as described below, neither Australia nor New Zealand chose (or was able) to bring all their health services under government control. This may reflect the fact that transferring hospitals that were typically owned and/or operated by charities or local authorities to state control was a far simpler proposition than 'nationalising' the many surgeons and physicians who operated, in effect, independent small businesses. (In contrast, other salaried health professionals, notably nurses, appear to have had little choice but to become government employees, and it was only in the 1990s that the concept of the independent nurse practitioner began to gain wide recognition.)

Governments in both countries continue to be the dominant providers of secondary and tertiary hospital care while allowing lively private markets to coexist in areas such as primary medical care and long-term care of older people. Table II.1 shows, for example, that although $19 out of every $20 of public funds spent on medical and surgical hospital services in New Zealand were spent in the public sector in 1996/97, almost 40 per cent of total government spending on health went to private or not-for-profit providers.

Table II.1 Government spending on selected health services (NZ, 1996/97)

	Market share by value	
	Publicly owned providers (%)	*Privately owned providers (%)*
Hospital, medical and surgical services	95	5
General practitioner services	0	100
Age-related disability support services	38	62
Other health and disability support services	46	54
Total	61	39

Source: Ministry of Health 1998: Appendix 6

As well as reflecting the historical legacy suggested above, this arrangement may also be a sign that public ownership is seen as assuring security of supply for vital hospital services. The higher costs of market entry for secondary and tertiary hospital services relative to primary and long-stay services is also a factor that might reasonably be expected to have influenced patterns of service provision. Similarly, the inflexibility of traditional funding systems in both countries has, until recently, guaranteed government-owned providers a virtual monopoly in some sections of the market.

Foley (Chapter 5) highlights the growing role of the private sector in financing and owning public hospitals and hence in delivering publicly funded hospital services in Australia (and countervailing moves by publicly owned hospitals to capture a larger share of the privately funded market).

New Zealand appears to have been less keen to seek a reduction in government's role as owner and deliverer of hospital services. It has theoretically been possible for government-owned purchasers to use public dollars to buy services from private hospitals since the introduction of New Zealand's purchaser/provider environment in 1993. In practice, however, the extent to which that has occurred has been very limited and largely restricted to the long-stay hospital area. Thus although the share of total government spending accessed by private and not-for-profit providers increased from 31 per cent in 1992/93 (the year immediately before the introduction of the purchaser/provider regime) to 39 per cent in 1996/97, the corresponding figures for medical and surgical services are only 2 and 5 per cent (Ministry of Health 1998a: Appendix 6).

In both countries, therefore, the long-established pattern of a core of publicly owned hospitals surrounded by largely private primary and long-term care sectors remains in place. Against that background, Australia appears to be moving more rapidly towards the development of a mixed economy in hospital service provision. It will be interesting to see whether that momentum is replicated across the Tasman.

In countries such as Australia and New Zealand, that rely heavily on taxes to pay for health services and on public sector agencies to deliver them, significant bodies of legislation are required to define how 'the system' should operate. Clearly, such legislation must change as organisational and/or operational developments occur. The chapters in Part II identify many such legislative changes that have taken place under the banner of reform—in essence, changes that define how governments will act in the sector.

In contrast, little mention is made in Part II of changes in government's role in regulating the health sector to protect citizens from risks—what might broadly be termed controls on risky activities. Such controls apply in areas as diverse as regulation of health-sector occupations, management of environmental hazards, treatment of communicable diseases, and licensing of hospital premises.

Despite the widespread winding back of regulatory controls in many other parts of the economy, health remains arguably one of the most highly regulated sectors in any developed country, and Australia and New Zealand are not exceptions. That is not surprising, given the potentially catastrophic impacts of an incompetent practitioner, a polluted water supply, or a hospital with inadequate fire protection. What is perhaps more remarkable is how, despite the massive changes that have taken place in organisational structures and resource-allocation processes, health reform has impacted so little on the fundamental regulatory approach to risk management in either country. Given developments in technology and the emergence of better-informed and more demanding consumers over recent years, questions may well be asked about the continuing relevance of at least some current aspects of regulation within the health sector.

Poutasi indicates that New Zealand has embarked on a comprehensive review of health legislation. This may signal the beginning of a new phase in the reform process that focuses more sharply on the transactions that make up health-service delivery than the organisational and operational environment in which delivery takes place.

One area where approaches to regulation are clearly different is the private health insurance market. In Australia the market is subject to a variety of controls (as described by Podger and Hagan). New Zealand, in contrast, places no requirements on medical insurers over and above those prudential safeguards that apply more generally in the wider insurance and financial services sectors. Arguably this reflects acknowledgment by Australian government and citizens that private insurance is an essential component of their country's health care system (which Podger and Hagan describe in Chapter 6 as being 'supported and regulated by the Commonwealth'). In New Zealand, however, the view appears to be that the state will provide for all, and so health insurance remains an 'optional extra' that is not a legitimate area for government intervention in support of health-sector goals.

Hindle and Perkins highlight another area where recent reforms appear so far to have had little impact in either Australia or New Zealand: the fundamental issue of how health services are financed. In both countries the mixture of user pays, charity, and limited government subsidies that prevailed in early years of the twentieth century has evolved into today's systems where tax revenues provide the lion's share of health dollars. Those dollars are supplemented by a variety of (compulsory) charges levied on the users of certain services and (optional) out-of-pocket payments made by those who choose to obtain services of a type or at a time that the public system will not fund.

Where changes in financing arrangements have been made during the last twenty or so years, they have typically focused on relatively minor fine-tuning of user-charge regimes. New Zealand's attempt to impose modest contributions towards the cost of hospital services in the early 1990s was perhaps the boldest recent move to modify the basis of health financing. The fact that it did not endure gives some indication of how deeply embedded tax-based funding has now become.

Australia has made some moves to induce better-off people to take out private medical insurance but has fought shy of requiring them to do so. As Hindle and Perkins explain, the arguments in favour of tax-based financing are strong from the perspective of both equity and efficiency. Nevertheless, it is perhaps surprising that the spotlight of reform has not yet settled more clearly on the financing issue.

The need possibly to revisit the issue of health financing becomes all the more pressing when demographic changes are considered. Australia and New Zealand are both fairly young countries that have undergone sizeable population growth as a result of immigration and the postwar baby boom. As a result, both countries will soon need to decide how best to meet the health care needs of an ageing population and to assess the extent to which it will be feasible to continue to rely on taxation to do so. Approaches such as Singapore's medical savings accounts, which reduce intergenerational transfers of health dollars (Hsiao 1995; Massaro and

Wong 1995) or increased reliance on user charges, may eventually need to be considered.

Despite the changes described in Part II, health is, and will remain, a highly labour-intensive industry. Remuneration of health professionals and other staff, whether by means of salaries or fee-for-service payments, is the largest single category of expenditure in any country's health system. Furthermore, health professionals also drive expenditure and the use of resources through the decisions they make as they go about their work. Any discussion of health reform must thus consider the role played by the health workforce as either advocates for, or opponents of, change.

Alexander describes the evolving role of clinicians (i.e. health professionals) in the Australian and New Zealand health systems (Chapter 9). While she points out that clinicians are not exclusively doctors, she argues that doctors constitute the most powerful group in the health care system and, as such, a group that merits special attention in the early stages of change. Policy-makers in both countries appear to have swung between the extremes of regarding doctors as part of the problem (to be addressed by reform) and recruiting them as key agents of change. The medical profession, likewise, seems to have taken some time to decide whether or not it wishes to engage in the processes of management. At present, however, collaboration has the upper hand, with all parties believing that successful change requires partnership across the policy/professional divide.

While doctors retain their central role in the delivery of health services, it is only fair and reasonable to expect that they should be involved in shaping the future of those services. Looking to the future, however, there is a risk that such involvement might hinder some desirable changes and, by so doing, delay progress towards a possible world in which, 'patients, not doctors, will drive the system' and 'doctors will be relegated to mere members of a wider health care team, which will include clever robots' (Anon. 1994: 16). How vigorously will the medical profession continue to support change in an environment where robotics and nanotechnology could deskill aspects of today's doctors' role, where genetic screening and manipulation might lead to entirely new patterns of disease, and where people might look to health services for caring rather than curing (Wyke 1997)?

Alexander points to many recent successes in involving clinicians in management at the hospital level. It remains to be seen whether those successes will be replicated and sustained in the wider health-policy arena.

Overall, the chapters in Part II confirm that health services in both Australia and New Zealand have undergone major change in recent years. Despite the differences between the two countries' health care systems, there are many similarities in the problems that reform has sought to address, the approaches adopted, and the results achieved.

Reform in both countries has focused strongly on issues of allocative and technical efficiency, and those issues have been tackled by means of wide-ranging structural and process changes. There have undoubtedly been many successes, numerous failures, and a great deal of individual and organisational learning along the way. Much has been achieved, but the future will surely present still more challenges as demographic, technological, and social factors combine and force the two countries to question some of the basic premises on which their health systems have been built.

4

Health Care Financing in Australia and New Zealand

Don Hindle and Rod Perkins

Conceptual Overview

There are three main issues in health care financing: how much money should be raised, how the contributions should be shared, and what methods should be used to obtain the contributions. Poor arguments are often used to justify particular approaches. This chapter asserts that the primary determinants of choice of financing methods are underlying views about society, and especially a society's fundamental beliefs about the appropriate balance between equity and privilege.

Before proceeding, it is appropriate to define key concepts. By *insurer*, we mean an agency that raises money (the *health budget*) from a group of people, and then pays their health care expenses in whole or in part. The group comprises the *insured community*. Its members are *contributors*, and the amounts they pay are *contributions* (or premiums). Contributors are also *beneficiaries*, and the services to which they are entitled constitute their *insurance benefits*.

How much should be raised to finance health care?

It is difficult to predict how much any community will choose to spend on health care (the health budget). But there are many obvious correlates, of which four are covered here.

One important correlate is the strong association between the health budget and the *wealth of the community*: wealthy communities tend to spend more. This relationship can be seen across communities, and within them over time. The efficiency of the financing process is related to how much money societies can raise. Countries that have effective taxation systems are likely to raise more resources for use in community services.

Society's *expectations* are also important: the extent to which the community believes it has a right to be provided with health care. Although historical factors play a part, the key factors influencing community expectations are consumers' knowledge and the community's sense of social justice.

A third important factor is *supplier-induced demand*. The health budget tends to be larger than one might otherwise expect where there are large numbers of influential service providers in relation to the population. The relationship may be particularly strong when service providers have financial incentives to encourage consumption by raising expectations and through other means.

Fourth, *health status* may have an effect on the level of health budget in some circumstances, particularly where society holds concerns that health status might decline. For example, health budgets tended to rise in most developed countries when there was a widespread fear of increased human immunodeficiency virus/acquired immune deficiency syndrome (HIV/AIDS). In general, however, the relationship between absolute health status and expenditure is fairly weak and shows few stable patterns.

No matter how much money is raised to fund health care, it will not be enough to meet all needs, much less expectations. Perfect health is an unattainable goal. Moreover, communities are willing to control expenditure on health in order to spend in other ways. Risks are taken, and individuals hope they will not suffer the penalties.

How should contributions be shared among members of the community?

There are four important approaches to determining shares. With the exception of the first, they all involve insurance of some kind—that is, the pooling of resources by a community in anticipation of expenditure.

First, contributions may be in proportion to *actual level of health service use*. This means decisions about health care financing are made at the point of delivery, and charges are related to estimated costs of the services actually received. This approach, commonly known as *user pays*, is advantageous to the wealthy and the healthy.

Second, contributions to insurance may be based on an individual's *ability to pay*. In this case, money is raised in proportion to the income or wealth of each member of the community. This is the approach commonly adopted in government-operated insurance schemes. Health care may be financed through a separate insurance fund, or it may be financed out of general revenue provided free or at a reduced cost. This approach may be implemented by private insurance agencies, though they may find it difficult to assess an individual's ability to pay. However, it is not unknown. In Japan, for example, private insurers are required by law to set contribution rates in proportion to the individual's income.

Third, contributions to insurance may be based on *anticipated service use*. This is known as *risk-based insurance*. Each individual is rated according to expected consumption of health services calculated by reference to variables such as age and previous health history, and charged accordingly.

Finally, health care may be financed through *fixed-rate* contributions to insurance. Australian private health insurance works more or less in this way. All members have until now contributed approximately the same amounts, regardless of their income, risk rating, or actual levels of use. This is often termed community rating. A recent adjustment is the introduction of *lifetime community rating* in Australia. Community rating is still applied, but people who enrol in private health insurance plans later in life pay a higher premium per annum than those who enrolled earlier.

There are many variants and combinations of these four basic approaches. One involves *co-payments*, or setting limits on insurance benefits. For example, the consumer may have to pay any costs in excess of a specified ceiling. Another approach involves a 'front-end deductible', whereby consumers have to pay a specified amount before insurance takes over.

How can insurance contributions be generated?

There are many options. For convenience, we will describe them on three dimensions: ownership of the insurance agency, number of insurers, and degree of compulsion to contribute to insurance.

Who should own the insurance agency?

Most Western *governments* own and operate health insurance schemes. The insured community may comprise all or only a subset of citizens. If the scheme applies only to a subset of the population, they will usually be people most at risk if left to their own devices (such as the isolated, the poor, or the otherwise disadvantaged). This may reflect a concern that non-government agencies are less likely to cater for them adequately. Or they may be a subset such as war veterans, who are deemed to qualify for special benefits.

Governments may choose to finance insurance through health-specific taxes or general revenue, or both. A claimed advantage of health-specific taxes is that they give a clear message about costs. A disadvantage is reduced budget flexibility for the government.

Virtually all Western European countries, and an increasing number of other nations, also allow some degree of *non-government* health insurance, which can take various forms. Non-government health insurance companies may be for-profit or not-for-profit. The latter type is more likely to involve some kind of affinity grouping, such as occupation or geography. A scheme that restricts its membership in some way (for example, to a particular occupational group such as teachers) is often called a 'closed fund'.

An apparent advantage of private insurance in the eyes of some governments is that it reduces government outlays, because people are effectively volunteering to pay tax in the form of insurance premiums. However, government insurers have a distinct advantage over private insurance because they tend to have lower administrative costs than private insurers.

One insurer or many?

The main benefit of having a *single insurer* is the potential to reduce administrative costs. Where there is a single insurer some tasks common to insurers may no longer be relevant (such as risk-assessment or marketing) and others may be greatly simplified (such as premium-setting, claims-processing, and care-provider audit). A single insurer enjoys economies of scale, and may find it easier to ensure equity of costs and benefits among contributors.

Estimates of savings in having a single insurer compared with multiple insurers vary widely. A typical view is that administrative costs of health insurance total around 3 per cent in countries with a single insurer (such as the United Kingdom and Canada), and at least 10 per cent where there are multiple insurers (as in France and the USA).

The *multiple insurer* approach is claimed to have two main advantages. First, it offers more choice, of both insurance agency and the level and pattern of insurance benefits. Second, it affords more competition, which may encourage cost containment and a greater sense of responsiveness to contributors' needs and expectations. But the benefits of both choice and competition are difficult to measure.

Where countries with a tradition of government insurance (such as the United Kingdom, Korea, New Zealand, and Japan) have encouraged private insurance, they have usually stressed the increased opportunities for 'customisation'. Australian private insurers are required to rate all members of the community at the same level of insurance risk—regardless of their actual risk rating. This is called 'community rating'. In fact, however, they have moved towards a greater degree of risk rating under the guise of providing opportunities for individualised coverage packages, including those where the beneficiary can choose to be insured for, say, trauma care but not for childbirth.

Compulsory or optional insurance?

The key argument in favour of *optional insurance* is that of choice. People may hold different views about the value of their health, and may therefore wish to make their own trade-offs in matters of cost and risk. A related idea is that governments should not intervene without good reason: compulsion reflects unwarranted paternalism and 'overgovernment'.

Optional insurance is often favoured because it 'rewards the prudent'. If a member of the community has the sense to insure, he or she should be able to profit. Mandated cover implies that the less prudent (and hence the less deserving) will have to be supported by the 'good citizens'.

An argument in favour of *compulsion* is that some people find it difficult to make the right decisions for reasons of uncontrollable financial difficulty, lack of knowledge about risks, and so on. In the interest of equity, it is argued, the civil society should support them appropriately.

Some of the cost implications of optional versus compulsory health insurance are unclear. For example, optional insurance tends to reduce the use of health services by the uninsured or under-insured, but limited access to preventive care may increase overall costs to the community in later years.

Putting aside the irrelevant arguments

It is difficult to identify the best approach to financing health care, but analysis is easier if some of the trivial, irrelevant, or illogical ideas are discounted. We believe there are six topics that deserve to be put aside at this stage.

First, contrary to what is often assumed, financing methods hardly ever dictate methods of providing health services. For example, it has been argued that capitation of GPs is a cause or consequence of government dominance of insurance, yet government can dominate in a private insurance model as well.

Second, there is no evidence that private operators are inherently more efficient than government operations. This belief originates in part from governments' tendency to be involved in the more problematic enterprises (such as health or education). This has led some people to conclude that the difficulties are caused by the managing agency (the government) when they are in fact inherent to the enterprise.

Third, no financing option can entirely avoid rationing. Eastaugh (1992: 502) contends that the problem with Canada's one-insurer system is that the government 'can ration care through inconvenience: long waits for elective surgery, tests, and checkup visits'. Lister (1986: 168) similarly argues that the US marketplace 'encourages demand and diversity, whereas the UK's controlled system leads to uniformity, rationing, and possibly mediocrity'. The reality is obvious. For example, private insurance has been dominant in the USA but rationing has been particularly vicious, as 40 million uninsured individuals can attest. It would be hard to argue that rationing by waiting lists is worse than rationing by price.

Fourth, uniformity of insurance is not inherently undesirable, nor an inevitable consequence of use of a single dominant insurer (and especially a government insurer). There are some obvious benefits of uniformity, including common information structures. Moreover, a single insurer can choose to have a variety of coverage levels. The opponents of uniformity tend to be more concerned about the compulsion for everyone to accept 'mediocrity' of access and care provision. Advantaged people would hardly wish to move down to mediocrity. But if you are poor and uninsured in the USA, you might well aspire to move from nothing to mediocre.

Fifth, choice of insurer is not always valuable in practice. A single insurer can provide variety in many respects. More important, much of the choice in communities with multiple insurers is difficult to exercise. The absence of major differences among Australia's various private health insurance companies, which cannot easily be evaluated by the average person, has meant that few Australians have ever had strong preferences for a particular insurer.

Sixth, health cannot be treated as if it were the same as any other product in the marketplace. As explained in depth by Hall and Viney (Chapter 2), there are many reasons for this being the case. Even the strongest proponents of market forces back off in the real world of health care. For example, during his presidential campaign Reagan promised to deregulate health in the USA, but within two years he had introduced more controls than any other president since Kennedy (including mandated hospital prices).

Thus it is not a matter of whether governments will intervene in the health market, but rather in what way. As a minimum, all of them legislate constraints over private insurance and provide some kind of subsidy for disadvantaged groups.

Finally, the debate on health care financing has been weakened by the use of loaded language. For example, it is common to refer to 'bureaucracy' with the deliberate intention of devaluing government involvement.

Bureaucracy is not restricted to government agencies and it is a desirable feature of some activities. On the other hand, terms like 'profit-driven' and 'capitalist' are intended to devalue the marketplace. No advocate of a public insurance scheme is likely to describe it as 'socialist medicine', and opponents are unlikely to call it 'social justice'.

The core factor in health care financing: equity or privilege

There are two extreme views about health care financing. On the one hand are proponents of the single government insurance scheme, to which all members of the community must contribute in accordance with ability to pay, and which finances free health care in accordance with need. Advocates of this approach are likely to use terms like 'collective responsibility', 'equity', 'community service', 'inclusiveness', and 'collaboration'.

At the other extreme are proponents of a financing model characterised by as many privately operated insurance schemes as the marketplace determines. Enrolment is optional, and anyone can choose to self-insure or have no insurance at all. In this case, advocates tend to use terms like 'individual responsibility', 'merit', 'freedom', 'opportunity', 'private enterprise', 'choice', and 'competition'.

These two views illustrate a matter that appears to be more important than any other in the health-financing debate: that of the balance to be struck between *equity* of benefits on the one hand, and opportunity to gain and retain *privilege* on the other. These views of society dominate the debate. Most people have a clear global preference for one or the other that affects their attitudes towards almost every detail of the design of a preferred health-funding model.

Five points need to be clarified here. First, privilege applies to care providers as well as care recipients, and there may be interactions between the two. Some medical groups have supported private insurance because it creates a privileged subgroup of the population which is more likely to use private medical services.

Second, equity is a value-laden concept open to various interpretations, and it is a dangerous term in some hands. For advocates of compulsory public insurance, 'equity' is likely to mean equity of access, service provision, and health status. But opponents are more likely to mean 'equity of opportunity'. *Access to* health and health care and *opportunity to seek access* are very different and can lead to very different situations.

Third, privilege can be conferred whether or not market forces are allowed to operate. That is, it is entirely possible for certain groups to obtain preferential access or treatment regardless of the market structure. However, the reverse does not hold: the unbridled impact of market forces in health is bound to increase the degree of privilege in respect of health care enjoyed by select members of society.

Fourth, every community will contain advocates of both extremes of health-financing model, and therefore the ultimate model will always be some kind of compromise. Few governments prohibit privilege altogether, though it may be well hidden. Nor will any democracy allow the wholly uninhibited play of market forces in health. Democracies differ, therefore, only in the extent and the nature of the methods they apply to control privilege and encourage equity.

Finally, if the financing of health care reflects core views about society, and if social attitudes are slow to change, then the same should be evident with respect to models of health care financing. This is clearly the case. Major changes are rare, and have usually been associated with upheaval in most aspects of society, such as immediately after the Second World War in Europe and during the civil rights period in the 1960s in the USA.

Financing Trends in Australia

During the first hundred years of the Australian colonies, most of the few available health services were available on a user-pays basis, and provided by private medical practitioners on a fee-for-service basis. Governments did little more than provide subsidies to a mix of public and charitable hospitals that delivered mainly means-tested care for the poor and chronically ill.

In the mid-nineteenth century private insurance became progressively more feasible and desirable. It largely took the form of not-for-profit self-help groups known as friendly societies. In return for weekly contributions, members had limited access to basic medical services and elementary hospital care. The period from 1870 to 1940 was characterised by a progressive increase in the capabilities of hospitals. One consequence was growth of the private hospital sector, which concentrated on care of the middle and upper classes. Public hospitals continued to provide free care to people with low incomes but also began to treat increasing numbers of middle-class patients. These trends stimulated the growth of private insurance for hospital services.

From 1900 until the Second World War, governments sporadically increased their financial support for health care, sometimes by accident. What were intended as temporary financing measures soon became the norm. Repeated attempts to increase public as well as private health insurance coverage and to improve efficiency met with little success. For example, legislation proposed in 1928 would have mandated compulsory contributions in equal shares by employers and employees for hospital care.

In 1938 legislation was drafted that would have enabled a mix of financing sources, including employers, employees, and government. The scheme would have been compulsory but applicable only to employees with low incomes. None of these measures ever came into force.

The views formed by the British (now Australian) Medical Association (BMA) during this period remain little changed today. Most doctors supported insurance, but only in the form of cash given to the patient to defray the charges levied directly by the care provider. Retention of the direct contract between patient and doctor would avoid third-party involvement and would further strengthen the commitment of each doctor to serve the patient's interests first and foremost.

By the end of the war, most medical services were provided by private practitioners on a fee-for-service basis. Most hospital services were funded and managed by the states and territories, with minor contributions by the Commonwealth. Services were typically means-tested, and involved significant co-payments for all but the most disadvantaged. The result was a relatively strong but highly fragmented private insurance sector covering both hospital and medical services.

Decision-makers and politicians continued trying to strike a balance between 'sympathy' and 'economic rationality'. The conservative parties (Liberal and later the Liberal–National Party Coalition) preferred choice of private insurer, and a mix of government, employer, and employee contributions. The Labor Party's long-time preference for compulsory over voluntary insurance had become a formal commitment by 1945, and the focus of debate shifted to how contributions might be raised. Labor favoured financing health services from general revenue, or possibly a health-specific tax, on the grounds that this structure would be administratively efficient and more equitable in terms of benefits.

A Labor government was elected in Australia in 1946. Strengthened by the social cohesion of the war years, it proposed the creation of a national health service similar to that in the United Kingdom. It wanted to establish a salaried medical profession and ensure that most people could obtain hospital care at no charge, or with only small and means-tested co-payments. The plan was never implemented, mainly because the BMA was able to convince many electors that a national health system was one step towards 'full-blown socialism'.

A conservative government was elected in 1949. Its Minister for Health, a medical practitioner by background, stressed that government-aided health systems tend to foster dependence at the expense of community responsibility. A system that required a direct financial contribution from each individual was therefore preferable. The 1949 government therefore did no more than re-establish the pre-war situation: slow expansion and rationalisation of private health insurance, with public insurance targeted to the disadvantaged.

Major changes promised by the wartime government did not eventuate until thirty years later. There were several reasons for the delay, including the difficulty of ensuring that the Commonwealth and all states agreed to the new system. But the main constraint was the absence of a government with a strong sense of social justice and enough power to persuade the electorate of the merits of universal health insurance.

These two conditions coincided with the first Whitlam Labor government in 1972. It proposed a health-financing model with a single national insurer, compulsory contributions, and no means test at the point of care delivery. In other respects it was a fairly conservative model. For example, it did not require all services to be free, it placed no restrictions on private insurance and private health care, and it made no specific proposals about the way in which doctors and others should be paid by the national insurer. Some of Whitlam's proposals would have been acceptable, but the national insurance fund (to become known as Medibank) was objectionable to conservatives. It was rejected by the Opposition-controlled Senate.

A general election was called, Labor was returned to office, and it was able to enact its Medibank legislation in 1975. The Health Insurance Commission (HIC) was established to administer medical benefits, which were funded from Commonwealth general revenue. There were two options for payment of doctors. First, the doctor could bill the HIC directly, in which case he or she would have to accept 85 per cent of the Commonwealth's Schedule fee (the approved fee on which government reimbursement is based), and the patient would be charged nothing. Alternatively, the doctor could invoice the patient directly, and the patient could then obtain 85 per cent of the Schedule fee from one of the newly established HIC offices. The hospital benefits component conferred free public hospital care on all. Patients could, however, choose to be treated privately, in which case they were liable for hospital charges. These could be paid by the patient's private insurer. No tax rebate was available for private health insurance membership contributions.

The conservative Fraser government, elected at the end of 1975, noted the growing public acceptance of Medibank and undertook to retain it with 'major improvements'. Over the next five years, however, the details of the scheme were adjusted to such an extent that its support for greater equity and integrity was considerably diminished.

Medibank was first substantially revised by the Fraser government in 1976. People without private health insurance continued to make contributions through the tax system, but a health-specific component of taxation was introduced and set at 2.5 per cent of taxable income. Those with private insurance were exempted from this levy. The last major change until recently occurred in 1981, when contributions to private health insurance were made tax-deductible and eligibility for free hospital services was reduced in scope.

The main consequence of Fraser's changes was to increase private health insurance membership, in accordance with the conservative parties' belief that citizens should look after themselves to the greatest extent possible. The Whitlam Labor government had taken health-financing policy in another direction, but residual gains were relatively minor.

It fell to the Hawke government, elected in 1983, to implement the main elements of long-established Labor policy. It had given the campaign promise to reinstate Medibank. In the event it created a major modification, called Medicare, which continues as Australia's health-financing model today. Its main features were

- a health insurance levy on all taxpayers, with no exemptions granted to the privately insured;
- all payments for private medical practice made by a single national agency at legislated national rates, but without constraints on the charges actually levied at the point of service;
- free public hospital care;
- predominantly free domiciliary and other community services;
- Commonwealth government contributions to the states and territories for the costs of operating hospitals and other services, with contribution levels of each party negotiated at five-year intervals; and
- constraints on private insurers, including community rating.

Public insurance expenditures rose significantly, and private insurance membership began a downward trend that continues today.

Medicare continues to be the main health-financing mechanism in Australia. Few changes have been made since 1983, and the differences in health care policy between the Labor and Coalition parties have become less marked. The Coalition periodically advised it would repeal (or at least extensively modify) Medicare, but had changed its mind by the mid-1990s in response to Medicare's popularity among electors. Incentives for private insurance have been revised upwards from time to time, in order to avoid too rapid a decline in membership, including a rebate of 30 per cent on health insurance premiums introduced by the Commonwealth government in 1999.

In summary, Australian health care was financed largely through user pays in the early years, with government and charitable support for the most disadvantaged. Increased wealth led to the growth of private insurance. Most of these early insurance funds were established by not-for-profit associations, friendly societies, and other affinity groups.

Governments progressively increased their involvement through both financial support for private insurance and growth of public insurance. For many years the latter was restricted to the more disadvantaged, but compulsory and universal coverage was finally achieved in 1983.

All of Australia's major political parties have accepted a mix of public and private insurance for most of this century. Views on privilege and equity determine the balance between public and private advocated by successive governments. The conservative political parties continue to prefer a larger degree of voluntary private insurance (except for the most disadvantaged), and the social democrats lean towards compulsory public insurance. Although the policies of the major parties are closer than they were a hundred years ago, the underlying conflicts remain.

Financing Trends in New Zealand

Before 1938 no coherent policy directed the funding or financing of health care in New Zealand, and different arrangements could be found in different locations. Individuals paid for primary medical care on a fee-for-service basis, to the best of their ability, whereas hospital and related care was jointly financed by local and central governments. In 1938 the first Labour government funded and directed the activities of what was intentionally a 'welfare state', in which the government took responsibility for the welfare of New Zealanders from the cradle to the grave. The enabling legislation, the Social Security Act, provided universal coverage for all New Zealanders, irrespective of their ability to pay.

While this system worked well in its early years, the policy of universal coverage has progressively been replaced by a system targeting government funds to those in greatest need. The major political parties have differed little in their support for government funding and provision of health care. Significant attempts to reform the health system in recent decades have usually caused adverse political reaction, with the electorate expressing their dissatisfaction at the polls.

The first attempt at reform after 1938 occurred in 1974, when the second Labour government developed a policy that would have provided a system similar to that of the United Kingdom's NHS. The second major restructure occurred in 1993, when the funding/purchasing role in health care was separated from the provider role. The remainder of this section addresses how financing of health care has developed in New Zealand, the types of insurance that have evolved, how NZ governments and insurers have addressed the issue of targeting and co-payments, and other features relating to the issue of financing and health reform. We conclude with our vision of how the systems in the two countries might develop in the future.

Financing health care in New Zealand

The early history of health care financing in New Zealand is similar to that in Australia. Demand for hospital services increased rapidly in the early part of the twentieth century, where hospitals developed in response to local advocacy. Private hospitals also emerged at this time, but were never to become as significant in New Zealand as in Australia. General hospitals received payment for each bed-day provided from local government. In each city and town in New Zealand, city or borough councils were required to finance their local (public) hospitals. Mandatory patient hospital fees were imposed. Beginning in 1875, central government provided matching funds for the majority of public hospitals. These payments, which took the form of direct grants, were equal to the revenues generated by the hospital from local government, charitable institutions, and patient charges combined. Mental hospitals were financed differently: from the outset, their financing and administration was the responsibility of central government.

The *Social Security Act 1938* provided public hospitals with a daily payment initially set at 6 shillings per bed-day. Although government increased this amount from time to time, as was the case with GP patient subsidies, the government's hospital bed-day rates did not keep pace with the rising costs of hospital care; an increasing and eventually unmanageable burden fell on local government and charitable agencies. There was no option but to change the basis of hospital funding, and by 1957 all responsibility for hospital financing had been transferred to central government.

By the mid-1960s the NZ government was having difficulty financing the extensive provisions of the welfare state created in the post-depression years. Patients found it increasingly difficult to gain admission to a public hospital for elective surgery, and were denied admission altogether if the hospital determined that the need for surgery was not sufficiently urgent. In principle, because (public) hospitals were entirely financed by central government at this time, the financial status of the patient, and their ability to pay, were immaterial. Admission was determined strictly by clinical need. Public hospitals in New Zealand at the time had no 'private beds'.

Expenditure on health services in New Zealand in this era, as a percentage of national income, was high by international standards. In 1961/62 New Zealand's expenditure on health services as a percentage of national income was 6.5 per cent, only 0.3 per cent behind the USA in the same year and 0.5 per cent greater than Australia's expenditure in 1960/61 (Abel-Smith 1967: 41).

Around 1967, the government required all departments to constrain public expenditure, and tough measures were adopted in all government services, including health care. Since then the New Zealand publicly funded health system has been required to live within allocated resources (Ward 1969). With government unwilling or unable to increase its funding for hospitals at a rate matching growth in demand, a deliberate strategy developed. Some of the demand for hospital services was diverted into the non-government, mostly not-for-profit hospitals: access to public hospitals was restricted, and public hospital waiting lists grew throughout New Zealand. The diversion of demand was made easier because of the growing affluence that accompanied expansion of New Zealand's economy. Ability and willingness to pay for access through the non-government sector grew.

By the 1980s New Zealand had a mixed health economy. Whereas the private sector had played only a minor role in financing and providing health care in the earlier years, the public sector had now become dependent on it to absorb an increasing proportion of the non-acute health workload. Nowhere was this more apparent than in New Zealand's major centres.

Types of insurance

Until the more recent involvement of physician proceduralists (e.g. gastro-enterologists, cardiologists, respiratory physicians, etc.), private medical insurance in New Zealand was limited in its coverage almost exclusively to surgical treatment. Benefits for patients seeking psychiatric and medical care were strictly limited. The traditional private health insurance policy in New Zealand has provided for part payment of costs associated with surgical procedures (i.e. part or all of a surgeon's fees and the in-patient hospital fees associated with the surgery). It was used largely to finance services that patients needed or wanted but which the public hospital did not or could not provide in a timely fashion. The privately insured had the best of both worlds: they were able to get urgent, acute treatment from public hospitals at little or no cost to themselves, and to obtain elective care at a time and location of their choice by using their private insurance. Until recently, all patients with private insurance enjoyed freedom of choice of surgeon without any influence on the part of the insurer. In the 1980s a family could obtain a basic private insurance package for less than NZ$1000 per annum.

At its peak in the mid-1980s, private health insurance in New Zealand covered around 40 per cent of the population. By 1998, however, coverage had declined to under 25 per cent, for much the same reasons as in Australia. First, in the mid-1980s, government removed tax-deductibility on private health insurance. Premiums have since risen, driven in large part by the technology cost-push, particularly in private health care. Having concluded that their rising premiums were being used to support the private surgical needs of New Zealanders in older middle life or old age, a disproportionate number of 'healthy young' began dropping out of private insurance. This reinforced a vicious circle: as more healthy policy-holders relinquished their coverage, premiums increased to cover the higher average cost of (more intensive) health care users who remain insured.

Targeting those in greatest need

The era of universal coverage, which commenced in 1938, provided government financing of primary health care without co-payments. Since then a plethora of payment arrangements in both the public and private sectors have developed. The NZ government has made several half-hearted attempts to reduce the level of co-payment since 1938, but never with the same degree of commitment to 'free' universal public insurance for medical services as in Australia. NZ governments have continued to believe that those who can afford to pay should fund their own primary care.

This view underpinned the government's increased emphasis on 'targeting' in the early 1990s. Rather than attempting to provide adequate medical insurance for all New Zealanders, government financing would focus on those with the greatest need for health care. In 1992 government created a Community Services Card (CSC) scheme, which gave people on low incomes access to health services at reduced prices. The cards were available to members of families with an annual income of less than NZ$35 000. Cardholders included a high proportion of students and older people. The actual level of co-payment for each type of service varied around the country, in line with variations in doctors' fees for identical services. For those eligible under the CSC scheme, co-payments were generally set at approximately 50 per cent of the service provider's fee. In 1996, at the instigation of the populist New Zealand First Party, legislation was enacted whereby children under the age of 6 became eligible for free health care from GPs.

In the early 1990s the government began to apply its targeting strategy to public hospital services. In order to subsidise reduced hospital costs for the more disadvantaged, charges were introduced for many hospital services for the population at large. The most visible of these was the $31 charge for each hospital out-patient visit, introduced in 1991. The objectives of the new fee were mainly to reduce utilisation and to reduce the barrier to greater and fairer competition among service providers and service settings. The government argued that there was little sense in maintaining co-payments for general practice and medical specialist services in other settings while hospital out-patient services were free of charge. The new charges made little sense to the community and proved very unpopular. After their introduction hospital managers reported publicly that the cost of collecting the new co-payments was approximately the same as the revenue they generated. The co-payments attracted such wide criticism that they were dropped shortly after they were adopted.

Australia and New Zealand have differed in their use of co-payments

New Zealand's private health insurers use co-payments as an effective and appropriate means of controlling use of health services. Co-payments easily took root in New Zealand, in part because the Southern Cross Medical Care Society, long the dominant private insurer in the country, operates its own hospitals. Southern Cross's hospital fee schedule ensures that Southern Cross policyholders' co-payments are exactly 20 per cent of the hospital fee. Other insurers, whose benefit rates are similar to those of Southern Cross, tend to charge about the same amount or a little higher. Consequently co-payments of at least 20 per cent have become the norm throughout New Zealand.

Other notable features of health care financing in New Zealand

Since 1990, private health insurers in New Zealand have become increasingly aggressive in applying other mechanisms to manage use of health services.

Insurers have been more willing than their Australian counterparts to embrace strategies prevalent in the USA, such as managed care. For example, one private health insurer has partnered with GP groups to contract with government to provide a range of primary-care services in return for a capitated fee. Other forms of private insurance funding for health services are likely to emerge in New Zealand in the future for many reasons. Of particular importance, government is attracted by the willingness and capacity of the private insurance sector to accept and manage the risk associated with the use of health services.

Government's restructure of health finance in the 1990s involved the separation of funder, purchaser, and provider. It also attempted to define 'core services', those essential, central, or fundamental services that would form part of the package of health care to which all residents are deemed entitled. Governments seek to define 'core services' in the course of health reform as a means of delimiting what government can reasonably be expected to finance. The definition of 'core services' differs across countries and at different points in time within any one country. A Core Health

Committee was established in 1993 to define services that would be funded under government contracts and, by implication, those services deemed to be of lesser value, which would have to be funded in other ways (e.g. through self-pay and private insurance). Not surprisingly, the committee never produced a list of services to be included or excluded. The technical complexities in rating services in terms of value for money was 'too hard', and conflict between sectional interests (both care providers and patients) made the list too politically contentious.

But the government's 1993 reforms were dependent on being able to define which services New Zealanders could expect government to finance, so the impasse of the committee undermined government commitment and action. The efforts of government then became concentrated on maintaining financial control, with little apparent interest in how best to ration health care resources. Despite the failure of the Core Health Committee in the early 1990s, its work remains central to future health reform in New Zealand.

A significant outcome of the 1993 reform program was the exploration of alternative private financing. One important initiative was the establishment of privately managed health plans, with partial payment of insurance premiums by government-supplied voucher. This scheme would have enabled New Zealanders to opt out of the public sector in exchange for obtaining treatment from the private sector. The scheme was abandoned by the National government but is still favoured by some conservative politicians.

Summary of health financing in New Zealand

The history of health care financing in New Zealand parallels Australia's experience. Health care was originally financed primarily through a user-pays system, with government and charitable support for the most disadvantaged. Government gradually increased its involvement in health funding, culminating in universal health insurance coverage 1938. But universal coverage began to erode in subsequent years and deteriorated to a critical point by the 1960s. New Zealand has never sustained public insurance coverage to the same extent as Australia. Instead it has maintained a much higher level of private insurance for procedural forms of health care than Australia. Even at its peak in the 1980s, private insurance coverage for hospital services in New Zealand remained lower than Australian levels.

New Zealand's approach to health care financing has been no more cohesive than Australia's. New Zealand has faced the same trade-offs and debates: between co-payments to suppress utilisation and fear that equity would be compromised; between private and public insurance, and so on. Like most governments, New Zealand's tends to be reluctant to lead the health-financing debate in the community as a whole: where they have tried (as in the early 1990s) they have encountered community backlash and lost their zeal.

Government interest in New Zealand has shifted towards the redesign of resource allocation processes and service delivery methods such as capitation and integrated care. New Zealand is not experiencing the degree of turbulence in health care financing that is evident in Australia. Nevertheless, it lacks a stable or widely endorsed health-financing strategy, and there is no strong sense that one is likely to emerge in the foreseeable future.

What, Then, is the Future?

Most clinical aspects of health care have been revolutionised in the last hundred years. There have also been changes in health care financing. In particular, more money is being raised, a larger proportion of care is covered by insurance, and governments are more deeply involved. But there is no clear strategic view about financing, and important structural problems remain. Governments tend to be reluctant to lead the debate in the community as a whole, and where they have tried they have run out of steam. Public insurance is efficient, but little has been done to encourage integrated care or establish explicit rationing of services. Private insurance continues to be relatively inefficient and still serves mainly to create an 'upper tier' of health care for the privileged.

Three major options

The first of three options is more of the same—or incrementalism. It involves no more than making minor changes at the margins in response to vested interest and political expediency.

The second means a serious attempt to design a mixed (public and private) system, rather than letting it evolve by accident and sectional pressure. If this is to succeed, however, it will probably require more formal and widespread support for a two-tier health system. One of the reasons reform has failed in the past is that many people who believed in privilege were afraid to say so—in part because of the fear that it would not be acceptable to the majority. Thus financing systems have effectively evolved by stealth rather than design, and this is technically inefficient.

The third involves moving towards a single public insurer system like that which Canada implemented in 1970. We are unashamed to say this is our choice. There are technical arguments, such as efficiency, but they are unimportant. The key is the view neatly expressed by Canadian economist Robert Evans: the health care system should serve as a fundamental expression of social unity. The people of both Australia and New Zealand have a strong sense of social justice. Thus, we predict, they will inevitably move towards a single public insurer as simplistic arguments about the marketplace are discredited. But the rate of change will depend on how quickly the community and health professionals at large join in the debate, reducing the dominant influence of politicians and private for-profit care providers, including doctors.

5

The Changing Public–Private Balance

Mary Foley

In Australia, the 1990s have seen significant shifts in the role of the private sector and private markets in health care funding and the delivery of services. Similar trends are evident in New Zealand, but this chapter will focus on Australia, where the shifting balance between public and private sectors has been more pronounced.

One of the distinguishing characteristics of the Australian health care system has always been its mixed economy. Australian health care comprises a tapestry of programs funded by federal and state government, private health insurance, government-owned institutions, private for-profit and not-for-profit institutions, private medical practice, corner-shop pharmacies, and large publicly listed and private corporations.

Commonwealth government health policies have focused on ensuring universal access to core, acute health services. The arrangements summarised here, as well as elsewhere in this volume, are the following:

- Acute hospital access is assured by arrangements with state governments under Medicare: the Commonwealth government provides a financial contribution to state public hospital systems, which are required, in return, to provide services free of charge to patients who elect to be treated as 'public' patients. The Commonwealth also regulates private health insurance for access to private hospital services.
- Medical services (consultations, procedures, diagnostics) are covered by the Commonwealth government, which pays a patient rebate of 85 per cent of a Medicare Schedule fee for services provided by medical practitioners in private practice.

- Affordable pharmaceuticals are covered through the Pharmaceutical Benefits Scheme, which subsidises prescription drugs dispensed through local commercial retail pharmacies.

In addition to these universal core services, which involve public and private sector providers, a host of other health services is provided in the private market and by targeted government programs for eligible groups, such as the aged and the disabled.

From a private market perspective, the Australian health sector offers enormous opportunities resulting from financial pressure on public sector delivery systems and growth in consumer demand and expectations. Over the last few years a plethora of market analysts' reports from the major merchant banks have highlighted health care as an attractive investment market.

For governments and public policy, these developments require a reassessment of policy and funding arrangements that have until recently been based largely on a more traditional split between public and private sector roles in health care.

This chapter focuses on the respective roles of the public and private sectors in relation to hospitals and medical diagnostic services as a means of exploring the public policy issues that arise from greater private sector participation in the health system. Specific topics covered include:

- growth in the size and significance of the private hospital sector;
- structural issues in private health insurance and shifting relationships between private providers and private health insurers;
- growth in public sector use of private capital through public hospital privatisation and co-location of private hospitals in public hospital precincts;
- emergence of major private, corporatised health care organisations, in both the charitable and for-profit sectors, and their pursuit of integrated service-delivery systems; and
- private investment in medical diagnostic services and the emergence of innovative funding models developed in partnership between private diagnostic providers and government.

Private Hospitals

Since the introduction of Medicare in 1984, the private hospital sector has grown to become a significant force in Australia's health care system. Private hospitals now account for about a third of acute hospital admissions (see Table 5.1, p. 101).

Table 5.1 Australian public acute hospital and private hospital admissions, patient days and beds, 1996/97

Category	Public hospitals		Private hospitals	
Patient days	15.2m	(72%)	5.8m	(28%)
Admissions	3.6m	(68%)	1.7m	(32%)
Beds	56 836	(70%)	23 996	(30%)

Source: Private hospital bed numbers form Private Hospitals Australia, 1996/97, ABS.
Other data from Australian Hospital Statistics, 1996/97, AIHW.

During the 1980s, private hospital use grew almost at three times the rate of public hospital admissions. This growth in use was supported by the steady growth throughout the 1980s in the take-up of 'supplementary' health insurance tables, which provided cover for private hospital care. Although Medicare ensured access free of charge to public hospitals, access to private hospital care continued to be an attractive option for a growing proportion of the population.

The complexity and acuity of private hospital casemix also increased in the late 1980s and into the 1990s, supported by changes in private insurance payment systems. The introduction of graded theatre fees, differential bed-day charges for advanced surgery, and fees for intensive care allowed differential payments between hospitals according to their level of infrastructure and case complexity.

Until the early 1980s, private hospitals (with some notable exceptions) were typically small 'cottage' hospitals offering basic elective surgery. Under the revised insurance arrangements, private hospitals became larger and offered a more comprehensive range of services, including accident and emergency services, intensive care and coronary care, and full in-house clinical support services.

These changes have dramatically affected the significance of private hospitals in public policy terms. From a marginal and therefore optional role, private hospitals have become essential to the totality of acute hospital service provision in Australia.

A comparison of the casemix of private and public hospitals demonstrates some market segmentation between the public and private sectors. The *Australian Casemix Report on Hospital Activity 1995–96* shows that almost 50 per cent of private hospital admissions were for surgical procedures, while fewer than 30 per cent of public hospital admissions were for surgery. In public hospitals, medical patients accounted for over 60 per cent of public hospital admissions (Figure 5.1, p. 102).

This differentiation in casemix is illustrated to some extent by comparison of the ten most frequent Diagnosis Related Groups (DRGs) admitted to public and private hospitals (Table 5.2, p. 103). It is interesting to note the similarities and differences.

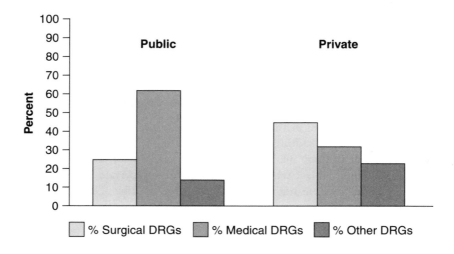

Figure 5.1   Percentage separations for surgical, medical and other AN-DRGs (v3.0); public and private acute hospitals, Australia, states and territories, 1995/96

Source: Australian Casemix Report on Hospital Activity, 1995/96,
Commonwealth Department of Health and Family Services

For some surgical categories the private sector is the major provider, as shown in Table 5.3 (p. 102).

The growth in capacity of the private sector has gone hand in hand with a reduction in private patient numbers in public hospitals. In 1989/90, 54 per cent of private patient bed-days were spent in private hospitals; by 1997/98 private hospital bed-days had increased to 76 per cent. This trend had the impact of reducing private revenues to public hospitals and increasing costs for private health insurance. Private patient charges in public hospitals are subsidised. The shift of private patients to private hospitals greatly increased the costs to private health insurance. As a result, the viability of private health insurance was a major public policy issue at the national level throughout the 1990s.

Health Insurance

When Medicare was introduced in 1984, the Commonwealth government was concerned to maintain the viability of private health insurance as an adjunct to Medicare. To this end, the original Medicare grants to the states for public hospitals included a $50 per day bed-day payment for private patients in public hospitals. The payment was intended to keep health

Table 5.2   The ten most frequent DRGs admitted to public and private hospitals, 1995/96

AN-DRG	Public hospital	No. of separations	Rank in private hospital
572	Renal dialysis	309 600	8
780	Chemotherapy	121 651	6
674	Normal delivery	112 612	7
332	Gastroscopy (non-major)	68 484	1
335	Colonoscopy	47 770	2
187	Bronchitis/asthma, Age <50	44 299	109
683	Abortion	39 018	9
484	Other skin, subcutaneous tissue & breast procedures	37 216	10
686	Other antenatal admission	36 683	68
252	Heart failure & shock	32 050	48

AN-DRG	Private hospital	No. of separations	Rank in public hospital
332	Gastroscopy (non-major)	93 798	4
335	Other colonoscopy	87 095	5
099	Lens procedure	53 510	14
128	Dental extractions & restorations	47 104	23
421	Knee procedures	46 787	32
780	Chemotherapy	37 305	2
674	Normal delivery	32 229	3
572	Renal dialysis	31 211	1
683	Abortion	28 653	7
484	Other skin, subcutaneous tissue & breast procedures	25 478	8

Source: Australian Casemix Report on Hospital Activity 1995/96, Commonwealth Report of Health and Family Services

Table 5.3   Surgical categories for which the private sector is the primary provider

		Patient separations	
AN-DRG	Procedure	Public hospital	Private hospital
099	Lens procedures	29 302	53 510
128	Dental extractions & restorations	24 091	47 104
332	Gastroscopy	68 484	93 798
335	Colonoscopy	47 770	87 095
404/405	Hip replacement	9 728	8 363
406/407	Other major joint & limb reattachment procedures	6 143	8 072
421	Knee procedures	19 054	46 787

Source: Australian Casemix Report on Hospital Activity, 1995/96,
Commonwealth Department of Health and Family Services

insurance premiums at affordable levels. The Commonwealth also maintained a bed-day subsidy for private hospitals. The subsidy was abolished during the 1980s, in response to fiscal constraints on government expenditure.

At the same time, health insurers began to market higher table or 'supplementary' private health insurance that offered beneficiaries higher-level cover for private hospital stays. Supplementary insurance enjoyed considerable growth in the 1980s, rising from 34 per cent of the population in 1986 to 39 per cent in the March quarter 1991. The economic recession in 1991/92 saw supplementary insurance coverage stall and then decline. Since that time there has been a steady decline in the proportion of the Australian population with any form of private hospital insurance, from 43.7 per cent (all insurance tables) of the population at June 1991 to 30.6 per cent in 1998. All insurance coverage data are drawn from the quarterly reports of the Private Health Insurance Advisory Council (PHIAC).

The main reason for the decline in health insurance fund membership has been the steeply increasing cost of health insurance premiums (see Figure 5.2, p. 105), which have risen at rates well above inflation.

In 1997 the report *Private Health Insurance*, by the Commonwealth Industry Commission, confirmed the substantial rise in health insurance fund members using private rather than public hospitals as the main factor driving increased costs for health insurers. The next most significant cost-driver identified by the commission is 'adverse selection', that is, the increasing concentration of high-risk members within private health insurance funds. As noted previously, increased insurance payments resulted in higher premiums, leading to younger, fitter members dropping their insurance, and hence higher average hospital use by remaining (less healthy) fund members.

Commonwealth governments have attempted a number of reforms to shore up private health insurance, but the fundamental structural issues remain unresolved. In 1995 the Labor government made extensive amendments to the regulatory framework for private health insurance, encouraging the use of case payment rather than *per diem* reimbursements of hospitals and the introduction of contracts among insurers, doctors and private hospitals. The main thrust of the 1995 reforms was to promote contracting for 100 per cent cover of private hospital charges, thus increasing the attractiveness of the insurance product to the consumer, while forcing hospitals to contain their costs within the funding cap negotiated with the insurer.

The legislation also sought to encourage doctors to contract with insurers to provide 100 per cent cover for their fees to in-patients. The medical profession strenuously resisted such contracting as a basic threat to their freedom to set their own fees. Nevertheless, some doctors at some private hospitals broke ranks with the general stance of their representative bodies and reached agreement with insurers. The result was a single, fully reimbursed hospital bill for the patient, incorporating all hospital and medical charges in the one bill, which was fully met by the insurer. These

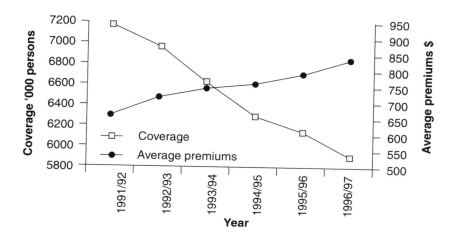

Figure 5.2   Private health insurance coverage and premiums

Source: Private Health Insurance, *Report No. 57*, Industry Commission, 2 February, 1997

initiatives sought to address a common patient complaint: that although private health insurance might fully cover the hospital bill, the patient still incurred numerous and substantial out-of-pocket expenses for medical bills associated with the in-patient episode, much of which was due to doctors' fees that exceeded the insurers' medical treatment.

The 1995 legislation radically altered the relationship between private hospitals and insurers. Insurers were now more likely to differentiate between hospitals and hospital groups on the basis of quality and value. Case payments for many categories of patient were becoming more common. The negotiations process between insurer and hospital, based on analysis of comparative data on utilisation and costs, was now far more sophisticated.

At the same time, the Industry Commission report suggested that the introduction of 100 per cent cover had contributed to the cost pressures on insurance.

Other measures that have been introduced to support health insurance include:

• use of 'front-end deductible' insurance products, whereby the insured pays an agreed initial amount of any hospital bill. There has been some increase in the take-up of these products, but this may be by conversion of existing members;

- use of exclusion tables, which exclude certain procedures or types of admission from cover as a means of offering cheaper premiums to attract lower-risk members; and

- introduction (by the federal Coalition government in 1997) of tax rebates for health insurance for specified income levels and a tax surcharge for people on higher incomes who do not take out health insurance.

Despite these initiatives, private health insurance has continued to decline. After the 1998 federal election, the re-elected Coalition government moved to introduce a more substantial tax rebate of 30 per cent for individuals with private health insurance. This initiative might curtail further fallout from health insurance but is unlikely to increase significantly the numbers of insured.

A major structural issue that is generally sidestepped by governments is the future of community rating. Under 'community rating', insurers are not allowed to risk-rate their products, and the government equalises funds between insurers through a 'reinsurance pool' so that insurers are not penalised for their numbers of higher-risk members relative to insurers with lower-risk profiles. Insurers must also accept all applicants to membership. Community rating is intended to maintain access to health insurance for the aged and other groups who are likely to need to access hospital services, but this measure also limits the ability of insurers to offer products attractive to lower-risk members.

The Industry Commission's report (*Private Health Insurance 1997*) recommended the introduction of lifetime community rating, whereby people entering insurance later in life pay higher premiums than those who take up insurance at an earlier stage. This is precisely what the Liberal government endorsed when it was re-elected in early 1998.

The difficulty for any Commonwealth government is that while private hospitals have greatly increased in importance in meeting the demand for acute in-patient services, the means of access to these services, namely private health insurance, has greatly diminished. The current situation is inherently unstable and will require further reforms.

Privatisation and Co-Location

The decline in private health insurance has not resulted in major adverse impacts on private hospitals. Private hospital growth has come largely from attracting the existing insured population away from public hospitals.

Those who have dropped their insurance are more likely to be lower-risk members who were less likely to require hospitalisation.

State public hospital systems have responded to the rise of private hospitals by attempting to harness private capital through public hospital privatisation and the co-location of private hospitals on the campuses of public hospitals (see also Chapter 13).

The first public hospital privatisation project was the NSW Port Macquarie Base Hospital, which opened in 1994. The first co-location project was the Melbourne Private Hospital (commissioned in 1995), constructed on top of the clinical services block at the Royal Melbourne Hospital.

Since these initiatives, all state governments have pursued similar options as a means of expanding public hospital infrastructure. Some of the major projects are listed in Table 5.4 (p. 108). On the basis of this list, over 4000 privately financed acute hospital beds come on line between 1994 and 2000 in association with state public hospitals. In addition, the privatisation of the Commonwealth government's war veterans' hospitals— Hollywood Hospital (300 beds) in Perth, Greenslopes Hospital (398 beds) in Brisbane, and Heidelberg Repatriation Hospital (part of the Austin Hospital privatisation) in Melbourne—has also increased the significance of the private sector.

The key driver in these developments is the unresolved problem of capital to finance public hospital infrastructure. Under Medicare, the Commonwealth government's payments to the states for public hospitals represent a contribution to operating expenses only. Capital funding must come from state government sources, in competition with other public works, on an *ad hoc* basis.

Under privatisation models, the private sector finances the construction of the hospital, and state governments enter into contracts for the private hospital operator to provide public hospital services. State governments pay off the capital costs of the hospital in respect of public patients over fifteen years or longer. As well as tapping private sector sources of capital, these projects are increasingly shifting the operating financial risk from government to the private hospital operator. Payment for public in-patients in privatised hospitals is generally by DRG on the basis of capped patient volumes. Outsourcing necessitates the development of explicit contracts for the quantity and type of services to be provided and for associated quality/performance standards. The risk for government is that such contracts make rationing of care more transparent.

As noted by Bloom in Chapter 13, co-location projects serve to enhance public hospital infrastructure as well as reducing state government capital outlays. In many cases private hospitals share plant and other capital infrastructure with the public hospital. The privately funded facilities also reduce pressure on the public hospital in relation to beds, delivery suites, operating theatres, and other services. The private facilities usually provide an income stream for the public hospital in the form of rent, purchase of diagnostic services, food services, security services, or other support

Table 5.4 Major privatisation and co-location projects

Project	State	Hospital and details
Privatisation	NSW	Port Macquarie Base Hospital (160 beds)—opened 1994
		Hawkesbury District Hospital (127 beds)—opened 1995
	Queensland	Noosa Community Hospital (100 beds)—under construction
		Robina Hospital (198 beds)—tender awarded
	Victoria	La Trobe Hospital (120 beds)—under construction
		Mildura Hospital (130 beds)—tender awarded
		Austin Public and Heidelberg Repatriation Hospitals (300 beds)— offered for tender
		Berwick Hospital (150 beds)—tender awarded
		Knox Hospital (150 beds)—offered for tender
	Western Australia	Peel Health Campus—(130 beds) opened 1998
		Armadale Hospital (160 beds)—offered for tender
	South Australia	Modbury Hospital (180 beds)—privatised 1995
	Tasmania	Mersey Community Hospital (130 beds)—privatised 1995
Co-location	NSW	Royal North Shore Private Hospital (168)—opened 1998
		St George Private Hospital (202 beds)—opened 1996
		Prince of Wales Private Hospital (162 beds)—opened 1998
		Armidale Private Hospital (40 beds)—opened 1998
		John Hunter Hospital (200 beds)—offered for tender
		Nepean Private Hospital (126 beds)—construction approved
	Queensland	Princess Alexandra (180 beds)—tender awarded
		Prince Charles (100+ beds)—tender awarded
		Redlands (45 beds)—tender awarded
		Caboolture (50 beds)—under construction
		Logan (60 beds)—under construction
	Victoria	Melbourne Private adjacent to Royal Melbourne (125 beds)— opened 1995
		Frances Perry House adjacent to Royal Women's (90 beds)— opened 1998
		Geelong Private (120 beds)—opened 1998
		The Alfred (150 beds)—offered for tender
	Western Australia	Joondalup Health Campus (50 private beds)—opened 1998
		Peel Health Campus (? private beds)—opened 1998
		Kalgoorlie (40 beds)—offered for tender
		Albany (40 beds)—offered for tender
	South Australia	Flinders (160 beds)—under construction
	Tasmania	Royal Hobart (120 beds)—tender awarded
	ACT	National Capital Private (120 beds)—opened 1998

Source: Courtesy Health Care of Australia

services. For public teaching hospitals, in particular, the co-located private hospital provides for their doctors an opportunity for private practice, thus assisting the public hospital in attracting and retaining doctors and maintaining their full-time presence and commitment to the teaching hospital campus.

For private hospital operators, privatisation provides an alternative revenue source to private health insurance, while co-locations represent very attractive market opportunities for capturing private patient referrals. Co-located campuses tend to generate major medical precincts, with associated medical centres and other related health services opting to locate adjacent to these campuses.

Again, these developments are entrenching the private sector in the Australian health care system and must be taken into account in public policy considerations about ensuring accessible and affordable health care for all Australians.

Emergence of Private Hospital Groups

The expansion of the role of private hospitals in Australia has gone hand in hand with the aggregation of private hospitals into larger ownership groups, both for-profit and not-for-profit. Statistics on the size and number of private hospitals belie the depth of capacity of the private hospital sector.

In relation to for-profit groups, the concentration of ownership and growth in private services has resulted in a significant number of groups listing on the Australian Stock Exchange. The Health Care and Biotechnology Index Sector of the All Ordinaries Index has expanded as health services companies, in addition to medical technology companies, have emerged for the first time as attractive investments.

Although the average size of a private hospital in Australia is still small—between fifty and one hundred beds—the capacity and management infrastructure of the private sector needs to be considered in light of the aggregated resources of these health care groups. Australia's main for-profit groups are outlined in Table 5.5, (p. 110). The sale of the hospitals owned by the Medical Benefits Fund (MBF) indicates that the process of consolidation of ownership is continuing.

Examples of major charitable groups include:

- St John of God Health Care Services Inc.: 9 hospitals; 1273 beds; pathology services; and
- the Sisters of Charity Group: 9 hospitals, 1800 beds; pathology and community services.

Table 5.5 Australia's largest private, for-profit hospital groups, 1999

Hospital group	Services	Listed/unlisted	Annual revenues 1997/98
Health Care of Australia: trading name of the health care group of Mayne Nickless Limited	44 hospitals (Australia); 4572 beds; pathology, radiology, medical centres	listed	$810.3m
Australian Health Care Limited	16 hospitals; 1879 beds	listed	$240m
Ramsay Health Care	13 hospitals; 1675 beds	listed	$215m
Healthscope Limited	11 hospitals: 919 beds	listed	$104.2m
Alpha Healthcare Limited	12 hospitals; 627 beds; medical centres, radiology	listed	$86m
Macquarie Health Corporation	5 hospitals; 341 beds; medical centres	unlisted	
Benchmark Mutual Hospital Group Pty Ltd	7 hospitals; 520 beds	unlisted	$97m

Source: Courtesy Health Care of Australia

The large groups have many advantages over individual private hospitals, including those outlined in Box 5.1.

Box 5.1   Advantages of larger hospital groups

- access to capital funding through the market and through private capital raising;
- corporate infrastructure with the capacity to undertake more complex development projects and new ventures;
- greater leverage in negotiations with health insurers;
- capacity to spread the risks of new, innovative ventures and service types, such as home care, diagnostic services or medical centres;
- more sophisticated and efficient systems development such as information technology and quality systems;
- performance improvement through internal benchmarking and sharing expertise across facilities within the group;
- vertical integration of services and increasing capacity to offer integrated care to patients; and
- quality of management resulting from management development opportunities and career paths offered by a larger group.

Diagnostic Services

In the 1990s the growth in private investment in health care extended beyond private hospitals into related health markets, particularly diagnostic services. The emergence of Sonic Healthcare Limited as a strong performer on the Australian Stock Exchange was indicative of this trend. Sonic Healthcare, with turnovers of $132.9 million in 1997/98, represented a merger of a number of previously doctor-owned pathology practices.

Since 1995 Health Care of Australia has also extended its reach from private hospitals into diagnostic medical services. By acquisition, this company has established a network of private pathology services with annual turnover of about $224 million. Other private hospital groups, including Alpha Healthcare Limited, St John of God, and the Sisters of Charity group have also moved into pathology services.

In 1997 business investment in private diagnostic imaging services also commenced, with investments by Health Care of Australia, Alpha, and other investment groups in established diagnostic imaging practices. Until then, most private diagnostic imaging practices had been owned by specialist radiologists in partnership.

Private pathology and private diagnostic imaging each account for about $1 billion in health expenditure in Australian each year. Most of this expenditure is funded by the Commonwealth government under Medicare, by the payment of patient rebates of 85 per cent of the Medicare Schedule fee for pathology and diagnostic imaging occasions of service. About 80 per cent of private pathology services are direct-billed (commonly known as 'bulk-billed') to Medicare. Under this arrangement, the private provider accepts 85 per cent of the Schedule fee as full reimbursement for the patient episode.

As previously described, under the Medicare Benefits Schedule, all medical services, except for medical services provided to public patients in hospital, are supported by the Commonwealth government for all Australian citizens. Traditionally, these services have been provided by medical practitioners in private practice. The corporatisation of private pathology and diagnostic imaging has extended the reach of private health care groups into this area of health service funding and delivery.

Corporatisation in pathology has occurred progressively since the 1980s in response to the increasing technological and logistical complexities of financing and delivering community-based pathology services. Funding pressure from the Commonwealth government under Medicare has also forced the pathology profession to embrace the disciplines of more corporatised models. These trends began to appear in relation to diagnostic imaging by 1998.

The private pathology industry has adopted a proactive approach in dealing with the Commonwealth government as the industry's primary payer. In 1996 the industry, the Royal Australasian College of Pathologists, and the government entered into a three-year funding agreement, under which the Commonwealth government's outlays for private pathology services were capped at an agreed growth rate for the duration of the agreement. This arrangement gave predictability to both providers and the payer, avoiding the previous expenditure patterns where runaway pathology service volumes would result in sudden, sometimes severe fee cuts by government. Under the funding agreement, the government agreed to provide regular fee increases if pathology service volumes kept expenditure below the cap. The industry, in return, agreed to develop targeted approaches to fee reduction and measures went reduce demand for pathology services if pathology expenditures went beyond the cap. The funding agreement was regarded as a success by both pathology service providers and government. Fee increases introduced throughout the agreement were intended to have two effects: adjusting the relativities in the pathology fee schedule and providing financial incentives to doctors to refer patients more appropriately for pathology services.

This funding model has been extended to diagnostic imaging, where the Royal Australian College of Radiologists entered into a three-year capped funding agreement with the Commonwealth government in association with the introduction of a Medicare fee rebate for MRI. The government was also seeking to negotiate a five-year funding agreement for general practice medicine.

Significance and Implications

This review of developments in the private hospital and diagnostic services sectors highlights the increasing significance of both private sector business interests and the large not-for-profit groups in the financing and delivery of Australian health care services. These shifts have occurred without major change to the philosophy or structure of national policies for health care financing and access under Medicare.

Private hospitals have greatly increased their sophistication and level of clinical services, not only offering a real alternative to public hospitals but also functioning as an essential safety valve in the demand for hospital admission for procedural services. The heavy demand on public hospitals to accommodate medical admissions through public hospital emergency departments means that public hospitals are forced to deal with patients requiring surgery and other procedures as the balancing factor—hence the problem of public hospital waiting lists. Private hospitals and private day-surgery clinics are an important source of supply for these services.

At the same time, the capacity of the private sector to tender for and operate public hospital services has increased the significance of private sector capital and management capability in considerations of public policy.

The involvement of private health care groups in medical services, notably diagnostic services, also positions the private sector and private investment as crucial components of national health policies. While trad-itionally federal funding of medical services has been in respect of individ-ual medical practitioners in private practice, the growth of large corporate players as health-service providers is again shifting the balance within these funding structures.

The most urgent policy consideration for national health policy is the position of private health insurance. If the Commonwealth government amendments, such as the introduction of 30 per cent rebates for private health insurance, are successful in stemming the outflow from health fund membership, the overall system of public and private hospitals will attain some stability. If membership of private insurance funds continues to decline, federal and state governments will eventually be forced to consider radical restructuring of health-financing arrangements.

One possible future scenario is that the private hospital sector's role will shift mainly to providing public hospital services under contract to state governments. In this way state governments would draw on the existing capital infrastructure of the private sector to cope with the increased demand for public hospitals in the face of the failure of private health insur-ance. Alternatively, the Commonwealth government could assume full funding responsibility for public hospitals from state governments, as occurred in the case of universities some decades ago. Under this scenario, hospitals, whether public or private, would derive their remuneration largely from the Commonwealth government, possibly using DRG-based case payments and the funding models that are developing under the Medical Benefits Schedule.

Some form of private insurance might also survive under these scenar-ios, but the difficulty for government would be the replacement of a large proportion of privately funded services by taxpayer-funded services. At a time when the thrust for all governments with developed economies is to reduce rather than increase the range of their funding involvement, a significant reduction in private funding for hospital services would present serious consequences for the Commonwealth government's economic policies.

Another set of strategies would entail changes to the insurance product and to the place of private insurance within the funding structures. In the past some reformers have advocated managed competition models between public and private insurers as the primary means of health care financing. Such reforms would take Australia's health financing a long way from its current arrangements.

Conclusion

There has been considerable stability in national health-financing policies in Australia since the introduction of Medicare in 1984. Nevertheless, the changing role and balance of private sector involvement, together with the problems of private health insurance, mean that major structural reforms are inevitable.

In considering reform options, governments will find that the traditional and usually ideological dichotomies of public versus private or insurance versus Medicare are unhelpful in finding solutions. The shifting balance of public and private sector roles, together with changing patterns of health care delivery, rising community expectations, and the intergenerational issues of financing health care for an ageing population will require new paradigms.

6

Reforming the Australian Health Care System: The Role of Government

Andrew Podger and Philip Hagan

Australians have good reason to be satisfied with their health care system—at least in terms of overall health outcomes and access to health care in relation to aggregate costs. On average, Australians are a healthy lot and getting healthier. This trend manifests itself in a declining death rate, increasing life expectancy, a low incidence of life-threatening infectious diseases and, for most people, ready access to health care when they need it. The cost is not exorbitant: Australia devotes around 8 per cent of gross domestic product to health, only slightly above the average for industrialised OECD countries. (This percentage of overall resources allocated to health has remained steady for a number of years, but it should be noted that Australia has a relatively young population structure compared with some OECD countries.) Australia cannot afford to be complacent, however, for a number of reasons: the ageing of the population will put increasing pressure on costs (and therefore resources devoted to health); good health is not enjoyed by all—indeed serious health inequalities persist (Aboriginal and Torres Strait Islander people's health is poor by any standard); and Australian governments face the continuous challenge of ensuring that the (mainly public) health care dollar buys as much health as possible for the citizenry.

Australia's health care system is extensive, loosely organised, complex and technically sophisticated. High standards of medical care generally prevail. The system is described elsewhere in this volume, but its most salient characteristics are:

- Australia's federal structure of government, with all three tiers—Commonwealth, state, and local—involved in the health system;
- the dominant role of private medical practitioners in providing care, mostly on a fee-for-service basis, but with governments increasingly influencing the structure of health services through their financing arrangements;
- universal access to quality medical care through Medicare, subsidised by both Commonwealth and state financing; and
- substantial private funding, particularly through private health insurance, supported and regulated by the Commonwealth, so that the system offers a degree of choice, particularly for hospital care.

Why Government is Involved in Health

There are several reasons for Australian governments being involved in shaping the health system (and reforms to it) at federal, state, and local levels (see World Bank 1993).

Several chapters in this volume consider the important differences between health and other aspects of a market economy. An essential feature of many health-related services, such as information about, and control of, contagious disease, is that they are *public goods*. Thus one person's use of health information does not leave less available to others; nor does one person's benefit from control of disease-carrying vectors preclude others enjoying the same benefit. Because private markets alone provide too few of the public goods crucial for health, government involvement is necessary to increase their supply. Other health services are associated with significant *externalities*: consumption by one individual affects others (for better or worse). Thus immunising a child slows transmission of disease, conferring a positive externality. On the other hand, polluters and drunk drivers create negative externalities. The task for government is to encourage cost-effective behaviours that confer positive externalities while discouraging those with negative ones.

Most countries view access to basic health care as a human right. This perspective is embodied in goals such as 'to improve the health of the worst off in society and to narrow the health gap' (UK Green Paper 1998). Provision of cost-effective health services to the poor is an effective and socially desirable means of addressing poverty and disadvantage, because it is effective in redistributing access to health-related goods and services independent of the distribution of income. Australian governments have historically held the view that private markets will not ensure that those who are economically or socially disadvantaged have adequate access to affordable, high-quality health care. Public finance of essential health care is thus justified to alleviate poverty—including the poverty that might result from having to pay unexpected large health bills. This is the rationale that underpins government involvement in major programs such as Medicare, even though a good proportion of the population may be able to pay for basic health care.

Government action may also be needed to compensate for problems generated by *uncertainty* and *insurance market failure*—uncertainties about long-term health costs challenge government and insurers alike. For example, technological and pharmaceutical innovations continue to increase the range of treatments available, and the pace is likely only to accelerate in the future. In the past few years it is these kinds of advances (rather than demographic factors) that have driven up the cost of health care. The considerable uncertainties surrounding the probability of illness and the efficacy of care give rise both to strong demand for insurance (especially long-term insurance) and to shortcomings in the operation of unregulated private markets.

The reasons are important, and are summarised again here. One reason for markets failing is that variations in health risk create incentives for insurance companies to refuse to insure the very people who most need it—those who are already sick or are likely to become ill. This problem is sometimes referred to as *adverse selection*. A second has to do with *moral hazard*: insurance reduces the incentive for individuals to avoid risk and expense by prudent behaviour, and can create both incentives and opportunities for health care providers (e.g. doctors and hospitals) to give patients more care than they need. A further rationale for government involvement in health arises from the problem of *asymmetry of information* between provider and patient concerning appropriate treatments and their possible consequences. Providers advise patients on choice of interventions; when a provider's income is linked to that advice there may be a strong incentive for overtreatment. If the last two problems are not addressed, costs can be expected to escalate without appreciable health gains for patients. Governments have an important role to play in regulating privately provided health insurance, and/or providing alternatives in order to ensure widespread access to health care and to hold down costs. In Australia these concerns provide a rationale for the government-subsidised Medicare program, as well as regulation of private health insurance and efforts to gather and disseminate reliable health information.

Challenges specific to the Australian health system

Special features of Australia and its history have generated additional challenges for government in regard to its role in health. For example, although the Australian continent is roughly the same size as Western Europe or the

USA (excluding Alaska), Australia's population is less than 19 million, and most people live in coastal cities. Vast areas of the continent are very thinly populated, so that providing health care services in rural and remote areas of Australia is logistically difficult and relatively expensive per service.

Australia's indigenous inhabitants, the Aboriginal and Torres Strait Islander peoples, were joined by a predominantly Anglo-Celtic population after European settlement in 1788. Since then, continuing immigration from around the world has produced in Australia one of the largest overseas-born populations in the world. Nearly one in four Australian residents was born overseas, a high proportion of them in non-English-speaking countries. Australians also exhibit a considerable diversity of cultural and ethnic backgrounds. These characteristics, and the complexity of the involvement of three tiers of government, present substantial obstacles to the effective and efficient operation of Australia's health care system.

Recurring themes in Australia's evolving health system

Four recurring themes have influenced Australia's evolving health system in recent years. They are identical to those confronting most industrialised economies, and for which developing economies must plan. They are: supply-side and demand-side controls; promoting competition; encouraging evidence-based health care interventions; and separating the roles of purchasers, providers, and regulators.

Supply-side and demand-side controls

The ability of a nation to control health costs through its health-financing system is an important factor in controlling growth in total health care spending. Increasing numbers of general practitioners and specialists, new medical technologies, and expanding health insurance, in combination with fee-for-service payments, constitute a potent brew. This obviously has the potential to generate demand for ever more costly tests, procedures, and treatments. Containing health costs within affordable limits is therefore a continuous challenge.

Various approaches have been tried to contain costs in Australia, including limiting the range of items subsidised under the MBS and the PBS (e.g. to medical interventions and drugs that have proved both to work and to represent value for money compared with alternatives), limiting the extent to which listed medications are subsidised from the public purse, and encouraging best-practice behaviour by providers of subsidised health care (e.g. via widely accepted treatment protocols, so that the knowledge of those at the leading edge of good practice is made available to others). Other approaches are being explored, such as budgeting a fixed amount for each person ('capitation') as practised by health-maintenance organisations in the USA and by the NHS in the United Kingdom. Demand-side measures have included the introduction of co-payments for pharmaceuticals. In addition, demand for health care interventions is mediated to the extent that consumers have to pay out of pocket for any 'gap' not covered by government subsidy.

Promoting competition

Two hundred years of experience with capitalist economies suggests that when it comes to supplying goods and services (including the delivery of health care), diversity and competition lead to better results than, say, purely public provision. In a competitive system, people seeking health services can choose from a variety of providers: public, private not-for-profit, or private for-profit. Because competition has the potential to improve quality and drive down costs, governments have encouraged competition and diversity in the supply of health services and inputs, particularly pharmaceuticals and medical equipment. Exposing the public sector to competition from private suppliers can also help to spur innovation and give more attention to patients as consumers.

The quality and efficiency of government-funded health services can be encouraged further through a combination of decentralisation, performance-based payments and other incentives, in combination with competition. But strong government regulation is also crucial, and includes regulation of privately delivered health services to ensure safety and quality and of private insurance to encourage universal access to coverage and to discourage over-use of services and unwarranted escalation of costs.

Another reason for governments needing to regulate private provision of health care is that the 'product' being contracted for is not necessarily easy to define. Light (1997: 299) explains the problem:

> Health care is often emergent as diagnosis and treatment unfold. Clinical decisions are contingent on what is found and how the patient reacts. Cases are highly variable, and the course of treatment is uncertain. These qualities mean that no clear product, with clear property rights, can be defined and its price set, as can be done for hotel rooms or computers. Put another way, health care has a large grey area in which services and products can be manipulated by the provider/seller, or by a contractor of services, so as to appear cheaper by treating less illness or by treating illness less.

Emphasising evidence-based health care interventions

No matter how health services are organised and funded, what is actually provided are health interventions: specific activities meant to reduce disease risks, treat illness, or palliate the consequences of disease or disability. In view of the potential for market failure discussed above, an appropriate role for government is helping consumers to get value for money in health care, whether they pay directly, or indirectly through taxes or insurance premiums. Clearly it is in the public interest to expand coverage of interventions with high cost-effectiveness, if necessary at the expense of less cost-effective ones.

In Australia, pharmaceuticals have long been subject to efficacy and safety evaluations and, more recently, to cost-effectiveness assessments for them to qualify for listing on the PBS. This, no doubt, has contributed to Australia's relatively low spending on pharmaceuticals. Additionally, a new National Prescribing Service supports and promotes high-quality, cost-effective prescribing of medicines.

Steps are now being taken to establish evidence-based medicine services funded under the Medical Benefits Scheme. A Medical Services Advisory Committee (MSAC) will provide advice on the inclusion of new procedures and services on the MBS and oversee the assessment of existing items, thereby ensuring that Medicare benefits fund only those procedures for which safety, clinical efficacy, and cost-effectiveness are firmly established.

Separating purchaser, provider, and regulatory functions

In recent years the Commonwealth government has moved away from its previous role as funder, purchaser, provider, and regulator of health services. Several formerly government-owned providers of health services have been either privatised (e.g. the veterans' health system, Commonwealth Serum Laboratories) or corporatised (e.g. Australian Health Services, which provides medical advisory and health assessment services to government agencies). Thus the Commonwealth is progressively relinquishing its previous role in direct service provision in favour of a more limited role as funder/purchaser and regulator of services provided by others.

As described by other contributors, the rationale behind the purchaser/provider split is much the same as in other countries, most notably to improve performance, enhance contestability, minimise conflicts of interest, improve operational efficiency, and shift the focus firmly from providers to consumers of health services. Examples in Australia include state government contracting with hospitals to provide acute-care services to specific groups, and the Commonwealth government contracting with public and private hospitals to provide services for war veterans (see Chapter 12). The move to contracting for health services from providers has meant having to specify in detail exactly what it is government wants to buy on behalf of Australians, and expected performance levels. This has led to intense interest in measuring performance in all its aspects (e.g. specifying outputs and outcomes, targets, performance indicators, and quality).

The separation of funding and purchasing from provision of health care has redefined the role of government. It has been transformed from an entity that merely subsidised the cost of inputs (e.g. reimbursing providers for services rendered) to an agency focused on desired outputs and outcomes of the health system, and on the impact of these on the health of Australians.

Increasing the emphasis on primary care and prevention

'Best at home' or in a community-care setting—rather than in hospital or residential care—sums up the emphatic preference of most Australians. Thus the Commonwealth government has strongly supported initiatives in health and aged care that keep older people, and people managing chronic conditions, in their own homes as long as possible. If they must be hospitalised, they are helped to return home as soon as practically possible and appropriate.

It is even better to prevent morbidity and disability in the first place, by investing in prevention and general population health. Yet striking an appropriate balance of funding between prevention and cure is difficult given the urgent, and some would say, insatiable, demand for acute-care services.

Better systems integration

The price of organising health spending along functional lines is to create islands of specialised care, which people then have to negotiate as they attempt to navigate their way around the health system. The result is fragmentation of the care process and unnecessary duplication since those seeking help have to supply personal details and recount their medical histories at every turn. Older people and those with chronic illnesses are perhaps the most acutely aware of the problem of lack of coordination, as Millar describes in Chapter 20.

Australia, like other countries at a similar stage epidemiologically and demographically, has addressed this problem in a number of ways, including the coordinated care trials described below. Continued funding is allocated to improve information systems, so that, for example, medical histories can follow patients around in the form of electronic patient records. These systems are progressively being built to convey timely information while respecting and preserving an individual's right to privacy.

Shifting emphasis and changing priorities

Shifting the focus from providers to consumers

Until fairly recently Australia's health-financing system, with its emphasis on subsidising health inputs, was more focused on providers than patients. This manifested itself in many ways. For example, in specialist hospital clinics, patients previously had to arrive *en masse* at 8 a.m., and perhaps wait all morning to see a specialist. Now specific appointments are the rule in most hospitals. Only a few years ago, 'Patient Charters', spelling out patients' rights and obligations, were rare. Now, reflecting the new focus on consumers, they are ubiquitous.

Empowering the patient (or the patient's agent) with information to inform his/her choice is one way to combat the problem of *information asymmetry*. An appropriate role for government is to act as the source of authoritative health information and to communicate it to target populations in cost-effective ways. The shift in focus from providers to consumers is also seen in Australia as a potential means of controlling costs, particularly through the better management of chronic disease, the driver of a substantial proportion of health care costs.

Responding to the continuing challenge of cost containment

Governments have an obligation to spend responsibly. Getting value for money for the public health dollar means allocating scarce resources so as to obtain the most improvement possible in the health of Australians. Because private health care markets can also fail to deliver value for money, government also has a policy role in providing information and incentives to improve the allocation of resources by the private sector.

Some practical steps are being taken in the Australian context to address cost problems from both the demand and supply sides:

*   modifying what was a fairly pure 'fee-for-service' system (e.g. by providing incentives for best-practice on the part of service providers, as well as throughput);
*   attempting to ensure that the health workforce is of the right size and composition, properly trained and equipped to do the job, and appropriately deployed to meet demand for health care; and
*   controlling the quality, range, and subsidy levels on government-funded services.

Addressing quality concerns

Quality and cost control can go hand in hand to a considerable extent as measures that might ensure greater consistency and discipline in the care process.

Tools for measuring and improving health care must address three broad kinds of quality concerns:

- over-use of unnecessary or inappropriate care (examples include the excessive or unnecessary use of x-rays and other diagnostic tests, unnecessary hysterectomies, and over-prescribing of antibiotics);
- under-use of needed, effective and appropriate care (examples include breast cancer screening and radiotherapy); and
- system failure of other types, including technically inferior and socio-culturally inappropriate care (examples include preventable drug interactions, failure to follow up abnormal test results, uncoordinated care, and failure to cater for patients of different ethnicity and cultural practices).

Promoting cost-effective health interventions

Government can better ensure that health financing is channelled towards cost-effective measures by supporting research to identify such practices and treatments, and by promoting their widespread adoption. During the late 1990s the Commonwealth promoted adoption of 'best practice' in clinical treatment in a variety of ways. One notable achievement was a substantially funded national program supporting re-engineering of the pre- and post-operative processes to improve efficiency and focus on what is best for the patient.

Collecting, disseminating and applying good information

Effectively functioning markets require that patients and other consumers of health care services are in the position to make informed decisions about their health, including the likely efficacy and cost-efficiency of proposed treatments. A central element of health reform in Australia has been increased monitoring and measurement, of the quality health care and the outcomes of that care.

For example, the technology now exists to track consumers systematically through the care network via a longitudinal patient record (in the form of an electronic patient record, or EPR). The instantaneous availability of information on a patient's vital health characteristics—chronic conditions, allergies, previous treatments, and so on—would ensure that every time that individual is treated, information on the problem, how it was treated, and with what outcome (if known) could be sent by the provider to be incorporated in the individual's EPR. Over time, individual EPRs would contain increasingly comprehensive information, including potentially vital information on which to base future decisions on appropriate care for the individual, and, through research, for groups of individuals. However, some information technology, such as EPRs, will raise questions about privacy, accuracy, and availability of personal information, and strategies will have to be in place to satisfy these legitimate concerns.

Focusing on priority health problems

Governments play a legitimate, and indeed essential, role when they target health investments to priority areas. Australia has identified six national health priority areas for special effort: cancer control, injury prevention and control, cardiovascular health, diabetes, mental health, and asthma. These health problems have been selected because they are significant causes of premature death and poor health, because there are marked inequalities in who suffers from them, because there is known potential to prevent or treat them more effectively, and because they are real causes for public concern.

Major Government Initiatives in Health Reform in the 1980s and 1990s

The Commonwealth government has also pursued reform strategies specific to particular aspects of health that are the responsibility of central government. These reforms have almost always been introduced incrementally, and after considerable consultation, to gain public acceptance, limit disruption, and manage the financial risks associated with change. This section examines some specific reforms.

Medicare benefits

MBS subsidies are set by government so as to contain public outlays and health-cost inflation, and to encourage high levels of bulk-billing (where health practitioners accept the government payment as their fee, in which case there are no out-of-pocket costs for consumers). Although this system is generally effective, cost pressures continually emerge and must be managed.

Recent initiatives include price-volume caps, for example limits on fees and volume targets negotiated with pathologists and radiologists, and restrictions on provider numbers (the number of doctors eligible to bill Medicare). Other options under consideration include 'reward-sharing' from better prescribing and referral patterns; and payments for achieving population health targets (e.g. incentives for child immunisation are now in place). 'Blended payments', another option, would reduce purely fee-for-service incentives which encourage maximum throughput, by including a component of doctors' remuneration that depends only on, for example, the quality of care provided (rather than remuneration depending only on the number of patients seen). All of these measures are designed to ensure that financing initiatives support improved quality and health outcomes, and do not only target costs.

Pharmaceutical benefits

Australia has a sophisticated system of approving, listing and subsidising drugs, and its record in containing prices and costs is excellent by international standards. Yet the the PBS remains the fastest-growing component of government health outlays, partly because some new medical technology uses costly pharmaceuticals, and partly because of the increased cost of new, more effective drugs generally. Supply-side measures to contain costs are now focusing on quality use of medicines and cost-effective prescribing practice.

During the 1990s the PBS has also been subject to a series of demand-side reforms aimed at increasing the efficiency and effectiveness of drug consumption in Australia. These include the introduction of 'catastrophe' insurance, whereby consumers make co-payments up to a nominated amount, beyond which further pharmaceutical consumption is wholly subsidised. Progress has been made on two other fronts: pharmacists are now able to suggest alternative drugs to consumers (generic substitution), and there has been (limited) aggregation of similarly acting drugs into classes that are subsidised to the same extent, so that consumers who wish to obtain the more expensive drugs in any class pay the difference.

Hospitals

There have been numerous Commonwealth-supported reforms aimed at the acute-care sector, but only the introduction of casemix is discussed here (see Chapters 8 and 11 for other perspectives).

Casemix in hospitals

There are several hospital casemix classifications (covering acute, non-acute and ambulatory episodes) in operation throughout the world. They tend to be concerned with measuring the 'products' of hospitals—that is, the bundles of goods and services provided for the diagnosis and treatment of illnesses—and are based on the assumption that commonalities exist among patients' attributes and medical problems on the one hand, and patterns of treatment, medical approaches, and levels of service on the other. Diagnosis-related groups represent the best-known casemix classification.

They consist of a manageable number of distinct classes that have been identified on the basis of their clinical meaning and resource-use homogeneity. Australia's DRG classification is known as the Australian National Diagnostic Related Groups (AN-DRGs) classification.

Beginning in the mid- to late-1980s, the Commonwealth was instrumental in supporting the development and dissemination of casemix systems in Australia. This method of paying for case-based costs rather than for individual inputs was seen as potentially invaluable, as a means of facilitating the management, monitoring, and planning of health services; providing a basis for funding, paying, and charging for health services; measuring outputs; generating information about quality of care; and comparing different care options nationally and locally. There was significant opposition to casemix at the time from many medical practitioners, who saw it as a threat to the independence of clinical practice, and from at least one state government, which identified it with 'American-style health care'.

The Commonwealth's support was pivotal to the introduction of casemix and to developing a variant appropriate for Australian conditions. The Commonwealth supported a broad range of casemix activity, including developing systems suited to Australian settings. The successful national casemix programs were an important element of reform. Partly as a result of the changed incentives involved in casemix-based payments (rather than the former system, which involved annual squabbling over budget bids to run public hospitals), the average length of stay in Australian hospitals is declining. There is evidence that those states that moved quickly and firmly to implement casemix-based purchasing of hospital services have achieved more substantial efficiency gains than those that did not.

Primary care

General practice remains the cornerstone of the Australian health system. Medical care outside hospitals is based on GPs in private practice who constitute the principal gateway to specialist services and hospitals (the GP 'gatekeeper' model).

The Commonwealth government's General Practice Strategy, which began in 1991, was aimed at enhancing the skills and quality of GPs to better meet the challenges arising from the increasing technological sophistication of medicine, the important relationships between primary and acute care, and the potential role of GPs in population health. The crux of the strategy was to encourage GPs to affiliate into geographically based divisions of general practice, on the ground that divisions could serve better as a conduit for training and peer interaction than could individual or small-group practices. Again, the Commonwealth committed resources and expertise to establishing and developing the role of the divisions. By 1996 there were more than a hundred divisions of general practice (of around 150 GPs each) covering the whole of Australia and involving most GPs.

Coordinated-care trials

At the core of an 'integrated' health care system is a model of care built around the needs of people rather than of providers or institutions. Its aim is to provide a seamless system of high-quality care that is reliable and readily accessible. The Commonwealth identified the need to trial new models of integration, and has devoted substantial resources not only to the trials but also to evaluating and comparing different approaches in terms of their clinical outcomes and cost-effectiveness.

Australians with greater than normal needs for health care, for example those suffering from a chronic illness, are a natural focus of these trials. They are the health care consumers most likely to use multiple sources of care, and are therefore most likely to experience the consequences of uncoordinated care, and benefit from a coordinated approach.

Thirteen very large 'coordinated-care trials' (programs demonstrating the feasibility and cost-effectiveness of different approaches to delivering and coordinating health services) are taking place across Australia, including four aimed specifically at improving the health of indigenous people. Although formal evaluations are not complete, early indications are that there are potentially enormous gains in patient care when that care is coordinated and funded more flexibly than is possible under separate programs such as the MBS and the PBS.

Aged care

Aged-care reform was a focus and priority for the Commonwealth in the late 1990s because of its responsibility for funding most aged-care services in Australia. Aged care in Australia is provided through residential care in nursing homes and hostels and through domiciliary and community support services. Health services are also available through the public hospital system and in the form of primary health care (especially GPs' services), funded through Medicare. Assistance is also available to carers of older people.

In order to increase the sustainability of the publicly funded aged-care system, the Commonwealth has introduced income-tested fees for care and allowed accommodation payments to be levied on those able to pay (to help fund capital requirements for nursing homes and hostels). It also encouraged initiatives designed to improve the quality of care. For example, the Aged Care Standards and Accreditation Agency was established in 1997 to ensure that residential aged-care facilities achieve and maintain high standards of care and accommodation. Hostel-type care, which would previously been available only to residents, is now available to people in their homes, enabling them to live at home longer. Other flexible arrangements include multi-purpose services (MPSs), where combined health and aged-care services increase the viability of these services in rural and remote areas.

Private sector reforms

As described in Chapter 4, the private sector has various roles in Australia's health care system, including private financing (through health insurance) and private provision of most services. It is difficult for private health insurance to compete with Medicare given the prices and other characteristics of the respective products. Nevertheless, the private sector manages to fund around a third of total health expenditure in Australia, including out-of-pocket payments for services.

The challenge for Australia is to build a sustainable public–private mix, offering both choice and universal access. The Commonwealth has been keen to arrest the decline in private insurance fund membership and so to ensure that Australia's health system offers adequate choice. Specific measures included a 30 per cent rebate on the cost of private health insurance (to lower the cost to consumers); moves to eliminate unexpected out-of-pocket costs through simplified billing and contracting arrangements with providers; and the establishment of an independent regulator for the private health insurance industry, with responsibility for overseeing premium setting, solvency rules, and takeovers.

Population health

During the late 1980s and the 1990s the Commonwealth acted to protect and promote the health of the population by initiating public health interventions guided by available evidence on leading causes of morbidity and mortality, and the availability of cost-effective measures of addressing them. Government has taken the view that initiatives at national and local levels can encourage people to make healthy choices, but it is finally up to individuals to choose whether to modify their behaviour in the interests of their health.

Initiatives that require people to change high-risk behaviours need to be supported by public policy that promotes the health and safety of the population. Examples are the maintenance of standards and regulations for water, milk and food quality, sewerage control, housing standards, road and vehicle safety, and occupational hazards.

The Commonwealth also devotes significant resources to reducing major population health risks, such as smoking, excessive alcohol consumption, use of illicit drugs, inadequate physical activity, communicable diseases, HIV/AIDS (in which Australia has achieved remarkable success as well as international acclaim for its innovative approaches), inadequate childhood immunisation, asthma, and malnutrition.

Population health initiatives at the Commonwealth level increasingly recognise the value of working collaboratively to formulate nationally shared goals, while still supporting the flexible delivery of programs that are adapted to local community needs. Many public health initiatives are now under the umbrella of the National Public Health Partnership, described in detail in a case study by Lin and King in Chapter 14.

Ongoing Issues

A fundamental role of government is to ensure, to the extent possible, equity in health status as well as equity in access to health care. Three areas in particular will require ongoing attention: Aboriginal and Torres Strait Islander health, the health of people living in rural and remote areas of Australia, and the health of an ageing population.

Aboriginal health

Australia's Aboriginal and Torres Strait Islander peoples continue to experience much poorer health than the general Australian population (see ABS and AIHW 1997 and 1999 for a detailed assessment). ATSI peoples can expect to live 15–20 years fewer than other Australians, and the infant mortality rate remains three to five times higher than that for the rest of the population. Government's response to this situation has been to allocate special funds—$136 million in 1997/98—for health services designed for and directed to indigenous people. To a considerable degree, the poor health of indigenous Australians is a reflection of their low socio-economic status generally, so it is difficult to make spectacular progress in just one area (health) without simultaneously addressing their general disadvantage. Nevertheless the Commonwealth is working closely with Aboriginal communities to put in place culturally sensitive initiatives to secure real and sustainable improvements in health.

Health of rural and remote populations

The health of people living in rural and remote areas of Australia is worse than those living in capital cities and other metropolitan areas (Mathers 1994). Mortality and illness levels increase as one travels away from metropolitan centres to rural areas and remote locations (Titulaer et al. 1998). Relatively poor access to health services, lower socio–economic status and employment levels, exposure to comparatively harsher environments, sparse infrastructure and heightened occupational hazards contribute to these inequalities. Attitudes towards illness, poorer responses to health promotion and self-care messages, and more frequent risky behaviour are other possible contributory factors.

At the same time, ensuring that Australians living in rural and remote areas have equitable access to high-quality health services is practically and financially challenging, and improving the delivery of health and community services to rural and remote regions continues to be a major concern and focus of action. Under the umbrella of the National Rural Health Strategy, a range of measures has been pursued, including new service prototypes, such as multi-purpose centres (MPCs), which ensure a core of services available at all times, and work towards improving recruitment and retention rates of health care workers and doctors, and establishing infrastructure to support the workforce in these areas.

Population ageing

The challenge of health and health care for an ageing population is addressed by McCallum (Chapter 19) and Millar (Chapter 20). In brief, the Australian population has been ageing since the early 1970s, and this trend is expected to continue for at least the next fifty years. Annual rates of population increase projected for the period 1976–2016 are significantly higher for the older population than for the overall population, with the rate of increase highest being among the very old (ABS 1996). In the 1970s, 9 per cent of the population (or 1.3 million people) was aged 65 years and over. By 1996 this had increased to 12 per cent (2.2 million) and by 2016 is projected to increase to 16 per cent or 3.5 million people. In 1976 one in six older people was aged 80 and over; by 1996 it was one in five and, by 2016, it will be one in four.

Ageing of the Australian population is a major issue in planning for health services and long-term care. The Commonwealth retains funding responsibility for significant components of health and related care for older Australians and, as described above, during the 1990s the Commonwealth introduced incremental changes to funding and programs in recognition that most older people can and wish to remain in their homes as long as possible, if appropriate support is available.

The Bigger Picture

According to the World Bank, advances in income and education have allowed households almost everywhere to improve their health. In the 1980s, even in countries in which average incomes fell, the death rate of children under five declined by almost 30 per cent. But the child mortality rate fell more than twice as much in countries in which average incomes rose by more than 1 per cent a year. Economic policies conducive to sustained growth are thus among the most important measures governments can pursue to improve their citizens' health. The bank went on to point out that 'policies that promote equity and growth together will . . . be better for health than those that promote growth alone' (World Bank 1993: 7).

A sound education has been shown in a series of studies to be central to better health and emotional well-being for all, particularly in helping children who are disadvantaged socially and economically (see, for example, Sylva 1997; Wadsworth 1997).

Thus a range of services—educational, social, transport, housing, environmental and leisure—has an important impact on health. For this reason it would be wrong to attribute wholly the improving health status of Australians over time to the health system and the services it delivers. And for the same reason, governments' efforts in support of health are not the only measures by which it contributes to a healthier population.

7

The Evolving Role of Government in Health Sector Reform in New Zealand

Karen Poutasi

Governments have an overarching interest in promoting and protecting people's health and in ensuring that related support systems are provided for people with disabilities. Governments also have equity and efficiency objectives. Certain intrinsic features of the health sector, including the potential for market failure, mean that governments cannot achieve these health sector objectives unless they intervene through some or all of the following mechanisms: raising finance; allocating finance; direct involvement in service delivery and ownership; regulation; and stewardship. The design and application of these mechanisms enables governments to intervene in the best way, given local conditions and values.

New Zealand's experience in reconsidering and redesigning the role of government through the course of health sector reform in the 1990s provides many instructive lessons. The shift of emphasis from structure to process in its reforms provides a foundation for New Zealand's health sector into the future. An important lesson from the reforms is that there is no single solution to the complex issues confronting health systems internationally. However, clear and strategic policy objectives, decentralised decision-making, and environments supportive of innovation are useful preconditions for successful reform. Transparency, flexibility, and accountability are mandatory, as are carefully designed incentives, 'enablers', and regulation. Government's challenge is essentially to give the 'right' people the 'right' reason for doing the 'right' thing. Nevertheless, ensuring that services are people-centred—as distinct from provider-centred—is an ongoing challenge.

Experience with health sector reform in New Zealand has shown how the *balance* of government intervention is crucial. Heavy-handed government intervention provokes reactionary forces and stifles innovation and local ownership of solutions. It is also likely to generate poor solutions, because the 'centre' usually lacks the information necessary for efficient and effective decision-making at local levels.

Equally, however, market-driven solutions are not guaranteed to deliver the outcomes sought by government and New Zealanders. Information asymmetry means, on the one hand, that consumer demand may not reflect actual need, and, on the other, that supplier-induced demand may lead to overservicing and other problems. The externalities inherent in health systems mean that one person's actions confer costs (e.g. passive smoking) or benefits (e.g. immunisation) on others. Fragmentation of delivery may mean that the vulnerable have difficulty negotiating and accessing services (e.g. mental health). Long experience has shown, however, that government intervention in health care, leading to 'quasi-markets' (i.e. having some but not all of the characteristics of a market as defined by economists), is a delicate business with no guarantee of success.

This chapter explores the role of government in health reform in New Zealand as it evolved through the 1990s. It demonstrates the need for understanding both the historical context of health and the contemporary environment within which health reform takes place. It argues in favour of a balance whereby an overarching strategic policy framework (top down) creates incentives for 'flax roots' (bottom up) initiatives owned by both communities and providers, and designed to provide better services as well as better service for the individual and the community: 'local solutions to local problems'. The chapter reflects on the complexity of health systems and the advantage of simple solutions that build on the past, and engage stakeholders in the reform process, but are responsive to the needs of individuals and populations. A genuinely people-centred health service provides good health outcomes and responsive, flexible service.

Background

The 1980s

New Zealand entered the 1990s searching for means to improve health care. This quest was driven by the events of the 1980s in both the health sector and in New Zealand society at large. The 1980s had seen a move towards population-based (capitated) funding for Hospital Boards. Hospital Boards then became Area Health Boards with public health responsibilities—that is, official responsibility for protecting and assuring the health of their populations.

Two seminal reports informed the search at the turn of the decade. The first, *Choices for Health Care* (Scott et al. 1986), examined problems in primary care, demonstrating that centrally managed benefit payments were fragmented and produced incentives for cost-shifting and barriers to innovation. The second, *Unshackling the Hospitals* (Fraser et al. 1988), highlighted inefficiencies in public hospitals and took up the debate on secondary care. Both reports stimulated significant discussion and provided an important context for the reforms of the 1990s.

New Zealand's experience of economic reform in the 1980s also contributed to the context of the 1990s health reform, as we have already seen (Chapter 1). Schick describes the conditions leading to the reform as a convergence of economic stress, perceived failure in government performance, new political capacity, and a set of novel economic and management concepts (public choice theory, new approaches to institutional economics, and managerialism). 'This convergence [of concepts and urgency for reform] was unique to New Zealand, which is why it alone has transformed the State sector so boldly and comprehensively' (Schick 1996: 11). The *State Owned Enterprises Act 1986* was enacted to reform the trading activities of government departments. These ideas and the cumulative experiences leading up to the late 1980s set the context for health sector reform in the 1990s.

Before the 1980s

The reforms have their origin in the relationship between government and medical practitioners established by the *Social Security Act 1938*. There was much debate over this Act, and the eventual outcome was that the legislation brought salaried hospital doctors under the wing of the state, but allowed GPs to remain self-employed and relatively independent; GPs received public subsidies but could also charge private fees. Over the years salaried hospital doctors retained some independence through optional part-time private practice. This relationship between government and medical professionals, whereby doctors had significant autonomy, continued into the 1990s.

From the 1970s it became evident that 'free' health care without queuing was impossible in New Zealand. There, as in several other countries, an implicit arrangement developed whereby in exchange for medical autonomy, doctors would help governments to allocate resources at a 'micro' level according to medical need. Klein (1990: 702) refers to this type of arrangement as 'the politics of the double bed'. This allocative decision-making at the micro level has increased in importance, with increased pressure on publicly funded budgets.

The 1990s

Financial pressure on New Zealand's health system had been building through the late 1980s. Area Health Boards had, on the whole, held expenditure within capped budgets. Although pressure on uncapped primary-care benefits led to cost-shifting, publicly funded real health expenditure remained fairly stable into the early 1990s. This financial pressure was aggravated by other pressures that included social and demographic change, changing disease patterns, advancing medical and information technology, and increasing public expectations and consumer demand. Simultaneously, government became increasingly frustrated with a sector—health—that appeared non-responsive and inefficient, and seemed characterised by sclerotic work patterns and perverse incentives. In 1990 the incoming government identified targeting and competition as promising approaches to the problems confronting the health sector.

A Green and White Paper of 1991 (Upton 1991) was the result of a ministerial committee called the Health Services Taskforce, whose terms of reference included:

> The basic goal of the Government's health policy is to ensure that everyone has access to an acceptable level of health services on fair terms. It is likely that the Government will continue to be principal funder of health services. Therefore, it has a continuing direct interest in ensuring that individuals' responsibility for their own health is recognised and fostered. (Upton 1991: 137)

The taskforce was given objectives in equity, targeting, efficiency, responsiveness, safety, individual responsibility, and public health. It was asked to 'identify and investigate options for defining the roles of the government, the private sector, and individuals in the funding, provision and regulation of health services which best achieve' those objectives. Subsumed under the 'funding' role were the dual functions of raising and allocating finances.

In his Statement of Government Health Policy that set out the new structure, the Minister of Health said that the purchaser/provider split would be adopted as a means of achieving a 'less centralised and less politicised way of allocating resources' (Upton 1991: 1). The Green and White paper concluded that extensive structural reform was necessary and set out a blueprint for implementation.

As described in Chapter 1, the government created four purchasing agencies, or Regional Health Authorities (RHAs), and a Public Health Commission (PHC). It split fourteen Area Health Boards into twenty-three Crown health enterprises (CHEs), all but one based on a major acute hospital, to function as Crown-owned providers. CHEs were established as limited liability companies with ministers as shareholders, consistent with the SOE legislation. Purchasers received merged funding streams from the following sources: disability support services (funded previously by the Department of Social Welfare), health benefits for the primary sector (previously funded by the Department of Health), and hospital and related services money (previously provided by Area Health Boards).

The National Advisory Committee on Core Health Services was established to assist government to define more explicitly, with community and provider input, those services 'to which we believe everyone should have access, on affordable terms, and without unreasonable waiting time' (Upton 1991: 75).

These structures took effect on 1 July 1993 but then evolved during the 1990s. The PHC was disestablished in 1996. Its policy functions were transferred to the Ministry of Health, and its purchase functions to the RHAs. The coalition government formed after New Zealand's first mixed-member proportional representation election in 1996 merged the four purchasers into one Health Funding Authority (HFA). It also converted the twenty-three CHEs into not-for-profit companies known as hospital and health services (HHSs).

Public financing of primary-care GP visits and pharmaceuticals is now targeted to all children under age 6 and subsidised for those people on low incomes or with high use, thereby addressing vertical equity issues. Hospital treatment is universally publicly funded, providing horizontal equity.

Mechanisms Available to Government

The New Zealand health sector reforms implemented in 1993, and adjusted subsequently, were the result of fundamental structural change that created decentralised 'quasi-markets'. In commissioning the major reports discussed above, government acted explicitly in its role to promote and protect people's health and to ensure provision of support services for people with disabilities. In its actions the government of New Zealand applied a mix of mechanisms available to any government: raising finance; allocating finance; service delivery/ownership; regulation; and stewardship.

Government's principal objective in health and disability systems is ensuring equity and efficiency of service delivery. Subsequent New Zealand governments employed each of the mechanisms listed to achieve this objective.

Government's equity objective has two aspects: horizontal equity requires equal treatment of those in similar circumstances, whereas vertical equity requires different treatment of different people in order to reduce the consequences of innate differences. Clarity of entitlement to services is an example of government's work on horizontal equity. Targeted Māori health initiatives are an example of government addressing vertical inequity. Māori health indicators, although improving, are still worse than those of non-Māori. Efficiency objectives are concerned with allocating and rationing resources efficiently (allocative efficiency) and producing services at minimum cost (technical efficiency).

The evolution of the role of government in health is evident, first, in the differing weights given to the use of each mechanism and, second, in how each intervention is applied. Balancing the multiple demands that are a feature of all health systems requires ongoing adjustments to the mechanisms used by government. This occurs ideally in a learning environment with ample feedback loops so that the empirical results of specific reforms can be appraised, and appropriate course adjustments made.

Raising finance

Securing finance for health and disability services is an important basis for government intervention in New Zealand, as it is in all countries with publicly accountable systems. The evidence suggests that funding public expenditure through general taxation is administratively simple, equitable, and effective. Raising revenue through direct taxation, the chief means by which the NZ government raises revenue, is believed to be equitable, since contributions rise with income. In 1996, 77 per cent of health expenditure in New Zealand was publicly funded (by general taxation), slightly higher than the Australian proportion.

If general taxation is the preferred method, then the fundamental questions in financing New Zealand health services are first, how much public resource should be invested in health (as distinct from, say, education), and second, to what extent should private insurance and out-of-pocket payments be used to increase the total level of finance available for health, to relieve pressure on public funds, and to influence the utilisation of health care? New Zealand experienced real per capita growth in government-funded (i.e. public) health expenditure in the late 1990s. There is a well-established positive relationship between economic growth and health expenditure, both public and private (Ministry of Health 1998a). New Zealand followed this pattern in that real GDP growth in 1993/94 coincided with the increase in government financing of health.

Allocating finance

The role of government in allocating finance for health and disability services was a focus of considerable attention through the 1990s. Allocation is central to government's effectiveness in discharging its responsibility for ensuring equity and allocative efficiency, strategic objectives and regulation. As described by Ham (1995), allocation decisions in the health sector are made at three different levels:

- the micro level, at which health professionals and other providers determine what service patients receive;
- the meso level, at which bodies such as the HFA or insurers determine priorities for population and patients; and
- the macro level, at which governments identify higher priorities that guide resource allocation.

It was in its role of allocating finance that the most significant evolution in government's role occurred in New Zealand in the 1990s. The main change entailed the decentralisation of decision-making within a clear framework of broad strategic objectives and regulation. New Zealand's purchaser/provider split focused serious attention on effectiveness and efficiency in allocation issues. The shift to such a split in turn significantly strengthened accountability, the quality and availability of information, and the flexibility of provider arrangements. The overall effect of these reform mechanisms on health outcomes is not yet known, but intermediate measures are promising.

With equity objectives and limited resources compounding pressures on health systems internationally, governments want fair approaches to the inevitable rationing. The learning environment of the 1990s reinforced the importance of understanding that allocative decision-making, prioritisation or rationing (terms with different emotive meanings but denoting the same process) take place at all three levels in any health system. As a result of the connectedness of the health system, decisions that affect one level affect others.

Because of the paucity of information available to stakeholders in the system, allocative decisions must be made at all three levels. The first problem is inherent to all health systems, namely the imbalance of knowledge whereby professionals know more detail than managers, providers know more detail than purchasers, and so on. This leads to what is known as the 'principal–agent problem', which occurs because agents know more about their performance than principals (for whom they are working) do. The second problem concerns the nature of medicine: it is not an exact science, in which all information essential to decision-making is necessarily known.

This latter problem has increased the appeal of 'evidence-based approaches' to medicine (see Chapter 18), whereby attempts are made to refine the evidence available regarding the effectiveness of any intervention.

The purchaser/provider split has helped with government objectives in relation to allocation. Accountabilities at each level are now clearer, and contracts aid that clarity. On the other hand, excessive attention to contractual specification can foster remoteness and 'disengagement' by providers, particularly where purchasers are overly wary of contracted providers. This arm's-length approach has been labelled 'hard-edged contracturalism', and may have limited application in the field of health and disability, particularly where specification is difficult and where flexibility is required. The evolving role is in government monitoring the effectiveness of the connections between the three levels at which allocative decisions are made. It is illustrated by changes to general practice in New Zealand.

General practice organised itself to respond to the 1993 New Zealand health reforms. It adopted a managerial approach, and many GPs regrouped themselves into independent practice associations (IPAs) in order to do business with the purchasers. There was a keen awareness of the need to 'engage' on both sides of the contractual process, and significant gains have been made. Budget-holding for pharmaceuticals and laboratory testing, peer review, and clinical guidelines have all resulted in practice that is more responsive to both government and community expectations of quality and efficiency.

In the hospital sector, by contrast, the 1993 restructuring was perceived as an imposed and unfriendly arrival. The diversion of management attention into the mechanics of establishing the CHEs as new business entities, struggling to secure revenue streams, distracted attention from the micro level. Hospital doctors were not necessarily formally involved in the contracting process between their hospital managers and the purchasers. Yet those same hospital doctors were, as part of their professional duties, making day-to-day allocation decisions on behalf of patients and on behalf of government. In such a structure, professional autonomy is inevitably threatened by the external accountabilities that are a necessary part of modern systems.

The government role at the macro and meso allocative levels is clear— governments can and should make the macro decisions in order to create the environment whereby it gives 'the right people the right reason to do the right thing'. This role requires more involvement than a hands-off quasi-market suggests. It is, nonetheless, more sophisticated than a command and control structure. The new role of government requires an understanding of the partnerships that are necessary to achieving shared objectives. Mant (1997) usefully contrasts two approaches: binary ('dog eat dog') and ternary (where two parties collaborate to achieve a shared over-arching goal). In largely publicly funded health systems a binary *modus operandi* fails to harness the objectives of the many players to the common goal of better health and disability support outcomes and better service for people. In New Zealand, some of the unexpected consequences of the first phases of reform served as a wake-up call to alert the country to potentially diverse agendas that might confound the reform process. Over time, a balance has been achieved between old-fashioned responsibility and the newer contractual accountability, so that the decisions can be guided by the goal of a people-focused service.

In his review of New Zealand state sector change, Schick (1996: 25) warned: 'In bilateral relationships it's hard for the third party to fit in'. In its evolving role, government's challenge is to steer a clear course between the Scylla of local anarchy and the Charybdis of central planning and dictate, which might not be responsive to local need.

This dilemma has been addressed in New Zealand, consistent with government's macro policy priorities and according to local features, including health needs. At the meso (allocative) level, the HFA has been given the role of assessing need and purchasing according to that need. The relevant legislation also requires the HFA to consult communities before implementing changes to the funding of services for which it contracts.

In the 1990s, government (macro-level) policy priorities have focused on Māori health, child health, mental health, and environmental health. These high-level priorities, together with a population-based allocation of resources to the four regions of New Zealand, have been stipulated in the funding agreements between government and RHAs/HFA. The regional population allocations (adjusted for age, sex, ethnicity, and rurality) are designed to engender a framework of equitable inputs across the country. Allocations within each region may vary, and are guided by local needs assessment: the outcome of the HFA's meso-level allocation of funding.

Of all five mechanisms available to governments, allocation of finances will probably be most interesting to watch in future, particularly as the shift from input control to output monitoring and outcome assessment begins to have an impact.

Service delivery and the ownership of health and disability service providers

Governments choose to be involved in ownership and delivery of health services for a variety of reasons. New Zealand, with 3.7 million people, is spread over a geographical terrain that can make for difficult access and security of supply, especially for acute hospital services. There would therefore seem ample justification for government to 'make' rather than merely 'buy', health and related services. A dearth of acute private hospitals is another factor encouraging greater government involvement in the provision of hospital services, in particular, in New Zealand.

With the possible exception of New Zealand's largest city, Auckland, there is limited scope for competition between HHSs, as currently configured, to drive efficiency objectives. Despite the existence of a more flexible contracting environment, secondary service markets remained concentrated over the 1990s, suggesting that scarce competition has resulted in little change to service provision (Ashton and Press 1997). Where alternative providers entered the market, they concentrated largely in areas such as community mental health services, disability support, and Māori-provided services.

In New Zealand, government-owned HHSs receive about 50 per cent of the total 'Vote Health' each year. As owner of the HHSs, government has encouraged its Crown-owned providers to concentrate on core business. HHSs also receive some revenue from the Accident Compensation Commission (ACC) and modest revenue from private insurers. As owner, government clearly has a role in ensuring both the clinical and financial viability of its HHSs.

With increasing specialisation of medical interventions arising from the development of new technologies, small country hospitals are less able to provide safe, modern secondary services. In sparsely populated regions, government's ownership role has evolved into ensuring a sound local capability for less complex primary services, backed by outreach services from neighbouring providers of secondary services. Service integration has occurred in rural areas, where GPs and 'district' and public health nurses have become central to the revamped services available in redesigned, multi-purpose health centres.

As noted above, the provision of health care in New Zealand is mixed, involving both public and private facilities and providers. Among the non-Crown (i.e. private) providers is a mix of provider types ranging from various forms of GP organisations (IPAs, union health clinics, etc.) through trusts that deliver disability support and mental health services and 'by Māori for Māori services', to private (for-profit and not-for-profit) rest homes and hospitals. As owner of HHSs, government's role is not only to ensure the appointment of competent boards of directors but also to encourage links between HHSs and other providers not under government ownership.

Government's formal role gives it influence when it expresses preferences for particular modes of service delivery, such as an expectation that services will be coordinated. Mental health services are a good case in point. Mental health hospital services have a keen interest in their relationship with community-based, non-Crown mental health services. The HFA role in allocating resources (meso level) is the key to accountability for ensuring services come together for the patient, but additional coordination is also required on the ground, at the micro level, by providers.

One of government's challenges is striking an effective balance between allowing decisions on service delivery to take place at the community level, which encourages local solutions to local needs, as against prescriptive contracting at a more central level by the HFA. The current approach taken by the NZ government is to require that HFA purchasing intentions are clear, so that providers are better placed to innovate in service delivery.

One of the prime risks of all health systems, supplier-induced demand, has been managed to some degree through contractual mechanisms: sophisticated contracting is specific enough to allow for accountability, but not specific enough to provide incentives for inappropriate delivery. For example, contracting has to provide incentives for keeping a child with asthma well managed in the community as distinct from providing payment incentives for hospital admission. Work continues in this area as the search goes on for a less prescriptive, more flexible approach that still allows for accountability.

Government as owner has a particular interest in technical efficiency. Hence decentralised management arrangements with clear accountability mechanisms are designed to facilitate efficient and effective management of resources. HHSs must produce at a minimum cost, and within specified quality parameters, the services contracted. Delivery on contract is monitored by the HFA.

Finally, government as owner has an interest in encouraging longer contracting time-frames while still complying with New Zealand's *Commerce Act 1986* requirements against anti-competitive behaviour. Longer-term contracts are more attractive to private investors and banks. They are essential if government itself is to invest wisely and to permit its boards of directors to access private capital. Because the quality of information has improved considerably throughout the 1990s, it is now feasible for the HFA to let longer-term contracts for particular services.

Regulation

Broadly speaking, government intervenes in market and non-market relationships in society on behalf of the public to help achieve society's social and economic objectives, including its objectives for health and disability services. The use of regulation as a tool is appropriate only where government's objectives cannot be achieved better in other ways, such as incentives, information disclosure, and persuasion. This is because regulation has hidden costs and unintended consequences: it can stifle innovation or restrict entry to the market, thereby reducing benefits to consumers. Resources may be spent evading it, or in proving compliance. Over time regulation tends to become dated and inappropriate.

In developing regulation, government must weigh trade-offs between the costs of administering regulation and the benefits arising from that regulation. The evolving role of government in health sector reform is compellingly evident in the changing use of regulatory interventions in New Zealand.

Indicative of the increasing focus on process reform, as distinct from structural reform, New Zealand now has a range of legislation pending: new legislation in consumer safety would repeal 1957 legislation; legislation in public health would repeal 1956 legislation; and amended occupational legislation would introduce nurse prescribing. Each of these bills would alter the regulatory environment affecting key dimensions of reform, such as medical technology, restrictions on the use of labour, and so on.

'Modern legislative approaches', employed to foster process reform in New Zealand, provide a further signal of the evolving role of government. Modern legislation in New Zealand means legislation that is enabling rather than prescriptive, under which the content of an Act tends to be broad but tight. The Act contains the regulatory principles, but the detail is regulated in subordinate legislation such as regulations, codes, standards, or guidelines. This approach allows for ongoing risk assessment and rapid action, as appropriate, through a menu of regulatory interventions or indeed non-regulatory interventions if they apply better.

'Enabling' legislation is more flexible, and avoids the problems arising from prescriptive legislation, which fails to control risks that were not envisaged at the time the legislation was drafted. Controls can be more readily reduced—or increased—if a hazard becomes a more or less significant risk over time. The modern legislative approach affords greater involvement of those regulated. It also establishes well-understood criteria in the principal Act for determining whether, and if so when, subordinate regulation is necessary.

This method of regulating reflects very well the evolving role of government: setting parameters that closely specify the contracting framework; flexible implementation; and in-built feedback loops leading to more responsive regulations, codes, standards and other guidelines.

Stewardship/convening power

The state may also play a coordination and facilitation role from time to time, as noted earlier, particularly in more advanced systems (World Bank 1997b). Government may act as a 'steward', promoting activity among the key players within the system to help achieve its objectives. Government stewardship is based first on expecting key players within the sector to manage their own relationships. However, there may be times when government itself may be best placed to facilitate policy implementation. In its stewardship role, government supports the implementation of strategies and programs that further policy objectives, particularly efficiency. It acts most effectively as a steward in its role as architect of the sector, facilitator of information and knowledge, and supporter of social capital development (see below).

Government's role as system architect involves not only design of the health system, but also monitoring of the effectiveness and relevance of the chosen structure. Government employs a number of feedback loops that elucidate such questions as how is the sector performing, should there be adjustments to structure or processes? In New Zealand, government's broad, democratic principles, which include a desire for greater accountability and transparency in decision-making, will guide the design of changes. Common issues that governments must consider include public versus private sector roles, central versus decentralised decision-making, diversity versus uniformity, and flexibility versus accountability. Availability of information is always a key to the efficient functioning of health systems. This, coupled with the desire for greater accountability and transparency in decision-making, means that information disclosure will be crucial. Consumer demand for information is beginning to have an effect—the Internet encourages consumer empowerment.

Government may also use legislation effectively to foster reform. For example, the *Health and Disability Services Act 1993* requires the HFA to consult communities on certain decisions. In addition, however, government can influence, in a less hands-on manner, how purchasers and providers execute their roles in order to encourage more information being made available. A specific example is government's requirement that clinical priority assessment criteria for elective surgery booking systems be developed and disseminated.

Social capital is another area in which government's role is evolving. Social capital refers to the networks, norms, and trust that facilitate coordination and cooperation in social organisations for mutual benefit. Networks of civic engagement have an influence over the quality of public life of both communities and individuals, and are widely valued as essential ingredients of 'healthy communities'. Researchers have linked improved health outcomes to an individual's level of social connectedness (Berkman and Syme 1979; Kawachi et al. 1997). 'Strengthening Families' is a NZ government initiative whereby the health, education, and welfare sectors are working together locally to coordinate services for families at risk. This initiative of coordination is also working within the civic network of local government and reflects collaboration and stewardship of social capital to encourage community support. International evidence supports the view that the level of local community involvement in planning, decision-making, and the practice of health promotion is positively related to the impact on health-related behavioural change (Gillies 1997).

Discussion and Implications

Government's overarching interest in better health outcomes and better services for people finds expression in its equity and efficiency objectives. In health, these objectives have remained constant in the face of ongoing pressures such as social and demographic change, changing disease patterns, advancing medical and information technology, and increasing public expectations and consumer demand. In New Zealand, government's role has evolved through selective use of the mechanisms available to it to intervene in the health sector.

The NZ government had several aims in establishing the new structures. It wanted to diminish controls over inputs, reduce the dominance of health care providers, and increase providers' accountability for the services they deliver. It also wanted to ensure that a central factor in decisions on the purchase of health care services was the measurable improvements those services could provide for the community. But health systems are dynamic, and governments must therefore continually monitor and recalibrate their roles. Maintaining the right balance between a central framework with effective incentives, and sufficient latitude to encourage local innovation, means that government's role will continue to evolve. 'How can we get better processes?' remains an ongoing question for government, as answers continue to percolate from the workforce and from communities. Thus health sector reforms will continue incrementally against historical and contemporary backdrops, against changing practices and cultures.

The challenge for government remains: to flexibly balance the mechanisms available to it, and create the environment within which health and disability services effectively match resources with needs. Achieving this balance, which is an art as much as a science (Saltman and Figueras 1998), is essential if New Zealand is to retain its focus on people-centred services.

Conclusions

The experience of government's evolving role in health reform in New Zealand has generated a large number of lessons. Governments considering or in the throes of reform would be well advised to consider the following:

- Understanding the complexity and interconnectedness of health systems is essential in order to achieve ultimately simple solutions.
- An understanding of both historical and contemporary influences is needed in order to build a positive environment for change. If imported ideas are used, they need to be translated into the relevant context. Solutions that work in one part of the country may not be applicable elsewhere. On the other hand, disseminating good practice based on local as well as international experience is invaluable, as the lessons learned may indeed be relevant elsewhere.
- Access to valid information for health promotion and disease prevention is vital to consumers if they are to self-manage their health effectively. Information is equally important for evidence-based practice, for measuring performance, for accountability, and, through transparency, for instilling public confidence. There will inevitably be a risk of provider capture and opportunism, but it is possible to convert mere antagonism into shared outcomes, and to channel energy into finding solutions rather than trying to outwit the payment system.
- The new accountability does not obviate the need for old-fashioned responsibility. Again, it is important to get the balance right.
- Flexible delivery, involving multiple organisations, has to be achieved while ensuring that any single organisation remains accountable for its actions.
- There is no 'magic bullet', no one right solution waiting to be discovered. Incremental change that draws on insight, wisdom, and energy is the key to successful health reform. It is a matter of hard work.
- Neither rigid central planning nor loose market arrangements work universally. Eclectic and pragmatic approaches have greater prospects of success. In general, New Zealand has found broad, central, strategic policy objectives coupled with devolved decision-making to be most successful.
- Successful decentralisation requires a supportive policy and legislative environment.
- Ownership of change is essential. When the change process is owned by those implementing the change, they will make it work. 'Local solutions to local needs' has become a central refrain in New Zealand: this includes the engagement of health professionals as a crucial component.
- Ongoing and incremental change is necessary for health systems to effectively adapt to changing populations, disease patterns, and technology pressures.
- People matter—the people who are served and the people who serve. This is the kernel of simplicity within the complexity that is a health system. As Māori say, '*E aha te mea nui? He tangata, he tangata, he tangata*' (What is the most important thing? It is people).

8

The Evolution of the Purchaser Role for Acute In-Patient Services in Australia

Stephen Duckett

A major area of reform in Australia has been to improve the technical efficiency of hospitals. The principal strategy to improve efficiency has been payment reform: moving to paying hospitals a benchmark price for the mix of patients (cases) they treat, a funding policy known as 'casemix funding'. Australia has a long history of casemix development. The first consultancy in this area was undertaken in 1985, aimed at testing whether the DRG classification system as developed in the USA was relevant to Australian clinical practice. Since that small beginning, Australia has embarked on an ambitious casemix development program. All states, with the exception of New South Wales, have either implemented casemix funding or begun a phased implementation process.

Briefly, before the introduction of casemix funding, public hospitals in all Australian states were essentially funded on an historical basis. As a result, to the extent that they could be measured, there were substantial variations in costs per patient treated. But measurement systems were crude, based on comparisons of cost per day of stay or cost per patient treated, neither of which was effectively standardised for the casemix of patients. The common response to any alleged differences in efficiency was that the comparison had failed to take into account the hospitals' patient mix.

Until the mid-1980s, hospital funding was increasing and any service problems were able to be solved with additional resources. The mid-1980s saw the development of clearer accountability relationships through the establishment of what came to be known in Victoria as health service agreements (HSA), essentially 40–50 page contracts. Agreements would typically include negotiated goals covering a range of aspects of hospital administration, including broad strategic objectives and targets about the number of patients treated, number of out-patient attendances and so on, together with a specification of the funds that would be available to that hospital in that year. In this regard, HSAs were very similar to the block contracts negotiated in the early stages of the purchaser provider reforms in the United Kingdom. However, health service agreements did little to change historical funding arrangements in terms of either patient flows or efficiency (Economic and Budget Review Committee 1992).

The next stage in development of funding arrangements was the transition to casemix funding, which occurred in the early to mid-1990s. Victoria was the first state to change in 1993/94, followed by South Australia in 1994/95 (a full description of Victoria's initial casemix funding system may be found in Duckett 1995). Casemix funding was introduced in Western Australia and Tasmania in 1996/97, and a phased process of implementation commenced in Queensland in that year. As in many other countries, the 'steering not rowing' nostrums of Osborne and Gaebler (1992: 'The state needs to row less and steer more') influenced public policy in Australia, and health policy discourse began to distinguish between purchaser and provider. The purchasing role was seen to be about ensuring that the 'required services in the right volume [are] delivered at the right quality and at the right price' (unpublished paper prepared in 1992 for senior health officials). The recognition of a purchaser role meant a reduction in autonomy for providers, who previously had unfettered control over hospital admission decisions. The loss of autonomy was also accompanied by a loss of legitimacy: previously providers had been seen as advocates for patients. The more closely government and health providers examined the purchasing function, the more providers were seen to be pursuing their own self-interest in their claims for increased funding.

Although the discourse of purchaser and provider was common, most states did not follow the UK model with formal organisational splits and did not establish separate purchasing authorities: the state health authority continued to act as both funder and purchaser. The exception was Western Australia, which established a separate purchasing bureau within the Health Department in 1991. But this experiment collapsed, probably because of the absence of a transparent purchasing methodology, and the presence of excessive bureaucracy in a state with a population of only slightly more than a million people. The policy approach favoured in Australia was to emphasise public competition (in line with reform approaches in parts of Europe; see Saltman and von Otter 1989) and to develop a common pricing policy using casemix measures rather than an 'internal market'.

The Development of Casemix Funding in Victoria

In most states the impetus for casemix funding was a desire to achieve substantial efficiency improvements. In Victoria, budget cuts of 15 per cent were being implemented; in South Australia, budget cuts were about 10 per cent. The governments in both states were keen that the budget cuts be targeted at inefficient hospitals rather than in the more traditional across-the-board manner. Casemix funding could also be implemented fairly quickly and could give certainty that budget reduction targets would be achieved (see Lin and Duckett 1997, which also analyses the contextual factors affecting the implementation of casemix funding).

New South Wales is the only Australian state that has not started a formal casemix funding approach for its hospitals, but even in that state, policy is that casemix 'inform' budget-setting processes and distribute budget cuts (for a review of the contemporary state of casemix funding in Australia see Duckett 1998a). Casemix funding arrangements are becoming more elaborate over time; this chapter concentrates on the evolution of funding in Victoria, but trends are similar in all states.

Victoria's interest in casemix had two main antecedents. In the early 1980s many states, Victoria included, were interested in the application of program budgeting to state financial arrangements. In its implementation process the then Victorian Department of Management and Budget argued that a single program for hospitals was an inadequate budget structure, especially since hospitals accounted for almost one-sixth of all government spending. One proposal for splitting the hospital allocation was to divide the hospital budget along speciality lines (medical, surgical, obstetrics and gynaecology, etc.). This required identifying the costs of the various specialities and output measures.

At the same time, some leading hospital managers were advocating the development of clinical costing systems to assist in managing hospital services in the state. A by-product of this approach would obviously be data to be used in speciality costing. These two developments came together logically in the first consultancy on casemix in Victoria, which was let in early 1995. The consultancy had two elements. Professor George Palmer of the University of New South Wales was asked to assess the feasibility of grouping the Victorian computerised discharge data into DRGs, and then to assess whether American DRGs provided an adequate basis to describe the Australian data. The second component of the consultancy was led by Professor Bob Fetter of Yale University and designed to develop relative costs of hospital care. This component entailed the first application in Australia of the 'Yale cost model', a method of estimating DRG-level costs without reliance on detailed, patient-level cost information (Chandler et al. 1991). These consultancies provided the basis for further development work in Victoria. Palmer's consultancy showed that the process of grouping the data was feasible, and that the American DRGs provided a good basis for description of Australian hospital care. The experience with the Yale costing model was not so positive, and the subsequent emphasis in Victoria was on the development and use of patient costing systems rather than the Yale cost model. For a number of years after that first consultancy, Palmer continued to have responsibility for grouping hospital data and for producing an annual report on Victorian hospital activity with comparisons with American length of stay.

The department continued to have an interest in casemix for a number of years and attempted to educate hospitals through the provision of data. Not only did it publish an annual report on casemix in the state, but it also provided detailed printouts to hospitals of their length of stay by DRG and comparisons with state averages. 'Top 30' DRG printouts showed hospitals the bed-day savings that would be accrued if the hospital had a length of stay equal to the state average. The department also published the so-called Rainbow Books, which compared the efficiency of hospitals in terms of costs per DRG-weighted patient.

Despite this substantial information effort, there was little evidence of any change in hospital practice. The information provision was seen as not being tied to budgets, even in regions where considerable effort was placed on drawing the attention of hospital managers to the efficiency opportunities during the course of the annual budget negotiations. Considerable efficiency variations were evident in hospitals across Victoria.

In the early 1990s the then Health Minister, Maureen Lyster, appointed a committee of review of Victorian hospitals (the so-called Victorian Health System Review) chaired by Dr Ian Brand. Although the main interest in this committee was whether or not Victoria should move to a system of area health services as recommended by the contemporary National Health Strategy, one of the key recommendations of the committee, which reported in May 1992, was that Victoria proceed to casemix funding for hospitals of more than a hundred beds. The government endorsed this recommendation and advised hospitals of a four-year phased implementation program. Because these decisions were taken in the last six months of the Labor government and it was clear that a change of government was imminent, hospitals took very little action to prepare for the introduction of casemix funding.

In October 1992 the Labor government in Victoria was swept out of power in a landslide election. The new Coalition government appointed a Commission of Audit to assess state finances shortly after its election.

The Commission of Audit (Victorian Commission of Audit 1993: v) claimed that Victorian acute hospitals were 18 per cent more expensive than hospitals in other states. These data corroborated data published by the Commonwealth Grants Commission (which assesses the performance of the public sector in all the states), which had also indicated that Victorian hospitals were relatively inefficient. This evidence was used by the state Treasury to justify imposing substantial budget cuts on the hospital sector in Victoria.

The new government appointed a new head of the Department of Health (renamed the Department of Health and Community Services), Dr John Paterson. As an economic rationalist with experience in price and work practice reforms, and in common with other economic rationalists who had come to dominate the bureaucracy (Pusey 1991), Paterson (1993) saw the health system as 'primitive' and 'Sovietised' and characterised the relationship between the department and the hospitals as one of 'co-dependency'. Although the new government supported a purchaser/provider split, Paterson saw the purchaser/provider system as creating bigger bureaucracies and preferred instead to use financial levers to create change. He was able to make use of two factors to convince the Minister for Health to defer the introduction of both area health authorities and purchaser/provider arrangements, and instead to introduce casemix funding. First, as outlined above, there had been a considerable investment that had led to the development of an information system that provided comparative hospital performance on the basis of DRGs. Second, the government intended to introduce 12 per cent budget cuts over two years, and there was the need for an equitable approach to pass on the cuts as the historically based global budgets had hidden numerous inefficiencies, if they had not actually penalised the most efficient hospitals. The government accepted de-emphasising a formal purchaser/provider split and instead gave priority to introducing casemix funding as a way of driving efficiency improvements.

A prerequisite for casemix funding was greater clarity in describing hospital activities, since product definition is the *sine qua non* of market reforms: without a meaningful definition of products comprehensible to both the purchaser and the provider, there can be no market. Clarification of hospital products occurred through 'unbundling' of hospital activity by first defining broad product lines. Casemix funding also required, for each of the major product lines, specification of prices for each product and limitation on volumes of activity to be funded to ensure that expenditure targets were not exceeded.

Three broad streams of hospital products were identified: in-patient services, out-patient services, and teaching and research functions (known as 'training and development'). Naturally, these broad streams of products could not specify the enormous range of other activities that were provided by hospitals, including home-care services and other services that have developed over time. Other services were captured in what were called 'specified grants' or 'site-specific grants' that continued to be made by negotiation (e.g. home dialysis—neither in-patient nor out-patient—and funds for special wards for treatment of prisoners).

In each case the broad product line needed to be further refined to classify the casemix or detailed functions within that broader stream. By far the greatest attention has been paid to the development of payment systems for in-patient services and the consequent need to describe in-patient activities of hospitals. The typical initial approach to in-patient payment was to implement a statewide standard contract with all hospitals.

The Development of the Purchaser Role

The development of DRGs meant that it was now possible to describe the activities of hospitals and hence pay for them rationally. Under casemix funding, the statewide standard contract typically provides for a fixed-base price across the state for an admission to hospital, with the actual price paid for an admission varying according to the DRG relative weight for that case. The contract also provides the rules under which funding varies with volume, a policy initiative which meant that the transition to casemix funding was also the end of the inflexible budget for hospitals.

A distinctive characteristic of the purchaser role is reduction in the autonomy of individual providers over hospital admission decisions and the volume of patients to be treated in particular diagnostic categories (Øvretveit 1995). The extent of autonomy reduction varies between different systems, and can range from requirements for 'pre-admission certification' for each admission to generalised guidance on the purchaser's preferred relative priorities. In Australia, the purchaser role in public hospital funding is still evolving and purchasers have eschewed strategies aimed at setting priorities at the level of particular diagnostic categories.

Focusing priorities

Implementation of casemix funding in Australia meant strong controls over expenditure but weak controls over both hospital-specific volume and hospital relative priorities. There were no specialty-specific or DRG-specific volume targets; rather payments were based on the total volume of patients treated in the hospital. The lack of specialty-specific targets was partly a response to the difficulty of interfering in patient flows and the aversion of the medical profession in Australia to the introduction of exogenous rationing processes (Crichton 1990).

The initial purchasing focus in Australian casemix funding implementation involved an attempt to bring hospital attention to patients on hospital waiting lists, and hence to change (or provide incentives for hospitals to change) hospital admission priorities. It built on a history of 'categorisation' of waiting lists where surgeons classified waiting-list patients in terms of the urgency of their admission; Category 1 was the most urgent, requiring admission within thirty days. (An example of a Category 1 patient would be a patient requiring open-heart surgery.) This categorisation also helped focus attention on the more appropriate measure of excess waiting times rather than a simple count of those waiting.

Casemix funding as implemented in Victoria provided that funding for additional activity would be through an 'additional throughput pool'. This was a single statewide pool that was used to pay for all increases in the number of patients treated compared with the base period. The amount of money in the pool available to pay for volume increases was fixed. Consequently the price paid per case varied inversely with volume. The additional throughput payments were on a quarterly basis with no speciality-specific or DRG-specific targets.

The additional throughput pool provided implicit statewide targets of throughput growth at the base price. Importantly, access to the pool was a reward (as many hospitals planned to offset budget reductions with additional payment for additional activity). Thus it acted as an incentive that allowed the application of other regulatory controls; in particular a critical condition related to elective surgery ('waiting list') patients. The focus on waiting lists was achieved by the fact that hospitals were not eligible for any payment from the additional throughput pool if they had any Category 1 patients waiting more than thirty days after 1 January 1994. Not surprisingly, Category 1 patients waiting more than thirty days declined precipitously over this period (see Street and Duckett 1996).

The government was not able to impose a similar elimination target on Category 2 patients waiting more than the target period, as there were substantially more of these patients waiting and hence elimination was not seen as feasible in the short term. Although there has been some reduction in Category 2 patients, this has not been sustained nor has it led to the elimination of long-wait Category 2 patients. Because categorisation is done by surgeons, it is often very difficult to audit the categorisation status; some of the reduction in Category 1 and 2 waiting has probably been achieved by reclassification rather than by ensuring that these patients are treated. This results in regular accusations of manipulation of categorisation (e.g. *Age*, 8 October 1996: 1).

The additional throughput pool thus provided a major incentive for hospitals to reassess their admission priorities to give greater priority to patients on the urgent waiting list (Street and Duckett 1996). The strategy was a rather crude approach to priority-setting, since definition of patients to be accorded priority remained in the hands of hospitals/surgeons through the definition of patients placed on waiting lists. There was no attempt to weight elective patients; for example, to give a higher priority to orthopaedic versus cataract patients.

A clearer purchaser role

The abolition of the additional throughput pool in the Victorian model, which occurred in 1995/96, was accompanied by a further refinement in the priority-setting process through the specification, for the first time, of hospital-specific volume limits: rather than volume of activity (and thus payment) being limited throughout the state, each hospital was given volume limits. This change marked the transition from a 'budget share' approach to a clearer purchaser orientation in payment policy, as the precise volume to be purchased at each hospital was now determined centrally. None of the other state casemix funding policies had adopted the flexible pool model, all having hospital-specific volume limits from the beginning.

Payment for additional activity (above the base and a small flexible margin) is now allocated to hospitals using approaches that involve making centralised judgments about where additional activity is warranted in the state. In this aspect of the Victorian model, hospitals are able to bid for additional throughput on top of their base target.

There has been no specification of particular DRGs or particular specialties for which additional activity is desired. Rather, decisions on relative priorities of admissions are still left in the hands of hospitals and their clinicians, albeit with the bonus program to address patients on waiting lists. This centralised process also gives some implicit weighting to those hospitals in locations experiencing population growth or those introducing new services as a result of a government-approved planning process.

Further experience of tendering is being seen in the choice of new providers for public hospital services. Most state governments in Australia have moved to seek private capitalisation of new public hospital facilities. This has involved private sector build-own-operate arrangements, where the relevant state government contracts with the private operator to provide hospital services to public patients. All of the casemix funding states have developed these arrangements, and the contracts with the private sector operators are normally expressed in casemix terms. The operators are generally selected after a competitive tender process, in some cases the tender specifying the price to be paid in advance and in others requiring the price to be specified by the tenderer.

These 'bidding' processes represent a distinct break from the public competition/market share approach that characterised the initial development of casemix funding in Australia. It marks a centralisation of control in the hands of the purchaser, with the allocation of additional paid activity being determined centrally rather than following patient preferences. The allocation decision forced hospitals to compete on price for the additional activity, which, in the absence of robust measures of quality, could also have allowed hospitals to skimp in this area. A 'variable price' approach also added complexity to the casemix funding arrangements.

The Transformation of a System: Casemix Funding Five Years On

Table 8.1 shows the key data on trends in acute health expenditure and separations from Victorian hospitals over the period 1991/92 to 1996/97.

Table 8.1   Activity and expenditure trends (indexed), Victoria public hospitals, 1991/92 to 1996/97

	1991/92	1992/93	1993/94	1994/95	1995/96	1996/97
Separations	100	105	114	124	127	131
WIES	-	-	100	106	107	109
Budgeted outlays	100	94	91	94	106	109
Budgeted outlays (real)	100	93	89	89	97	98
Budget/separation	100	89	80	75	84	83
Budget (real)/separation	100	89	78	72	77	75

Source: Author's calculations from data supplied by Victorian Department of Human Services

Budgeted expenditure

It can be seen that budgeted expenditure for acute health services in 1996/97 was 9 per cent higher than the budget in 1991/92, thus verifying political statements that more is being spent on Victorian public hospitals than ever before. (The table shows total outlays, including both Commonwealth and state funds. Over the period shown in the table, the Commonwealth has increased its share of funding and the state has correspondingly reduced its share.) The trend line for outlays, however, would reveal a significant dip, bottoming out in 1993/94 with the impact of the initial budget cuts. After taking inflation into account, the increased expenditure in later years has not offset the effects of these initial cuts and so there has been a real decline of 2 per cent in outlays on hospitals over the period.

Activity

Hospitals have responded to the introduction of casemix funding by significant volume increases: overall the number of separations has increased by 75 per cent over the period 1991/92 to 1996/97. The standard payment unit in Victoria is weighted inlier equivalent separations (WIES), a measure introduced in 1993/94. The rate of increase in WIES is slower than the rate of increase in separations.

The increase in recorded separations overstates the real growth in activity in Victorian hospitals. Some of the increase in separations is undoubtedly a nominal increase resulting from reclassification of activity that was previously undertaken on an out-patient basis but is now recorded as in-patient activity. The extent of actual versus nominal growth is difficult to estimate. Assuming that all the activity increase is real, the costs per separation have declined by 25 per cent over the period 1991/92 to 1996/97.

A decline of this magnitude raises the question of whether funding per patient is adequate. Unfortunately, the data on this issue do not give an unequivocal answer. On the one hand, there are still significant variations in costs per patient treated for patients in the same DRG between hospitals, suggesting that efficiency gains in the more expensive hospitals are still achievable. On the other hand, the recent report of the Auditor-General on casemix funding in Victoria (Auditor-General of Victoria 1998) gave moderate evidence of financial stress in hospitals and networks, citing information such as the following:

- there has been a significant decline in net current assets of hospitals and networks (from $76 million on 30 June 1993 to $4.4 million on 30 June 1997;
- current assets are less than current liabilities in most networks; and
- aggregate surpluses in the health system are declining ($80.8 million in 1992/93 to $6 million in 1995/96).

Hospitals and networks are not business organisations, and the standard financial ratios and measures are not as relevant for hospitals as for businesses. Accordingly, the Department of Human Services has challenged the relevance of these figures (Auditor-General of Victoria 1998: 215). However, financial stress can also be demonstrated by the extent that 'bail-outs' have been required for significant parts of the system, including the Western and North Eastern Networks and Ballarat Health Services.

Waiting lists and times

The increase in activity in public hospitals has led to a decline in some aspects of waiting lists. Although, overall, the total number of people on waiting lists is virtually unchanged from 1993 to 1997, Category 1 patients waiting more than thirty days have disappeared from the system (a decline from 1141 in January 1993 to none in 1997). There has also been a significant decline in Category 2 patients waiting more than 90 days (from 6870 in January 1993 to 2597 in September 1997, a decline of 62 per cent).

Quality

The evidence of the impact of the changes on quality of care is quite mixed. Unfortunately, there is almost no before and after information to demonstrate any impact on quality, but staff certainly believe there has been an adverse impact on quality (Auditor-General of Victoria 1998). Patients, on the other hand, are by and large satisfied with their experience in hospitals (77 per cent of patients surveyed in the statewide patient satisfaction survey reported that they were 'very satisfied' with their care). Importantly, hospital data show significant differences between hospitals in level of patient satisfaction, giving confidence that patients are able to distinguish satisfactory from unsatisfactory care, and so the patient data should not simply be dismissed.

There have been two studies that have looked at quality of care over time. Brown and Lumley's (1998) analysis of data from 1989 and 1993 surveys of patients' views of maternity care showed that, for example, the extent to which the patients felt they were given a say in their care and the extent to which midwives and doctors were perceived to be helpful had deteriorated between the two surveys. MacIntyre et al. (1997) examined trends in rates of potentially avoidable readmissions from 1987 to 1995. Although readmission rates increased over this period, neither the introduction of casemix funding nor the budget cuts appear to have caused any change in the overall trend in readmission rates.

Discussion

The transition path to casemix funding in Australia has paralleled the development of more explicit purchaser policies in other countries, such as the internal market in the United Kingdom. The common policy design has primarily been one of fixed-price contracts, with common contracts applied across the whole state. Although one state (Western Australia) flirted with a purchaser/provider split with detailed contract specifications, contemporary state policies do not involve detailed purchaser-driven contracts. To some extent this reflects the 'success' of the implementation of casemix in Victoria, which showed that the technical difficulties of developing casemix funding arrangements can be overcome, that implementation can occur fairly quickly, and that transition and transaction costs are relatively low (Lin and Duckett 1997).

The various state casemix policy measures have concentrated on simple description of the product in output terms, and measurement of quality of care has not been emphasised. Although the initial Victorian introduction of casemix funding was associated with an emphasis on analysis of readmission rates and the development of a statewide patient satisfaction survey, the results of analysing these data were not released until 1997 and 1998 respectively. Use of administrative data, such as comparisons of case fatality rates in cardiac surgery, has not been widespread, even though the technologies to do this are available (Hannan 1998).

The two states that introduced casemix funding first, Victoria and South Australia, were both involved in significant budget reductions, and the chief policy objective was presented as being about increasing technical efficiency very rapidly. The alternative economic objective, of improving allocative efficiency (see Mooney 1996; Segal and Richardson 1994), was not a high priority in the implementation process, reflecting the market-oriented rather than planning-oriented emphasis of government in both states. The technical efficiency orientation of the changes in hospital funding meant that they relied on the development of good measures of output, mainly casemix measures, and on such methods being widely accepted in Australia. A policy focus on allocative efficiency would have required use of measures of outcomes or cost effectiveness, where the measurement technology is still under development (e.g. the Australian Quality of Life measure [AQoL] was not released until 1998). Further, there are still major technical difficulties in applying cost-effectiveness analysis to priority-setting processes, as was shown in Oregon (Tengs et al. 1996). There are also considerable political difficulties in introducing formalised (explicit) rationing strategies, especially when these appear to be counter to the values of the general public (Nord et al. 1995).

Despite regular calls in the professional literature to fund on the basis of health gain (e.g. Braithwaite and Hindle 1998), policy-makers have not followed this course. As outlined above, the elaboration of the purchaser role in Australia has mainly been in the form of more sophisticated pricing policies rather than the development of policies to influence hospital priority-setting at the level of particular diagnostic categories.

What then made it possible to change fundamentally the way hospitals were funded and hence to centralise decision-making?

The first prerequisite was a technical one: as far as possible, all the products of the hospital needed to be described, counted, and paid for. As would be expected, based on transaction cost economics, market allocation can be preferred to internalised processes only if these preconditions, relating to product definition, are met (Williamson 1975; Ashton 1997a). Hospital products needed to be described, and it was here that casemix and DRGs were essential. It was not appropriate to describe hospitals simply in terms of specialities, as there can be considerable casemix variation within such speciality groupings. It was also necessary to set prices. At first these were set on a statewide basis using relative weights for the various DRGs, but subsequently government has encouraged hospitals to compete by tendering services to establish a benchmark price.

Second, it was important to recognise that not everything was done by simply relying on market effects, and there had to be a regulatory environment to incorporate other objectives (such as a focus on waiting lists through the additional throughput pool or through bonus programs) into the hospital funding policy arrangements.

Third, as Lin and Duckett (1997) pointed out, there needed to be political will. Casemix funding for hospitals meant that government funding reduction targets were able to be achieved through efficiency improvements rather than through reductions in services. This helped to ensure political will. Importantly, in the first two states in which casemix funding was implemented, this occurred in the early period of new governments elected with substantial majorities and major reform mandates. This alignment of political will and technical ability was thus essential to ensure that the changes could overcome both sets of obstacles (political and technical).

As argued above, casemix funding has led to a change in the balance of power in the health sector, advantaging purchasers over providers. The power shift is partly the inevitable result of the more centralised priority-setting process inherent in a purchaser/provider arrangement. It also results from an increase in accountability of providers, because the better hospital output can be measured, the easier it is for central authorities to compare performance of providers and refute arguments about inadequacies of funding. Further, the more elaborate and complex the purchasing arrangements become, the more difficult it is for providers to explain the details of funding arrangements to the public and to mobilise political campaigns against the funding formulae. (The complexity of the Victorian casemix arrangements has been criticised by providers and by a recent review of Victoria's casemix funding arrangements; see Auditor-General of Victoria 1998.)

Elaboration of the funding formulae has not only further centralised decision-making (e.g. over where additional activity will be funded), but also the very process of regular changes to the formulae strengthens the purchaser's knowledge of the system and demonstrates the purchaser's ability to change the *modus operandi* of the system. This power shift to the purchaser involves a transfer of risk for provider efficiency variation to the provider and has been associated with significant improvements in productivity. Together this means that this approach to funding is attractive to governments. Government has also been able to use the improvement in technical efficiency to achieve its budgetary goals, thus reducing its immediate need to address allocative efficiency for budgeting (rather than economic) reasons. Ironically, the centralisation of power has been accompanied by a decentralising discourse about consumer empowerment, 'money following patients', and so on.

The future path of hospital funding policy is likely to involve a continuation of this evolution of the purchaser role. Hospital products that are not currently well specified (e.g. out-patient services and training and development) will need to be specified, and the proportion of activity will need to be subject to tender processes. The most likely trend in the future will be priority-setting by central authorities. However, there are no signs that the purchaser role in Australia will develop into one that involves explicit priority-setting at the level of diagnostic category.

9

The Changing Role of Clinicians: Their Role in Health Reform in Australia and New Zealand

Jennifer Alexander

Experience during the 1980s and 1990s in Australia, and to a lesser extent in New Zealand, suggests that not only are clinicians, as providers of health services, key targets of many reform processes, but also they can and do play a significant role in bringing about change. Indeed it is unlikely that anyone involved in health reform would ignore the role of clinicians, or fail to harness their energies and ideas in the interest of change. To do otherwise would be a recipe for failure. Thus no discussion of health sector reform can ignore the importance and potential contribution of clinicians, who are now central to reform in the health arena. This is particularly evident in management, where clinician involvement in most aspects of reform is being bolstered to improve the efficiency and effectiveness of health service delivery.

While the term 'clinician' can be applied to doctors, nurses, and allied health professionals, in this chapter most of the discussion will focus on doctors. This is not because they are the only clinicians, or the only clinicians of importance. In particular, it should be noted that this is not to deny nurses' influence in the reform process (Cochrane 1989). Through professional organisations and the activities of senior nurses and nurse academics, nurses have been directly involved in developing and implementing a range of reform initiatives, including casemix funding, clinical pathways, and quality assurance programs. Moreover, management is now an established career path in nursing (Gardner and McCoppin 1989), and along with medical managers and lay managers, nurse managers are taking a leading role in hospitals (Degeling et al. 1998). Nonetheless, few would deny that doctors constitute the most powerful group in the health care system (Willis

1989). Securing their cooperation is therefore crucial for health sector reform.

Doctors traditionally have made the important resource decisions and wielded the most power, usually to block changes they oppose. Without their cooperation, much change is unachievable. Indeed experience has shown that once doctors do become involved in management and change, they quickly demand the involvement of other clinician groups, such as nurses and allied health professionals, and forge new and more productive partnerships with clinician colleagues whom they might, in the past, have viewed as providing subservient assistance to them. For all of these reasons, doctors are usually seen as the most significant potential barrier to change in health systems (Palmer and Short 1994), so they constitute a group that merits special attention in the early stages of change.

In this chapter I shall explore the changing role of clinicians during the 1980s and 1990s, with particular reference to Australia, though some mention will be made of changes in New Zealand. I shall also discuss why clinicians are important in health reform, and review the lessons of almost two decades involving clinicians in the management of health services. Hospital doctors are the main focus of this chapter; although reference will be made to the changing role of general practitioners, this topic is discussed in detail in Chapter 10.

For many decades, the health literature has demonstrated how the decisions made by clinicians, mainly doctors, have profound resource implications for the health system as a whole. In most industries, those who make decisions with resource implications are also responsible for the consequences of those decisions. In that sense the strategic and operational parts of the organisation are connected through a management hierarchy. In the health sector, until recently, clinicians have remained fairly free of responsibility for the resource implications of their actions. Indeed others, such as health managers and bureaucrats, were, and still are, held accountable for the implications of clinicians' decisions. Making clinicians more cost-aware, and developing organisational structures that make them more accountable for the resource implications of their decisions, bring them into the managerial process, especially in hospitals. This process has been a central feature of health reform in Australia, and to a different degree in New Zealand, in recent years.

In most organisations, the operational delivery function is subordinate to the strategic epicentre, and responds to changes initiated at the apex. In health, clinicians, especially hospital-based medical clinicians, have remained organisationally disconnected from the strategic apex of most hospitals and from the central policy functions of the publicly funded health services. As a result of this 'disconnected hierarchy', the major restructurings and other reforms involving the strategic apex have had limited impact on changing clinical practice.

The focus of many 'strategic' actions by clinicians has been at the political level, usually through direct lobbying for additional resources. They usually initiate these actions independent of, and often without informing, the formal management structure of their organisation. Clinicians, individually and collectively, have historically worked 'around' their managers. Their ambiguous relationship with the hospital and their undoubted political clout have given clinicians great freedom, and they have used this freedom to exert their influence directly, through the media, on politicians and other important stakeholders, including the public.

An implicit and poorly understood intention of many recent reforms is to reconnect the hierarchy in health, and in so doing, to link clinical practice with strategic decision-making. Although many clinicians welcome this, they do not intend to relinquish their political and clinical freedom.

Health Reform and Changing Clinical Practice

A common view is that the *raison d'être* of health reform is the desire to get maximum benefit from the available resources: to make health care cheaper and more cost-effective, fairer, or more responsive. Reforms in Australia and New Zealand have been promoted under various guises: as casemix accounting in Victoria (as a means to increase technical efficiency in care delivery); as 'population-based restructuring' in New South Wales (as a means of improving allocative efficiency), and as the introduction of an internal market in New Zealand (to make purchasing decisions more transparent and thus get better 'leverage' for change).

At the heart of reform, however, is an implicit (or explicit) desire to change clinical practice. Health systems cannot be effectively 'reformed' unless there are changes in clinical practice. Change may be more urgently required in how the care is given, or where it is given (e.g. in a community setting or at home, rather than in hospital), by whom it is given (e.g. by a nurse practitioner rather than a doctor, or by the patient or the patient's family, in the case of some nursing care), or to whom it is given (e.g. to parts of the population that have traditionally been less well served in health care, or whose health status is poorer). The first three changes, by definition, will always involve changing the behaviour of the caregivers themselves, the clinicians. The last two will involve patients or health care clients, as well as the providers, and may even involve a patient's carers and family. But these changes also inevitably involve clinicians.

However, many of the instruments of reform that aim to change clinicians' behaviour, such as casemix systems or structural reforms intended to drive changes in clinical practice, originate 'outside' the clinical process. In that sense, from the clinicians' perspective they are imposed changes, or 'outside-in' changes. Bristling under externally imposed change, clinicians have sometimes used their considerable power to thwart such changes, irrespective of whether they in fact support or at least have sympathy for the reforms. This has been the case especially in Australia, where professional dominance is still very much alive.

Clinical practice can also, however, be reformed from within. Many health reforms have been driven by technological changes, such as the introduction of laparascopic instruments, new drugs, or new diagnostic procedures. But as more clinicians have been required to become involved in the management of their services or institutions, we are seeing reforms of clinical practice that are driven by the clinicians themselves, who are now integral to developing new and better processes of care. These are 'inside-out' changes (Berwick 1994), and clinicians are using their power in positive ways to effect change. Clinician-managers are much more likely to bring about change within the clinical ranks, including better clinical practice, than non-clinicians acting independently.

The Changing Role of Clinicians

The 1970s and early 1980s—professional dominance and the Greek chorus

The 1970s and early 1980s were the golden era of medical professional dominance in Australia. Like most other health systems in Western countries, Australia and New Zealand had not yet really started to experience the significant resource constraints that became evident in the late 1980s. The relationship between clinicians and managers was one in which each party knew its role. The relationship was usually not antagonistic, provided each party understood and adhered to its role. In the case of managers, this meant keeping up the supply of resources to the clinicians, who 'got on with the real work'.

To the extent that doctors were involved in management, their role was advisory. They commonly influenced decisions through a medical advisory council (which often recommended substantial expenditure but bore no accountability for the consequences) or expert committees that advised on clinical policies. Such committees have been described as 'functioning as a sort of Greek chorus', commenting on what was occurring on stage 'but not taking part in the play' (Chantler 1994: 17).

Nevertheless, resource pressures were starting to affect the relationship between clinicians and managers (then called administrators) and the general climate in hospitals. Meanwhile, pressure to redistribute resources from city centres to the growing urban fringes of Australia's large cities, especially Sydney and Melbourne, was beginning to affect hospital budgets. The impetus for change was most evident in hospitals, where what were once comfortable relationships between hospital managers and clinicians were beginning to fray.

The mid-1980s—following an international lead towards decentralised management structures in hospitals

In the mid-1980s one of America's most prestigious medical journals published an article describing a new decentralised management structure at the Johns Hopkins Hospital in Baltimore (Heyssel et al. 1984). A little later, similar changes were reported at a prestigious London teaching hospital, Guy's Hospital (Chantler 1990). Copies of these articles circulated widely. The organisational structures at the two hospitals were highly appealing to influential senior clinicians in Australia. Some Australian clinicians visited the overseas institutions and returned with reports that clinically led restructuring would reduce internal tensions and allow hospitals to cope with the growing resource constraints without unnecessarily diluting doctors' autonomy.

Some clinicians in Australia advanced proposals to restructure their hospital management systems along the lines of Johns Hopkins and Guy's hospitals. Their enthusiasm was based on a somewhat innocent assumption that management was a matter of common sense, and provided that the current managers could be 'tamed', removed, or replaced by clinicians, the tensions mounting within the hospitals would dissipate.

There was little understanding of the complexities of organisational change as a process, nor of the management skills required in complex, professionally based institutions. The focus was on organisational charts, with little regard for the more fundamental and difficult issues involved in changing organisational culture. As a result, change was usually thought to occur when a new organisational chart was adopted, and a few difficult managers replaced with clinician-managers. Few clinicians grasped the implications of becoming a clinician-manager.

The late 1980s—the tripartite institute model

In 1988 a management consulting firm began to promote a similar model of a decentralised management structure in which a hospital was comprised of numerous units (or 'institutes' or 'divisions') of approximately one hundred beds, each headed by a trio of executives (a doctor, a nurse, and a business manager), and all reporting to a single CEO (Hickie 1994; McCaughan and Piccone 1994). Faced with mounting financial pressure, many teaching hospitals restructured a part—or all—of their organisation according to the tripartite model. Thus there would be a CEO for the whole hospital and a tripartite model for the operational parts of it. At precisely the same time, New Zealand was moving to introduce a general management model, appointing a single CEO to replace their tripartite model (doctor, nurse, administrator), which had been in place for the management of the hospital as a whole.

Benchmarking also commenced in earnest. Although it focused mainly on the catering, diagnostic, and allied health departments, hospitals were also given comparative data on their staffing levels vis-à-vis similar institutions. The benchmarking program, introduced as it was at the very beginning of organisational reform, encouraged more rational and efficient deployment of staff, and succeeded to some extent. As the downsizing and restructuring continued over the years, efficiency gains became increasingly more difficult, and hospitals developed and employed other benchmarking processes.

Most managers reluctantly embraced the restructuring, which they saw as a threat to their future career prospects. Many believed that the outlook for full-time health managers was bleak, and that eventually hospitals would revert to a bygone era when doctors, and to some extent nurses, managed hospitals, combining their management role with ongoing clinical responsibilities. Hospital boards embraced, and in some cases initiated these changes; restructuring seemed to hold the promise of overcoming resource constraints. Some boards simply wanted to keep the clinicians happy.

Despite concerns on the part of full-time managers, or in some instances as a result of these concerns, the new management structures were adopted by a number of Australia's most prominent teaching hospitals. But the restructure usually did not result in any real sharing of power. In most cases managers devolved power in name only. Many hospitals established divisions, institutes, or clinical programs (the names varied but the intent was basically the same). These were similar in nature to the clinical directorates that were being introduced in British hospitals as a result of the policy initiatives underpinning the NHS Reforms.

About this time, the (then) Royal Australian College of Medical Administrators (RACMA), one of the postgraduate medical colleges, began a program of management education for clinicians to support the emerging cadre of clinician-managers. This was in addition to their already established education programs for full-time medical administrators. Other 'Management for Clinicians' programs began during the next few years.

The early 1990s—clinicians at the 'Top Table'

Faced with continuing resource pressures, some clinicians and managers realised in the early 1990s that genuine decentralisation involved more than the adoption of a new organisational chart. They began to understand that it was necessary to develop an agenda for change that was shared by top management and clinicians. This would inevitably involve a more radical restructuring, and led to the establishment of some form of 'Top Table' around which clinicians and full-time managers gathered to deliberate and decide on the future direction of the hospital. This forum was additional to the divisional, or similar, structure put in place to manage the ongoing delivery of current services.

Some clinicians, however, still saw these changes as imposed by management, despite their success. Some believed clinicians had not been given sufficient management training and development opportunities to play their new roles effectively. In hindsight, wider availability of such opportunities would have ensured that more clinicians understood the basis of the changes and constructively participated in their development.

The then Commonwealth Department of Human Services and Health was not directly involved in the management of hospitals, nor in driving the hospital restructuring that started to involve clinicians in management. However, the department stimulated the change process by funding a three-year program, the 'National Program of Management Development for Australian Clinicians' (1993–96), conducted through the RACMA. It enabled Australian clinicians and managers to participate as management teams in four-day off-site workshops in which they explored the pressures for change and discussed options for their hospital's future. Many of these teams returned to their institutions to introduce seminal changes, usually entailing more extensive involvement of clinicians in management.

The mid-1990s—the AMA endorses the changing role of clinicians

In recognition of the emergence of a growing number of Australian medical clinician-managers, in the mid-1990s the RACMA introduced a new category of college membership, specifically geared to meeting the management education needs of this group. The college also began conducting management programs in association with other clinical colleges.

Also recognising the changes that were spreading across the country, the AMA released a position statement in 1995 supporting and encouraging the involvement of clinicians in management (AMA 1995: 8). Their six-part statement advocated participation by medical practitioners in all levels of health care management; endorsed management structures that provided for clinicians' participation in planning, development and management decisions; and requested appropriate training and development opportunities to assist doctors in management.

The late 1990s—networking of clinical services 'beyond the hospital walls'

By the late 1990s, Australian hospitals contained a plethora of management models and structures. Most featured, to varying degrees, clinicians as managers of clinical services, and many institutions showed a real sharing of power between managers and clinicians in the overall management of the institution. Business manager roles were established in clinical units, and many institutions eliminated the traditional medical administration departments, devolving many management functions to clinical divisions or departments.

Although Australian hospitals have always engaged a large cadre of medically qualified, full-time health managers, the late 1990s also saw the re-emergence of the clinician–manager as CEO. Their numbers were still small, but this new development was, perhaps, an indicator of changes ahead.

Other developments emerging in the late 1990s included the development of specialist services networked across a specified population group. This presented new challenges for clinician–managers, as the hospital walls became more 'permeable' and the model of the 'boundaryless' hospital emerge (Braithwaite et al. 1994). Networks challenged traditional clinical rivalries and intensified the complexity of budgetary arrangements.

Further complications were introduced by moves to sharpen the community focus of traditional hospital services. Ambulatory and home-based services highlighted the need for better linkages between community-based GPs and hospitals. These forces for change, and the continued drive for technical efficiency and improvements in service quality and reliability, are the future challenges for clinician–managers.

The clinical colleges

By 1999, in addition to the RACMA, other clinical colleges such as the Royal Australasian College of Surgeons and the Royal Australian and New Zealand College of Psychiatrists had started to review their college training programs, taking into account the increasing involvement of clinicians in management.

Clinicians observed that expectations of their role were changing: 'Clinicians must now not only have good clinical skills', one said, 'but are also required to understand and have acquired skills in management.'

Another said, 'Once I thought that my role was to be a good clinician, to treat patients and to be a good surgeon. Now I see that I must also have a wider role and must involve myself in a management role in order to be a good clinician' (Pers. comm.). Although not all clinicians were expected to become clinician-managers or leaders, all clinicians who did not were expected to become good followers.

Progress of reform

As indicated earlier, the changes in the roles and functions of clinicians have been by no means uniform across the country or across all institutions. Indeed, in the late 1990s it was still possible to visit teaching hospitals that were in the early phases of change. In other hospitals, with different cultures and structures, clinicians were involved in both the management of the delivery of services, and the strategic management of their institutions, for almost a decade.

Some hospitals changed clinicians' roles in name only. They adopted new organisational structures but did not make fundamental changes in culture, systems, and procedures. These superficial changes may be counterproductive in the long term without a commitment to real change.

The most significant changes occurred in those institutions with a large full-time medical staff (either because of salaried positions or a large full-time academic staff). Rural institutions and those with a predominantly part-time, visiting medical staff embraced change with less enthusiasm.

New Zealand

The picture in New Zealand has been somewhat different, though it appears that hospitals there are now embarking on a path of change similar to Australian hospitals. One feature of the health reforms introduced in New Zealand in the early 1990s was a concern about the 'provider capture' and the influence of the professions (see Chapter 7). Although some managers who were appointed to new health management roles had prior training and experience in health, many managers appointed at that time had little or no health experience. Non-health managers with a strong emphasis on a business culture were actively recruited into New Zealand's hospitals. They came from diverse backgrounds and generally had very strong business credentials.

But the efficiencies expected to flow from the new 'managerialism' did not eventuate, or at least not to the extent required. By the mid-1990s resource pressures were still evident and the tide had begun to turn: clinicians were brought into management roles in their institutions. In 1995 the NZ Ministry of Health reviewed how management education for clinicians might be introduced, and whether a medical management clinical college should be established in New Zealand, along similar lines to the RACMA. It was eventually decided by clinicians and managers in New Zealand that the RACMA would be invited to extend its sphere of interest to include New Zealand. In 1998 it became the Royal Australasian College of Medical Administrators. By this time various 'management for clinicians' programs had begun in New Zealand.

The personal journey of the clinician-manager

Clinicians who embraced a management role during this period experienced a series of transformations that was unique for each individual. Anecdotal comments from a wide range of Australian clinicians suggest that they also had much in common.

Most clinicians have commented that they felt unprepared for their new management roles; they felt overwhelmed, especially with management jargon. For many, the ambiguity and complexity that surrounded many management decisions contrasted powerfully with their formal training in science-based, clinical decision-making. Many addressed these conflicts by attending management courses, or by reading. Their experiences led many to rethink their role within the overall health system, and, for some, long-held assumptions about clinical priorities.

Seeing the 'bigger picture' presented new problems for some clinicians, especially in their relations with their clinical colleagues. Often there were tensions between new clinician–managers and other clinicians who did not share the new 'bigger picture of health', or who resented the control exercised by their clinician–manager colleagues, who now held budgetary authority. For many of these new managers, resolving day-to-day conflicts was a major, and often very draining, part of their new role. Some also described tensions with managers who, they believed, had devolved accountability for a range of key resource decisions without fully devolving responsibility and control. Many clinician–managers also experienced a personal tension between their role as manager (and therefore budget-holder), and their role as clinician, because the two roles were not always aligned. For example, the 'clinician' might have felt ethically obliged to recommend a treatment or intervention that the 'clinician–manager' knew the current departmental budget could not afford. These conflicts needed to be recognised and addressed. Yet clinician–managers found little support as they grappled with these dilemmas. By contrast, health managers who did not simultaneously maintain a clinical practice did not commonly face such role conflicts.

A tension between clinical work and managerial work arose from the conflict, confronted by clinician-managers, between the essentially autonomous, short-term perspective of many clinical decisions and the 'collective, long-term, team based, resource procurement nature of formal management' (Burgoyne and Lorbiecki 1993: 253).

'Clinicians as Managers'—Current and Future Issues in Health Reform

In Australia, as in the USA and United Kingdom, the involvement of clinicians in management has yet to have a profound impact on the prevailing medical culture. This is not to say that change might not be imminent, especially through some of the clinical colleges, but rather that attention to date has concentrated on institutional restructuring of hospitals, and to some extent hospital culture, with little significant impact on the culture of the medical profession *per se*.

Writing in the *Medical Journal of Australia*, Perkins et al. (1997) reported a study of the perceptions of medical specialists in Australia, New Zealand, and the United Kingdom on recent changes in health services in their countries. They found that British specialists saw themselves as having greater influence on management priorities than did their Australian or New Zealand colleagues. This might reflect the greater scope for clinician-managers in the United Kingdom, or the extent to which such managers have permeated the British health system.

Writers such as Burgoyne and Lorbiecki (1993) also observe that reforms initiated to change the role and behaviour of clinicians have not (yet!) fundamentally altered the prevailing medical culture in the United Kingdom. They predict that conflict within the system will increase in the future 'if the consequences of management control systems and objectives percolate down through the management hierarchy and cross into the medical domain' (1993: 248). At the heart of the conflict is a struggle for additional resources within perpetually constrained national and regional health budgets. This dilemma can never be resolved at the level of hospital management or clinical directors. Conflict between managers and clinical directors is thus avoidable only if fundamental decisions about health system resources are resolved by higher authorities at national, state and regional levels. Alternatively, clinicians may have to opt for professional regulation by clinician-managers. These issues pertain equally to Australia and New Zealand.

Key Lessons

There are several important lessons from more than a decade of experience in involving clinicians in management in Australia.

1. Clinicians must become involved in health reform, and must be helped to do so. In a recent editorial in the *Medical Journal of Australia* on doctors and health reform, Duckett (1997) says 'the medical profession (and other health professionals) must be given the opportunity to engage in the reform process'. Doctors have had a long history of obstructing processes of reform, or even stopping them outright. They should be encouraged to use their powers to support reform. This is most likely to occur when the clinicians themselves are included in the development of the agenda for change, where they have developed a broader vision for health, and where they already have a significant management role.

2. Engaging clinicians in hospital management will facilitate reform at the micro level (e.g. the introduction of casemix, new quality-management systems, and clinical guidelines and pathways). Some clinicians will also become involved in wider aspects of health reform at the state and national level. This will generate a group of clinicians who will bring to policy debates and other discussions a wider range of clinical and managerial experience than might emerge from either group alone.

3. Clinician-manager roles in the operational aspects of service delivery must be differentiated from a wider role in the overall management of the institution. Some clinicians must be involved in this wider role. But senior managers are mistaken who think that because clinicians are involved in management at the service delivery level they are effectively involved at the institutional level; they will soon find that these clinician-managers become frustrated. Some clinician-managers will even forsake their management role, and confrontation between clinicians and managers in the institution will result. At the hospital level, clinicians must be engaged in both the operational management of service delivery and in the strategic or corporate management of their institutions. To achieve this, changes will be required on the part of both managers and clinicians, and the agenda for change must be

developed and shared by both groups. Hospitals in which cultures have been characterised by a 'them-and-us' attitude will not survive in the complex changing environment that now exists in health.

4. To successfully integrate clinicians into management, it is not enough to change organisational structures by introducing new organisational charts. Changes are needed in institutional culture, as well as in delegations of authority and other policies and procedures. Implementation of change of this kind will require a sustained program of organisational development. Superficial changes will be counterproductive in the longer term.

5. Though highly educated in clinical areas, many clinicians will be encountering management terms and concepts for the first time. They will require a program of management development offering opportunities for formal and informal learning.

6. Clinicians must be warned about the likelihood of a 're-entry' problem after returning from management education programs. They will need support to reassimilate and maintain their enthusiasm for change. These programs are likely to heighten enthusiasm for change and generate many new ideas. When they return to the workplace clinicians will quickly identify ongoing problems, but they may confront apathy and ignorance in clinical colleagues who have not been exposed to the same new ideas. Many will become frustrated and will need support.

7. Because clinical and management paradigms differ, individuals must be supported to understand and work through these differences. Medically qualified people who move into full-time management roles may adopt a predominantly management paradigm. In contrast, clinician-managers will continue to operate in both worlds, and may not always cope easily with these conflicting paradigms, which full-time managers do not have to face.

8. Especially in the early stages of their management responsibilities, clinician-managers may need time and support to work through the personal issues that confront most such people. These include juggling the time demands of a clinical load with managerial responsibilities and family commitments, and accommodating pressures to keep up with the literature in their clinical area.

9. For some, the time spent in management will be at the expense of their clinical work, and they will experience a loss in income as a result. Clinician-managers must be adequately compensated for their management work.

10. It is vital to identify, encourage, and support emerging leaders among the clinical ranks in the early stages of any organisational change involving clinicians in management roles. These leaders will be effective role

models for other clinicians, and will gather around them clinical colleagues who will form the early vanguard of clinician-managers in the organisation. These agents of change will usually be identifiable by their interest in management and broader issues of health, and they will have earned the respect of their clinical colleagues, usually because of their clinical expertise. Some might already have been identified as leaders. Even for such keen and talented individuals, however, the early stages of change will be difficult, and they will need a great deal of support from senior management.

11. Clinician-managers are much more likely to bring about change within the clinical ranks, in both management matters and in better clinical practice, than will full-time managers acting alone.

12. Managers themselves might well feel insecure, and might be threatened by already powerful doctors moving into management. Managers, too, must be supported and encouraged to understand that, contrary to their expectations, the power that clinician-managers can bring to their management roles is most likely to provide additional support to the full-time manager.

13. Experience to date suggests that some clinicians adopt a formal clinician-manager role for a few years and then return to full-time clinical work. It is therefore imperative to identify and encourage other clinical leaders to take on a clinician-manager role, if only for a few years.

14. Attention tends to focus on the development of senior clinicians, but it is important to develop a succession plan, and to provide opportunities for younger clinicians to develop their management and leadership capabilities, thereby avoiding a gap in managerial levels in future years. Many younger clinicians will already display qualities of leadership, and their potential will be evident both to their clinical colleagues and to managers.

Conclusion

In contrast to other health reform initiatives, the introduction of clinicians into management was not the result of an explicit policy. Unlike other aspects of reform discussed in this book, the changing role of clinicians is a story of uncoordinated and incremental change against a backdrop of convergent ideas. Australia's incremental approach to change in this area has been influenced by, and has responded to, broader domestic and international trends.

The shift from clinician to manager in Australia and New Zealand has been more characteristic of a grassroots process of decentralisation than a centrally driven policy shift, as was the case in the United Kingdom. There the 'resource management initiatives' that brought clinicians into management were explicit NHS policy (Burgoyne and Lorbiecki 1993).

The important exceptions to incrementalism in Australia are the changes introduced in primary care. Australia has never had an explicit policy of organisational change for primary care such as exists in the NHS GP Fundholding initiatives in the United Kingdom. Nevertheless, some initiatives have successfully fostered major organisational change. These include the 'Better Practice' grants sponsored by the Commonwealth Department of Health, and changes to the basis of primary-care funding.

Change in the clinician's role was often supported and encouraged by actions of central agencies, such as the state departments of health and other bodies. For example, it could be argued that the casemix reforms introduced in Victoria in 1993 to increase the technical efficiency of Victorian hospitals hastened the involvement of clinicians in management. At the national level, the Commonwealth funding of the National Hospitals Demonstration Project and funding of the National Program of Management Development for Australian Clinicians (1993–96) also provided support.

It can also be argued that involving clinicians in management has been a means to an end, not an end in itself. It was not, in Australia or New Zealand, merely a veiled attempt to change the current medical culture. The means was encouraging clinicians to share in the difficult task of decision-making within a resource-constrained environment. The end was restraining the growth in the cost of health care. Since health systems can no longer afford unfettered clinical autonomy, it is argued, involving clinicians as managers might do better in aligning clinical decisions with the health system's priorities and constraints.

In conclusion, the transition from clinician to manager has been a central feature of health reform in Australia and, to a lesser extent, in New Zealand. Is the involvement of clinicians in management an end in itself, or a means to an end—to close the gap between resource consumption and resource constraints, by introducing accountability at the point where the decision is made to consume resources? Regardless of the answer, clinicians, particularly doctors, are fundamental to the success of health reform. They can wield their power to expedite or to derail reform. Experience in Australia and New Zealand has shown that they must be included as part of a deliberately designed process that gives them the additional skills and expertise to participate in a partnership to manage resources as well as health care.

PART III

MODELS OF HEALTH SECTOR REFORM

Introduction

Abby Bloom

This section contains a series of case studies illustrating and analysing the experience to date in health sector reform in Australia and New Zealand. The chapters have been selected not only to illustrate common priorities in reform—primary care, hospital services, and the increasing role of the private sector—but also to consider other aspects of health that may have an equal or greater impact on health outcomes, public health and health promotion. Health care finance, a major aspect of health reform, is not included in this section (see Chapter 4). The reason is that the mixed public/private models of the two countries, both incorporating elements of a universal health insurance mechanism, do not offer up any compelling lessons at this time. As stressed by several authors in Parts I and II, notably Somjen, despite a fixation on finance issues throughout the reforms, little of import has been achieved. Readers interested in understanding more about the features and limitations of Australia's Medicare health insurance system are referred to Swerissen and Duckett (1997).

In Chapter 10 Malcolm describes the New Zealand experience in primary care, where improvements in the effectiveness and quality of care have been introduced as a central component of reform. There, as in so many other countries, primary care is dominated by GPs. In true participant-observer style, the author documents the measures introduced at different levels to preserve and strengthen this essential 'gatekeeper' role. He contrasts the New Zealand experience with simultaneous events in Australia. In Australia reform of primary care also had the object of containing costs, and was designed to influence GPs' capacity to trigger other health care costs (notably pathology, diagnostic radiology, and pharmaceuticals) and manage others (notably hospitalisation).

Underlying Malcolm's observations is a strong endorsement of general practice. The case study emphasises how strong clinical and social values persist in general practice in New Zealand, despite the intrusions of reform. Most GPs wish to preserve their professional independence, and fear the stigma associated with for-profit commercial enterprise. Of particular interest for reform of primary care in other settings is the substantial variation in the structure and commercial linkages of the IPAs of New Zealand. Malcolm considers this to be the most significant achievement of general practice reform to date.

The author emphasises the time needed to implement reforms, reminding us that even reform of a single level of service delivery has many dimensions. Improving and installing information systems in doctors' surgeries, developing continuing education courses and incentives, and improving coordination between primary care and other levels of service delivery are just a few examples.

Chapter 11 examines the different paths of reform adopted by Australia's two most influential states, Victoria and New South Wales. The chapter is designed to illustrate how political values, expressed in policies, 'ideas in good currency', and formulae, can precipitate very different reform processes in two adjacent states. Stoelwinder was formerly chief executive in a large public hospital and health care network. Viney was a senior policy adviser to the NSW government through the process of reform.

Writing about the state of Victoria, Australia's most fervent adherent to the principles of economic rationalism during the 1990s, Stoelwinder adopts the theoretical approach of Alford to examine how 'ideas in good currency' ('convergent ideas') can influence health reform. He describes clearly how the enthusiasm for economic rationalism led to reforms that focused on improving technical efficiency, and emphasised hospital-based services. Viney contrasts the experience of New South Wales, which, through the tenures of both Labor and Liberal (conservative) governments, has placed a higher priority on equitable access to quality health care (allocative efficiency) than on optimising the cost-effectiveness of health care finance and delivery (technical efficiency).

In Chapter 12 Lyon addresses the rationalisation of 'parallel health systems'. The author was the architect of Australia's most successful 'parallel' health system reform, undertaken by the Commonwealth Department of Veterans' Affairs (Repatriation Commission). Parallel health systems are systems that coexist to serve defined groups of people, usually through entitlement, and usually serve different, though potentially overlapping, populations. They are nearly ubiquitous, having developed over time to provide a broad range of health services to military veterans, police officers, railway employees, social security beneficiaries, and others, depending on the country. These complete health systems coexist with services funded by ministries of health and are valued for the speedy access and sometimes superior service they provide.

As in most countries, the veterans' health care system is a publicly funded and operated health system that parallels, and duplicates, the public hospital system. The reform of the veterans' hospital system in Australia in an impressive and successful process with international relevance. When this case study was described to observers of the Veterans' Administration hospital system in the USA, their reaction was, 'Impossible. It can't be done!'.

Lyon's chapter describes not only the rationale for the reform, and the important steps, but also the crucial success factors in undertaking similar reforms. Unlike many other hospital reforms, it has been carefully documented and nurtured independent of political vagaries. The reform of Australia's veterans' health system is ongoing, has not yet been evaluated in terms of health outcomes, and is by no means perfect, but stands out as a reform success story.

Chapter 13 examines the multiplicity of privatisation options available in just one arena of reform, hospital services. Privatisation is often the first recourse of health reformers trying to break the impasse between resource constraints and incessantly increasing demand for, and cost of, health care. An initial reaction may be 'Privatise—sell assets!'. This chapter illustrates the many creative options available under the umbrella of privatisation. Citing the experience in Australia during the 1990s, the case study demonstrates that governments can foster a very varied response from the private sector, and that 'privatisation' has many more meanings than 'sell the assets to the private sector' or merely 'buy private services under contract'.

The chapter identifies two factors that appear to be crucial to successful involvement of the private sector: a partnership-like relationship that enables each party to achieve its objectives, and very carefully crafted contracts that operationalise each party's obligations and commitments. The variants include public sector purchasing of health services from existing private hospitals; privately financed construction and operation of hospitals strictly for the purpose of public provision; and private construction and operation of a new facility on an existing public hospital site. The chapter focuses on the third variant, called 'co-location', and examines why it has become the preferred approach for both public and private sectors in Australia.

Amazingly, Australia's experience in hospital privatisation has never been catalogued or analysed systematically, in spite of the fact that it has become the principal engine for the redevelopment, expansion and reform of the nation's hospital system. The author, who has been involved in the growing participation of the private sector in Australia since the first co-locations of the late 1980s, also advises on privatisation internationally. She does not promote a particular view on privatisation, seeing it instead as governments' inevitable response to lack of funding for health care, particularly for capital infrastructure development.

Chapters 14 and 15 are case studies illustrating how governments can embed public health objectives and mechanisms in the health reform process. Public health and health promotion have been chosen for case studies because they are not often considered essential to the course of reform, and are often pushed aside as governments focus on more pressing elements of health systems (e.g. hospitals and primary care). Yet they are crucial to the ostensible goals of reform—improvements in health as well as in the technical and allocative efficiency of health care systems.

As noted in other chapters, health insurance and hospitals tend to become the almost exclusive focus of reform because they are cohesive, tangible facility-based organisations with a hierarchical reporting structure, and are more amenable to reform. They also make urgent claims for attention, because they highlight the life-and-death nature of health care and have highly vocal and politically influential stakeholders. Yet downsizing, closing, or relocating hospitals—the very thought of which may cause bureaucrats to run for shelter—is far easier than defining and implementing a role for public health and health promotion.

Chapter 14 describes in detail the process through which diffuse and sometimes competing public health initiatives were coordinated under a single umbrella, Australia's 'Public Health Partnerships'. The themes of the case study can be generalised to most health reform settings: public health goals can get lost in the reform process because of the forces that focus attention and effort on treatment services. The reform process provides both the opportunity and the obligation to reassess and align reform efforts with public health goals. When public health initiatives are examined, however, they are seen to be well intentioned but usually fragmented and overlapping—leading to uncoordinated, disparate and sometimes wasteful efforts.

Lin and King are strong advocates not only for public health, but also for what is known as 'the new public health'—a more activist, comprehensive approach to contemporary health problems such as heart disease, mental health, and other major causes of morbidity and mentality. Yet the rhetoric of nearly all health reform includes the exalted goals of improving the population's health status, and often redressing inequities in health and health care. Certainly the health policies of Australia and New Zealand have maintained these aims throughout the period of reform.

Chapter 15 is one of the most challenging in the volume, especially for those who consider themselves veterans or doyens of health reform. Galbally argues that many health reformers have lost sight of the ultimate aim of reform—improving health. Allocative and technical improvements are means to an end, and, although probably necessary, are insufficient to achieve that end when the real determinants of health status are fundamental environmental and behavioural factors.

Galbally, a well-known and highly respected practitioner of health promotion, uses the pioneering case of VicHealth, the Victorian Health Promotion Foundation, to show how governments can incorporate, within reform mechanisms, structures that influence some of the principal determinants of health. She is a strong supporter of the principles of health promotion embodied in the 'Ottawa Charter', and is highly critical of more traditional approaches for changing health behaviours.

10

Primary-Care Reform in New Zealand: Key Contrasts with Australia

Laurence Malcolm

It is now widely recognised that New Zealand's recent health reforms have been possibly the most radical of any OECD country. Implemented in 1993 and based on the purchaser/provider split, the reforms emphasised commercial goals and competition. The unrealistic expectations of these earlier reforms have now been largely rejected, even by government. The reform process is now refocusing on health outcomes and professional incentives.

The most striking success story of the reforms has been the rapid progress towards integrated care. Integrated care has been initiated and largely driven not only by general practitioners, through independent practitioner associations, but also by a range of community-based providers, Māori among them. IPAs, similar in many respects to Australia's divisions of general practice, now represent more than 70 per cent of GPs. The key goals of IPAs are to promote better health outcomes for patients and communities, to ensure the best use of primary-care resources, and to improve the quality of care in general practice.

As discussed in detail below, IPA funding has come mainly from savings retained from holding and managing budgets for pharmaceutical and laboratory services. IPAs are now establishing a wide range of joint ventures with hospital-based secondary care providers, in a move towards integrated care that may be as extensive as in any country.

Overview of New Zealand's Health Reforms

The main features of New Zealand's health system, and the process of health reform, have been described and analysed elsewhere (Laugeson and Salmond 1994; Malcolm and Barnett 1994; Hornblow 1997; Malcolm

1997a; and see Chapter 3). Reform, under various labels, has been a feature of the health system since 1980. The most recent reforms, announced in 1991, were initiated by the National government in 1993. These radical reforms were based on the purchaser/provider split. Four regional health authorities were formed and given fully integrated budgets to purchase all health and disability services from a wide range of competing public and private providers. The existing area health boards, which provided hospital, community, and public health services, were converted to Crown health enterprises and expected to function as commercial entities.

In 1996 the newly elected National–New Zealand First coalition government, recognising that the commercial aspects of the health reforms had failed, announced the amalgamation of the four regional health authorities into a single Health Funding Authority. The HFA, implemented on 1 January 1998, instituted a major review of primary-care policy. As a result of the review's recommendations, CHEs are being restructured once again as hospital and health services, and the government is shifting its emphasis to better health outcomes as the 'bottom line' for all services.

The largely unsuccessful attempts to reform the secondary-care sector have overshadowed much more important and successful developments in New Zealand's primary-care sector. The latter reforms are the main focus of this chapter.

The Organisation and Financing of the Primary Medical-Care Sector in New Zealand

Both organisational and management issues have received much attention in New Zealand. Organisationally, health providers in New Zealand fall into four broad groupings, the defining characteristics of which are summarised in Table 10.1 (p. 185). The groupings are hospital and related services, primary medical care and related services, disability services, and public health services. Only the primary medical-care services are discussed in detail in this chapter.

Primary medical-care services include those services provided by GPs, associated investigations such as laboratory and radiology, and the dispensing of pharmaceuticals. Key providers in this grouping are GPs, practice nurses, midwives, pharmacists, physiotherapists and, in a few situations, social workers.

Primary medical-care services are now provided by about 3000 GPs, some solo practitioners but most now in group practices. Attempts were

Table 10.1 Main defining features of the four health and related service divisions (NZ$1 = A$ 0.85, 1998)

Feature	Hospital and related services	Primary-care services	Disability services	Public health
Scope	Hospital and community-based services	General practice, pharmaceutical and diagnostic	Assessment, rehabilitation and long-stay care	Health protection and health promotion
Ownership	Mainly government but small private specialist component	Almost entirely private	Mixed government and non-government agencies	Mainly government
Source of financing	Almost entirely government insignificant fee contribution	Largely government-subsidised with one-third private fees	Mixed government and charitable donations	Almost entirely government
Type of financing	Capitation for geographically defined population	Fee for service but moving to capitation	Individual social welfare entitlement	Contracting with Public Health Commission
Annual government expenditure	$2.3 billion	$1.4 billion	$0.8 billion	$89 million
Organisation	Boards of management	Individual entrepreneurs	Mixed including boards of management	Mostly within CHEs
Focus of service	Population served	Individual patient	Individual client	Population served
Main type of care	Acute	Episodic	Long-term	Public health
Community involvement	Significant	Increasing	High	High
Budgetary control	Tight with no growth in last decade	6% annual growth in decade to 1993	Related to individual entitlement	Tight with recent decline in expenditure
Emphasis	Specialised medical treatment	Generalist	Maximising independence and autonomy	Improving public health
Place of the hospital	Central but decreasing	Useful	Seen as threatening	Minimal
Preventive public health focus	Increasing	Important	Essential	Essential
Main barrier to access	Long waiting times	Financial	Lack of community services	Finance

Source: Malcolm and Barnett 1994

made, with the passage of the *Social Security Act 1938*, to make these services a full charge on government, preferably by capitation, but these moves were strongly resisted by the medical profession, which saw them as a threat to its independence. As a result, GPs have remained free to charge their patients on a fee-for-service basis, at levels higher than the general medical services (GMS) benefit or subsidy.

GMS subsidies, along with pharmaceutical subsidies, are subject to patient co-payment, which is pegged to age and income level of the patient. Apart from government subsidies, general practice is also paid for the treatment of accident victims by the Accident and Rehabilitation Compensation and Insurance Corporation (ARCI), which provides for the treatment, rehabilitation, and compensation of accidents on a no-fault basis. Financing of general practice has, until recently, been largely on a fee-for-service basis.

Table 10.2 (p. 187) summarises expenditure on primary medical care and related services in New Zealand for the year 1997/98; Table 10.3 (p. 187) contrasts similar expenditures in Australia for 1994/95. Organ imaging is not included in the New Zealand figures as this is almost totally unsubsidised, patients either paying privately or receiving free services from a hospital. Although the years and currencies are different, the contrasts are still important. Total GP revenue per consultation, from government and private sources combined, is higher in New Zealand ($33.50 with the inclusion of the ARCI), compared with $22.90 in Australia. The most notable difference between the countries is the level of pharmaceutical expenditure, which is very much lower in Australia, presumably due to the much lower amount paid by the Australian government for pharmaceuticals.

Primary medical-care services are complemented to a varying extent by services provided by non–government agencies, such as private physiotherapists, the Family Planning Association, and the Plunket Society (which provides most preventive child health services).

Reform of the Primary-Care Sector

Apart from relatively minor changes in subsidy levels, organisation of primary-care services was unchanged for decades. But reform in these services is increasingly being seen as the key to the current reform process, with significant moves towards budget-holding and increasing accountability, and a major shift from fee-for-service to capitated funding (Malcolm and Barnett 1994; Malcolm and Powell 1996, 1997; Health Funding Authority 1998a).

Table 10.2 Government and patient expenditure (NZ$) in New Zealand on primary medical care and related services for 1997/98 (GST-inclusive)

Category	Expenditure per capita ($)	Expenditure per GP ($)	Expenditure per consultation ($)
Patient fee			
GP	91.8	130 712	17.8
Pharmacist[a]	91.8	130 712	17.8
General medical services	55.1	78 427	10.7
Accident Compensation Corporation (ACC)	21.5	28 086	5.0
Laboratory	27.3	38 834	6.2
Pharmaceutical	145.7	207 326	37.3
Practice nurse	8.9	12 649	1.6
Total	442.1	626 746	96.4
Private	183.6	261 424	35.6
Public	258.4	365 322	60.8

a Estimate only. Figures are GST-exclusive.

Source: Figures derived from HFA Funding Formula and unpublished data from a recent study for the HFA Northern Division and ACC statistics.

Table 10.3 Government and patient expenditure (A$) in Australia on primary medical-care and related services for 1994/95 (NZ$ 1.0 = A$ 0.85)

Category	Expenditure per capita ($)	Expenditure per GP ($)	Expenditure per consultation ($)
Medicare benefits			
public	119.1	146 000	21.1
private	9.8	11 000	1.8
Laboratory	29.7	34 000	5.4
Organ imaging	26.8	31 000	4.9
Pharmaceutical	90.8	108 000	17.1
Total			
Private	264.6	319 000	48.5
Public	9.8	11 000	1.8

Source: Based on data from Commonwealth Department of Health and Family Services 1997

These developments have arisen out of concern by government that utilisation and expenditure in the primary medical-care sector have been largely uncontrolled. Total expenditure on primary-care services increased, on average, at a rate of 6.1 per cent annually over the decade to 1993 (Malcolm 1993). More recently, large increases in total expenditure have continued, especially in pharmaceutical and laboratory costs. The establishment of RHAs in 1993, with fully integrated budgets that include primary-care services, meant that for the first time GPs could negotiate new initiatives with a decentralised funding body that included budget-holding.

The emergence of IPAs

A number of primary-care pilot projects had been established in 1991. Most of these employed a budget-holding approach to the management of primary-care resources, akin to the GP fund-holding approach in the United Kingdom (Glennister and Matsaganis 1993). These initiatives led to an increasing number of independent practice associations throughout the country (Malcolm and Powell 1996, 1997). About thirty IPAs now exist throughout New Zealand, ranging in size from large general practices of 6–8 members to the 340-member ProCare Health in Auckland, and covering more than 70 per cent of GPs.

A recent development has been the formation of Carenet, a contracting entity representing the interests of those GPs who do not wish to enter directly into budget-holding contracts with the HFA. It is expected that eventually almost all GPs in New Zealand will be in some form of contractual relationship with the HFA.

IPAs have provided leadership in several areas that have increased the level of collective professional accountability in general practice, or what is now being called 'clinical governance' (Scally and Donaldson 1998). They include alternatives to GMS such as capitation; encouraging the development of patient age-sex registers and patient registration; increased awareness of quality of care issues; improved information systems; and progressive budget-holding for laboratory, pharmaceuticals, maternity, and secondary-care services (Malcolm and Powell 1996, 1997). Nearly 100 per cent of IPA practices now have computerised age-sex registers, largely as a result of IPA involvement. Computerised practices now routinely provide data to IPAs, which use the data to analyse and feed back to GPs information on variation in per capita expenditure, and to monitor the effects of budget-holding strategies.

One important step in the development of the practice register has been the extension of the unique national patient number, the national health index (NHI), to practice registers. Initiated in the secondary sector, a NHI has now been allocated to 95 per cent of New Zealanders. The NHI is attached to all claims, prescriptions, and laboratory requests. It thus serves as the key identifying piece of data enabling linkage of all health events and all health care expenditure. It makes it possible to identify patients and their characteristics and to assign patients to practices, and it permits patient data to be linked with utilisation and expenditure of both primary and secondary services.

Māori and community trusts

The reform process has stimulated a range of other primary-care initiatives. These include contracting (including budget-holding) by community groups and Māori tribal organisations, and the progressive empowering of communities both to provide and to contract for their own primary health care services. About 6 per cent of all primary care is provided by groups owned and managed by the community, and their coverage is increasing.

Some of these groups serve disadvantaged populations. Some employ their GPs and other staff directly. This is an important innovation, because utilisation of primary-care services has historically been low, and serious equity problems exist in access to care (Malcolm 1997).

Factors promoting primary-care reform

The initial impetus for IPAs came from a few enthusiastic GPs. They were also supported by the newly formed RHAs, though with some reservations. With their limited and capitated budgets, RHAs were persuaded that giving budgets to IPAs to manage fee-for-service expenditure, especially for pharmaceutical and laboratory services, offered the best strategy to reduce their risk from cost escalation in those expenditure areas. Despite the obvious need for collaboration between IPAs and RHAs, however, relationships between them were often conflicting and even destructive.

RHAs initially offered contracts to IPAs for laboratory and pharmaceutical services. Funding levels were based on historical expenditure, adjusted for projected growth, plus financial support for development costs. As an incentive, IPAs were able to retain all or a significant proportion of savings from budgets held to cover administrative costs, information systems, new services, and educational programs. Budget-holding involved a series of new activities: guideline development of personal feedback to IPA members on prescribing and laboratory use, peer group reviews, and educational programs to improve prescribing and laboratory use. The main aim of these programs was improving the quality of general practice rather than cost savings.

Early results of budget-holding in general practice

Most IPAs are now involved in budget-holding for laboratory and pharmaceutical services. An evaluation of laboratory budget-holding by Pegasus Medical Group, an IPA in Christchurch with 208 members, showed savings of over 23 per cent of total laboratory expenditure, as well as a reduction in the wide variation in laboratory expenditure per consultation

(Kerr et al. 1996). These savings are being used to improve patient services, such as improving access to care for children and the terminally ill, health promotion programs, and education and training. Immunisation rates among Pegasus Medical Group patients increased to 93 per cent in Christchurch, largely as a result of recall systems instituted by the IPA (Bell et al. 1997). Pegasus Medical Group substantially funded a new chair in general practice in the Christchurch School of Medicine in 1996 to support education and research programs in general practice.

Evaluations of pharmaceutical budget-holding in a number of IPAs have shown much more modest savings (only 5–10 per cent) than the laboratory services savings in the Pegasus Medical Group (Malcolm 1997b). ProCare Health, the largest IPA based in Auckland, with 340 members, began an extensive program of pharmaceutical management in 1995. Twenty-two cell groups, each with fifteen members, met monthly to formulate guidelines for prescribing practice. The guidelines covered twenty-eight clinical conditions. Clinicians receive and discuss personal feedback on prescribing behaviour and compare their costs with the ProCare mean cost. Attendance in cell groups reached 80 per cent. The program is supported by a central information system, pharmacy facilitators who visit each practice, and an incentive system that enables the IPA to retain savings. In spite of these efforts, ProCare pharmaceutical expenditures were only 5 per cent less than the national average in 1995 and 1996 (Malcolm 1997b). Similar results were found in a number of other IPAs.

Almost all IPAs have rejected the use of savings for personal gain (e.g. payment of dividends to members as shareholders). Although debate continues, it is generally agreed that savings from government-funded primary care should be directed into improved services. Most GPs see retaining savings for personal use as both unprofessional and unethical (Malcolm and Powell 1996). However, several IPAs, totalling about 200 members, are financially supported by First Health, which in turn has been established by Aetna Health, a large US insurance group with strong commercial interests in IPA development. These and other IPAs tend to take a more commercial approach to management. For example, First Health GPs are funded on a capitated basis.

Although they are made up of private, entrepreneurial and competing members, IPAs claim to be professional bodies seeking to advance the status and standards of primary medical care and, in doing so, to manage increasing amounts of public money to achieve public goals. This has not stopped accusations of a profit motive. Many IPAs are anxious to avoid the appearance of using their profit-making powers for personal gain. Some have deliberately become not-for-profit entities.

The growth of capitated primary care

Capitated funding for GP consultations (i.e. a fee for each enrolled patient) as an alternative to the fee-for-service system was introduced to New Zealand with the *Social Security Act 1938*, but very few GPs took up this option. Capitation of GMS was introduced as a means of payment in Otumoetai Health Centre in Tauranga in 1979, and subsequently adopted by a number of general practices, such as union health centres in the 1980s (Malcolm 1998a). In the 1993 health reforms, it became a preferred funding method for general practice in many centres serving Māori.

The main thrust towards capitation of GMS payments came from the Midland RHA where, as at June 1997, 45 per cent of GPs were paid on capitation. This contrasted markedly with other regions, in which payment by capitation ranged from 4.8 to 12 per cent (Ministry of Health 1998).

Support for capitation from IPA leadership has strengthened, particularly for capitation inclusive of referred laboratory and pharmaceutical services. A survey of IPAs in late 1994 showed 30 per cent supported this option, but the level of support had risen to over 50 per cent by the end of 1996 (Malcolm and Powell 1997). Strong support was evinced for an inclusive model of capitation at a meeting of representative IPAs in April 1998.

HFA policy, capitated funding and the response of general practice

The HFAs' directions for general practice were set out in 'The Next Five Years in General Practice' (Health Funding Authority 1998a). They included the following objectives:

- community confidence in the provision of quality primary care to meet needs, and based on the Treaty of Waitangi;
- proactive, population-focused, and well managed;
- better outcomes/effective and efficient use of resources;
- continuity, teamwork and coordination; and
- targeting services to those with the greatest needs, who have a potential to benefit.

Other aims included contracting consistency, service quality, population-based funding, equitable allocation of resources, and workforce development. The new funding arrangements stressed population enrolment, equitable funding based on need rather than historical funding, performance incentives, and collective accountability.

As with other proposed changes to a health system, and especially those that involve philosophical as well as financial issues, the proposals sparked

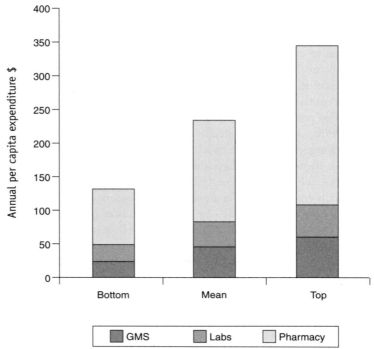

Figure 10.1 Comparison of annual per capita expenditure on GMS, laboratory and pharmaceutical services in bottom and top 10% of practices, as compared with the mean, in IPAs serving an average population

Source: Malcolm 1998a

vocal opposition from general practice, particularly from GPs who do not belong to IPAs. Although IPA leadership is supportive of capitation for the most part, the rank-and-file membership of some IPAs expresses misgivings. Their main objection is to compulsion, rather than choice, in moving from fee-for-service to capitated GMS. Experience in Midland, however, indicates that these objections may be based as much on philosophical as financial grounds. Few GPs would have the detailed statistical understanding of their practice populations to have calculated the financial consequences of capitation.

Obstacles to implementing capitated funding

Defining the denominator population
A major impediment to the implementation of capitated funding is inability to define the denominator population. Denominator population refers to the number of people in a population who constitute the defined group used as the basis for calculating per capita rates. For example, a

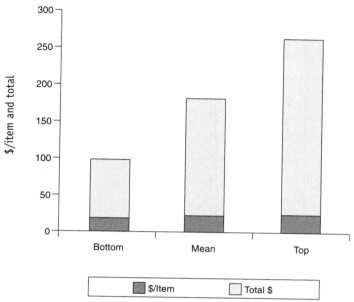

Figure 10.2 Comparison of the expenditure per item and total annual per capita expenditure in bottom and top 10% of practices, as compared with the mean, showing that the variation is almost entirely due to volume differences

Source: Malcolm 1998a

population of 1000 with an annual expenditure of $200 000 on pharmaceuticals has a per capita rate of expenditure of $200 ($200 000/1000).

In order to define their registered populations for capitation purposes, many IPAs, especially in the northern region of the HFA, have merged their practice registers by name, gender, and date of birth. Through this process, IPAs have assigned each patient to a practice within the IPA, usually on the basis of the practice where the patient was last seen. However, analysis of HFA merged practice and IPA data has shown significant overlap between IPAs in patient registration (Malcolm 1998a).

Although NHI registration might be a definitive solution to this problem, formidable impediments exist. These include the formalisation of patient registration/enrolment, patient acceptability for such enrolment, updating the NHI, and removing duplicate NHIs from the allocation system.

Achieving equity within and between IPAs

Despite adjusting for characteristics of practice populations such as age, gender, etc., recent unpublished work has shown that there is still wide residual variation in per capita expenditure when top and bottom practices in IPAs are compared (Figure 10.1, p. 192). Analysis shows that the

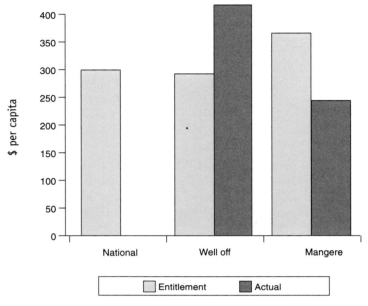

Figure 10.3 Comparison of expenditure patterns per capita in three populations on total of GMS, laboratory and pharmaceutical services: comparison of actual and HFA funding formula levels

Source: Malcolm 1998a

variation in both laboratory and pharmaceutical services is due almost entirely to variation in the volume of items prescribed or tests ordered, not in price (Figure 10.2, p. 193). High-expenditure practices see their patients more often, request more laboratory tests, and prescribe more drugs than low-expenditure practices. There is some evidence that better-quality practice is associated with lower rather than higher expenditure (Malcolm 1997b).

Thus far, efforts by IPAs to address this variation (e.g. through budget-holding) have had little measurable effect in achieving savings or reducing variation. Although laboratory budget-holding appears to be more successful in both achieving savings and reducing variation, evaluation of pharmaceutical budgets appears to achieve much more modest savings (Malcolm 1997b).

Wide variation also occurs between IPAs in per capita utilisation and expenditure on GMS, laboratory, and pharmaceutical services, even when adjusted for patient characteristics. Preliminary unpublished work in the Auckland sub-regions using the HFA funding formula has shown that, despite their greater health needs, poorer populations, such as those in the most disadvantaged areas of South Auckland, have much lower levels of primary-care utilisation and expenditure than better-off populations (Malcolm 1998a). The research revealed that primary-care expenditure on disadvantaged populations (inclusive of GMS, laboratory, and pharmaceutical) is about 30 per cent below their entitlement level under the HFA funding formula, whereas expenditure on well-off populations is 40 per cent above their entitlement (Figure 10.3, p. 194). This under-use and underfunding of primary care is almost certainly a factor in the much higher use of hospital in-patient services by poorer populations (Malcolm 1998a).

The main issue arising from these figures is how best to address the issue of equity, especially given the relative lack of success so far by IPAs in controlling, let alone significantly reducing, pharmaceutical expenditure in well-off areas. HFA policy at present is that equity issues are to be addressed largely through the redirection of savings from high-spending IPAs to underfunded populations. At present, however, no effective strategies are in place that might achieve the level of savings required to address fundamental equity issues, either within or, especially, between IPAs.

The Future

Prospects for capitation

The key to improving quality in primary care is better management of clinical activity. The painful experience of the recent health reforms has shown that the market alone does not address this issue. In contrast, well-supported and committed clinical leadership appears to work. But this requires financial and organisational commitment by IPAs and similar groups to support change by means of training, promoting the development of information systems, and expanding rather than withdrawing investment.

At present little is known about the factors that influence clinical behaviour, why the large variation within and between IPAs exists, or what works in changing behaviour. In the case of prescribing, the present faith in evidenced-based medicine may be misplaced, because prescribing may be a far from rational activity. The evaluation of pharmaceutical budget-holding demonstrated that even comprehensive strategies, including personal involvement in guideline development, have a relatively modest impact on prescribing behaviour (Malcolm 1997b). Much more investment is needed in research and development into health services, in particular to illuminate the factors that influence clinical decision-making and the reasons for wide variability in utilisation and expenditure, primary as well as secondary.

Concerns of IPAs

Doubt and uncertainty are widespread about the ability of the restructured HFA to provide the leadership in primary-care development sought by IPAs, including moves towards capitation.

A survey of IPAs in late 1998 (unpublished), with responses from twenty-eight IPAs/groups out of a potential thirty, has shown that IPAs have over 2000 members—about 70–75 per cent of all GPs in New Zealand. IPAs are wary about taking on risk and even less enthusiastic about retaining savings as personal benefits, but they strongly support better management of the clinical activity of members. The most important achievements of IPAs were identified as establishing an infrastructure, achieving collaboration between members, and developing information systems.

Continuing IPA and political commitment to the goals of better health outcomes, to be achieved through capitation and integration, appears to contrast markedly with a current lack of HFA leadership. IPA development has occurred in spite of, rather than because of, RHA and now HFA support (Malcolm et al., in press).

Towards integrated care

'Managed care', a key word in health sector development in 1996, has now been replaced by 'integrated care'. Integrated care has less of a commercial emphasis, and more explicitly defines the process of exploring models of integration.

Integration of services is occurring in a number of directions, including integration of primary care, with GPs, nurses, and midwives working more closely together. Its main thrust, however, is the integration of primary and secondary care in major age groups (e.g. child health, elder care), disease groups (e.g. asthma, diabetes, heart failure), and whole populations (e.g. provincial areas). The new HFA is now tentatively promoting and evaluating eleven national pilot projects involving integration of services (Health Funding Authority 1998b), similar to programs being implemented in Australia (Powell Davies et al. 1997).

In two provincial centres, specialists and GPs have formed joint-venture integrated-care companies to contract with the HFA for the full range of primary and secondary-care services. In Christchurch, Pegasus Medical Group, together with geriatricians, has initiated what has become a broadly based, relationship-building process now involving the HSSs and a wide range of agencies providing care for the elderly. The overall aim is to develop comprehensive health services for older people in Canterbury

(Steering Group Elder Care Canterbury 1998). A joint venture between a West Auckland IPA and the Auckland Children's Hospital claims to have reduced asthma admissions in children by 40 per cent.

Integration between primary care and public health is another development emerging from the primary-care sector, and concerns those services most closely associated with primary-care services (immunisation, cervical screening, etc.).

Key Contrasts with Australia

Table 10.4 summarises some contrasting features of the primary-care systems of Australia and New Zealand. Despite the obvious opportunity to benefit from each other's experience in reform of primary care, neither seems to have shown much interest in the lessons learned across the Tasman.

Table 10.4   Key contrasts between the Australian and New Zealand primary-care systems

Feature	Australia	New Zealand
General practice organisation	Divisions of general practice	IPAs
Funding	Fragmented between federal level and states	By single authority with almost fully integrated budget
Computerisation of practices	Still 'primitive'	98.8% computerised age-sex registers in IPA practices
Purchasing of primary-care services	Largely open-ended reimbursement	Contracting for service outputs within agreed budget
Medical accountability for health expenditure	Not yet addressed	Largely accepted
Accountability for primary-care expenditure including pharmaceuticals	No direct accountability	Majority of this expenditure now in IPA budgets
Ability to shift primary-care resources from low- to high-priority services	Nil	Substantial
General practice funding	Fee-for-service	Wide acceptance and support for capitation by IPA leadership
General practice accreditation	Well advanced	Little progress yet
Unique identifier for health information linkage	Medicare number family only	National health index for 95% of population
Models of integration	Selected high-risk diseases	Wide range including full practice population, age and disease groups
Relative power balance between primary and secondary care	Little change	Shifting from secondary to primary care

IPAs and Australian divisions of general practice share many features. A key contrasting feature, however, is the now widespread acceptance by New Zealand GP leadership of accountability for cost as well as quality of care. The report of the General Practice Strategy Review Group (Commonwealth Department of Health and Family Services 1998) contained no reference to GPs' accountability for resource expenditure in Australia. Whereas general practice leadership has almost universally accepted the goal of making better use of primary-care resources, including laboratory and pharmaceutical services, neither the Australian vision for general practice in the twenty-first century nor the description of core roles for the divisions of general practice to the year 2001 made any reference to this responsibility.

Capitated general practice does not appear on the horizon in Australia. Although the General Practice Strategy Review Group report refers to exploring new funding arrangements, including funding models for services ordered by GPs, there is no suggestion of budget-holding models such as the ones that are now well developed in New Zealand.

In contrast to Australian divisions of general practice, IPAs have recognised their responsibility in managing increasingly large amounts of public money, and the power this gives them to achieve their health outcomes and equity goals by redirecting savings into alternative higher-priority patient services. They also recognise that utilisation of laboratory, pharmaceutical, and other services may bear little relationship to quality and outcomes.

IPAs have led to a high level of computerisation among GPs in New Zealand, whereas computerisation of general practice is still in a primitive state in Australia. The recent survey of IPAs indicated that 98.8 per cent of practices in IPAs now have computerised age-sex registers. This is in striking contrast to Australia, where 'between 30 and 50 per cent of GPs have a computer in their practice but only a small proportion—between 3 and 15 per cent, depending on the source—use computers for clinical applications' (Commonwealth Department of Health and Family Services 1997: 222). On the other hand, Australia may be well advanced in addressing the question of quality in general practice through accreditation, an issue New Zealand has yet to consider.

A focus on integration of care in many IPAs has caused a shift in the power balance between primary and secondary care. IPAs are exploring new relationships with CHEs and with specialist service groupings within CHEs, and a productive dialogue is occurring. Progressive CHEs have recognised that better management of acute care in the primary-care setting could diminish the rising tide of acute admissions (Ministry of Health 1998).

Progress towards integration, particularly of primary and secondary care, appears to have been much more rapid in New Zealand than in

Australia, where the focus of integration has been more on communication, collaboration, and coordination of care for high-risk diseases, and change has been driven more by government funders than by care providers. By contrast, in New Zealand, the impetus for integration has come much more from general practice and clinicians generally than from government. An important example of clinician-led integration is the Elder Care project in Canterbury (Steering Group Elder Care Canterbury 1988) as discussed in Chapter 20.

Conclusion

In summary, the key achievements of the New Zealand experience in primary-care reform of relevance to Australia and other countries are the following:

- the rise of clinical leadership, or to use the vogue term, 'clinical governance', in general practice with a strong influence on clinical behaviour, including quality and resource management;
- the development of collective professional accountability in managing new internal and external relationships;
- collaborative approaches to integration of primary care (involving GPs and other professionals such as nurses and midwives), and integration of primary and secondary care;
- extensive development of information systems, including merging and managing practice registers, analysing laboratory and pharmaceutical data, and providing personal feedback to members;
- formulation and monitoring of guidelines on pharmaceutical and laboratory services;
- only modest savings from budget-holding thus far; (wide variations are observed to remain in certain age and socio-economic cohorts, and among those whose health is poorer to begin with);
- success in collective/collaborative action to improve clinical decision-making, which requires much more than dissemination of evidence-based practice guidelines; and
- emerging issues include achieving equity in IPA and practice budgets, and adjusting IPA budgets to counter low per capita use of primary care among New Zealanders of certain age and socio-economic cohorts, and among those whose health is poorer to begin with.

In recent years, general practice in New Zealand has been through what some consider a cultural revolution. Most GPs are now actively supporting policies and practices they previously condemned. The management of clinical activity such as primary-care resources within a framework of clinical leadership would have been unthinkable five years ago. The key achievements of IPAs go beyond achieving savings from budget-holding. More important has been the development of a new sense of collaboration, accountability, sensitivity to quality, and peer review among members. Many IPAs have now established a platform from which major future achievements in quality, cost control, and integration of care can be expected.

Two crucial lessons for successful health reform emerge from the New Zealand experience—lessons that could be of considerable importance to not only Australia but also many other countries. The first is that market strategies do not work if they are in conflict with the real incentives driving clinical behaviour. In the case of New Zealand, GPs' underlying motivation is the desire to achieve better health outcomes for their patients. Clinical leadership, with the support of management, might be able to achieve not only better outcomes for patients and the wider community, but also cost containment through the integration of clinical and resource management.

11

A Tale of Two States: New South Wales and Victoria

Just Stoelwinder and Rosalie Viney

Australia's publicly funded health system allows for innovation and difference between states and territories within the bounds of a uniform national health insurance scheme. This is possible because, in the Australian federation, states have the major responsibility for funding and operating health institutions (hospitals, community health), whereas the Commonwealth is responsible for the national health insurance scheme. The relationship between the states and territories and the Commonwealth is primarily mediated through five-year agreements, termed the Australian Health Care Agreement (AHCA). Provided states and territories meet their obligations under the AHCA, they have a considerable degree of autonomy in the design of state-funded or state-operated health services. How, and why, have states changed their health services during the late 1980s and the 1990s? In this chapter we describe the reforms in Australia's two most populous states, New South Wales and Victoria, which encapsulate the general range of reforms that have been undertaken during this time throughout Australia.

Because the main institutional components of the health system are largely owned and operated by state and territory governments, reforms are inextricably linked with local political processes, geography, and history. The process of reform is primarily political; major changes to the system are possible only when the government is politically strong. The content of reform is essentially an expert construct; ideas about good practice in health service policy and management emerge from time to time, often as international phenomena. The organisation of service providers on an area basis, hospital accreditation, casemix funding, and purchaser/provider splits are just some examples of these international ideas. Central health authorities continually need to develop their health services to respond to perceived pressures and to achieve their strategic vision of a good service. The major health service reforms in Victoria and New South Wales demonstrate the ideas that have been in 'good currency' and how these have been incorporated into efforts to bring the health system under control. The pattern of implementation of reforms that has emerged shows how ideas in good currency are shaped and modified by the culture and politics of health systems.

A New South Wales Case Study

In retrospect, reform in the New South Wales health system during the 1990s has been much more a process of consolidating a consistent set of principles guiding funding and management than it probably appeared to be to many players in the system over that time. It is certainly the case that the system looks very different now from that in the mid-1980s and the beginning of the 1990s. It is also the case that the process of creating the current system has been one of almost constant organisational change and restructuring, with all its associated upheaval, uncertainty, and changes in personnel. Some key ideas and catch phrases have waxed and waned in prominence in response to changes of government ('customer focus', 'privatisation', and 'health gain', for example, have either been replaced by new terms or have become less important). But despite a change of government and significant shifts in underlying political philosophy, many distinguishing features of the New South Wales system have been strengthened, and it is possible to identify a single direction of reform towards population health management. It is difficult to assess whether the structure of the system has been explicitly designed to reflect this philosophical approach, or whether the emphasis on population health management has emerged from the architecture of the system. Probably both are true.

The main features of reform in New South Wales include the development of area health service (AHS) structures, the introduction and subsequent redefinitions of a population-based funding formula, the use of casemix as a management tool, and the health outcomes 'movement'. While other reforms have been important and have in some cases complemented these developments, these central features have together formed a package that has resulted in a strong orientation towards population health across New South Wales. This approach is not without weaknesses, and has certainly not averted the gaming and cost-shifting that seem prevalent throughout the Australian health system (and indeed internationally). But there is a real sense in which the management of health services in New South Wales is at last beginning to represent population health management rather than management of hospital services. It is interesting to note, however, that New South Wales has held back from some more radical reforms, which might have led it down the same paths more quickly and more definitively (but with greater risk). The tension that has characterised the reform process in New South Wales is between devolution of management and responsibility, and maintaining structures that allow central control.

In this case study the four key reform thrusts are described and documented, and broad consistency of direction is demonstrated. The links between the reforms and other key developments are examined, and the strengths and weaknesses of the system that has emerged are assessed. Relative consistency of direction of reform in New South Wales has not prevented health policy within the state being driven by the party-political process. The impact of this process on the implementation and success of reforms is examined.

Area health services

The AHS approach was adapted from the UK model of district health services. The idea of integrating health services under local area management was first introduced in New South Wales in a pilot project in the mid-1970s, but it was not until 1986 that the area health services model was introduced widely. At that time, twenty-three AHSs were established. They covered metropolitan Sydney, the Central Coast, Newcastle, and Wollongong.

Many of the features that have since become central to AHS management were articulated in the legislation as objectives: population focus, services planning, integration, coordination, and a spectrum of treatment and prevention services. But the key achievement was widely recognised as the abolition of individual hospital boards. The boards had been powerful advocates and lobbyists, particularly in the larger teaching hospitals. The introduction of an AHS model, with a chief executive officer (CEO) and a single board, reduced the involvement of the Department of Health in day-to-day management, and inevitably meant less of a voice for parochial interests. Whereas the CEO effectively reported through the department, the CEO and the board were directly accountable to the Minister, breaking the direct link between the department and individual service development decisions within hospitals.

However, even this significant structural change had only limited effect on day-to-day operations. The AHSs were still generally defined around a large hospital (often a teaching hospital). Some included only one hospital.

Thus the twenty-three AHSs were still strongly identified with a particular hospital, and the regional offices of the department still had a significant role in management at the local level.

In 1988 the new government abolished the regional offices and restructured the AHS into ten much larger units. Over the next two years, more services were incorporated in the AHS structure and more functions devolved to area management. An important complementary development was the establishment of public health units, providing the beginnings of the skill base in epidemiology necessary for services planning at a population level. But it was still the case that area health services represented 'a good corporate model for running hospitals or groups of hospitals' (Read 1991: 25).

Introduction of AHS management in rural New South Wales was more problematic and was really achieved only in the late 1990s. Country hospitals are central to the identity of country towns and are often the largest employer in each town. The outcry against some hospital amalgamations and downgradings in 1989 led the then Minister for Health, Peter Collins, to declare there would be 'no further forced downgradings or board amalgamations' while he was Minister (Collins 1990: 5). The initial step towards AHS in rural New South Wales was the dismantling of regional offices of the department, and their replacement in July 1993 with twenty-two rural district health services (generally managing services across three to five local hospitals in a geographic area). Although some of these districts were large in geographic terms, most had relatively small populations. The district health service model offered some of the advantages of area-based management, particularly those that could be captured in the phrase 'a good corporate model for running hospitals', such as capacity to network services and achieve some efficiencies in administration of hospital services. But managing the health of a population requires a population that is of a meaningful size in epidemiological terms, and many services are better targeted at a larger population. Thus the district health service model contained some anomalies, for example the public health units sat outside the district health services, with one unit serving a number of districts.

Since 1996 the district health services have been replaced by rural area health services, and there has been some redefinition of metropolitan AHS boundaries. There are now seventeen AHSs, with populations ranging from just over 50 000 to over 700 000, of which nine are in greater metropolitan Sydney (including the Blue Mountains region and the cities of Newcastle and Wollongong), and account for 76 per cent of the state's population.

The CEOs of area health services have performance contracts with the NSW Department of Health that specify targets across a range of health outcome measures, reflecting the increasing focus on population health. In practice, however, the key performance indicator for an area CEO has tended to be the ability to keep within budget, reflecting a continued emphasis on managing services rather than population health.

The key question is whether or not AHSs have become more than a good model for running hospitals—that is, whether they have fulfilled the objectives set out in the legislation. One of the weaknesses of the AHS model is that it invests in the CEO a dual responsibility for managing a group of health services and the health of a population. The task of managing the health services is the one that creates day-to-day demands, and potentially leaves little room for focusing on improving the health of the population, even though the CEO is one step removed from internal hospital management issues. This is reinforced by funding arrangements, which tend to relate more to the services within an AHS, as discussed below. The extent to which AHSs have successfully attended to population health has largely resulted from other reform initiatives.

Population-based funding

Concurrent with the introduction of AHS there has been a shift towards a weighted population basis for funding of health services in New South Wales. Despite the ten-year period over which the principle of population-based funding has been explicitly espoused and enacted in New South Wales, it is still not fully implemented. There have, however, been significant shifts in funding allocations. Another important result is the subtle shifts in the mindsets of both the older, more established AHSs and the newer ones towards a different mix of service provision for populations with differing needs.

Population-based funding was first articulated in a resource allocation formula (RAF) introduced in the 1989/90 budget year. The RAF was adapted from the UK National Health Service Resource Allocation Working Party (RAWP) formula. It was based on the principles of self-sufficiency of areas and regions for primary and secondary services and preservation of funding for existing tertiary referral services. The in-patient and out-patient components of the first version of the RAF related largely to age and sex-weighted population, with some adjustments for resource use. These activity-related adjustments to the population-based formula took three different forms, but all used casemix-based information. The age and sex weights were adjusted for resource consumption using DRG cost weights, other activity-based adjustments (for private hospital activity and interstate flows) were based on DRG cost weights, and 107 DRGs were classified as tertiary, and directly funded based on DRG cost weights (Gilbert 1990; Viney et al. 1991).

Three points are worth noting with respect to the first version of the RAF. First, it was never intended to be the means of allocating funds, but rather served to establish the goalposts for future funding shares. The RAF provided a ten-year plan for redistribution of funds and signalled the end of historical-based allocation, which favoured more established hospitals and AHSs in the centre of Sydney. In practice, however (and in fact as an explicit component of the policy), the redistribution of funds was to be capital-driven (Gilbert 1990). The newer areas of Sydney, where there was significant population growth, simply did not have the infrastructure to provide services to meet the local population's needs locally. An immediate shift to true population-based funding would have required a complex set of cross-border funding arrangements or may have risked the possibility of substantial underprovision of services. Thus funding to AHSs continued to be on an historical basis, but the RAF provided a measure of the gap between actual and indicative funding shares, and sent clear messages to health service managers about inequities in funding.

Second, the RAF was introduced in a fiscal environment that favoured health. Over the period 1989/90 to 1993/94 there were real increases in funding to the health sector in New South Wales, making it possible to shift towards the RAF shares without significantly reducing funding to other services. It is perhaps not surprising that moving towards the targets has proved more difficult as funding has become more contested (because of other impacts such as Medicare cost-shifting penalties and the demands on resources such as the waiting list program).

Third, in providing a transparent basis for funding, the RAF also became the focus of dispute about equity in resource allocation. The release of the first version of the RAF was followed by considerable debate about the appropriateness of the definition of tertiary DRGs and the needs-based adjustments in the formula. There was possibly as much emphasis on this as on the gap between actual and indicative allocations.

Once goalposts are established, effort tends to be divided between reaching them and moving them, and this has certainly been true for population-based funding in New South Wales. Thus there have been two main areas of effort in terms of resource allocation to AHSs: refinement of the formula and development of proposals to hasten implementation of the funding shares implied by the formula. Refinement of the formula has included development of improved measures of need and development of population-based formulae for other programs, such as mental health and aged care. Several versions of population-based funding formulae for NSW Health have been developed. The last publicly released version was in 1992. Thus although the implied shares from the resource distribution formula (RDF) have routinely been made publicly available, the basis for calculating them has not been subject to the same scrutiny as was the first RAF.

Implementation of the implied funding shares constitutes a case study in itself. As noted above, the RAF was always intended to guide rather than determine resource allocation. With the change of government in 1996, from Liberal to Labor, the will to implement population-based funding appeared to increase. A key component of the *NSW Government's Economic Statement for Health* (NSW Health Department 1995) was a proposal for a new RDF that would be used to determine the actual budgets. Gaps between current and 'equity-based' allocations were to be eliminated by 1998/99. This was to be achieved by introduction of cross-border funding arrangements that would be implemented either by direct adjustment by the department (based on benchmark costs per case) or by bilateral service agreements between AHSs for the provision of particular services.

However, implementation of the new formula required transitional arrangements to make the significant shift in funds feasible. The problems associated with the location of hospital infrastructure, which are common to many health systems, were also present in New South Wales. The population-based formula was designed to fund services for geographically defined populations, but the hospitals were located in the wrong places. The inner city was oversupplied with tertiary-level services, and outlying areas of population growth were undersupplied.

In 1996 the NSW government embarked on an ambitious attempt to shift resources within metropolitan Sydney. This included release of a recommended RDF and proposals to move St Vincent's Hospital, a major teaching hospital, to the St George campus to rationalise the provision of tertiary referral services in South-Eastern Sydney AHS. The process was marked by a very public, and media-driven, battle between the major stakeholders that ultimately led to most of the proposals being abandoned.

Although work has continued within New South Wales on development of population-based funding shares and methods to implement these (including the development of explicit casemix cost weights across New South Wales hospitals), the impetus to shift to equity-based shares seemed to evaporate. This episode not only exemplifies the persistent gap between implied and actual funding shares, but also demonstrates the problems that emerge when resource allocation is the explicit objective of policy initiatives. A clear policy direction based on sound and widely agreed principles of equity of access can disintegrate when translated to the reality of closing or downgrading facilities, particularly if these decisions are perceived as being imposed from above. Explicit attempts to introduce equitable funding seem to stall on debate about what is fair.

The St Vincent's–St George episode also demonstrates the tension between devolution and central control of policy. Through its direct control over funding allocations, the Department of Health has maintained the principles of equity of access and self-sufficiency as key components of policy. But control has impeded the full implementation of the policy—the department and the Minister for Health can be held directly responsible for any perceived reduction of service provision associated with shifts in funding. If government relinquishes control (for example, by relating funding to activity), radical changes in funding shares can occur, with the resultant shifts in hospital infrastructure. The approach New South Wales has adopted has been to maintain historical funding until a clear path to population-based funding emerges. Despite a decade of commitment to population-based funding, in New South Wales AHSs are still funded on an historical basis. But under historical funding, only marginal shifts towards equity-based funding are possible.

Casemix

Whereas New South Wales has placed emphasis on equity of access in its funding models, in other states in Australia there has been a shift towards using funding arrangements to encourage technical efficiency, particularly through the use of casemix funding. Such a model has also been considered within New South Wales, but there is a tension between activity-based funding at any level of the system and population-based funding at the AHS level. If activity-based funding is to operate within hospitals or from AHS to hospitals, then at some point there must be a reconciliation between population-based shares and activity-based shares. This implies the necessity to set up funding arrangements for cross-border flows and to some extent imposes the need for the cost per case to be comparable across different hospitals. In practice, costs are rarely comparable. The tension between funding services at the facility level and at the population level has been a major part of the problem New South Wales has encountered in fully implementing population-based funding. An RDF is meaningful for populations, but at the service-delivery level it is activity which consumes resources and output that must be managed. How has New South Wales approached this conflict, and what role, if any, has there been for casemix?

The NSW Health position on the role of casemix information during the 1990s has fairly consistently been one of 'approach with caution'. The emphasis has been on casemix as a 'management tool' rather than a funding tool. Nonetheless, casemix information has had a growing role in the allocation of funds. Casemix information has been an important component of the RAF and the RDF, and in the current version of the RDF 'the overall impact of casemix on the distribution of funding to Areas as implied by the RDF is in the order of about $300 million per annum' (Gibbs 1998: 39). At AHS level, there has been increasing encouragement for hospital budgets to be determined by their casemix, and some AHSs have been doing this for a number of years.

The *NSW Government's Economic Statement for Health* included an explicit policy to introduce casemix budgeting at the AHS level, with casemix-based payment for cross-boundary flows. Progress on this has slowed since the other components of the proposal (discussed above) were abandoned. However, detailed casemix standards have been published for New South Wales hospitals, and the department encourages hospitals to use these for budgeting, for benchmarking, and for development of cross-area purchasing arrangements (Casemix Policy Unit 1998). This includes providing guidelines on how to develop budgets for different components of hospital services.

Thus although there has been a subtle shift in emphasis away from the role of casemix as a management information tool towards its use as a funding tool, New South Wales has stopped short of embracing the policies adopted in other Australian states. This ambivalence relates both to the continuing strong support of an area-based approach to population health and to the tension between funding for population health and funding on the basis of activity. What is interesting to note is the relatively widespread acceptance that the use of casemix to fund facilities is essential to improvements in technical and allocative efficiency. Although it has an essentially historical funding model in which hospitals have global fixed budgets, there have been reductions in length of stay and in costs of casemix-adjusted episodes in New South Wales that are comparable to those that in other states have been cited as evidence of the efficiency gains from casemix funding (Commonwealth Department of Health and Family Services 1997a).

Health outcomes

The final element of reform that has been a crucial component of New South Wales health policy during the 1990s has been the emphasis on 'health outcomes' (i.e. on monitoring and assessing the impact of health services on health status, at both the individual and the population level). Health outcomes or health gains are by no means unique to New South Wales, and indeed in New South Wales (and elsewhere) there is an element of rhetoric to outcomes-oriented reform. But the combination of population health management through AHSs, continued emphasis on implementation of population-based funding, and active development of a health outcomes approach to policy has had a major impact on the way services are planned and managed across the state. The notion of establishing and measuring performance against health goals and targets for the population seems so integral to health services management now that it is easy to forget that it was a fairly new idea not long ago.

A health outcomes approach in New South Wales was adopted as the Health Outcomes Initiative in 1992, and between 1992 and 1994 it was formalised as the NSW Health Outcomes Program. The concrete components of the program included the funding of demonstration projects, identification of priority areas for health outcomes (which were closely related to the national health priority areas), and the establishment of health outcomes councils at the AHS level. However, an important element of the success of the outcomes approach in New South Wales was the work that had already been undertaken and has continued towards establishing a public health infrastructure across the state, which includes a training program for public health officers. This has been crucial to providing the resources to support outcomes-based monitoring and planning, but also to shifting the mindset within the health system to thinking in terms of population health indicators and evidence-based decision-making.

AHSs had a great degree of scope in how the health outcomes councils were formulated, what their role would be and on which health areas they would focus. Thus, across New South Wales AHSs, the extent to which an outcomes approach has been incorporated in the planning and management of services has been fairly varied. More recently the emphasis has been on the development of health outcome performance indicators. This allows performance of the health system at various levels to be measured not in terms of inputs or outputs but outcomes, and on progress towards goals in population health.

Perhaps the most important long-term impact of the various health outcomes initiatives in New South Wales has been the extent to which an outcomes approach has been incorporated in the performance agreements of AHS CEOs.

A question remains, however, regarding how far a health outcomes or health gain approach can be taken. There is increasing capacity to monitor health outcomes, but there is still a major challenge for health systems in using health outcome information in planning of services and in building a direct link between resource allocation, activity and outcomes. Other attempts to build this link in health systems have been beset by problems (Hall and Haas 1992), and in New South Wales the health outcomes approach has never been fully integrated with other policy instruments such as the RDF or statewide services planning. Similarly, the approach to setting goals and targets in New South Wales has been subject to the same problems encountered elsewhere, that there is no direct link between objectives, resources available, and targets. The goals and targets do not emerge from a priority-setting process in which assessment has been made of what can be achieved with available resources.

Part of the problem is the paradox of how to link funding (which provides the most direct incentive) of health services to their outcomes. This requires a more sophisticated understanding of the relationship between funding, activity, outputs, and outcomes than is yet available, but it is well recognised that there cannot be a simplistic approach of rewarding achievement of health improvement at the population level. Again, the challenge is whether a needs-based population health approach to funding is consistent with providing incentives to improve health outcomes.

Within AHSs there have been some attempts to link funding and health services planning to achievement of health outcomes through the technique of Program Budgeting and Marginal Analysis. A number of pilot projects have been undertaken with limited support from the NSW Health Department, and with mixed success. Some AHSs are continuing to use Program Budgeting and Marginal Analysis in small projects, but it has not been widely adopted.

Summary

Three features stand out from the health sector reform in New South Wales in the 1990s. First, the approach adopted in that state has progressively strengthened the focus on population health within the state health system, but this has possibly been at the expense of other reform initiatives that have been implemented in other states, particularly casemix funding of hospitals and health services. Second, in a health system founded on area-based management there is a tension between devolution and control. Area health services have been empowered and encouraged to manage their population's health and the range of health services they provide, but within a fairly tightly defined structure with clear boundaries. Arguably, the persistence of some key features of the New South Wales health system, particularly the use of historical funding, has limited the capacity of AHSs to manage population health rather than manage services. This is particularly notable where there are significant inequities in resource distribution. Unless the underlying problems, which go deeper than mere allocation of funds and include issues about workforce and referral patterns, can be addressed, it is not possible to relinquish control to the AHSs, but nor does it seem possible to address these problems centrally. Third, explicit approaches to health sector reform, particularly addressing issues of equity and efficiency, have proved problematic and have sometimes stalled. The explicit nature of the process of shifting resources has, at a number of stages, left the government open to direct political action from those affected.

This is in marked contrast to Victoria, where quite radical shifts in policy have been implemented with much less (initial) resistance. In Victoria, casemix funding was introduced with equity as part of the explicit rationale, and budget cuts (or possibly technical efficiency) as part of the implicit rationale. The nature of the policy meant that the attention of health service managers and clinicians was focused on the operations of the new funding mechanism rather than mounting the sort of resistance to policy change that has been seen in New South Wales.

Reforming Victoria's Public Hospitals: A Case Study of Managerial Control

Reforms in the Victorian public hospital system during the 1990s reflect the inexorable march of managerial rationalism. These reforms have included the introduction of hospital services agreements, a process designed to establish a contractual approach to hospital accountability. Casemix funding followed, a technique designed to improve hospitals' technical efficiency. More recently the metropolitan hospitals were aggregated into a smaller number of governance units, called networks. Born out of a crisis in casemix funding, the main aim of the networks was to address the maldistribution of metropolitan hospital services and to achieve further technical efficiency. With a desire to lead national competition policy, the Victorian government has also opened all major hospital development to private sector financing and operation. By the transfer of risk to the private sector it assumed that the associated discipline would result in further efficiency gains, particularly through reformed work-practice.

The assumption often made is that the content of these reforms reflects the different ideological approaches of the state government in power at the time. Although ideology undoubtedly affects the rhetoric of reform, and politics its timing, this case study will argue that the reforms make more sense as part of the ascension of managerial rationalism.

Managerial rationalism gives prime value to technical efficiency and provides the rationale for managers, of both health care facilities and health authorities, in their ongoing struggle to gain control of the system. Alford (1975) referred to this group as 'corporate rationalists'. This view argues that in a complex professional organisation such as a hospital there is a constant struggle for dominance of control between organised stakeholders represented by the managerial group on the one hand, and the health professions, especially doctors, on the other. The actual content, or idea, of the reform is immaterial. In their bid to incrementally gain more control over the health professions, managers latch onto any rational idea, or 'idea in good currency', that happens to be around at the time.

We should not be surprised at this state of affairs. Managers value order, control, and rationality. Stakeholders will not knowingly proffer change that is not in their self-interest, as they understand it. There are not many new ideas to go around. Change is inevitably incremental, as social systems are inherently conservative.

Each of the reforms in the Victorian hospital system during the late 1980s and the 1990s has demonstrated this struggle in action. The need for reform is inevitably called for by government bureaucrats and eventually finds support among enough managers in the field before implementation. The ideas contained in the reforms reflect those that are in good currency in health care or in public sector management at the time. Each reform has increased managerial control of the system, with a concomitant decline in professional autonomy and influence.

The reforms

A variety of system reforms has been implemented in Victoria. In this section the most important—Health/Hospital Service Agreements, casemix funding, metropolitan hospital networks, and private sector involvement in public hospitals—are briefly described. Not covered is the introduction of a uniform chart of accounts in the early 1980s, the introduction of program budgeting in the mid-1980s, and clinical costing in the late 1980s. Each of these advanced managerial control of hospitals as a prelude to the reforms described below.

Health service agreements

The Victorian Health Department trialled health service agreements in four hospitals over 1986/87. Within two years eighty-seven HSAs had been signed, covering more than 50 per cent of hospital funding (Health Department Victoria 1989). Agencies entering into a HSA were required to develop role statements, management objectives, plans, and strategies, and to specify the services to be provided and the resources allocated. From the department's perspective, negotiation of HSAs 'is the major link between increased management autonomy and responsibility and ensuring accountability of the system to the community' (Health Department Victoria 1989: 35). Hospitals and other agencies expecting that the use of the words 'negotiate' and 'agreement' would allow them to hold out for a better deal from the department soon had those delusions corrected. In 1988 the government enshrined HSAs into legislation. It determined that any agency failing to enter into an HSA would be subject to an interim funding statement, in which the Minister unilaterally set the funding, nature, and throughput of an agency's services.

HSAs, which still operate in Victoria, are a logical administrative tool to specify the funding arrangements between a hospital or health agency and the funding authority. But the rhetoric of two parties entering into a voluntary contract in the name of decentralised autonomy and community accountability is clearly false. On the contrary, it is not a tool of autonomy, but a mechanism of control. Standard Conditions of Funding and Schedules determined by the department now constitute 96 per cent of the 230-odd pages of a typical network HSA. The power to negotiate is as one-sided as the flow of money. The agency's only token influence is to delay signing all, or part, of the 'agreement'.

Casemix funding

The government introduced casemix funding into Victorian public hospitals in July 1993 as part of health policy reforms to 'enhance and expand the excellent hospital system in Victoria by developing a system that was free from bureaucratic control, that engendered competition and economic incentives for hospitals and that rewarded efficiency and growth in services' (Tehan 1993: iii). The Minister for Health further wrote, 'casemix funding means that funding for hospitals [sic] services will follow patient demand. In a very real sense it involves putting patient needs first.'

Driving the introduction of casemix payment at this time was the department's need to implement a 10 per cent reduction in funding as part of the state government's strategy to reduce its debt burden. This followed a 4 per cent reduction in funding the previous year. A clear risk to government was that these funding cuts would cause politically sensitive waiting lists to grow. As an incentive to maintain throughput, hospitals could gain more revenue from an additional throughput pool, provided they also achieved waiting list performance criteria. This penalty/bonus feature subsequently became a dominant part of performance management by the department.

That casemix funding improved hospital technical efficiency is now generally accepted (Duckett 1995). By 1995/96 Victoria was judged to be the most efficient producer of casemix-adjusted public hospital throughput in Australia (SCRCSSP 1998). But the impact of casemix funding on quality of care remains a concern. The Victorian Auditor-General reported that there was a *prima facie* case to suggest that casemix funding in Victoria had adversely affected the quality of care (Auditor-General 1998). This view was based on a questionnaire of senior clinicians. Although many would seriously question the reliability of this methodology, there will continue to be concerns about the potentially adverse impact of casemix funding on quality.

The introduction of casemix funding, with its concomitant budget cut, represented a massive change effort, and it is not surprising that there were some unintended consequences. An important one was the introduction of hospital networks.

By the second year of casemix funding, hospitals had so effectively responded to its incentives that the utility of the additional throughput pool was put in doubt. The increase in throughput was double that anticipated by the department, which now faced the conundrum of discounting the case payment from the pool, by perhaps 50 per cent, to ensure that the pool operated within its budget. Of concern was whether many hospitals would maintain additional throughput and waiting-list performance at such a discounted payment. At the request of the Minister, the Victorian Hospitals Association, together with senior hospital managers, devised a plan to limit any hospital's call on the pool to 5 per cent of its base throughput target. At this level the casemix price of the pool could be maintained without further discount. This plan was to the advantage of the majority of hospitals that could not sustain a competitive price war. The department readily adopted this plan, seeking no doubt to co-opt hospitals to an agreed budget outcome.

As a result of this decision to cap throughput, most of the large city hospitals had to reduce in-patient activity for the remainder of the financial year. The very political problem that the additional throughput pool was meant to prevent—a reduction in patient throughput due to budget cuts—came to the forefront. Within two weeks of this decision, the media were reporting health union and Opposition claims of massive bed closures, staff sackings, and the predicted blowout of waiting lists. Despite valiant efforts by the Minister and the department to blame the hospitals for the crisis, for pursuing the 'high-risk strategy' of a 'dash for cash', the media, leading public opinion, saw it differently. This was well illustrated by the radio compère Ranald Macdonald, who interviewed the Minister: 'you've said to them [the hospitals] we will reward you if you actually increase productivity . . . and now you're changing the rules of the game, you are capping the amount of money they can get' (Radio 3LO, 19 October 1994).

This discourse led to a major shift in public perception. With casemix funding the public view was that poor financial performance by a hospital was because it was inefficient. It was the hospital's fault. When government capped throughput the perception changed. Now government was at fault for limiting the throughput of efficient hospitals. Government opponents, of course, heavily promoted this revisionist view. Political pressure mounted over the next months as more and more hospitals identified the need to reduce bed capacity to meet budget. Following a round of post-Christmas visits to hospitals, this pressure caused the Premier to establish the Metropolitan Hospitals Planning Board and led ultimately to the creation of hospital networks.

Metropolitan networks

The Metropolitan Hospitals Planning Board (MHPB) structure and process was modelled on the government's successful reform of local government over the previous twelve months. The concept of a 'network' of hospitals was incorporated as a condition of its terms of reference, which required it, *inter alia*, to 'advise on positions for aggregation of existing hospitals under new Boards and a process of rationalisation of administrative functions and clinical divisions within these aggregations' (Metropolitan Hospitals Planning Board 1995: 73).

As in the local government reform, the structural outcome of the hospital review process was a given. This forced hospital stakeholders, as local governments before them, to make submissions on how hospitals should be aggregated. No hospital contested the idea of aggregation itself, as opposition could compromise a hospital's fate in the new structure. The government's approach of imposing a single, clear structure proved extremely successful. Thirty-five individual hospitals, large and small, special and general, meekly coalesced into seven metropolitan health care networks. As a change process, this cycle of crisis, an available rational managerial idea, and strong political leadership, stands as an exemplar of the implementation of structural reform in the hospital system.

According to the MHPB, the main goal of aggregation was 'to facilitate the integration of health services and allow more localised, detailed and rational planning of a range of services for a given community . . . within a framework that is accountable and responsible for performance' (MHPB 1995: 40). Networks have taken diverse approaches to achieving this goal.

Since their introduction, four of the networks have restructured. The Inner and Eastern Networks voluntarily merged with an aim of relocating a city hospital to the outer eastern suburbs. This initiative stalled when the intended target, St Vincent's Hospital, mounted an effective public defence. The network has not yet been able to redistribute resources. It continues to function as a group of independent hospital providers, structured to operate in a competitive environment, but not to integrate services. The Western and North-Eastern Networks have been merged, withdrawing the Austin and Heidelberg Medical Centre from the network model to enable the government to put it to tender for private sector redevelopment and management. Both groups have been beset by chronic financial difficulties that would seem to preclude attention to restructuring service delivery. The Women's and Children's Health Care Network is a speciality grouping with limited functional interdependence. Southern Health Care Network and Peninsula Health Care Network have sought to develop integrated service systems, though the latter's long-term outlook is constrained by its relatively small size.

With this diversity of approach, hospital networks in Melbourne will continue to evolve. A return to independent hospitals is unlikely, for, as the American Hospital Association (1994) pronounced some time ago, 'the era of the go-it-alone hospital is over'. Integrated service systems are, as discussed below, an idea in good currency. They are being expressed in a variety of forms in managed care in the USA, in the proposed primary–care structures in the NHS, and they have a track record in Australia in various regional health service configurations. Their catch phrase is 'providing the right care, at the right time, in the right place, for the right price'.

Private sector involvement in public hospitals

The Victorian government has been an enthusiastic proponent of national competition policy as a means of ensuring that resource allocation is not distorted because of public ownership. The implementation of competition policy in health care has, however, been restrained. Unlike the local government sector, which was required by government to market-test its services, health care facilities have been left to develop individual strategies to meet the competition policy requirements. Most have progressively put to tender functions such as hotel services, which can be provided by the private sector in a competitive environment. Market testing of clinical support services, such as pathology and pharmacy, is just beginning.

The department has sought to implement competition in some of its funding arrangements. Mental health services and an array of community services have been subject to competitive tendering. Hospitals seeking additional acute hospital casemix funding have had to compete on the basis of price. These initiatives are limited by the lack of an established provider market and ambiguity in the department about the loss of direct control over public hospitals when they secure explicit service contracts. As a result, the packages put to tender are small and not part of an integrated health service strategy. This limitation could be addressed by more aggregated purchasing based on sub-populations or per capita funding. There are suggestions of some movement by the department in this direction.

The main form of private sector involvement in public hospitals has been in the finance, construction, and operation of new or redeveloped hospitals under the government's ambitious hospital development plan. About a quarter of the scheduled $900 million capital required over five years from 1997 was to come from the private sector. Three hospital projects were to be financed and operated by the private sector—the new hospitals planned for Berwick and Knox, and the redevelopment of the Austin and Repatriation Medical Centre.

The fundamental concept is now well accepted. Similar approaches to hospital development are being used throughout Australia. Both the Tory and Labour governments in the United Kingdom are using this method for large hospital development projects. As a source of capital, the private sector offers many advantages and was indeed used successfully to develop the Monash Medical Centre, Victoria, in the early 1980s.

Long-term operating contracts for the private sector to provide public hospital services, however, are yet untested. There would appear to be no theoretical reason for their not succeeding. But it remains to be seen whether the department, as purchaser of hospital services from private operators, will develop the sophistication necessary to incorporate system control and service adaptability within a long-term contractual relationship. Market development and significant purchasing reform will be needed if a competitive private sector system is effectively to meet the long-term expectations of government.

The struggle for control with ideas in good currency

Hospitals are contested domains. The nature of hospital work is complex, difficult, highly valued in the community, and reliant on a workforce made up of influential, autonomous professionals. This gives health professionals, and medical staff in particular, significant power within hospitals and in the public arena.

As the technology of hospital care has developed, so has its appetite for funds. In Victoria, as in other Australian states, the state government faces an unenviable dilemma. As owner of over 70 per cent of the hospital beds (and all of the most prestigious technologically advanced hospitals) and the payer for all public hospital care, it faces continuous demand for both capital and operating funds. With health care consuming typically 40 per cent of a state's expenditure, it is clear that controlling this pressure for funds is a major task. Stakeholders will perpetually demand more health funds, and the effort of state governments to control costs leads to a hotly contested public process in which the government is politically vulnerable.

In this contest those responsible for funding and managing the system will continue to seek rational ideas for reform, not necessarily because the system is seen to be broken, but to counteract the claims of the other stakeholders for more resources. This is where ideas in good currency play their part. If they are around when an idea is needed, they have a good chance of being implemented.

Casemix funding was such an idea in good currency, hovering around while waiting for its time. DRGs were first trialled for the purpose of regulating hospital fees in the state of New Jersey in 1980. In the USA they shot to prominence with their serendipitous adoption by the Health Care Financing Administration for hospital payments under Medicare, a clear example of an idea in good currency. This action responded to a need to demonstrate a plan for cost reductions as mandated by prospective tax savings legislation.

The first public discussion of DRGs in Australia occurred shortly afterwards with a descriptive article by Palmer and Wood (1984) and an accompanying commentary by one of the present authors in the *Australian Health Review* (Stoelwinder 1984). The Australian health services research community adopted DRGs with robust enthusiasm, supported by the most generous Commonwealth government research funding ever made available for research into health services. A veritable DRG research industry resulted. The development of a series of Australian cost weights, medical record coding practice, clinician co-option, and clinical costing was but some of the focus of this work. The national investment in casemix continues with an ongoing Casemix Development Program in the Commonwealth Health Department, which also arranges an annual Casemix Conference.

Victoria embraced DRGs with special enthusiasm. By 1986 the Victorian Health Department was publishing Victorian Hospital DRG data (length of stay comparisons) retrospective to 1982/83 (Health Department Victoria, Health Statistics Unit 1986). By 1987 the department was already foreshadowing the use of DRGs in hospital funding. 'The Victorian Government will make greater use of DRGs in funding hospitals', declared the first Victorian Health Plan (Health Department Victoria 1987). Support for DRGs, if only as a management tool rather than for funding hospitals, gradually developed in Victoria (Victorian Hospitals' Association 1988). The last health system review conducted by the then Labor government, published the month before the change to a Liberal government in 1992, observed: 'The Review believes that case-mix funding provides the most appropriate mechanism for achieving such goals and could fit well with the Health Service Agreement program which is currently in place' (Victorian Health System Review 1992).

So the ground was well tilled for the introduction of casemix funding by the new state government in 1992, with its fresh mandate to improve the Victorian economy by reducing public sector debt. Massive funding reductions were achieved by obfuscating them in casemix funding rhetoric of hospital competitiveness and complexity of formulation. Even though the political wheels fell off in their second year, leading to the next round of change in the form of networks, they served their purpose well.

They are still not being used as economists had hoped: 'The desirable outcomes of case payment may be summed up as being first, that hospitals which produce more output will earn more revenue and secondly, that their financial results will depend on their average costs per case' (Scotton and Owens 1990: 1). Rather, they remain in force because they are managerially rational, as a logical hospital funding control that articulates resource distribution in terms of normalised clinical efficiency. This pre-empts clinical complaint and redirects it to disputes about DRG weights. Tinkering with the weights is an effective safety valve that keeps the funder in control.

Reform in the conflict-ridden hospital system is a political process, not that of a particular ideology of the government in power but one based on the play-out of the power structure within the system. As the Victorian reforms during the 1980s and 1990s show, there is a constant struggle for rational administrative control over what is otherwise a hotly contested domain. Ideas for reform get implemented if they are available at politically convenient times when the opportunity for greater managerial control arises.

Conclusion

Reform of health services in both states shows interesting similarities and differences. The 'content' or ideas of the reforms have tended to be similar. The 'process' of reform, in essence the politics of implementing a desired idea of change, has reflected the power of government at the time to deal with disaffected stakeholders. Significant reform, such as casemix, severe budget cuts, and restructuring in Victoria has reflected the perceived political strength of the state government at that time. With small political margins, change has been more incremental, as demonstrated in New South Wales. Whatever the pace, the reforms have in common the progressive strengthening of managerial control. This has occurred because it is these common managerially rational ideas that are seen to be the answer to pressures of cost, quality or appropriateness that governments face. The structure and funding of state health care services demonstrate these dynamics.

The aggregation of providers into geographically based systems of care had early implementation in New South Wales. Clear models were available in the NHS in the United Kingdom with early Australian proponents (Hospitals and Health Services Commission 1974). The New South Wales model incorporates both a decentralised health authority function and a geographic aggregation of service providers. The espoused aim is to improve the coordination of service delivery while maintaining a uniform system of control. While tightly coupling the provider institutions with the centre, this model has led to internal ambiguity about competing obligations to the central authority, the local institutions, and the community. A number of national health services have sought to resolve this conflict in role through a purchaser/provider split. In Victoria, the central health authority was 'regionalised' in 1984, but health care institutions retained their separate governance structure. Not until 1995 were metropolitan provider organisations aggregated into geographic structures, the networks, still separate from the regional health authority, which continues to operate as the purchasing agency. Because of this separation of roles, Victoria has had to invest in the development of HSAs to retain control over the distributed provider organisations. It can be argued that this separation of roles has contributed to Victoria's success in implementing more rigorous hospital cost-reduction strategies. The purchaser has been able to distance itself from the pain and suffering of implementing budget cuts in the provider organisations.

The difference in structure of the health services in New South Wales and Victoria is reflected in their funding arrangements. The quasi-contractual relationship between Victorian hospitals and the department facilitates the use of casemix as a payment, or pricing, arrangement. In that environment it has demonstrated its role in driving technical efficiency. New South Wales has not ignored casemix but has relegated it to a lesser role. This reflects a broader role for its decentralised area health services, leading to greater interest in population-based funding with an emphasis on equity and a greater policy interest in health outcomes. It also reflects differences in geography. With a more geographically dispersed population, the trade-off between efficiency and equity in health service provision in New South Wales has been more cogent. This has possibly been at the expense of gains in technical efficiency: the increase in throughput in New South Wales hospitals has not been as great as in Victoria, and since 1992/93 the level of per capita health services expenditure has been higher (and increasing) in New South Wales (AIHW 1998a).

While these common themes of a more managerially rational health service play themselves out, the timing and pace of change is bounded by the capacity of the local political environment to resist counter-pressure from disaffected stakeholders. Ironically, in both states this limitation has been most cogently demonstrated by efforts at relocating their inner-city St Vincent's Hospitals. In New South Wales the relocation of St Vincent's to St George's Hospital was seen to rationalise tertiary services and allow for the redistribution of resources to areas of greater need. Intense public stakeholder opposition led the government to abandon the plan. In Victoria a major purpose of developing hospital networks was to facilitate the redistribution of hospital services from the inner city to the outer sub-urbs. Not to be deterred by the New South Wales experience, the burden of redistribution fell on a proposal to move St Vincent's Hospital to the outer suburb of Knox. A very brief but intense campaign from disaffected stakeholders was enough for the government to abort the idea.

State government health services will continue to be subject to pressures for reform. The conflicting interests of its stakeholders will ensure it. In general, most reforms will reflect well-canvassed ideas to make the service operate in a managerially rational way. Local implementation will remain constrained by the political will or capacity to reject disaffected stakeholders. These dynamics predict a continued incremental reform of the health system.

12

They Said It Couldn't Be Done: Contracting for Veterans' Hospital Care in Australia

Keith Lyon

One of the most comprehensive and successful examples of health reform in Australia over the past decade has been the transition of the Department of Veterans' Affairs (DVA) from a provider of health care to a purchaser. Buying from both the public and private sectors, DVA has emerged as the first and largest national purchaser of health care. The department is also the only publicly funded organisation with responsibility for all aspects of health and aged care. It funds the entire range of services from budget, enabling it to assemble the best mix of services for an individual's circumstances. The reform of veterans' health care has been strongly supported by veterans' ex-service organisations, who are keen to expand the scheme.

DVA's progress in refining contractual arrangements with 40 000 health providers provides a valuable model of coordination and management of the full range of health care. Specifically, DVA's experience offers lessons in the implementation of health reform and provides a model for ensuring both quality and cost efficiency in health care services for the elderly, the heaviest users of health and community services.

The Department of Veterans' Affairs and health care for veterans

DVA is responsible for providing compensation, income support, health care, and commemorative services to Australia's veterans, their widows, and their dependants. In this respect, its role and functions are similar to publicly funded veterans' organisations in many other countries, for example the USA and Canada. DVA's annual budget is $7.3 billion, of which the health care component (including aged-care accommodation and support) is $2.3 billion.

Most Australian veterans served during the Second World War and/or the Korean War. Australia had one million people in uniform in those conflicts, of a total population of under 7 million. Approximately 400 000 of these war veterans are alive today and their average age is approaching the mid-seventies. Consequently, they and their widows use health care services extensively.

The veterans' population also includes a small number who served in the First World War and about 100 000 younger veterans who served in Vietnam, Malaysia, and numerous peacekeeping missions. Published analyses of veterans' mortality and morbidity studies (Crane et al. 1997; Commonwealth Department of Veterans' Affairs 1998a; Commonwealth Department of Veteran' Affairs 1998b) show that many veterans have substantial health problems resulting from their military service.

The Factors Leading to the Reform

Australian veterans previously received most of their health care in repatriation hospitals, which operated as a special category of public hospital. Dedicated veterans' hospitals were established in March 1921 when hospital care and the control of defence hospitals passed to the Repatriation Commission. A number of Second World War defence hospitals was transferred to the commission in 1947, thus increasing the total number of dedicated veterans' hospitals. Over the years, the repatriation hospitals gained a reputation for providing high-quality health care. In the 1970s many became teaching and research hospitals. The hospitals were strongly supported by the veterans' community and were widely valued as the 'bricks and mortar' of the repatriation system.

During the 1980s DVA recognised the need for change in veterans' health care arrangements and initiated several studies to assess the future impact of an ageing and eventually declining veterans' population. In June 1985 the report of the Brand Committee, which illustrated concerns at that time, concluded:

- Separate high-quality repatriation hospitals could not be financially justified indefinitely because the ageing veterans' population was dwindling.
- The hospitals would not continue to attract and maintain quality staff. Consequently, the breadth of treatment needed to sustain quality of care in modern acute-care facilities could deteriorate.
- One option was to permit repatriation hospitals to treat a progressively increasing number of public patients from the general community in order to maintain acute expertise. However, most repatriation hospitals required substantial capital investment for modernisation.

- Negotiation with state governments should start to provide for the integration of repatriation hospitals into the state public hospital system.
- Geriatric services should be developed in repatriation hospitals, but these should be in addition to, not instead of, acute speciality services.

By 1988, considerable capital redevelopment of some of the repatriation hospitals had occurred. However, the Commonwealth government decided to transfer the hospitals and their operation to the states. This decision was motivated by the Australian Defence Force's recognition that it would have to rely increasingly on a civil infrastructure organised primarily to meet civil needs for defence logistics and support. The option of treating civilian patients in hospitals run by the Defence Department was rejected on the grounds that it was not the department's business to assume the states' role of providing hospital services for civilian patients.

At the time of these deliberations, the scale of operations of repatriation hospitals and related institutions serving the veterans' population (e.g. artificial-limb manufacturing facilities) was substantial. Altogether, the hospitals employed 9000 people directly and had an annual budget of more than $500 million. This was nevertheless a minor part of the size of a major city's hospital services. Nationally, veterans accounted for fewer than 3000 occupied beds and just under a million outpatient occasions of service per year. The commission decided that a separate, parallel health system for veterans was no longer justified.

But a wide range of interests was involved in the decision. Whatever the logic underlying the case for policy change, the implementation process would have to proceed very deliberately. Many stakeholders needed to be persuaded of the merits of dismantling the veterans' hospitals system. Initially the Returned and Services League (RSL) and other ex-service organisations were united and vocal in their opposition to the transfer of veterans' hospitals to the states. Understandably, they feared that the government would no longer be able to ensure that veterans received quality and timely health care in already overstretched state facilities. Health employee unions and hospital staff also opposed the change. State governments themselves were very wary of taking over large and expensive facilities, with no guarantee of continuing operational funding in addition to their current budgets.

The Reform Process

DVA recognised that such fundamental change had to be driven from the top—by the Minister, the Repatriation Commission, and senior DVA officials. The issues of each stakeholder group were carefully analysed and considered, and a reform strategy formulated.

A Veterans' Repatriation Private Patient Scheme (RPPS) was designed to enable veterans to obtain hospital care at private hospitals (see Box 12.1, p. 226). The DVA communicated its advantages directly to veterans and ex-service organisations. As veterans began to understand the mechanics and implications of the proposed changes, elderly veterans quickly perceived the benefits of local treatment, greater freedom of choice, and more immediate medical and community support. Legislation introduced to guarantee implementation of the scheme assuaged any lingering doubts.

DVA reached agreement with the Australian Council of Trade Unions (ACTU) after designing innovative arrangements to transfer staff to state employment (see Box 12.2, p. 227). But the wide range of staff employed (specialist doctors to blue-collar workers) raised complex issues that required detailed implementation arrangements. A crucial issue was DVA's decision to match the local state's pay and conditions of service for key employment categories (e.g. medical and nursing). Legislation was required to implement this provision because no mechanism existed then to transfer staff sensibly and economically between levels of government.

Box 12.1   The Veterans' Gold Card Repatriation Private Patient Scheme (RPPS)

Under the RPPS, veterans and war widows receive comprehensive health care regardless of whether their illness, injury, or disease was war-caused. Their benefits include:

- Free medical treatment from 14 000 participating general practitioners (called local medical officers), who agree to treat veterans and to use the DVA-contracted network of specialists, hospitals, and other health providers.
- Access without prior approval to specific services at the former repatriation hospitals, including those privatised, and to any state hospital, as a private patient. They also have access to private hospitals when prior approval is deemed necessary, and when timely treatment is not available within the state systems.
- Access to pharmaceuticals, nursing care, auxiliary health services, and transport geared to meet veterans' needs.

The Scheme is monitored by a joint ex-services/DVA committee reporting independently to the Commonwealth parliament annually on actual performance.

DVA also had to negotiate on financial arrangements with those states willing to absorb repatriation hospitals into their hospital systems. This required it to understand each state's health system and the local factors that would influence the prospect and consequences of absorption into the state system. DVA also had to accept that not all of its hospitals would fit sensibly within a state's hospital strategy. It therefore had to consider alternatives, including closure of hospitals that had no future and privatisation of those hospitals with commercial prospects. Because of differences in the quality of DVA hospital infrastructure, and the fit within each state system, DVA's transfer of financial arrangements varied from state to state. One state received significant capital funding to construct a new rehabilitation centre.

Box 12.2   DVA hospital staff arrangements for transfer of staff into the state health systems

Under specifically drafted legislation, if staff members were offered an equivalent position by the states (essentially same duties, same pay), they were required to transfer or were deemed to have resigned. Staff members who were offered non-equivalent positions could take redundancy and were not required to transfer, but DVA provided income support for a period if they did agree to transfer.

Most professional staff members were offered equivalent positions. Long service leave, sick leave, and holiday leave were transferable, as were retirement benefits. These arrangements were negotiated with the key unions, the ACTU, and the DVA unions.

In each hospital, agreement was reached to maintain certain services deemed important for veterans. The chapel and identified commemorative activities and sites were also maintained at all hospitals.

Payment arrangements for the treatment of veterans in each repatriation hospital and in other state hospitals were made in the form of block grants for periods of four or five years. In most cases the block payments were progressively reduced, which meant that the states gradually picked up the bill for treating publicly funded veterans. Funding of veterans' hospital care at the end of the initial period would be provided to hospitals on the basis of casemix.

The success of the reform strategy relied on the full commitment of DVA's management, and on political support. The latter occurred quickly, facilitated by grassroots veterans' support for the RPPS.

The disposition of veterans' hospitals and privatisation issues

All hospitals were privatised, closed, or transferred to state governments (see Table 12.1), with one exception, between July 1992 and January 1995. Veterans' artificial-limb and appliance centres were all closed or transferred to the states.

Table 12.1   Disposition of Veterans' hospitals, 1992–95

Activity	Number of beds	Number of hospitals
Closed	260	3
Privatised	900	3
Transferred	1770	6
Total	2930	12

Source: Commonwealth Dept of Veterans' Affairs

When the WA State Health Minister advised DVA in August 1992 that the 330-bed teaching repatriation hospital in Perth would not fit into that state's public health system, the Commonwealth government approved the sale of the hospital. A further two repatriation hospitals were later sold— Greenslopes in Brisbane (a 440-bed teaching hospital) and Lady Davidson Hospital at Turramurra in Sydney (a 120-bed specialist rehabilitation and palliative-care hospital). In 1992, however, there was no Australian precedent for a sale, privatisation, or service contracting on this scale.

DVA again consulted ex-service organisations. They agreed to the private sales, which were essential to ensure that the hospitals continued to offer veterans a range of specialised as well as general acute services.

Objectives and outcomes for sales of hospitals

The Repatriation Commission stipulated clear outcomes from the sale of veterans' hospitals:

- a satisfactory agreement for each sale;
- health services agreements to ensure continuous provision of quality and cost-effective hospital services for veterans;
- optimal net financial benefit to the Commonwealth from the combination of hospital sales and contracting back of veterans' care from each purchaser;
- satisfactory employment opportunities for as many DVA staff as practicable; and
- smooth transition of ownership.

Achieving these objectives meant striking a balance between maximum immediate value from the sale of assets and the economical purchase of quality health services for veterans, which would continue to be required for many years. To protect quality of care, the contractual arrangements called for infrastructure upgrading, accreditation, and a range of access measures to ensure that veteran patients were treated speedily.

Arrangements for DVA staff: transfer to the private sector

The government's objectives in relation to staff were:

- to avoid DVA staff taking both a job with the new private sector owner/operator and full redundancy payment ('double dipping'); and
- to avoid transferring to the private sector the obligation to meet DVA's higher public sector pay rates and more generous conditions of service.

DVA conducted lengthy and difficult negotiations with the unions. Agreement was eventually reached to permit staff to resign before taking a position with the new owner/operator in return for a termination payment that was significantly less than standard redundancy benefits. Long-service leave beyond ten years was paid in full. Payment was made when employees had close to ten years' service but not for comparatively short service.

These arrangements were not popular with staff. Many experienced and skilled staff members elected to take redundancy rather than employment with the new operator. The strong market demand for health staff at the time enabled most to do so. However, the employment market had changed by the time the last repatriation hospital (in Sydney) was sold. Staff members were then allowed to take both voluntary redundancy and a job.

The tender process

Tender documentation was prepared for each sale following discussions with potential buyers. Four separate tender documents were released:

- A Request for Tender that set out the general conditions of the tender.
- A proposed Land Sale Agreement covering the sale of the land and improvements and tailored to the local terms and conditions. Each agreement incorporated special leasing and accommodation arrangements; for example, the continuation of the Red Cross's voluntary work.
- A proposed Business Sale Agreement covering sale of the business of each hospital. This agreement included provisions for staff members who were to resign from the Australian Public Service to take up positions with the new operator.
- A proposed Hospital Services Agreement that included a contract for hospital services, requirements to meet the specific interests of the

ex-service community, and provision for quality standards. Price would be negotiated annually and would include financial and performance guarantees by the operator, who was to be given the opportunity to share in the proceeds of efficiency savings.

DVA's aim was to attract commercially advantageous bids by minimising uncertainty and maximising commercial opportunities. Competition among multiple bidders was desirable and encouraged, and negotiation with many other stakeholders was necessary. Discussions were held with the state branch of the AMA, the relevant universities, the Red Cross and veterans' carer organisations, and state government planning bodies. Each of the sales was concluded successfully, in terms of service quality and access, savings or returns to the government, and level of client satisfaction.

The Results of the Reforms

The new DVA purchasing model: strategies underlying the current veterans' health system

The veterans' health scheme now funds—rather than provides directly— treatment by GPs, specialists, hospitals, community nursing, and allied health providers, in addition to aids and appliances, transport, and pharmaceuticals. It also finances health care. The department has a single budget for a huge volume across the entire range of health services and goods, and therefore has reasonable leverage to negotiate reasonable fees with providers.

The current veterans' health care model rests on six principles:

1. Treatment must match an individual's requirements, that is, thorough analysis of the individual's condition and needs. It usually means directing care to selected providers in circumstances where there are substantial variations in provider quality and coverage.
2. Where veterans are treated by multiple providers, provider cooperation and stored information that is easily retrievable are essential. This presents a considerable challenge in Australia's current health system, where health care providers are generally not geared to communicating with each other to ensure continuity of care. Billing and fee structures for health services often work against efficient treatment, especially for chronic illness. As a single funder across a broad range of care, DVA can link information on the treatment received by veteran patients, and intervene on the patient's behalf where necessary. For example, it is often necessary to consult the relevant doctor and patient about appropriate pharmaceutical usage.

3. It is recognised that GPs are crucial to an effective health care system. About 13 500 GPs or local medical officers (LMO in DVA terminology) have agreed to use the DVA referral networks of specialists, contracted hospitals, and other providers. That is, they have effectively agreed to use DVA's 'preferred providers'. LMOs prepare annual care-management plans for each chronically ill patient—an important initiative for the elderly, who often have multiple conditions requiring a range of health services and providers. Ancillary service support in addition to GP care is important as many veterans are, or will become, frail aged.

4. Cooperative partnering relationships with all providers are beneficial. Partnerships are based on sound understanding of contractual obligations and often entail excellent personal relationships.

5. Cost control is fundamental. DVA believes that competitive and selective tendering and contracting arrangements are effective tools for improving the cost-effectiveness of services.

6. Service contracts must be carefully designed. Developing appropriate contracts with small business and private-sector providers also involves particular challenges. DVA uses standardised documentation but has learned to take the initiative in negotiating fees with provider groups.

7. DVA funds all treatment costs. Co-payments are limited to some pharmaceuticals, high-cost dental treatment, and high-cost eyeglasses. DVA's approach is based on Australian evidence that 'price signals' may have undesirable impacts. Older people, including veterans, may conclude unnecessarily that they must choose between diminished quality of life and co-payments.

Veterans' reaction to divestment and the RPPS

The veterans' health scheme was reviewed in depth in 1998. The RPPS review (McLaughlan and Preston 1998) concluded that the scheme was successful overall. The volume of services provided to veterans in those states where the former repatriation hospital was integrated into the state system has decreased over time. Nevertheless, with the possible exception of Hobart, the former repatriation hospital remains the single largest provider of hospital services to the veteran community in each state.

According to the RPPS review, privatisation gave an opportunity to improve the quality of hospital care through better integration of hospital-based services. In each case, a preferred private provider is delivering a more holistic service comprising allied health and ancillary services. The privatisation of the former repatriation hospitals in Western Australia and

Queensland is considered very successful by veterans, local residents, and the ex-service organisations (McLaughlan and Preston 1998).

The review recommended some refinements to the scheme: increased access for veterans to private hospitals (without prior approval); a more explicit communication strategy aimed at increasing the medical profession's understanding of the scheme; and more accurate understanding of transport arrangements for veterans' health service delivery. It also urged DVA to maintain a closer relationship with the health insurance industry.

In recognition of the scheme's success and popularity, the Commonwealth government extended its coverage to an additional 50 000 Second World War veterans in January 1999.

Performance outcomes

The single most important objective of the reform was the provision of timely access to quality medical treatment for veterans. The initial performance indicator was waiting times for elective hospital care; waiting times in the repatriation system were previously often lengthy. The new system soon delivered much better results, largely a result of greater access to private hospitals. Improvements in access were powerfully demonstrated by the decrease in waiting times for elective surgery at the first of the privatised hospitals (see Table 12.2).

The privatised repatriation hospitals also helped set higher standards for efficiency, cost, and quality.

Table 12.2   Changes in waiting times for elective surgery at privatised Perth Hospital

Surgical procedure	Before sale 31/1/94	Waiting time in weeks Post sale 30/6/94	Post sale 21/9/94
Orthopaedics	30	up to 6	6
Urology	40	up to 6	8
Ophthalmology	41	up to 7	8
Vascular	nil	up to 2	4
ENT	2	up to 2	4
Plastics	18	up to 2	10
General	4	up to 2	1–2

Source: Commonwealth Dept of Veterans' Affairs

Financial outcomes

Divestment provided very substantial financial benefits to the government. The number of veterans' separations increased by 28 per cent. Use of surgery increased significantly, but the average cost per separation (in constant prices) fell by 12.6 per cent from $5032 in 1992/93 to $4397 in 1996/97. DVA's total annual hospital expenditure fell by 10.7 per cent between 1994/95 ($858 million) and 1996/97 ($766 million) (Nicol et al. 1998).

DVA's total funding for public hospital treatment of veterans declined substantially after implementation of the reforms. In 1992/93, 83.3 per cent of DVA's expenditure on hospital services was channelled to public sector hospitals, including the repatriation hospitals; only 16.7 per cent financed treatment in private hospitals. By 1996/97, 54.5 per cent of DVA's expenditure was allocated to the public hospitals, and the private sector (including the former repatriation hospitals) accounted for 45.5 per cent. Excluding the privatised repatriation hospitals, DVA expenditure in the private sector increased by $118 million (Nicol et al. 1998).

Critical success factors

The new veterans' health arrangements have succeeded for several reasons:

1. For more than ten years the DVA has maintained a consistent policy direction based on consultation with relevant stakeholders at all important levels—ministerial, ex-service organisation, and the Repatriation Commission.
2. Commitment and leadership have also been continuous.
3. The range of services provided under the RPPS is seen to match veterans' health needs, and the scheme is supported by both health care providers and government. Specific measures were taken from the earliest days to gain and maintain this support.
4. The new arrangements have a solid commercial foundation and adhere to a partnership model of contracting between the DVA and health care providers.
5. Performance against contracts is assiduously monitored by purchaser, provider, clients, and veterans' service organisations.

Lessons Learned

DVA's experience provides important lessons for all purchasers of services to government. Perhaps the most salient are the importance of identifying outcomes and processes at the outset, continually reassessing priorities, consistently monitoring costs, and fostering competition. Specific lessons include the need to:

- *define health care broadly* Strategies to improve health care outcomes should include research, prevention, transport, and community-based care. They should include help in the home as well as the more obvious medical services and pharmaceuticals. Integrating these activities into an effective holistic approach has required more attention than DVA originally contemplated.

- *continuously improve contracts*   DVA's contracts for the sale of repatriation hospitals to the private sector, and with ongoing provision of hospital services, have proved flexible and robust. But arrangements with state governments, which took over the former repatriation hospitals and continue to provide hospital care for veterans, need to be improved. Improved arrangements are introduced each time an agreement is updated. For example, incentive payments are now being introduced to help achieve better treatment outcomes and information.
- *improve information*   Although DVA can relate services and costs to individual veterans and specific providers, more efficient information systems are needed for planning and budgeting. Progressive improvements in data collection are being included in new contracts, and the department's own information-processing and analytical capabilities are being improved.
- *introduce competition*   Health care, like any other service, can benefit from appropriate competition. DVA will continue to increase competition. Arrangements with the state governments for acute care will now be converted to a full-cost basis, so that value for money can be compared across public hospitals and funding provided accordingly. This will open the door for a more competition and is expected to lead to cost savings as well as better data-gathering and performance-monitoring.

Conclusion

Government funder-providers can make an effective transition to the role of service purchaser. Commitment, continuous leadership, and well-developed strategies are essential for major reform. For DVA, the introduction and incremental improvement of the RPPS have demonstrated that increasing private sector involvement, accountability, cost-effectiveness, and improvements in quality can be achieved within a flexible and adaptive model. Moreover, the precedent set by the veterans' model has the potential to stimulate similar structural changes in the management of health care nationally, especially for the elderly. In 1999 DVA aims to start selective competitive tendering between public and private hospitals. Integrating these activities into an effective holistic approach is ongoing and has required more attention than originally contemplated.

13

Hospital Co-Locations: Private Sector Participation in the Hospital Sector in Australia

Abby Bloom

Co-location has emerged as the preferred means of increasing private sector involvement in Australia's predominantly public hospital system. It refers to the establishment of a privately owned hospital within or adjacent to an existing public hospital campus. The co-located facility or facilities might be owned and operated by an investor-owned corporation or by a not-for-profit entity. It might be physically distinct from, or linked with, the existing public hospital; it might provide comprehensive or selected services; and it might or might not involve formal sharing of facilities, staff, or services. Its two distinctive features are its independent, private ownership and operation, and its position on or near an existing public hospital campus.

This chapter examines the phenomenon of co-location, assesses the benefits and risks for both the public and private sectors, and considers the issues raised by co-location. The examination of co-location illuminates how markets respond to new opportunities for competition from the private sector, and how both the public and private sectors seek to gain advantage and minimise risks in the course of health reform.

A salient feature of health sector reform is how generic policies, concepts, and theories are interpreted and applied to fit local circumstances (Bloom 1988). Australia has proved a fascinating laboratory of private sector participation in the hospital sector, demonstrating colourfully how the role, structure, and functions of the private sector in health care delivery respond to local incentives, barriers, and opportunities. A variety of forms of private sector participation has emerged in response to new market conditions.

Background: Co-Locations in the Context of a Mixed Public–Private Hospital System

The Australian health care system is a mixed public–private system, and has always incorporated a mix of public and private service provision and financing (Peabody and Bickel 1996; Palmer and Short 1994). The balance between the two has varied over time and between states, depending on local circumstances, history, and political ideology. As Foley describes in Chapter 5, a marked trend towards increased private sector participation in health care delivery began in earnest in the late 1980s. The trend gathered momentum through the 1990s, as every state and territory introduced policies and incentives aimed at attracting private capital and service providers to complement and enhance existing publicly funded health care services.

Historically, private sector participation in Australia's hospital system has involved both the not-for-profit sector (largely but not exclusively hospitals owned and operated by religious organisations) and the for-profit sector. Although most teaching and super-speciality hospitals were public hospitals, some noted large specialist teaching facilities were owned and operated by not-for-profit religious organisations (e.g. St Vincent's Hospitals in Sydney and Melbourne, and the Wesley Hospital in Brisbane), and by some for-profit hospitals (e.g. Epworth in Melbourne). The typical private hospital was (and remains) small (under a hundred beds, with many private hospitals as small as fifty to eighty beds) and offered limited general medical or surgical treatment, or selected specialities. They differentiated themselves from public hospitals by offering faster access for elective procedures, access to the doctor of one's choice, and (often but not always) better amenities. However, because Medicare provides every Australian access to sophisticated, high-quality treatment in public hospitals, private sector investment in acute hospitals was modest until the late 1980s.

Private sector participation in hospital service provision accelerated in the late 1980s for several reasons. First, Liberal (conservative) state governments sought to reverse the limited role to which private enterprise had been relegated. In 1988, for instance, a new policy was announced by the Liberal government in New South Wales, which actively promoted the construction of large new, sophisticated private hospitals. The fulcrum of the policy was the announcement of tenders for twenty-four hospital co-location opportunities on public hospital campuses throughout the state.

Australian governments were also monitoring policies and experience in the United Kingdom, USA, and elsewhere that seemed to suggest that the state could fulfil its essential responsibilities by *ensuring access* to services, but not necessarily *owning all assets and actually providing all services* (Osborn and Gaebler 1992; Domberger 1998). Accepting the concept that private sector involvement could be useful in achieving public sector goals, Liberal governments also believed that private sector involvement could stimulate improved efficiency in public sector facilities by providing direct competition, particularly for government organisations resistant to change.

The most persuasive factor encouraging greater private sector involvement in the hospital system was pragmatic, and purely financial. State governments simply could not get enough infrastructure capital for the construction of new hospitals and the redevelopment of existing ones. Not only were they unable to raise capital in the market, but also their requests for a share of government's development capital had to compete with requests from all other government departments. The wait was long and uncertain. Government capital works lists typically had a waiting time of ten years until funds were approved.

In the 1990s state governments, led by Victoria, began to sell or privatise government-owned infrastructure to retire debt and stimulate public sector productivity. In response, the private sector began to provide increasing amounts of investment capital for new privately owned and operated hospitals. Private sector participation in hospital services took many forms, including build-own-operate-transfer (BOOT, where the private sector constructs and operates a hospital for a stipulated period under conditions agreed with government, and then transfers the facility to government).

By 1999 more than forty-five substantial private hospital developments were under way nationally, involving upwards of $1 billion in capital. Of these, nearly twenty were co-locations. By the same year most of the prime public teaching hospital campuses in Australia's largest cities had new co-locations operating or out to tender. This included six campuses in Victoria (four in Melbourne), six in New South Wales (five in Sydney), and five in Queensland (three in Brisbane).

Distinguishing Features of the New Wave of Co-Locations

The co-location of a private hospital within the campus of a public hospital was by no means new in Australia. Until the late 1970s, public hospitals commonly had a separate private wing, building, or floors where attending doctors could give their patients private accommodation. The earlier co-locations were well accepted by the community, medical profession, and government. They differed from the current wave in that the facilities were owned, operated, and staffed by the public hospital. All attending physicians were also engaged part-time in the public hospital.

The new co-locations differ in one important respect: they are operated by a wholly independent, private owner/operator, at arm's length from government. This was deliberate government policy, and part of the ideology that the private sector must be unencumbered by interference from the public sector.

The new arm's-length arrangements for private sector involvement on public hospital campuses provided advantages and disadvantages for both parties. Most importantly, they meant that no relationship between the public and private co-located hospital could be assumed. Any relationship between the two—whether it concerned sharing services or other features—would have to be negotiated and formalised in a commercial contract. The public sector would have to identify the potential risks and benefits in a co-location arrangement, specify them, quantify them, and negotiate a mutually agreeable, enforceable commercial contract.

It also placed the two effectively in competition for a share of the private patient market. The first wave of co-locations, which took place in the Sydney metropolitan area, reflected the inexperience of the public sector in commercial dealings in general, and in public–private partnerships in social services in particular. But the initial tenders also occurred at a very early stage in the evolution of corporate hospital groups in Australia. At that time the public sector had no local experience as a basis for predicting what the private co-location partner would try to extract from the relationship. It knew little about what the private operator would do to establish its business and bring it to profitability. The American experience suggested that the private sector might be expected to 'cream skim', that is, to capture profitable patients who would otherwise attend public facilities.

Public sector planners and negotiators in Australia, however, did not as a rule go to the same length as the private sector to model and quantify the implications of the new arrangement. Most importantly, they did not estimate and plan for the probable commercial impact of the private co-location on the public hospital. In contrast, the private hospital had ample incentive to do so: it had to argue their case for debt finance, explaining to lenders how the hospital project would perform under different assumptions and scenarios. It also had to judge for itself, of course, whether the private hospital would generate enough revenue and profit to satisfy its shareholders.

This gap in knowledge, experience, and commercial accountability has been the public sector's Achilles heel in co-locations and other private hospital projects, and was painfully revealed when an audit was conducted of an early privatisation, the Port Maquarie Hospital (NSW Auditor-General 1997).

Co-location opportunities generate diverse and creative alternatives

New opportunities to build and operate private, co-located hospitals on prime teaching hospital campuses unleashed an innovative range of options for public–private partnerships in hospital care. By far the largest number of co-locations has been proposed or constructed directly on a public hospital campus, though at least one co-located hospital is situated near, but not immediately on, the publicly owned site. The land is usually leased from the government for twenty to thirty years in exchange for a financial payment, plus regular payments linked with performance and other concessions (e.g. a car park, stipulated services). Most existing co-locations are freestanding, but many are physically connected to the public hospital either by a covered walkway, or, in the case of one, by a short connecting corridor on each floor. This same co-located hospital was constructed on top of an existing publicly funded hospital.

Another co-located hospital owned and operated by the same company in a different state has also been carefully integrated within existing buildings on the public hospital campus. In this case, the co-located hospital's construction occurred as part of a simultaneous redevelopment of the campus. A conceptual scheme, designed with the participation of all parties, unified the new campus and enabled patients of both hospitals to use a common underground car park and other facilities. Part of the redevelopment was the integration of a women's hospital within the campus. The outdated women's hospital in another part of Sydney was closed and its service capacity transferred to the new site. The public buildings within the campus now offer a full range of adult, obstetric and paediatric care. The private hospital offers similar services, and the public hospital continues to treat 'private' patients (fee-paying and privately insured patients) as well. While financial data are not available, it would appear that the private hospital has indeed diverted private patients from the public hospital (especially obstetrics patients), but that it has not achieved its expected throughput targets in other specialities.

This co-location was the catalyst for a comprehensive upgrading of an existing campus, as well as rationalisation of a maternity and gynaecology facility. The amalgamation was designed to generate efficiencies and other benefits not directly associated with the co-location. Not all have been fully realised to date, but other opportunities have arisen, demonstrating the need for some flexibility and receptivity as the relationship between public and private hospitals matures.

Most of the major urban teaching hospitals across Australia by now have a co-located private hospital planned or in operation. The competition for these sites among for-profit and not-for-profit hospital operators is compelling evidence of their attractiveness. The few remaining significant teaching hospitals are likely to have co-located private hospitals constructed within the next few years.

Benefits and Risks in Co-Location

A major theme in the literature on privatisation of public infrastructure and service provision is the complex balance between benefits and risks. Hospital co-locations have emerged as the preferred form of private sector participation in hospital care in Australia because they are perceived to offer the best available combination of risks and benefits. Thus they provide a useful canvas for analysing how a mixed public–private hospital system satisfies the different, and sometimes conflicting, needs of its stakeholders.

A substantial literature exists on risk and risk management in service-contracting in other sectors, including the means used by contracting organisations to avert and minimise risk (Domberger 1998). In contrast, there is scant but growing evidence on risks and risk management in con-tracting health services (Mills 1998; Øvretveit 1998; Saltman and Casten von Otter 1998). Co-locations offer the prospect of considerable benefits, as well as significant risks, and an understanding of the respective interests of each party is crucial to understanding the appeal of this particular public–private mix.

Benefits: public hospitals

A co-location enables the public sector to trade off assets they have (good-will, land) for assets and services they need. The state government already owns the land on which public hospitals currently stand. Although much of it is surplus, asset sales are often constrained by communities and activists who wish to retain disused government land for use by the local commu-nity. The sites often have zoning restrictions, but hospital use (private or public) is usually compatible.

By bringing capital investment onto the campus, a co-location can physically reinvigorate a site with no capital outlay by the government being required. Parking stations, amenities (cafés, indoor and outdoor public space, etc.), and sometimes costly new technology (e.g. diagnostic radiology), can make the public hospital campus a more modern, access-ible, pleasant, and comfortable place.

Co-locations can also absorb excess patient demand by offering an alternative source of care, with the private hospital attracting patients away from the pressured public hospital. Of course, unless specific arrangements are made, only those patients able to pay out of pocket, or through private health insurance, can elect for treatment in the private hospital. Proponents of co-location claim that it can also result in cost savings to the government if, as patient numbers decline, beds are closed and overall capacity is reduced.

Co-locations can potentially enhance the range and quality of services available on a campus. The combined volume achieved through the two hospitals may achieve the critical mass that makes it feasible to offer a more complex level of services in certain speciality areas. An example of this is the co-location of the Holy Spirit Hospital on the campus of the Prince Charles (public) Hospital in Brisbane. New, comprehensive services are then available in principle to public patients who would previously have had to seek them elsewhere. In addition, the broader mix of patients, who will in theory be attracted to the campus, provides greater scope for education and research.

Co-locations provide staff incentives, particularly for doctors, by offering additional valuable opportunities for private practice. Private consulting rooms, modern in-patient facilities, linked diagnostic facilities, and other amenities all make it easier for doctors to treat private patients in a modern, high-tech, customer-focused environment. And, of course, the new private consulting rooms in the co-located private hospital give doctors a strong incentive to concentrate their efforts on the single site by eliminating travel between the public hospital campus and private rooms.

A co-location is considered an insurance policy against closure of a public hospital. In an era when the unthinkable—closing historic and revered public hospitals—is now a real threat, a co-location reinforces the future of the campus. With a private hospital on site, the public hospital may be downsized, but it is likely to survive.

Benefits: private hospitals

Co-location provides the private hospital operator with several competitive advantages. These include affiliation with a prestigious institution and a site that is already a magnet for referring doctors and for private patients. Established teaching hospitals usually occupy valuable land—centrally located sites within a medical precinct that was set aside many years ago. Purchase of a comparable site would be prohibitively expensive and often impossible now.

The most important benefit of co-location for the private hospital is immediate access to two of the key factors that determine its profitability: referring doctors and paying patients.

The biggest challenge facing any new hospital in its first years is building up its throughput—the number of patients treated and its occupancy rate. Throughput and casemix, plus costs, determine the point at which the new hospital is trading profitably. Any partnership—whether co-location or service contract—that rapidly pushes a new private hospital's throughput to the margin and beyond is commercially extremely valuable.

A co-located hospital is a valuable form of partnership because the new entrant instantly benefits from extant demand from private patients. Some of them are 'new' patients who would have sought treatment elsewhere; others would have been treated as 'private' patients in the public hospital next door. The latter are 'diverted' from the public hospital, alleviating pressure on the one hand, but, on the other hand, sifting out a casemix that benefits the private hospital, possibly to the detriment of the public hospital. Still other patients may be redirected from other hospitals within the operator's network—a distinct advantage that corporate groups have over stand-alone, unaffiliated private hospitals.

Most co-locations will be preceded by intensive negotiations with the doctors employed in the public hospital. A variety of inducements may be offered to ensure their commitment, including consulting and procedure rooms, specialised equipment, and commercial advice.

Another advantage in co-location for the private hospital operator is the benefit they may gain from complementary services offered by the public hospital. These complementary benefits typically include access to residents and registrars, very sophisticated emergency units, super-speciality services, and diagnostic equipment (e.g. MRI and PET). The availability of the public hospital infrastructure also enables the private hospital to offer low-volume/high-cost clinical services within the private hospital, relying on, for instance, the intensive-care cover that can always be tapped at the public hospital.

Risks for the public hospital

The first risk the public sector faces is the possibility that co-location may disadvantage—or be perceived to disadvantage—the public interest. Two scholars, one from the USA and the other from Ireland (pers. comm.), have recently remarked that they have never seen a country where health and hospitals are as prominently and frequently covered on the front page of major newspapers as they are in Australia. Stephen Leeder stated with fervour in the *Sydney Morning Herald* (8 December 1998):

> Rather than abolishing the Medicare levy it should be seen for what it is: a flag that symbolises who we are and what we believe in, the way we care for our

people in sickness and in health. If this flag is ripped down and burnt, rather than gently repaired, washed, and raised in a fresh colour, Australians should grieve, for something precious will have died in our soul.

This interest in health policy also means that the slightest misstep affecting the Australian public health system is a catalyst for very public and heated debate. The increasing role of the private sector in health has generated continuing debate and controversy. The lack of transparency resulting from commercial confidentiality clauses imposed on every co-location agreement fuels political and public suspicion.

Probably the greatest immediate risk to the public sector concerns the potential loss of revenue that may result from the diversion of patients from the public hospital to the private hospital. There is little doubt that co-located private hospitals attract lucrative patients that the public hospital might prefer to retain. The same risk applies to staff members. Instead of retaining them, the public hospital may lose them altogether, as has already occurred in some instances.

The obvious challenge to the public hospital is establishing the right balance of patients—commercially, clinically, and in terms of research and teaching. With a new, attractive, effectively marketed private hospital next door, how can the public hospital ensure that it retains that balance? What measures can be put in place—before as well as after the fact—to ensure that the public hospital retains a viable patient mix?

Risks for the private sector

Co-locations do not automatically carry a guarantee of patient throughput. Guarantees of patient numbers must be stipulated explicitly in the contract, and to date this is not common. Thus the private hospital is at the same type of risk as any start-up operation—namely that it will not attract enough patients of the right mix. But as discussed above, co-locations provide a very keen market advantage. On the one hand, they are in an ideal position to take a share of the existing market of patients who would previously have been treated as private patients in the public hospital. Alternatively, they can obtain patients from the external market—patients who might have been treated at other private hospitals, or who represent unmet or latent demand for elective hospital treatment.

Miscalculation of costs, revenues, and capital and operating expenses is always a risk to a start-up business, including a new hospital. The risk for the private hospital operator is heightened by the strong policy and regulatory influence of government in health, in particular its control over private health insurance (on which effective demand for private hospital treatment is so dependent).

Benefits and risks for the other stakeholders: private insurers, consumers, and the Commonwealth government

Consumers too face both benefits and risks. The benefits of co-locations for consumers have already been stressed, including greater choice, easier access, improved amenities (car access and parking, modern, patient-centred facilities, etc.). Risks include the unintended weakening of the public hospital. And, for consumers reliant on the public system, the co-location might contribute towards the emergence of a two-tier system, exaggerating the gap in health care between those who can pay and those who cannot.

Private health insurers and private hospitals are mutually dependent. Affordable private health insurance is vital to the commercial success of private hospitals. Access to treatment in private hospitals provides a strong incentive to retain private insurance. But a greater supply of more attractive private hospitals, including co-locations, might also encourage more people to use their health insurance. The current crop of private hospitals, particularly co-located private hospitals, supply a more cost-intensive mix of services than the older private hospitals they are forcing out. It is also likely that the charge to insurers per episode in these hospitals exceeds the comparable charge for private patients treated in a public hospital. This cost push is already being felt by the major funders of private hospital treatment in Australia, private insurers and the Commonwealth government on behalf of veterans.

For Australia's Commonwealth government, greater reliance on private hospitals, including co-locations, might increase the total percentage of GDP spent on health, but it also shifts at least some proportion of costs from central Treasury to individuals (e.g. through payments for private insurance). Total hospital costs might also increase as costs are shifted from one provider to another. On the other hand, the remaining casemix in public hospitals might be more costly to state government.

Issues Emerging from Co-Locations

The main issue in hospital co-location in Australia is the surprising lack of attention to the medium-term and longer-term impacts of these arrangements on the public sector and on consumers. Most of the analysis and preparation for co-location appears to have focused on the commercial agreements rather than on the longer-term impacts.

To understand the issues that arise in a hospital co-location, it is essential to understand the incentives and other factors affecting each party's needs and behaviours. The private sector must cover all costs and make a profit sufficient to amortise debt and, among for-profit operators, to make a profit. Any listed company must account to its shareholders for the value and growth of their equity investment, whether the hospital's proprietor is a religious order or a large corporation listed on the New York Stock Exchange.

A private operator might have other objectives: they might wish to build the organisation's reputation, enhance its 'brand', and increase its market share. A key element in its success is enlisting the support and services of doctors and, with them, patient referrals. Those doctors might currently be employees of the public hospital. Sharing, caring, and protecting the well-being of the public hospital is at best a secondary objective. However, as in any mutually dependent relationship, the welfare of the 'host' is integral to the progress of the co-located private hospital.

The factors motivating the public sector are many. As Poutasi has described in Chapter 7, government must be seen to be providing equitable access to quality health services at an appropriate price. It must also be seen to behave prudently and responsively on behalf of its constituents.

Lessons Learned from Co-Location

The knowledge lag

The knowledge lag is a well-known hazard—practical knowledge gained in one co-location experience is not transferred to those who would benefit from applying it to the next co-location. This nearly always places government at a disadvantage in public–private partnerships, at least at the beginning. In hospital co-locations in Australia, unfortunately, the asymmetry of information can be seen clearly to favour the private sector, which has done its homework well. It has predicted alternative scenarios for patient flow and caseload, and converted these into financial models. These have been subjected to sensitivity analyses, and judgments made about how best to configure, operate, and market the new private hospital. Private hospital operators have a clearer strategy. They learn from each others' experience and use this information to inform their next co-location.

In contrast, the public sector typically has neither analysed thoroughly the impact of the co-location nor shared this valuable commercial insight systematically with other public hospitals considering co-location. Moreover, the rapid build-up of the private hospital sector in Australia, as elsewhere, has meant that private operators have recruited staff vigorously from the public sector, but the traffic has not been two-way. Consequently, rarely would the knowledge of the private hospital environment be transferred back to the pubic sector. Whereas impressive commercial expertise is assembled to advise on the initial agreement, there is a lack of systematic data on what tends to happen two, five, or ten years on. Many of those responsible for assessing and managing co-locations would have had no commercial experience whatever.

This is not to say that experience has not been a valuable teacher. As one private hospital negotiator recently told his colleagues, 'I'm really glad we negotiated our contract back then. I wouldn't want to be negotiating with the same authorities today.'

Proponents of increased private sector participation are quick to point out that government has a natural advantage in its cumulative knowledge through experience in operating hospitals. They cite one Australian privately built and operated hospital, intended to provide public hospital treatment. In this instance, it appears that the operator's knowledge about pricing and delivery was insufficient, and the hospital has experienced acute financial problems.

But the knowledge gap nearly always disadvantages the public sector. This is a strong argument for more thorough and commercial analysis by the public sector before contracts are negotiated, including the construction of financial models predicting how different co-location arrangements will affect the public hospital, right through the implementation and management stages.

A cooperative, respectful relationship is essential

Private and public hospital operators point to the importance of complete independence on the one hand, but to 'friendly, respectful neighbours' on the other (Schmiede 1998). Although tone and degree of mutual regard in relationships is something that cannot be enforced, they certainly can be encouraged through the efforts of both parties, and they can formalised in contract preambles, as they often are in service contracts.

Private operators differ in business strategy, implementation and collaboration

As experience accumulates on co-locations and other forms of privatisations, palpable differences are emerging among operators. One of the interesting differences is in the degree of collaboration above and beyond the essentials of the contract. For example, the underlying corporate values of some of the hospitals operated by religious orders will differ from the for-profit, publicly listed hospitals: listed, for-profit companies must maximise returns to their shareholders, whereas other entities, although still functioning commercially, might placer higher value on other objectives. It is important for the public sector to be aware of these differences and use them to best advantage.

The devil is in the detail: the importance of the contract

A co-location is at heart a symbiotic relationship, with each party obtaining different benefits, but each dependent on the other. However, as the early experience in hospital privatisation in Australia has shown, many of the anticipated 'sharing and caring' benefits of co-locations will remain hypothetical unless they are stipulated in the contract. Although not everything can be specified within a contract, there is ample scope to formalise all commercial relationships, and to at least set out in writing the values and objectives expected of each party. At the end of the day, if a party is not obliged by contract, there should be no expectation that it will provide any added services or benefits.

A lack of strategy diminishes the value of the mechanism

Until recently, governments have not always had clear strategies to match the objectives they wish to achieve with co-locations. Thus if the phenomenon of co-location has succeeded, contends one senior expert, it has been by accident rather than design (Smythe 1998). In fact there is sufficient cumulative experience to be able to specify strategies that will maximise revenue, minimise risk, or achieve other common public sector objectives. Unfortunately, it is not shared systematically.

Privatisation by stealth?

Some co-locations are clearly being used by government as catalysts for the consolidation of the public (and private) hospital system. This is clear from tender specifications that state a preference for solutions that relocate existing hospitals, closing down facilities in overserviced communities and relocating them where access is lower. One such tender was awarded in Queensland, and another very large tender for amalgamation and privatisation was undertaken in Melbourne.

There are several questions we can legitimately ask. Are co-locations a covert means of downsizing or even closing existing public hospitals (virtually impossible to achieve overtly), and replacing their ageing capital stock with new, private services, subtly shifting the public–private mix of the entire system? Shouldn't it be evident from the outset that a private hospital will substitute its capacity for that of the public hospital? Is rationalisation by stealth deliberate? Is government an active party or an innocent bystander to this process? Is there a not-so-hidden agenda, encouraging the private sector to replace public facilities in the full knowledge that what will emerge is a two-tiered hospital campus—top amenities and modern equipment for those who can afford it, and a continuously deteriorating public hospital for those who cannot?

Why is co-location so popular?

Co-location is the most popular form of private sector participation in hospital care in Australia because it provides a mutually beneficial 'win-win' model that best meets the needs of both public and private sectors. It offers the private sector immediate access to a lucrative market as well as the prestige of association with a leading public institution. The proximity is invaluable—it is a unique asset that cannot be duplicated by a competitor. This propinquity has tangible financial value, as will be explained below. From the private sector's perspective it is quite straightforward: co-located hospitals provide much better margins (profits), more rapidly, than most alternative forms of privatisation. They deliver an immediate supply of doctors and other staff, and patients (referred through doctors or diverted from patients who look to the local teaching hospital as their preferred source of care). Coupled with the attraction of a new building and up-to-the-minute equipment, and backed by skilful marketing, a co-located private hospital is a potentially lucrative and highly competitive business.

Although the private hospital operator still runs the risks of any business start-up, these risks are greatly reduced in a co-location as compared with a freestanding hospital somewhere else in town. Not only are the profit margins of a co-location higher in principle, in comparison with an identical stand-alone hospital, but also the period for reaching 'break-even' should be shorter. Moreover, co-locations have been shown to have tangible financial value. In 1999 Health Care of Australia's parent company, Mayne Nickless, securitised the rental cash flows from a co-located hospital; they were placed in a trust (Health Care Trust No. 1), creating A-rated bonds (annuities) that were then sold to investors. The tangible government support behind the co-location, and the rental streams, are not usually available in freestanding hospital projects, making co-location a valuable form of privatisation for yet another reason. It is expected that this creative new annuity product will be applied to other co-located hospitals as well (*Australian Financial Review* 21 June 1999: 47).

There are undoubtedly some risks associated with being on a public hospital campus, and concessions or collaborative agreements are needed to win the tender and maintain the relationship. Obviously, however, these risks have not deterred private operators, and must be considered minor in the broader context of risk undertaken in opening any new private hospital.

Co-location offers the public sector the possibility of generating capital reserves not otherwise available to them. The public hospital can attract to its campus new facilities, such as a safe modern car park and the attraction of a modern new hospital, as well as new equipment. The public sector has a better prospect of retaining its doctors, who will have obtained a convenient and modern venue for treating their private patients.

The potential risks to the public hospital are, unfortunately, considerable. Any misstep by the private hospital can be sheeted home to the public hospital, too—either by association or because the government is responsible for monitoring and managing what occurs on its campus. Benefits and risks are a double-edged sword: although the private hospital might help to alleviate the 'excess burden' on a public hospital, it might do so to such a point that the public facility is irreparably damaged. For example, if patient numbers in a department such as cardiology or cardiac surgery fall dramatically, the throughput might fall below the level at which quality care can be guaranteed. With new, convenient private rooms, doctors might reduce the hours they allocate to treating 'public' patients, and even abandon public employment altogether in favour of working full-time in the private sector. And, as we have seen, a co-location might erode the public hospital's financial picture, leaving it with a residual casemix that is much more costly per unit.

Conclusion

Hospital co-locations have become the preferred approach to private sector participation in hospital development in Australia because they offer each party the best available balance of benefit and risk within the local market conditions. But for the public sector, it is also potentially a Trojan horse. Public–private partnerships will inevitably involve a degree of mutuality and interdependence as well as an element of 'gaming' (i.e. trying to maximise advantage within prevailing rules). To maximise the benefits it obtains on behalf of the public, government must improve its ability to predict and avert the undesired by-products of hospital co-locations and ensure that, to the extent possible, ample provision is made within the agreements and contracts.

Have the benefits expected from co-location materialised? Have the shared infrastructure and resources delivered the expected benefits? Unfortunately, the details of the numerous co-locations remain undocumented and little shared. While this is not unique to the privatisation experience in Australia, it leaves all—but particularly government—at a disadvantage in planning, appraising, negotiating, and managing these very desirable but very delicate collaborations.

In conclusion, co-locations are like arranged marriages. They are most likely to succeed when adequate preliminary investigations are made by those with the skills, knowledge, and experience to judge how each partner is likely to behave under the inevitable strains of a long and sometimes tense union.

14

Intergovernmental Reforms in Public Health

Vivian Lin and Cathy King*

Reforms to health and related community services, initiated by the Council of Australian Governments (COAG), are changing the guidelines by which the health system operates and is funded in Australia. The reforms' theoretical underpinnings are similar to those underpinning reforms introduced in New Zealand. What is of interest in the Australian context, however, is how Commonwealth–state relations have had a bearing on their shape.

In Australia, public health is a useful example of how intergovernmental relations can influence the course of reform. Policies in public health, like other areas of public policy, reflect the period of history in which they have emerged. The set of reforms in public health considered here reflected the convergence of political and technical rationality that characterised much of public policy in the mid- to late 1990s. The public health system in Australia rests on a complex set of intergovernmental and community interdependencies, which have both shaped the direction of reform and been shaped by them.

Over the period 1996–98, Australia's Commonwealth, states and territories negotiated two separate but linked public health reform processes. The first, the introduction of a multilateral National Public Health Partnership (NPHP), between the Commonwealth and all states/territories, provided a mechanism for greater cooperation and coordination between jurisdictions on public health policy and practice.

The second reform was the 'broadbanding' of specific-purpose payments (SPPs) for the transfer of public health funding from the Commonwealth to the states/territories into bilateral Public Health Outcome

*The views expressed in this paper are the authors' own and do not necessarily reflect those of the Commonwealth Department of Health and Aged Care, the National Public Health Partnership, or the Department of Human Services.

Funding Agreements. Broadbanding means pooling specifically allocated program dollars into one block grant. The aim of this reform was to create greater flexibility and administrative efficiency in Commonwealth–state financing arrangements in public health.

In this chapter we argue that the parallel introduction of these two reforms changed the context in which Commonwealth–state relations in public health are conducted. In combination with the diversity of interests that have shaped public health over its history, the parallel reforms have, in turn, set the scene for a stronger environment to advance health policy. What lessons can other elements of the health system draw from the experiences of reform in public health? What lessons can be drawn for public health itself in its interactions with other elements of the health system?

Public Health in Australia

Public health has been defined as an 'organised response, by society, to protect and promote health and to prevent illness, injury, and disability' (NPHP 1998). The central characteristics of public health interventions include a focus on the population as a whole (or groups within it), and on managing the determinants of health and ill health. The word 'public' is also significant in three respects: for the public, by the public, and in the public interest.

There are generally three main components of public health work (NPHP 1998):

- *public health intelligence:* the gathering and analysis of information about health, the causes of ill health, and the patterns and trends of health and ill health in populations;
- *public health interventions:* the development of policy and action aimed at prevention, protection and promotion of the health of the community; and
- *public health infrastructure:* the administrative, legislative and informational systems developed to ensure that the entire public health system is sustainable.

Government intervention in public health in Australia can be traced back to colonial times. Most early government interventions in the health field were public health measures introduced to reduce the level of disease and prevent epidemics from occurring or spreading. The types of public health activities undertaken are illustrated by the following examples:

- introduction by the New South Wales colony of measures to improve sanitation and to address outbreaks such as the 1881 smallpox epidemic in Sydney;

- cooperation between the Commonwealth, New South Wales and Queensland to establish a school of tropical health;
- implementation of a campaign to eradicate hookworm;
- development of the Commonwealth Serum Laboratories during the First World War to produce serums and vaccines;
- Commonwealth grants for the provision of free milk to primary school children;
- the anti-tubercular campaigns; and
- broad vaccination programs such as that introduced to eradicate poliomyelitis in the 1950s.

Public health developed primarily as a local activity because environmental hazards in the early days of industrialisation and colonisation tended to be local in nature. Consequently, the Australian Constitution does not cite public health among the express powers of the Commonwealth government. Commonwealth influence in the development of public health policy across Australia was first observed in the passage of the *Quarantine Act 1908* to prevent the introduction and spread of infectious diseases, which might occur as the result of international movements of people and goods.

In more recent times, Commonwealth influence has increased mainly through the Commonwealth government's use of a number of specific-purpose payments (SPPs). These SPPs, which emerged in the 1970s and continued into the early 1990s, were made possible by changes to Commonwealth revenue-raising powers in 1946.

States and territories have remained largely responsible for local policy, planning and program implementation, regulation, disease surveillance, and enforcement of standards affecting public health. Local government has in the main been the vehicle in most states and territories for food inspection and environmental health services, and in some for the implementation of immunisation and child and maternal health services.

Between the mid-1980s and the early 1990s, the Commonwealth began to assume greater importance in supporting public health programs, and as such began to shape state and territory priorities in public health. Commonwealth expenditure on public health in 1998/99 was budgeted to be $274m, with 51 per cent of these funds transferred to states and territories by way of SPPs for public health purposes. Comparability of Commonwealth and state and territory expenditure on public health is difficult due to differing definitions of which activities to count. In many jurisdictions, however, the Commonwealth contribution is close to half of state/territory public health expenditure.

The politics of public health have meant some contests among the Commonwealth, states, local government, and community organisations over who has the main role in defining the parameters of policy debate and

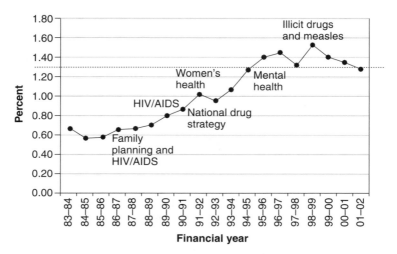

Figure 14.1 Commonwealth health promotion and disease expenditure as a percentage of Commonwealth health expenditure

Source: Commonwealth Department of Health and Aged Care Budget Papers

development. However, beginning in the early 1990s, as conservative governments took hold across states and territories, the commitment to 'small government' and debt reduction resulted in significant cuts to health budgets. With increasing proportions of public health budgets tied to cost-shared programs (i.e. funding arrangements under which it is a condition of grant that the state match the Commonwealth contribution), the traditional infrastructure shouldered most of the cuts.

As Considine (1998) points out, much of public policy in the 1990s was influenced by a pattern of increasing government control. To some extent this signaled a shift from the 1970s and 1980s, when public policy was largely influenced by social movements, and from the 1950s and early 1960s, when professional dominance was most influential. But public health is made up of policies that emerged throughout all of these periods. The result has been a complex set of interdependencies that have served the Australian population well in a number of areas, but in which inherent tensions have emerged.

The Context for Reform

After 1991, attempts were made at all levels of government to reform the functional relationships within Australian federalism, in order to bring clarity to the roles and responsibilities of each level and to the relationships between governments. By 1994 COAG had proposed that health reform be constructed around three major streams: acute care, general care, and coordinated care. There was subsequent unresolved debate about the location of public health within health reform. Propositions were put forward that population health should constitute a fourth stream, but at the same time there were suggestions that public health was the overall umbrella framework for the three streams of care.

In 1995 the Commonwealth Department of Human Services and Health, under a Labor government, announced its intention to develop a national public health policy and action plan. Until this point there had been little coordination in Commonwealth–state relations across the broad spectrum of public health activity, other than the adoption of general principles about the broad health and community service system.

After the 1996 federal election was won by the Liberal–National coalition, a set of neo-liberal reforms was pursued by the Commonwealth. The June 1996 COAG communiqué set the tone for the overall reform agenda (COAG 1996). But the public health reforms had been gathering impetus since 1995 through various different forums involving public health officials. Despite government changes, health ministers supported reforms in public health. The Liberal reforms had two main fronts: reforms to the system within which public health priorities and policy were considered by decision-makers, and reforms to the financial arrangements between the Commonwealth and states, framed by a focus on outputs and outcomes.

The reform agenda posed particular challenges for public health. Within the context of federalism, it was difficult to identify and advance shared priorities. This was, first, because states and territories were often in competition with each other and with the Commonwealth. It is also a consequence of differing political imperatives associated with different electoral cycles and issues in each jurisdiction. It proved nearly impossible simultaneously to introduce reforms to financing mechanisms (including the realisation of efficiency savings) at both state and Commonwealth levels in public health as well as other areas of health. In public health, introducing reforms that reflected the mutual interdependencies and shared policy agendas of jurisdictions was a particular challenge.

A key facilitator in meeting these challenges was the public health officials' shared concern over distortions in resource allocation arising from the growth of time-limited, cost-shared programs. Many cost-shared programs helped establish services on which the community had come to rely, and for which demand was strong. With increased financial restraint, funding for newer programs was at the cost of diminished resources for existing programs. This raised concerns about both the sustainability of newer programs and the decline of existing infrastructure.

Furthermore, public health professionals shared a commitment to meeting health needs across the population, and recognised the complexity and national significance of many public health issues. For instance, problems such as HIV and substance abuse affected all states; drug distribution and HIV infection occurred across state borders, and concerted national effort was required to bring about acceptance of harm-minimisation principles. Similarly, new emerging disease outbreaks such as bat lyssavirus necessitated mobilisation of expertise from around the country.

Policy Reform: A National Public Health Partnership for Australia

Following the 1995 announcement of the Commonwealth's intention to develop a national public health policy and action plan, concern among chief health officers about the lack of coordination in the public health system led to a new proposal for collaboration. The proposal aimed to integrate the public health system through a new mechanism, a national public health partnership, which would bring together key stakeholders who had a contribution to make in strengthening the public health sector.

Although there were significant achievements by all jurisdictions in the various areas of public health, there was a shared perception of major structural weakness in the system. Vertical programs, developed around SPPs, or in response to other Commonwealth and state initiatives, had been integral to the success of public health. But boundaries between programs had tended to develop, mitigating their impact. Boundaries did not always foster integration of public health services and messages across settings, populations or groups, or between issues with common health determinants. For example, separate recruitment, education and outreach strategies existed for breast and cervical cancer, though older women and non-English-speaking women were priority target groups for both. Schools and GPs were being bombarded with requests to conduct educational programs from different sources—Commonwealth, state and NGO—on skin cancer, drugs, and sexually transmitted diseases.

The boundaries became increasingly problematic after a period of financial restraint in most jurisdictions. Health budgets were progressively squeezed. Dollars in public health locked into cost-shared programs were temporarily protected, leading to disproportionately large cuts in traditionally state-based public health activities. At the same time, the limited duration of cost-shared programs made them fundamentally unstable.

Decline in public health infrastructure (and therefore system sustainability) thus became the major focus for the discussion around the National Public Health Partnership.

In the spirit of intersectoral collaboration, public health officials proposed at the outset that a partnership be broadly inclusive of all government, non-government and other key stakeholders. But by the time senior government officials became involved, the NPHP had become an intergovernmental partnership, with a strong interest in coordination of operational issues rather than a single focus on system development. After all, governments simply working together would represent progress. Local government in Australia, however, is a creation of state legislation and therefore is not enshrined within the Australian Constitution. Consequently it was not incorporated in the NPHP, despite its central (though highly variable) role in the delivery of public health services.

By November 1996 health ministers across Australia endorsed the concept of a NPHP between the Commonwealth, the Australian Institute of Health and Welfare (the national health statistics agency), the National Health and Medical Research Council (the national health and medical research body), and all states and territories. The work of the NPHP was overseen by a group consisting of the chief health officers or directors of public health from each of these jurisdictions, who have the day-to-day responsibility for policy development and operational management of public health activity in each jurisdiction. The Partnership group advised the Australian Health Ministers Conference through the Australian Health Ministers Advisory Council, which comprised the chief executives of the various health authorities.

The main aim of this national effort was to improve the health of Australians, particularly population groups most at risk, through improved collaboration in the national public health effort, through better coordination and sustainability of public health strategies, and through strengthening the infrastructure and capacity of public health. Key priorities identified for work included information, legislative reform, workforce development, research and development, planning and practice improvement, and the coordination of national strategies.

In recognising the importance of the non-government sector in public health, an Advisory Group was established comprising key NGOs concerned with public health policy and service delivery. The vision articulated by the Advisory Group was to offer

> effective timely advice to the Partnership Group on the public health issues the Advisory Group has determined to be priorities for Australia. Its advice will reflect community perspectives and those of the multidisciplinary membership of the Advisory Group. Through its advice it will influence public health

agendas being followed by the National Public Health Partnership and promote public health debate, community interest and political will. (NPHP Agenda Paper, Item 3.1, 26 November 1998)

In similar vein, another forum was established to convene the chairs of Australia's national health strategies. About twenty national strategies or programs were developed, ranging from the pre-existing cost-shared programs through to emerging policies and action plans in diabetes, physical activity, and child health. Until the NPHP, chairs of the groups managing these strategies had never met. Each strategy group designed and negotiated its own program of activities in relation to data collection, community interventions, workforce training and research, in spite of the obvious overlap and potential synergies among them. With the new forum, joint projects were developed where shared investments could bring greater returns in efficiency.

Funding Reform: Public Health Outcome Funding Agreements

The second arm of public health reform was a change in the financial transfers from the Commonwealth to the states for public health, intended to simplify administration and create greater programmatic flexibility.

Until the 1997/98 financial year, SPPs in public health consisted of funds to the states for HIV/AIDS, a national drug strategy, women's health, cervical and breast cancer screening, alternative birthing, childhood immunisation, and a national education program on female genital mutilation. Separate administrative and programmatic arrangements had developed for each of these SPPs. These included separate agreements between the Commonwealth and the states/territories incorporating the terms and conditions under which funds could be spent, approval mechanisms for projects, and financial and statistical reporting requirements. The agreements reflected focus on detailed input controls in intergovernmental financial relations in public health.

As Swerissen and Duckett (1996: 7) point out, SPPs followed a particular life cycle. Generally those 'which remain locked in their early stages of this life cycle with joint Commonwealth–state approval of the individual project level are those most criticised by states both in terms of their intrusiveness and in terms of wasted resources because of duplication of management approval'. SPPs in public health are at varying stages of this life cycle: some are new, others have matured, and most have been in existence for five to ten years.

For some years after the beginning of debates over reform of Commonwealth–state relations, states argued that the Commonwealth should move from input controls to outcome monitoring. The adoption at the Commonwealth level of the concept of funder/purchaser/provider separation (Department of Finance 1995), and ensuing contractual arrangements, influenced the direction of policy discussions and sharpened the focus of reform. On the surface, separation of funder/purchaser/ provider and an output-monitoring approach was appealing: it allowed for a clearer delineation of the roles and responsibilities of the Commonwealth and states, explicitly recognised what was the 'best buy' in terms of health gain, and attempted to separate decisions about what should be purchased from decisions about from whom and how it should be purchased, and who should deliver services.

However, introducing such a system to public health financing arrangements between sovereign entities was problematic (Oceania Health Consulting 1997). Each level of the system had elements of funder, purchaser, and provider roles in its relationships with the other. Although it would have been possible to separate them, states and territories would have found it highly offensive to be seen as purchasing arms of the Commonwealth in a system in which they shared responsibility for public health policy.

The other issue raised in the context of reform to financing arrangements was the move towards focusing on outcomes rather than inputs. Despite the emphasis on health outcomes in public health practice, practical problems were encountered in quantifying government and program accountability due to intervening variables and policy time-lag, which made it difficult to measure cause and effect. Because public health outcomes might stretch across a decade and be the responsibility of several sectors, it was difficult to develop specific objectives and indicators.

The 1997/98 financial year saw the first Public Health Outcome Funding Agreements (PHOFAs) signed between the Commonwealth and states. Essentially the agreements transferred the pool of public health funds to each state via one funding agreement. States agreed to be accountable against a set of outcome indicators. Given the two problems discussed above, the PHOFA indicators remained a mixture of outcome, output, process, and input indicators. They remained largely focused on the original eight programs, with some scope for innovation through a pool of incentive funds. The agreements spelt out the shared interests of the signatories, and represented agreement on the amount of funding to be transferred, the principles under which the funding was to be expended, the specific undertakings of the Commonwealth in relation to administration of the funds, and the specific undertakings of each state in relation to the agreed level of performance against outcomes. For a number of reasons, the final agreements were negotiated bilaterally. Tactically, it was easier to conclude negotiation by accommodating variations across jurisdictions. Practically, a bilateral approach could take into account differing needs priorities and systems of service delivery. As a matter of reform principle, it was also important to keep financial bickering out of a multilateral policy forum. Although the broad principles and clauses of each agreement were similar across all states and territories, they remained bilateral agreements between the Commonwealth and each state, with negotiations occurring state by state.

The broadbanding of public health dollars into a single funding agreement between the Commonwealth and each state/territory received mixed views. In a joint communiqué after COAG in 1996, state premiers said that their preferred position was that all payments from the Commonwealth to the states should be in the form of untied financial assistance grants from the Commonwealth to the states. Alternatively, they recommended that the area in which the funding was to be spent could be identified but not actually tied (identified funding grants), with states remaining accountable to their electorates for the outcomes—and voted in or out of government according to their achievements. Other states individually put the position that the money should be rolled into the renegotiated Australian Health Care Agreements (general tied funding assistance for hospitals and other health services).

This approach, although appealing to the states, did not correspond with the Commonwealth's own accountability requirements. Commonwealth governments have been vulnerable to criticism when outcomes in health decline or the Commonwealth has been unable to demonstrate what it can deliver, such as the decline in immunisation levels after the program's transfer in 1988 to financial assistance grants. Community groups, and indeed some program officers within states and territories, expressed anxiety over the broadbanding of public health dollars into a single public health agreement. Many saw it as a mechanism through which their particular program funding would be diverted to other public health or personal health care issues. Alternatively, others argued that creating a strong and clearly identifiable mechanism for the transfer of public health funds lessened the likelihood that limited public health funds could be diverted to the tertiary health care sector, thus further weakening Australia's public health efforts. The removal of matching requirements also caused particular concern in the face of continued budget constraint. However, states and territories themselves argued that outcomes agreed in the PHOFAs would be difficult to attain without the current levels of state and territory expenditure.

Early Impacts and Lessons

The existence of simultaneous but separate reforms (i.e. policy coordination through the NPHP and pooling of funding via PHOFAs) has been important in setting a new climate for managing intergovernmental relations in public health. In combination, they have also created an enabling environment for enhanced coordination efforts at various levels in the public health system.

The creation of the NPHP has strengthened the environment in which the new financial mechanisms operate. By addressing broader issues, such as reporting mechanisms, information development, and accountability in a more systematic way, the NPHP provides a policy forum in which debates can be undertaken on public health priorities and public health practice, and coordinated responses to emerging issues can be formulated.

Some of the early impacts of the NPHP have seen the Commonwealth and the states and territories develop several strategies: an issues paper on partnerships with industry; a planning and practice framework that provides jurisdictions with a common currency for describing the business of public health; guidelines for the development of public health strategies and coordination leading to a reshaping of national strategies; joint papers and reviews in areas such as health and medical research, food safety and drug strategy; joint working parties on mental health and general practice; and a public health information development plan that foreshadows a coordinated national survey program.

The changes that were made to public health financing mechanisms were mainly incremental. States and territories have generally continued the same programs and practices as under previous arrangements, with indicators still largely constructed around the eight programs. The first set of PHOFAs allows for innovation through an incentives component, but funding for infrastructure development (e.g. improved data collection, improved planning and better integration at the local level) has remained as an expectation within the overall funding provided (i.e. that funding comes from the global budget). Experiences with PHOFAs have seen the Commonwealth concentrate more heavily on broad policy development and less on day-to-day control of funding. Relationships between the federal and state and territory governments and community organisations have also been changed by the new arrangements and have opened the door for community-based organisations to become a stronger voice at the state and territory level.

If the public health system had to rely on changes to financing mechanisms for broad policy reform to be introduced, change would have been a fairly slow process. When health system reform has been attempted in the context of AHCA negotiations, policy progress has traditionally been minimal (Painter 1998). Financing negotiations generally involve a fair amount of disagreement—with a tendency to focus on the bottom–line amount: states and territories argue that they are not getting enough; the Commonwealth argues that the states are not spending it where it should be spent. There is also a degree of one-upmanship, so these negotiations are probably the worst possible forum in which to attempt to come to a shared policy agreement on matters as important as public health.

As far as intergovernmental relations in health are concerned, they have been characterised by battles over funding levels, so there would have been every reason to expect the same dynamics to apply to public health funding reforms. Without a broader policy forum, there would have been little incentive for jurisdictions to work together to strengthen infrastructure and generate a more sustainable base for public health.

It can be argued, to some extent, that the nature of public health is different from government provision of health care to individuals. Public health has more of the characteristics of a public good, and there appears to be less conflict of interest around whether or not to fund it. Nevertheless, some lessons are emerging for public health that might have broader application. Lessons for public health have included recognition of the usefulness of a permanent policy forum to provide a context for reforms to financial mechanisms. This forum seems to avoid the tendency of reform to concentrate on the *mechanism* rather than the actual *improvements* in policy.

For public health itself and its relationships with other fields, mechanisms for the development of shared policy directions with other areas might also be needed. While the provision of funding might help public health to gain some leverage externally, policy forums that facilitate the development of shared language and relationships might prove a firmer and more sustainable foundation.

It is also interesting to consider the limitations imposed by confining the NPHP's membership to government representation. Although contrary to the original ideals of public health officials and professionals, this might have served the NPHP well in its formative stages. Governments, as major investors in public health, operate with similar constraints and imperatives. This has helped bridge the language and culture gap between representatives to the NPHP, and has expedited identification of shared priorities and progress on them. There remains the challenge, however, of bringing the broader health industry along, and ultimately moving to a more inclusive partnership.

Conclusion and Remaining Issues

Public health in Australia in the 1970s and 1980s made many strides. But illness, disease, and the need for preventing these do not respect jurisdictional boundaries, and hence the absence of a mechanism for whole-of-system coordination in public health became a pressing issue in the mid-1990s. Health issues confronting the community also change, and the distortions created by intergovernmental financing arrangements in public health became an increasing constraint on the capacity of public health services to respond to actual need.

Had the pooling of funding occurred on its own without a policy coordination mechanism, the national public health effort could have been greatly diluted. Had a policy mechanism been instituted without reforms to financing, there could have been a divergence between policy priorities and financing incentives. Thus it was crucial that the NPHP and PHOFAs be implemented simultaneously but separately. Each constituted a major reform for both public health and intergovernmental relations. Together they created the environment for even more significant reform.

Some important challenges remain. These relate both to population health as a specific stream of health services and to the construction of population health as a broader framework for health system management and broader health system reforms. There are some important tasks to be done:

* instituting a rigorous approach to public health risk assessment, intervention selection and design, and risk communication at all levels and across all public health issues;
* developing local-level partnerships for public health, i.e. involving government, non-government, other sectors, professional, and community interests;
* developing appropriate indicators that are valid and reliable for measuring progress towards public health objectives;
* identifying effective mechanisms for funding public health priorities;
* designing appropriate financing incentives for the whole-of-health system, thereby shifting the service-delivery system upstream towards prevention; and
* adopting public health methods to measure health outcomes as an integral part of health system management.

The way in which public health has attempted to cast a new approach to Commonwealth–state relations through the separation of funding negotiations from policy development, its attempt to build on a shared commitment to public health between the Commonwealth and the states, and its initial focus on improving intergovernmental relations while brokering new relationships between other partners are the lessons that are emerging and that make public health an area worth watching.

It remains to be seen whether broader health reforms will be informed by public health perspectives. But the reforms in public health will certainly provide a stronger platform for reorienting the health care system to one that focuses on population-health outcomes.

15

Placing Prevention at the Centre of Health Sector Reform

Rhonda Galbally

In this chapter I argue that models, strategies, and processes of health care reform in Australia have neglected the main objective of reform: improving the effectiveness as well as the efficiency of the health sector, particularly in the areas of greatest potential health gain, promotion and prevention. The chapter presents the rationale for including prevention and promotion in health reform strategies. It describes how a successful model for addressing prevention and promotion was developed in Australia parallel with, but not as an integral part of, the reform process. The chapter describes and analyses the key dimensions of a successful prevention and promotion model, and concludes that unless these strategies are incorporated into reform, it is unlikely to achieve its aims.

The Challenge of Health Reform

The rationale and therefore the starting point for health sector reform in many countries has been cost-cutting in the name of efficiency. Most governments would assert that effectiveness (as evidenced by impact on health status) is of equal importance. In most cases, however, the definition of what would constitute an effectively reformed health sector has never been clear.

The values underlying health reform agendas are usually not clearly expressed. The competing claims of the major contenders in any reform scenario are rarely adequately articulated. Consequently health reform tends to occur against a backdrop of dynamic tension between implicit values: between public and private interests; between high-cost, high-tech medicine and primary care; and between a focus on providing curative services and one on prevention and health promotion.

Second, the main social, political and economic factors responsible for major change in Australian society do not appear to have been incorporated into the core of health reform strategies.

The first of these factors is globalisation. As a consequence of globalisation, geographically distant economies, cultures, and diseases are now more than ever interconnected and interdependent. Globalisation has influenced health in many different ways. For example, multinational tobacco and alcohol companies have deployed vast resources on selling cigarettes and alcohol, targeting young people, and, for cigarettes, aiming particularly to capture young women.

The next is the revolution in gender roles, which has had a significant impact on health status, and which must be considered in developing an effective strategy for health sector reform. For example, whereas women's health status in Australia (as measured by disability-free life expectancy) continues to improve, men still appear to be locked into historically determined roles that prevent them from maintaining their health, and dealing with the emotional component of health, or, more generally, the emotional component of their lives. This transition offers opportunities as well as dilemmas for health reform. The disparities between the health of men and women are well documented. Yet reform has so far neglected cultural constructs of masculinity and femininity, the primary underlying issue in many male risk behaviours. On the other hand, the reform agenda has thus far missed the opportunity to harness the more responsive and humanistic modes of organisation that women bring to their roles as principal guardians of health within families, and as the majority of the workforce in many health systems. Any health reform agenda should continue to support increased literacy—the most potent single means of raising the health status of disadvantaged populations (World Bank 1997)—among women and girls in disadvantaged communities, especially Aboriginal communities.

Next, new communication technologies have made available an enormous quantity of information to everyone with access to a computer. The potential for more informed health decision-making has thus exploded—for some people. But the growth of information technology has also increased inequality for those who lack access to computers, the 'information-poor', thus exacerbating their already disadvantaged position. The reform agenda must take into account information poverty alongside socio-economic inequity as a threat to health status, and incorporate strategies to address growing disparity.

Australia's labour market has undergone profound change in recent years. The country now faces the conditions that many developing countries have faced for decades: constantly changing labour markets—a steady rise in the proportion of short-term contract work, job insecurity, part-time work, unemployment, and a future in which many young people will never gain full-time, secure employment. Both the very nature of work, and the skills necessary to gain employment, have changed significantly, and probably irreversibly. The skills and support that individuals need to withstand the insecurity and stress of occasional, casual work or unemployment are not well understood. Yet health experts have long since known of the links between employment status, work environment, and physical and mental health (Stansfeld et al. 1997; Lewis 1998).

Health sector reform that is genuinely aimed at safeguarding and improving health will incorporate practical strategies involving education systems, retraining, and employment programs, as well as advocacy on behalf of these programs, based on their impact on health status. The reform agenda must include practical methods to develop skills among children and adults, enabling them to become resilient in the face of these massive changes and uncertainties. Inclusion of these 'non-health' initiatives, which have a strong impact on health status, is usually called 'intersectoral collaboration', and is all too often considered as an after-thought to the 'real' core activities of health.

An example of why (and how) the health reform agenda must develop effective intersectoral capacity is mental health. Rates of suicide and depression have become epidemic in Australian society, particularly among the young, and among middle-aged men. In order to address the underlying causes of this tragic pattern, the health sector is increasingly becoming involved in disciplines and sectors that can have an impact on the development of life skills and self-esteem, and ultimately suicide risk. Effective collaboration with other sectors has also proved essential to development of effective public policies that affect health, such as reducing the environmental health impacts of intense urbanisation, or rearranging transport systems to minimise road trauma and pollution while increasing exercise levels.

Addressing the Health Impacts of Broader Social Change

To date health sector reform in Australia has not formally addressed the health impact of fundamental societal trends and patterns that have a significant impact on health. Many of these factors have, however, been addressed in a parallel model that has demonstrated how health prevention and promotion can be incorporated into reform effectively. The approach has had impressive impacts on health status in the state of Victoria.

The model of health promotion was pioneered by the Victorian Health Promotion Foundation (VicHealth). VicHealth was established in 1987 by the Victorian government as a statutory authority, with an independent board of trustees and with bipartisan support. It was the first organisation of its kind in the world to be funded with proceeds from a dedicated tobacco tax.

Multisectoral Inputs into Health Sector Reform

The focus of VicHealth is solely on the prevention of disease and the promotion of health. An organisational structure was therefore developed to enable it to function effectively in the context of the multisectoral determinants of health. The necessity of multisectoral involvement in health is often asserted. Yet it is extremely rare to find practical mechanisms to achieve intersectoral collaboration, let alone implement strategies that produce measurable improvements in health.

From its inception, VicHealth epitomised a multisectoral approach that was both practical and effective, and that also ensured ownership of health promotion by key sectors. At the core of VicHealth is its Board of Trustees. The board was deliberately established to represent health concerns from multiple perspectives: medical research, cancer prevention, education, sports, arts and culture, marketing, and the corporate sector. This broad focus was related to the immediate objectives of the organisation.

An initial, primary focus for VicHealth was tobacco control. VicHealth's specific goal was replacing tobacco company sponsorship (funding) of sports, arts, and culture with health sponsorship. The primary means of raising revenue to replace tobacco company sponsorship was a dedicated tobacco tax.

Successfully negotiating the tobacco tax through parliament was lengthy and complex. Through the process, however, parliament was drawn into the issues surrounding prevention and health promotion. This had two major benefits. First, parliamentarians came to understand and support health promotion, previously a fragile and underfunded area. Second, it provided the opportunity to win bipartisan support for health promotion in the form of board members: the appointment of representatives from the three parliamentary political parties to the board of VicHealth added a valuable dimension to the organisation.

VicHealth's multisectoral character and strong base of support provided a solid foundation for an organisation directed at influencing the diverse settings in which people spend their lives—the organisations and communities where they learn, work, and play. These settings, which include schools, workplaces, health facilities (including primary health care), sports, arts and cultural organisations, and local communities, have the respect of participants because the participants have insight into how best to design and implement systems and structures that can lead to safe and healthy environments.

An Institutional Approach to Health Promotion

The very structure of VicHealth thus acknowledged local expertise and experience in improving health. The VicHealth philosophy is that the people within each setting are most likely to know what works best in that sector and setting to promote healthy and supportive environments. VicHealth's endorsement of this 'lay' expertise challenged the dominance of the health sector as the sole source of health knowledge. VicHealth's multisectoral approach to reform effectively eroded the hegemony of the health sector and of health experts, replacing it with a partnership of many sectors, with a higher probability of preventing many lifestyle diseases.

This contrasts with the usual assumption that health knowledge, residing exclusively in health experts, can be communicated to the 'target audiences' most effectively by sophisticated social marketing and/or information, education and communication (IEC) methods. IEC methods of health promotion are analogous to the one-way curative medical model: medical professionals hold the essential wisdom, and they alone apply knowledge to treat patients. In IEC, it is assumed that the IEC expert knows best how to impart relevant knowledge about prevention. This is what I call 'the injection into the head method of health promotion'. Yet the essential knowledge about what will work best in schools, for example, is far more likely to be held by the classroom educator, whose understanding of how to work in that setting is both subtle and practical.

The 'expert' health content in the field of prevention is relatively simple. For example, that smoking is a deadly habit causing cancer and heart disease is well known and easy to understand. The knowledge about how a school environment, or a workplace, can be organised to enable children or adults to decide not to smoke is far more complex. Health experts are not needed to impart this message. The challenge is how best to design communication of the message within a particular environment or organisation. An organisational approach to the promotion of healthy behaviours involves the expertise of members of the specific organisation— that is, it is an approach that works 'with' people rather than just 'for' people. They participate in the redesign of the environment and the systems that make healthy behaviours possible and likely in that particular setting. In schools, for example, the 'experts' are teachers, students, administrators and parents. In sporting clubs, they are the athletes, coaches, club officials, and families.

The Inclusion of NGOs in Health Promotion

Extensive evaluation of costly and sophisticated IEC approaches that attempt to impose their views on a passive community audience show that these approaches have low effectiveness and a lack of sustainability (Syme 1986). This is because a one-way informational approach basically cannot build a community's capacity to deal with their health issues. Communities that work together to address health issues have the best hope of ensuring that effective preventive measures are developed and that, most importantly, individuals, families and organisations within those communities will cooperate to implement them. Community participation in setting priorities, and in designing and implementing interventions, is the only approach likely to generate sustainable improvement in risk behaviour in poor and disadvantaged communities (Syme 1997).

Moreover, research conducted in the 1980s and 1990s has shown that once an individual's basic needs have been met, the most important factor determining one's health is degree of control over one's life. People who have a sense of control, who are able to set their own directions, can resist health threats that destroy people without this 'immunity'. Infusing a sense of coherence and control into people's lives is consistent with a focus on community and organisational participation (Stansfeld et al. 1997; Marmot et al. 1998).

Community involvement in health is part of the process of developing social capital—replacing or restoring traditional social roles and relations under threat from the new economic and cultural pressures. New systems of social support are intrinsic to the development of social capital and are essential solutions to the most important risks to health status: lack of control or coherence in one's life, and hopelessness.

Effective and innovative responses to these challenges are far more likely to come from an interface between government and non-government capacity. VicHealth has successfully demonstrated how the non-government sector can be facilitated by a body which is sufficiently outside government bureaucratic controls and thinking. One of VicHealth's primary tasks is to work with NGOs to focus their creative capacity on developing innovative trial projects and programs aimed at the underlying determinants of behaviours that place health at risk. Government also has a role to play: identifying successful trials for replication on a state and national scale. VicHealth's role included initiating funding for trial projects, highlighting their importance, and then ensuring that government is sufficiently involved in the trials to use the findings for the widest applications.

Governments often have ambivalent views of NGOs. But NGOs have a number of essential roles, including advocacy and service delivery. With their community focus, they are far more skilled in community development, and are thus far more likely to generate authentic participation than is government, which is often viewed with suspicion.

Many attempts have been made to coordinate (some say control) Victoria's abundant non-government sector, usually in the name of efficiency. The underlying rationale is unease about NGOs' community mobilisation, organisation, and advocacy skills.

VicHealth offered distinct advantages in this environment. Established as a statutory authority, it was a welcome broker, able to position itself among the major health sector players, relating to each but independent of all. It could relate equally well to the health department, the non-government sector, and other government departments whose domain affected the development of healthy public policy.

Some trial projects implemented by NGOs will be challenging and provocative. One advantage of a body like VicHealth is it that can be positioned at arm's length from government, where it is more likely to survive the inevitable attacks that the funders of innovative research and projects always seem to attract.

Advocacy: A Key to Health Promotion and Health Sector Reform

Some prevention strategies require vigorous advocacy from a body that is close enough to government to indicate government approval and distinct enough to use media and other advocacy mechanisms to tackle powerful opponents. An example from VicHealth's first decade is advocacy involving tobacco companies, which predictably resisted tobacco-control measures.

Judicious support for a range of advocacy initiatives is essential if health promotion is to improve the health status of the population in keeping with the Alma Ata Declaration and the WHO global strategy of Health For All By The Year 2000 (WHO 1978). Some of these initiatives will be unpopular with parts of the wider community (for example interventions to promote safe sex); or with specific corporate interests (for example, tobacco). Others may simply never gather enough support.

An example of the last is Aboriginal health in Australia. In every country, the best predictor of life expectancy is the degree of inequality. The more equal the distribution of wealth, the longer people live (Wilkinson 1996). In every country, socially and educationally disadvantaged groups have a higher mortality rate than affluent and educated groups (Turrell 1995: 119).

The relationship between poor health status and attacks on self-determination fuelled by endemic racism is also well proved (Saggers and Gray 1991; Kennedy et al. 1997). Aboriginal communities have poor health because history has forced them to respond to an adverse social environment. The outcome is that they are poor and poorly housed, poorly nourished, poorly educated, and have a high rate of unemployment. Successful programs to address these determinants of health usually involve advocacy, and may therefore be controversial, because they are unpopular with the mainstream.

An arm's-length funder of advocacy initiatives is more likely than government to survive the inevitable interest-group attacks these initiatives will provoke in political forums. Most governments are cautious about inciting controversy, particularly when they seek political support from many factional interests. Interest groups will inevitably cite controversial initiatives when considering whether or not to support the government of the day.

A body such as VicHealth can provide a source of funding and ongoing support for advocacy programs while insulating government from criticism. Deliberately insuring bipartisan and corporate participation in its board is further insurance for the continuation of important, albeit controversial, health promotion initiatives.

The Integration of Vertical Programs

Risk behaviours cluster in risk situations. Situations containing clusters of risk factors—not merely one or two risk factors—generate behaviours that increase people's risk of poor health and injury. For example, people who smoke are more likely to be poor than their fellows (Marsh and McKay 1994). People who are poor and unemployed are more likely to be depressed and even suicidal (Jin et al. 1995). People who consider suicide tend to have low self-esteem. People with low self-esteem are more likely to smoke.

Risk behaviours do not result from isolated decisions, but arise from an individual's total life circumstances. Single-issue approaches that do not address underlying issues may be highly effective in placing important issues on the political agenda, particularly when advocacy is deftly used. Single-issue approaches can also be effective for general populations. But they are rarely effective for disadvantaged groups, whose health status is poorest. Different lifestyle risk behaviours have common roots in the population, the community, the environment, and local culture. Among adolescents, for example, suicide, binge drinking, unsafe driving, unsafe sex, and drug-taking are all associated with social class, depression, and poor mental health (Patton et al. 1996). Single-issue campaigns in all of these areas need to be linked together to develop programs that take account of these relationships.

Therefore an important role for a body such as VicHealth is providing a forum to bring together vertical programs supported by government and non-government organisations (e.g. cancer councils, heart foundations, diabetes organisations). The forum's purpose is to develop an integrated strategy leading to joint programs based on a contextual view of health.

A practical example is health education in schools and workplaces. Vertical programs, often reinforced by government funding for single issues, generate single-issue campaigns. These initiatives have created a bewildering array of programs competing with each other for limited curriculum space in schools, or for the attention of workers at lunchtime breaks. The single-issue approach does not improve the health of poor and disadvantaged groups because it has no impact whatsoever on the systems and structures necessary to develop healthy organisational and community cultures. A vertical approach can never instil the self-esteem and self-efficacy that enables children and adults to resist risk, nor do these programs address the clustering of risks.

Mobilising through the Development of a Learning Network

In Australia, as in most countries, thousands of prevention and health promotion projects, funded through a variety of mechanisms, have been completed or are under way. Attempts at coordinating these projects to avoid overlap or, worse, double funding ('double dipping') almost always fail because of the pluralism intrinsic to Australia's culture and political system.

Moreover the singular focus on coordination has diverted attention from the equally urgent need to learn from past experience, so that the wheel does not have to be reinvented anew on each occasion. Failure to divert some energies and resources to assimilating 'lessons learned' is wasteful because practitioners remain ignorant of which strategies work, how, why, and for whom, and which do not.

An important role for VicHealth was establishing an informal learning network, supported by forums in which the findings of various projects were presented. The program of workshops and symposia had strategic and practical importance. Not only did it generate an opportunity to promulgate the details of new approaches, but it also offered a forum in which the collective wisdom of participants could be used to improve current and future programs aimed at similar issues.

The forums were part of a broader learning strategy that employed an organisational network, interactive communication technologies, and a variety of bulletins, to accumulate lessons from domestic projects and provide access to international experience. A learning forum offers other opportunities: to transfer strategic knowledge that can be usefully applied in different settings, and to discourage proliferation of vertical programs.

Private/Public Interface for Health Sector Reform

The private sector plays a central role in the Australian health sector reform agenda. But the private sector's role, as currently envisaged, is restricted largely to finance and provision of health care services and infrastructure. From the perspective of prevention and health promotion, the potential role of the private sector is much broader.

A focus on the workplace for promotion of health generates immediate involvement of the corporate sector in essential health issues. The experience of VicHealth has shown that with the implementation of successful workplace health promotion programs, the corporate sector begins to take health promotion seriously. The corporate relationships, awareness, and programs facilitated by VicHealth have established a robust and sustainable corporate commitment to occupational health and safety. There have also been benefits for VicHealth in developing these relationships: it has been challenged to approach health issues in novel ways. For example, working with business has meant using its concepts, such as benchmarking and best practice, and transferring them to workplace health programs. In the process, new techniques and models have been generated that can be used throughout the corporate sector. Linking the corporate world to health in a way meaningful to business encourages the private sector to value health as a high priority, not only in general but also for the prosperity of the corporate sector itself.

Developing Regional and Local Organisational Infrastructure for Health Sector Reform

A central health promotion body can increase its local and regional impact by encouraging the development of effective organisational structures. This is particularly important in order to address the health promotion needs of rural communities. Although the central body can offer management support and initial funding, this is preferably done with matched funding arrangements that encourage local contributions. This is also more likely to spur local ownership of the issues, and therefore more viable and sustainable local programs. Local structures increase the likelihood of successful local networks, cooperation, and exchange of strategies and information to address underlying risk behaviours.

Regional and local infrastructure for health promotion, as part of a network serviced by a national or state body, means that local needs can be measured and used as the basis for program design. Local learning networks can be used to collect information about projects operating at the grassroots. Regional and local infrastructure, which may take the form of health promotion committees, also provides a structure for decision-making at these levels.

Experience has shown that funds for health promotion can be generated from local business, and, where appropriate, from religious groups, local service clubs such as Rotary and Lions, and, most important, from local government. When these traditional regional and local authority structures become involved in lifestyle issues they are more likely to support primary-care organisations politically and financially.

Alternative Financing Models for Health Sector Reform

Health promotion is most successfully delivered within a multisectoral framework, and thus alternative funding mechanisms can be developed to reflect the variety of sectors and stakeholders. Development of alternative financing models for health promotion is always a high priority. Prevention always struggles for resources, perhaps because the imperative of immediate results inevitably sees resources channelled to curative services in preference to prevention—to hospital development and high-tech medicine, despite government's support, in principle, for the efficacy of prevention.

A long-term financial commitment to prevention and promotion is necessary to finance the long-term prevention and promotion strategies that must be put in place. Even where government commitment to health promotion is strong, the short-term nature of politics means that financing of health promotion can be vulnerable to the vagaries of changing policies.

VicHealth's experience in using the dedicated tobacco tax as its main source of funding for nine years is instructive. This tax ceased in 1997 when the tobacco industry mounted a successful High Court challenge to state governments' rights to tax. But the concept of this type of tax, dedicated to health prevention, had become so ingrained that the Victorian Treasury subsequently made a direct allocation of funds to VicHealth, bypassing the Victorian Health Department and thus ensuring that funds for prevention and health promotion could not be diverted for other uses, such as treatment.

There is, of course, an exquisite irony in using a dedicated tax on a most harmful substance to promote good health. Taxing tobacco, alcohol, and gambling, and directing the revenue to control of these health risks, and to wider, more integrated health promotion programs, provides many health promotion benefits at once. Taxing cigarettes, alcohol, or gambling increases the cost of access to these harmful substances or practices. This operates as a disincentive, particularly for young people, who are far more likely to be price-sensitive (Biener et al. 1998).

Once the Victorian government saw the strong public support for the dedicated tax, and the popularity of VicHealth's programs, it was confident enough to later increase the tax on tobacco, which was used to fund the promotion of health throughout the state. The levy funded a range of health promotion initiatives, such as tobacco control, injury prevention, food and nutrition, drug and alcohol prevention, reproductive and sexual health, mental health and well-being, and environmental health. As a result of these highly visible programs, health promotion became a top priority for the community.

The Future

There are now many variants on the VicHealth model of infrastructure for health promotion throughout the world, financed by a variety of sources. The Clearing House at the Australian International Health Institute (University of Melbourne) Ltd (AIHI) tracks the performance of these differing approaches and models, and offers training and advice to governments, aid agencies and development banks interested in devising new models or adapting existing ones. The AIHI is also establishing new structures for health development in developing countries with the private sector.

The VicHealth experience provides several key lessons for health sector reform:

1. Reform is ultimately about better health, not just more efficient health services. Decision-makers undertaking health reform must therefore articulate the health goals of reform, and incorporate measures known to deliver improved health. This means that prevention and promotion must be integral parts of reform.

2. Any reform process must incorporate strategies that are structured around major social transitions, as well as disease trends, such as the changing nature of work and employment, the roles of men and women, and the potent role of new forms of information and communication.

3. One of the central lessons is the need to examine and learn from the experiences of pioneering models and programs, such as the VicHealth model.

An institutional approach to health promotion offers a practical as well as strategic means of achieving through health sector reform improvements in effectiveness—improving health—not just improvements in efficiency.

PART IV

THE NEW WAVE OF HEALTH SECTOR REFORM

Introduction

Abby Bloom

This section examines major topics in the next wave of health reform. Each topic is introduced with a theoretical discussion of varying length and illustrated by specific materials drawn from the Australian or New Zealand experience. Each author is intimately involved in the reforms she or he describes, and thus brings to the subject a detailed knowledge of the practical as well as theoretical challenge of reform.

The latest wave of reform in Australia and New Zealand has generally followed the trajectory described by the World Bank's model (World Development Report 1997: 152). In this model, a first stage of reform is typically precipitated by genuine financial and social crisis. The crisis mentality provides fertile ground for drastic reforms, for example severe budget cuts, liberalisation, some privatisation, and in general a crisis mentality. This initial period, which can be said to have occurred in New Zealand but not in Australia, gives way to a second stage or generation of reform, characterised by reform of the civil service, restructuring of social ministries, large-scale privatisation, and restructuring of the relationships between central and local governments. For a fuller understanding of recent developments in Australia and New Zealand, however, the model proposed by Ham (1998) is more helpful.

What characterises the next wave of reform in Australia and New Zealand? According to Ham's phases of reform, the third (and final phase), experienced in the 1990s in the USA and Western Europe, involves a focus on public health, primary care, managed care, evidence-based medicine, and assessment of the efficacy of health technologies. For Australia and New Zealand, the next phase, effectively the fourth phase of reform, is more specifically focused on yet another set of issues.

First, there is a concern with stabilisation of the health system's financing, and, in particular, the dilemma of funding stability in a mixed public–private system. Although some are supporting changes to private health insurance in order to reinforce private funding sources, other experts are advocating a single, universal insurer—Medicare only.

With regard to service provision, intensive work is under way at both the macro and clinical levels to identify better models and structures for service delivery. As noted previously, in Australia there is a sense of inevitability about 'managed competition', and the next phase of reform will undoubtedly involve numerous experiments in its interpretation. As several authors have remarked, the current phase of reform has also entailed numerous pilot studies of delivery models under the umbrella of 'coordinated care'.

One of the gaps in health reform during the 1990s has been an absence of measurement, evaluation, and comparison in order to better inform decisions about resource allocation in health. This is a major focus of the next phase of reform, as illustrated by three chapters in this section.

Specifying and ensuring quality is emerging as an elusive and urgent issue for health systems globally, and is especially important as health systems have shifted to purchasing health services under contract. The lack of proximate quality measures, and the need therefore to resort to proxies or processes, has proved unsatisfactory. Without quality measures, governments (or other funders, including insurers), have little basis for comparing alternative providers: they are unable to judge value for money because although they may compare price, they cannot compare quality.

Many countries are encouraging the accreditation of health care facilities (e.g. hospital accreditation) or processes (ISO 9000 Standards or other quality measures of processes or equipment), coupled with retraining and certification of health professionals (e.g. Australia's vocational registration of GPs). Another approach is the encouragement of quality improvement from within professional associations (e.g. the establishment of IPAs in New Zealand and divisions of general practice in Australia).

But quality of health care is more than the sum of its parts: it is more than well-trained, registered professionals working in high-quality facilities in which systems and processes are clearly documented. Even in the presence of all of these quality indicators, health outcomes—the ultimate 'product' of health care—can be poor, or may vary inexplicably from place to place.

Lapsley (Chapter 16) has been involved in the study of health quality and the introduction of quality measures for many years. She guides readers through the development of quality measures in Australian health care, noting the role government can play and flagging the potential influence of information available through the Internet, much (though by no means all) of it from reliable sources.

Government is the main funder in most Western health care systems, and therefore must have the tools and measures to determine how best to allocate resources. Corden and Luxmoore (Chapter 17) consider this dilemma under the term 'performance management'. Performance management is most often a euphemism for supervision or control. Its meaning here is much more direct: what role can government play, with what mechanisms, to foster better performance through the application of government funds where they will generate the greatest economic growth and social gain? As the authors describe, these questions are of particular import where there are significant differences in performance, and where they cannot be entirely explained—or excused—by differences in situational factors. They describe a very specific structure, developed by the Australian government's Productivity Commission, which designed and implemented a framework to address these issues.

Evidence-based health care, the topic of Chapter 18 by Frommer and Rubin, is an important new direction in clinical practice and health care finance. Frommer and Rubin have extended the concept to embrace health care, not merely medicine. Its premise is straightforward: health care should consist of those interventions the effectiveness of which have been established through clear, scientifically gathered evidence. To the lay person, of course, it may come as a surprise that a scientific enterprise such as health care might *not* be based exclusively on evidentiary proof of effectiveness. In reality it is not, for many reasons, such as the inability or lack of incentive for clinicians to update their skills and knowledge, the persistence of beliefs that may have represented 'best practice' long ago but have since been disproved, or simply the fact that ineffectual practices are more lucrative. A prime example of the last is the overprescription of pharmaceuticals—patients expect them (in Australia many 'shop around' if they don't get them) (Bloom 1996), and in many countries doctors rely on the sale of pharmaceuticals for their basic income.

Frommer and Rubin examine the principles behind evidence-based health care, consider how it can be implemented, describe its potential impact on health care provision, funding, and consumers, and use the Australian experience to show how it can be used to improve quality (and technical efficiency) on a large scale.

McCallum (Chapter 19) challenges the prevalent belief that the crisis in health care is caused by older people consuming more and more resources. He suggests instead that health reform might look at the 'problem' from several quite different perspectives. He reminds us that the longevity enjoyed by people in Western societies is one of mankind's major achievements. He then systematically dissects and dismisses the arguments behind the scapegoating of older people, and suggests how a more thoughtful and selective approach to the funding, provision, and coordination of health care would better address many of the real issues.

Millar (Chapter 20), an active practitioner in New Zealand, is involved in one of New Zealand's most successful examples of integrated, client-focused health care for the aged. The emphasis of his case study is on *why* and *how* the process of health care was re-engineered. He provides a fascinating model for managers and clinicians in virtually any area of health care delivery, since the questions the Millar team confronted, and the techniques they used, are widely applicable.

Together the chapters in this section illuminate the several directions that health reform is beginning to take in its next phase in Australia and New Zealand. Once again, many different players are at work at different levels in the health system, and on different functions of the two health care systems: financing, provision, regulation, and quality.

16

Quality Measures in Australian Health Care

Helen Lapsley

Change is an integral part of the Australian health care system, and will continue, probably with increasing pace. Technology, pharmaceuticals, anaesthesic techniques, and operating procedures are all rapidly evolving. At the same time, public expectations of access to and outcomes of health care services remain high, some would argue unrealistically, while governments and insurers increase budgetary pressures and financial scrutiny.

Quality is also an integral part of the Australian health system. The development of formal, codified and mandated quality processes can be clearly traced from the mid-1970s. This chapter will concentrate specifically on those formal processes, but it is important to recognise that hospitals have always undertaken a range of quality activities. Many of these activities were not quantified, measured and evaluated, as is the current expectation, but were nevertheless an important part of the health services culture. Hospital quality activities included hospital grand rounds, death committees and autopsies, shift handover procedures in wards and intensive care, journal clubs, and scientific meetings. More formal processes have evolved, and some of the processes that were formerly voluntary have been mandated. Additional quality activities have been developed specifically for the health care sector, often adopting and modifying techniques from industry and the service sectors.

The structural, economic and professional changes relating to the assessment, assurance and outcomes of quality measures in Australian health care will be identified and discussed in this chapter.

Background to Formal Institutionalised Quality

It is useful to identify and clarify some of the terms most frequently used under the umbrella of quality assurance. There are several terms, activities, techniques and formalised processes, each with its own advocates, or even devotees. Many terms and acronyms are used in Australia to describe quality techniques, programs, and mechanisms. These change in fashion and popularity, and there appears to be no particular legitimacy for any one. The most useful and workable definition of quality is 'degree of excellence'. Quality programs that have been used in Australian health care have included 'quality improvement' (QI), 'continuous quality improvement' (CQI), 'total quality management' (TQM), and 'quality circles' (QC). The umbrella term 'quality assurance' has been defined by the Institute of Medicine (1990: 46) as 'a formal and systematic exercise in identifying problems in medical care delivery, designing activities to overcome the problems and carrying out follow-up monitoring to ensure that no new problems have been introduced and that corrective steps have been effective'. Each of the two largest health professions, medicine and nursing, has developed its own quality initiatives and activities in different ways, which will be discussed later. First, the most formal, widely recognised, and financially underwritten system of quality measurement will be discussed: the process of hospital accreditation in Australia.

Institutional Accreditation

In 1974 a voluntary program of hospital accreditation was established under the authority of the Australian Council on Hospital Standards. This name has now been changed to the more contemporary Australian Council on Healthcare Standards, with the same acronym. The first ACHS Accreditation Guide enumerated a series of standards against which hospitals were to be assessed by surveyors in order to obtain the formal quality recognition of accreditation. Public and private hospitals responded enthusiastically to the challenge of demonstrated quality. An ever-increasing number of hospitals applied to be surveyed for accreditation, and undertook the review of facilities, staff organisation, and the development of the requisite committees.

In the early years of hospital accreditation the focus of the ACHS was on standards of physical facilities, including appropriate record-keeping and documentation. This approach was similar to that taken by its US counterpart, the Joint Commission on Accreditation of Hospitals (JCAH), on which the Australian accreditation system was modelled. The JCAH has now been renamed the Joint Commission on Accreditation of Health Care Organisations (JCAHO). One significant difference between the JCAHO and the ACHS is that in the USA health facilities must be accredited in order to receive federal subsidies and reimbursement, whereas in Australia the accreditation system, now widespread among health care facilities, has remained voluntary. But there is a financial incentive for Australian hospitals to seek accreditation, since private health insurers pay a higher reimbursement per patient day to accredited facilities. While ACHS accreditation is the most accepted and widely disseminated quality activity by health care providers in Australia, it is by no means the only one. Many health care organisations have undertaken system-wide quality management based on programs from other service sectors, such as TQM, and have also introduced comprehensive risk management programs with significant quality aspects. This is consistent with a similar trend in the USA where quality and risk management have often been combined.

The ACHS has recently moved from its initial emphasis on structure and process as evidence of quality to include an outcome focus, which is again similar to the change of emphasis of its counterpart organisation, JCAHO. There is also an increasing focus on improved documentation and measurement of both processes and outcomes, which suggests a welcome move towards more rigour in assessing institutional quality.

The name change of ACHS recognises that complex and sophisticated health care services are now provided in a number of locations, including free-standing day-surgery facilities and community health centres, which now undergo the process of accreditation. The intensity of care within nursing homes has increased, and now nursing homes are also eligible for accreditation.

Quality Measurement and Health Professionals

The introduction of hospital accreditation in Australia provided a stimulus to the health professions both to formalise and extend their existing quality activities, and to develop new ones. Although it is possible here to discuss the activities of only the two most numerous of the health professional groups in any detail, doctors and nurses, it is important in the quality context to acknowledge the contribution of medical record managers, previously known as medical record administrators. Medical record managers have long been responsible for ensuring the maintenance, collection, and storage of an adequate medical record for every person receiving care in a hospital or health facility.

Both JCAHO and ACHS Accreditation Guides emphasise the responsibilities and necessary involvement of medical record managers in quality assurance. The role of these managers has now been enhanced and further developed through aspects of casemix payment and through provision of data and skills for quality assurance activities, particularly the evaluation of the processes and outcomes of patient care.

Quality measurement for medical practitioners

Until fairly recently, Australian doctors, in common with their colleagues in other countries, believed that their rigorous formal training, professional ethics, and the regulatory environment of the registration system were sufficient to ensure the maintenance of appropriate standards of care. Although some might still hold this belief, there is now wide recognition within the medical profession, and within its professional associations and its learned colleges, that rigorous and continuing assessment of the processes and outcomes of care is a necessary component of quality medical practice. As mentioned earlier, there has always been a number of ongoing quality processes within the practice of medicine, though without specific quality nomenclature. Most of these processes, such as grand rounds and clinical audit, were associated with the assessment of institutional care, and related particularly to clinical activities in teaching hospitals. Despite these longstanding quality-assurance activities in teaching hospitals, quality assurance is still not an integral component of all undergraduate and postgraduate medical education.

Although most hospital medical staff, particularly those in teaching hospitals, have regular involvement in aspects of utilisation review, the same still cannot be said for medical staff within private practice. Colleges require their members to engage in continuing medical education (CME), and to document and report on these activities, but of course not all CME activities are associated with quality, and not all practising doctors are members of colleges.

The absence of adequate formal quality activities within private practice, and the lack of knowledge of peer review activities, were recognised soon after the start of the ACHS. In response to this need, the Peer Review Resource Centre (PRRC) was established in 1979 under the joint auspices of the AMA and the ACHS, with funding support from the Commonwealth government. The objectives of the PRRC included the provision of assistance, training, advice and support for peer review activities. It provided a major catalyst for the development of formal processes of peer review by medical and other health professionals during the seven years of its existence. By 1986, when the AMA and the ACHS decided to close the

PRRC, it had undertaken education for clinical review and provided support for other quality-assurance activities for thousands of health care professionals in all Australian states. When the PRRC closed, the AMA and the ACHS divided and shared its functions, though mechanisms for peer review have continued to be a difficulty and in some cases are still non-existent for doctors in private practice. The rate of participation in continuing education within medical specialities has been increasing, with positive implications for quality, but there is as yet no accessible peer review structure outside hospital practice.

In 1982 the ACHS first developed a policy requiring evidence of clinical review activity as a prerequisite for hospital accreditation, and by 1985 all public and private hospitals seeking accreditation were expected to provide evidence of documented clinical review activity. Against this background, it may be reasonable to argue that the need for a PRRC was irrefutable, but this was not the prevailing view of its funders and sponsors. To some extent its activities have been assumed and developed by accreditation and quality-assurance consultants, and through the continuing education resources of the various medical colleges.

Quality measurement and nursing

As with medical practitioners, nurses have traditionally conducted quality review activities, though these were often contained within processes described as shift handover, and not readily measurable. Nursing care was traditionally task-oriented, and adherence to recorded standards has been an important aspect of nursing practice. In Australia, the introduction of hospital accreditation required nurses to demonstrate to surveyors that the care they provided was measured and evaluated. Nurses and their colleges responded to this requirement of accreditation very positively. As the great majority of nurses is employed within hospitals and other health care institutions, the profession was able to assert by the early 1980s that a range of formal quality measures had been incorporated into nursing practice. Nursing quality measurement has included nursing audit, retrospective and concurrent patient surveys, and performance indicators. Until the present time, however, most nursing quality activities have been focused on documentation and process and rather less on the outcomes of care. A very wide range of nursing quality activities has been undertaken, some initiated and developed at ward and unit level, and others centrally organised. But there are issues still not completely addressed relating to the evaluation of nursing quality-assurance activities and the incorporation of all the identified quality changes into nursing practice.

The quality facilitators, quality coordinators, and quality managers now routinely employed in many hospitals have nursing backgrounds, often supplemented by additional qualifications in health service management, so that the contribution of nurses to quality extends beyond their activities in their original discipline.

Multidisciplinary quality measurement

Provision of comprehensive health care to patients requires a wide range of health care professionals applying very specific skills and having distinctive educational requirements. Some aspects of quality measurement and peer review are specific to only one discipline. For example, errors in diagnosis can be addressed within medical peer review, while the existence of pressure ulcers is an appropriate subject for nursing quality audit. Other topics may be less readily categorised and may require a multidisciplinary approach. For example, medication errors may be the responsibility of doctors, nurses, pharmacists, or even the patient, and an adequate review of such errors requires the participation of all relevant professionals. Unfortunately, quality assurance in Australian health care settings has frequently been subjected to 'ownership' and 'turf' debates. On the one hand, there has been an effort at government and health-funding level to ensure that quality is the concern of all health managers and professionals, to avoid the various processes of quality assurance being seen as 'the business of nurses', or 'that is what doctors do'. On the other hand, some of the findings of the Quality in Australia Healthcare Study (Wilson et al. 1995) suggest that quality may continue to be everyone's concern but no one's responsibility.

Quality Measurement and the Role of Government

Quality-assurance activities are continuing within the Australian health care system, and continue to develop in rigour and methodology. The impetus given to the measurement of health outcomes through government support and funding should lead to improvements in the process of quality measurement, and in turn to improvement in health outcomes. There are many positive and welcome signs that other aspects of quality measurement are being incorporated into the health care system, leading to better and, one hopes, measurable health outcomes. At the same time, the dynamic nature of the health care system is such that new structures, processes of care, and methods of measurement require constant and ongoing evaluation.

AHMAC has accepted a major coordinating role to improve hospital quality and safety and has commissioned a National Expert Advisory Group on Safety and Quality in Health Care to produce a national action plan to recommend ways of improving and coordinating health care safety and quality activities. Governments at Commonwealth and state levels continue to support professional self-regulation. More specifically, they require that the professional registration bodies provide evidence that appropriate standards are maintained. The maintenance of standards by registration bodies has resulted in the development of processes that, while not formally described as quality activities, nevertheless include aspects of quality assurance. As some of the medical colleges move to promulgate recertification, it can be expected that such directions will be approved and ultimately mandated by governments.

Health Outcomes

Further developments relating to outcome research in Australia include the relationship between technology assessment and quality assessment, links between process and outcomes, and links between evaluation of access to pharmaceuticals and health outcomes. Evidence of health outcomes, although essential, cannot be the only dimension by which quality of care is evaluated, since not all patient outcomes are directly related to the quality of care provided. Patient outcomes are complex, often dependent on time of measurement, sometimes subjective, and may be subject to variables outside the health care system. Outcomes may include not only 'the five Ds'—death, disease, disability, discomfort, and dissatisfaction—but also return to work, readmissions, quality of life, and general health status.

The focus on health outcomes has been supported vigorously by the Commonwealth Department of Health, whose Health Service Outcomes branch has financed and supported activities including Coordinated Care Trials, reduction in adverse drug events, and the application of best practice.

Evidence-Based Medicine

The National Health and Medical Research Council (NH&MRC) has supported the development and dissemination of evidence-based guidelines as a national activity. The momentum of the move to develop clinical practice guidelines is one very positive aspect of continuing efforts to measure and improve quality. Evidence-based clinical practice guidelines are important tools in achieving quality assurance because they assist and promote professional accountability, facilitate an evidence-based approach to clinical decision-making, and improve the process and outcomes of clinical and preventive care. A number of guidelines has been developed in Australia, or adapted for Australian conditions. The monitoring of their implementation and their effect on health outcomes will provide important information for quality measurement and improvements in clinical practice.

It has been recognised that local adaptation of nationally developed evidence-based guidelines is likely to increase practitioner acceptance and use of guidelines, so a number of Australian projects are currently being undertaken to ensure that guidelines are appropriate to local conditions. The Australian guideline process acknowledges resource constraints, and thus recommends that if alternative interventions differ markedly in cost but have similar outcomes and similar acceptability, the guidelines should support the less costly alternative. Australian Commonwealth government subsidy for the Australasian Cochrane Centre has contributed to the ability of that organisation to prepare and provide information on systematic reviews of the effects of health care interventions, supporting the development of evidence-based guidelines.

Patient Complaints

The role of complaints in the measurement and improvement of the quality of health care has been widely acknowledged, but there is little evidence that the data generated through the complaints process are actually analysed and incorporated into systems improvement. Most Australian states have developed complaints commissions and structures of varying effectiveness, but that effectiveness itself is not always understood. For example, in New South Wales, where the Health Care Complaints Commission is widely known and generally supported, the number of consumer complaints is increasing, as the public knowledge of and faith in the Commission process increases. This does not mean that the quality of individual health practitioners is necessarily either improving or declining, but rather that the complaints process has increasing public support. The existence of credible and independent complaints procedures should be recognised as part of a quality structure.

Location and Continuity of Care

In Australia, as the delivery of health care changes, the location of care for acute interventions and for chronic long-term illnesses is shifting to settings other than hospitals. This shift has exposed the need for quality-assurance criteria appropriate to the process of care in different locations. The development and selection of such criteria also have economic implications. Both the structure and process of most existing quality-assurance programs are predicated on the assessment of quality within one institutional environment, appropriate to that facility. The accreditation of health care facilities certifies the standards of care only within the particular environment. Care delivered outside the institutional environment has not been subjected to the quality-assurance processes that apply to institutional care. It is clearly impractical economically and logistically to transfer all quality-assurance programs and activities that are appropriate for institutional environments to the range of alternative locations of care, such as community centres, day centres, and homes, but optimal care may be compromised without adequate quality-assurance mechanisms. Pilot projects currently focusing on continuity of care for groups such as the elderly and people with chronic mental illness are expected to provide results to inform future policy on care delivery, including quality.

The Role of Information for Quality Measurement

Despite all these initiatives, deficiencies in quality measurement persist. More comprehensive clinical information systems are needed to monitor both process and outcomes of care. Comprehensive and effective systems require the combination of information from general practice, specialist, and diagnostic services, together with records of hospitalisation. Most of the data required are already collected and stored, but are neither integrated nor readily accessible. Commitment and electronic databases will facilitate necessary development. Quality issues associated with electronic health records include data security, legal implications, patient access to health records, and the roles and responsibilities of health professionals. Initial and ongoing support for data collection and review is required to encourage and facilitate data management and validation by clinicians. The collection, analysis, and dissemination of quality data have a cost, but the absence of data also has a cost.

The identification of avoidable complications of care, for example adverse drug reactions and post-operative wound infections, which may result in longer hospital stays and additional therapies, will be helped by better information systems. Access to objective data should result in improved patient management and better health outcomes. The front sheet of the medical record has been promoted as a National Front Sheet (Reeve 1993), which could be transmitted by electronic means and would provide a consistent and validated database, with valuable quality information.

Quality initiatives at state levels and national coordination mechanisms by the Commonwealth are both needed to improve the processes and outcomes of patient care. But resources should not be diverted from patient care to fund a quality bureaucracy. National commitment to quality health services, and support for appropriate education and incentives to ensure continuing improvements in quality of care should make an already good Australian health system an excellent one.

The Future

Formal quality-assurance processes will inevitably become more visible, and quality assessment and measurement will be fully incorporated into clinical and managerial accountability structures within all branches of the health care system. Public expectations of service quality and timeliness increase continuously, perhaps unrealistically, and Commonwealth and state governments and professional registration bodies will be under public pressure to demonstrate the effectiveness of quality processes. The increasingly litigious environment will provide a possibly unwelcome catalyst for further development of quality-assurance structures.

It can be expected that health outcomes will continue to be used as a measure of quality of care, though perhaps with increasing recognition that many health outcomes are only partially a reflection of the effectiveness of health service delivery.

Information technology can be expected to play an enhanced role in quality of health care, to inform evidence-based clinical decision-making, to reduce the adverse effects of remote and isolated practice, and to support formal and continuing education for health professionals. The development of evidence-based guidelines will continue, with an increasing emphasis on their dissemination and evaluation, focusing on better-quality clinical outcomes and more effective and appropriate use of resources.

Whether information readily available to patients through the World Wide Web results in better decisions about appropriate health care, leading to higher-quality health outcomes, remains to be seen. More rigorous and comprehensive evaluation will, one hopes, include the effective use of evidence by both patients and providers.

Conclusion

This brief review has demonstrated that a considerable range of quality measures has been developed within the Australian health care system. The assessment of quality continues to be a dynamic and developing area, within both the processes of care and the formal and continuing education of health professionals. Patient expectations of improved quality, the increased complexity and sophistication of pharmaceuticals, less invasive and more accurate diagnostic technologies, therapeutic advances, and improved communications all interact to foster a culture of more rigorous measurement and evaluation of quality processes and outcomes.

It may prove difficult to disaggregate and assess the relative effectiveness of the increasing range of quality initiatives, but given the advances and improvements that have already occurred, it would be reasonable to assume that quality of care in the Australian health system will continue to improve.

17

Managing Performance for Better Results

Simon Corden and Jenny Luxmoore*

Governments allocate funds across a range of widely differing portfolios such as education, defence, health, and housing. The specific activities that governments fund, and their grouping in portfolios, vary from country to country, across the states and provinces of each nation, and over time. Governments must also allocate funds within each portfolio to competing priorities—for example, in health, between preventive and early detection services and interventions, including those delivered in hospitals—and they must choose between alternative means of delivering services.

Most governments, however, including those of Australia, are compelled to make these key strategic decisions with inadequate information. Although information is often plentiful, it usually is neither structured nor available promptly enough to facilitate comparisons across service providers or jurisdictions, so as to help in strategic decision-making. In health this has meant that there has been little basis for determining whether even basic administrative functions, let alone clinical activities, are more cost-effectively performed by some hospitals or in some jurisdictions, compared with others.

Australia's Productivity Commission (an independent statutory body that advises Australian governments on all aspects of micro-economic reform), in its role as Secretariat to the Review of Commonwealth/State Service Provision, has been working since 1993 with Commonwealth, state, and territory government departments responsible for a wide range of services to improve the available information. The short-term aim of this cooperative effort has been to bring together the best set of information possible to inform policy choices across a range of services. The

*The views of the authors do not necessarily reflect those of the Productivity Commission or the Steering Committee for the Review of Commonwealth/State Service Provision.

longer-term objective has been to hasten development of better and more timely information on government services that will be useful to both the agencies directly responsible for each service and the central agencies (the departments supporting heads of government and treasurers/finance ministers).

This chapter describes the ongoing efforts of the Productivity Commission to help governments define and compare variations in the performance of services (including health) across jurisdictions (states, territories, and the Commonwealth). It illustrates the rationale, difficulties, and benefits of developing performance measures across a wide range of government services.

Information to Inform Strategic Analysis and Decision-making

Most current information on health services is designed to meet the needs of clinicians, health service operators, or individual government departments. The information needs of central agencies involved in contemplating broad strategic questions are not being met particularly well. The available information also tends to focus on existing process and input levels, rather than outputs and outcomes. Among the fundamental changes brought about through health reform have been changes in service delivery (such as separating the purchasing and providing functions, including in conjunction with competitive tendering) and funding methods (such as introducing output-based budgeting). These changes have forced agencies to address the question of how best to measure the production of outputs and the achievement of outcomes, and from there, how to apportion funding.

Governments must make many decisions annually through their budget processes, and when examining new policy proposals. Should existing health funding be allocated to hospitals on the basis of the outputs produced? Should additional health funding be used to raise the average price paid to hospitals for each patient, or should it be used to increase the number of patients being treated? More broadly, should governments allocate more resources to health, implicitly at the expense of education, aged care, police, or roads? A wide range of information that reflects all aspects of performance—including the outcome of service provision—is needed to address these questions.

Casemix funding of public hospitals, introduced in a number of Australian states in the early 1990s, and described by Duckett in Chapter 8, provides an instructive example. There seems to be agreement that the cost of care has declined as a result. For example, funding of acute-care services in Victoria rose by only 2.2 per cent (in real terms) between 1991/92 and 1996/97, but the level of throughput increased by 24.5 per cent (in terms of WIES) (Richardson 1998).

The debate continues about why. Were savings achieved through more efficient resource use, or by reducing the quality of care and access of patients to services? Casemix funding strengthens incentives for hospitals to reduce the length of stay, and some argue that this has been to the detriment of good patient care. The media have drawn on anecdotal evidence of such failures, including claims that patients have been discharged 'quicker and sicker'. Yet the absence of performance data made it difficult to assess these claims. The Victorian Auditor-General relied on a survey of the opinions of doctors, nurses and other health professionals in assessing the impact of casemix funding, but acknowledged the difficulties of making a thorough assessment due to the lack of robust indicators of quality of care and access (Auditor-General of Victoria 1998).

The problem of poor data to inform analysis and decision-making has not been confined to the activities of public acute-care hospitals. Performance information has been poor across a wide range of government services—education, police, aged care, and emergency management, to name a few.

A broad set of data is particularly important for government services, where multiple and often competing objectives are the norm. Any assessment of performance will depend on the importance placed on each objective. Thus the Productivity Commission has worked with governments to establish a process of annual national reporting in all of these areas.

One aim of coordinating the reporting process across a range of services is to encourage those who manage individual services to learn from the achievements in other areas. For example, many performance measurement issues are common across services. The commission's work on the treatment of superannuation and payroll tax when costing government services is relevant to all the diverse services in the project (SCRCSSP 1998b). This work should improve the comparability of unit cost measures across jurisdictions. Other challenges, such as measuring waiting times, targeting, and outcomes for clients using a range of separate services, arise in a number of areas.

A second aim of coordinated reporting is to permit readers to examine the links between related services in a single sector, such as the various components of the justice system (police, courts, and corrective services) or health system (hospitals and GPs), and, potentially, the links between different but related sectors, such as mental health and the justice system. Those responsible for managing each service area have been encouraged to develop performance indicators that are both comprehensive in terms of performance against key services objectives, and suitable for comparisons across jurisdictions. This simple approach produces a robust structure that forms the basis for development of better, nationally comparable performance measures in future.

Encouraging comprehensive reporting

Performance indicators are typically used to assess whether a service has achieved its main objectives. Governments' objectives for public acute-care hospitals are outlined in Box 17.1. They are common across jurisdictions, though the importance placed on each objective may differ between jurisdictions and over time. It is often difficult, however, to convert these objectives into specific and measurable aims.

Box 17.1   Objectives for public acute-care hospital services

    The common government objectives for public acute-care hospital services are to provide ready access to high-quality, cost-effective acute and specialist services that are responsive to individual needs.

Source: Report on Government Services 1999

Ideally, a robust set of indicators would capture all aspects of performance. This is particularly important where governments face trade-offs between competing funding priorities—for example between programs designed to prevent future illness and those that care for people who are already sick—or between the number of people treated (that is, access) and the quality of each person's care.

The framework for performance indicators developed for public acute-care hospitals assesses performance in terms of effectiveness (how well a service achieves its desired outcomes) and efficiency (how well governments use their resources to generate units of output). Effectiveness indicators are broadly grouped into four major categories: overall outcomes; access and equity; appropriateness; and quality, though clearly there are quality aspects to outcomes and appropriateness. In practice, 'quality' in the frameworks for each of the services in the *Report on Government Services* has often included measures such as level of accreditation, assessments against service standards, and client views. Where possible, inputs by government per unit of output are used as indicators of efficiency.

The actual indicators developed for each service differ to take account of the characteristics of the service, such as features of clients and providers. The framework for public acute-care hospitals (developed in conjunction with the National Health Ministers' Benchmarking Working Group, which is made up of Commonwealth, state and territory health officials and chaired by the Commonwealth Department of Health and Aged Care) groups indicators under the broad aims of quality, appropriateness, accessibility, and efficiency of care (Figure 17.1, p. 298).

The framework also indicates progress to date. It specifies, for each aspect of the service, whether there are nationally comparable performance information, non-comparable data, or no indicators yet defined. It highlights the partial nature of the current performance reporting, the gaps, and progress in filling those gaps. It also effectively sets out a work program for the future.

Filling the gaps in this framework is a slow process, especially for health. There is no agreement on indicators of equity of access, for example, that would shed light on some aspects of performance, such as whether people from ATSI backgrounds are getting the health care services they require. By contrast, nationally comparable, if imperfect, information on indigenous people's access to services is now reported for government school education, disability services, children's services, and vocational education and training.

Governments and individuals will have different values or policy priorities that lead them to place different weighting on the various objectives of the health system. Publishing the framework of indicators, along with relevant information on the characteristics of each state and territory, allows each to apply their own weighting and make their own assessment.

If the main challenge is determining the appropriateness of services provided in public acute-care hospitals, then one would be most interested in differences in the number of separations per 1000 people. Across Australia, the number of separations per 1000 people ranged from 160.8 in Tasmania to 260.6 in the Northern Territory (Table 17.1, p. 299). In understanding this difference, it is important to take account of the characteristics of each jurisdiction. For example, the Northern Territory has a small population spread over a large area. Lower population density in rural areas and greater distance between towns may increase the use of public acute-care hospital services for a number of reasons:

- first, fewer specialist medical and surgical practitioners may mean a delay in diagnosis such that patients are admitted later, and sicker; and
- second, some medical practitioners may admit some patients from isolated areas to reduce the risk that their condition may worsen unnecessarily if not treated very early (NSW Health n.d.).

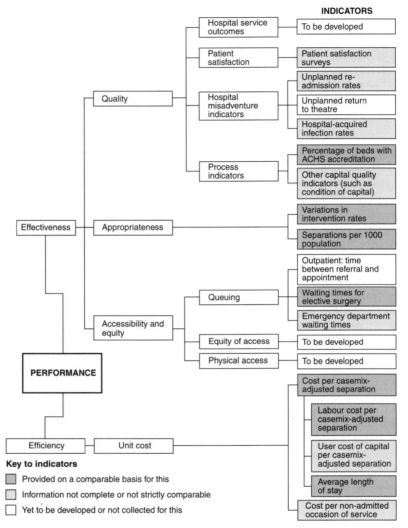

INDICATORS

Figure 17.1 Performance indicators for public acute-care hospitals

Source: Report on Government Services 1999

Information on the ratio of separations per 1000 population sheds some light on the appropriateness of public acute-care hospital services in aggregate. (Disaggregated data are also useful, and are discussed below.) But appropriateness is only one dimension of performance, and it says nothing about the quality of care provided. At present, only very imperfect quality indicators are available for comparison nationally, such as the proportion of public beds that are accredited and hospital–acquired infection rates (Table 17.1).

Table 17.1 Selected effectiveness indicators for public acute hospitals, 1996–97[a]

	NSW	Vic.	Qld	WA[b]	SA	Tas.	ACT	NT	Aust.
Hospital-acquired infection (%)									
post-operative wound (clean)	na	na	1.9	na	1.5	na	1.0	3.3	na
post-operative wound (contaminated)	na	na	1.8	na	2.7	na	0.7	6.5	na
hospital-acquired bacteraemia	na	na	0.2	na	0.3	0.3	0.6	0.5	na
Emergency patient readmission rate (%)	na	10.3	na	na	4.6	1.0	2.7	4.0	na
Public hospital beds accredited by ACHS as at year end (%)	75	86	53	71	68	87	99	0	72
Separations per 1000 people (no.)	196.6	192.5	191.7	193.4	219.9	160.8	182.2	260.6	196.6

a Comparisons should be made with care as some data are not strictly comparable. See notes in the relevant chapter and attachment of the Report on Government Services 1999.

b Data on hospital-acquired infection rates for WA were available for a sample of teaching, non-teaching metropolitan, and non-teaching non-metropolitan hospitals, but not aggregated across all hospitals.

na Not available.

Source: SCRCSSP 1999

Appropriateness—looking for clues

Appropriateness relates to how well service provision directly relates to client needs. That is, are clients receiving the correct service? Appropriateness indicators also seek to identify the extent, if any, of under-servicing or overservicing of clients (Renwick and Sadkowsky 1991).

In other sectors, measurable (albeit subjective) standards of service have been introduced against which current levels of service can be assessed. For example, in public housing, the appropriate-sized house for a couple with two or three children is considered to be three bedrooms. Larger houses are considered underused, smaller ones overcrowded.

Equivalent standards have not been established for many health care services. For some treatments, the appropriate level of service would have to be determined for particular populations. This has not been done.

Differences in service levels can indicate possible underservicing or overservicing, and further examination of service patterns is usually warranted (Table 17.2, p. 300). Where comparable information is available, it can encourage decision-makers to ask appropriate questions about performance and how it may be enhanced. For example, given the risks and costs of surgery, it may be worth further investigation of why such large differences in the number of tonsillectomies occur across states and territories.

Table 17.2 Difference in age- and sex-standardised separation rates (% difference from average of other states and territories)

Sentinel procedure[a]	NSW	Vic.	Qld	WA	SA	Tas.	ACT	NT
Appendicectomy	−3.3*	9.9**	−3.8**	6.0	−6.0	9.1*	−17.9	−40.5
Coronary artery bypass graft	22.3**	−0.1	−0.6	−43.1**	−3.4	−13.6**	−12.8	−41.7**
Angioplasty	−9.9**	36.7**	−39.4**	7.1*	22.6**	12.8*	−35.3**	−25.1*
Caesarean section	−7.5**	−3.4**	11.6**	−3.3*	15.9**	8.7**	−8.9**	−13.5**
Cholecystectomy	4.1**	0.6	2.3	−20.2**	11.9**	−4.5	−4.5	−36.3**
Endoscopy	7.5**	7.3**	5.9**	−15.3**	−17.9**	−7.8**	−44.6**	−43.3**
Hip replacement	−9.5**	13.2**	−14.9**	2.4	10.4**	37.4**	21.3**	−62.2**
Hysterectomy	−7.2**	−1.8	−2.0	0.0	25.2**	26.1**	5.0	−36.7**
Lens insertion	1.6*	−3.6**	29.5**	−2.4*	−25.8**	−25.6**	−51.8**	−14.8**
Tonsillectomy	−19.7**	22.8**	1.2	−2.7	38.1**	−29.4**	−11.0**	−74.1**

a Sentinel procedures are common surgical operations provided for serious health conditions in acute-care hospitals, for which alternative non-surgical treatments are often available.

*less than 5 per cent probability that the observed difference occurred by chance.

**less than 1 per cent probability that the observed difference occurred by chance.

Source: AIHW 1998b

Facilitating comparisons across jurisdictions

Indicators that allow comparisons across jurisdictions help identify which innovative approaches in one jurisdiction may be worth pursuing elsewhere, as well as fostering yardstick competition—which is particularly important where market forces do not operate (SRCSSP 1998). Government expenditure on hospitals in Australia was almost $12 billion nationally in 1995/96. But until recently, it was not possible to make reasonable comparisons of many aspects of performance of state hospital systems. What was included as a cost (for example, superannuation or depreciation) and what constituted an output varied across jurisdictions. Hence available unit cost information was not directly comparable.

This point was highlighted in Victoria in the early 1990s where performance reports by the Economic and Budget Review Committee (1992) and the Victorian Commission of Audit (1993) were heavily criticised by the Victorian department, on which they were reporting: 'In the absence of reliable comparative measures of costs and output, those reports are so fundamentally flawed as to be scarcely worth the paper they are written on, at least in regard to hospital performance' (DHCS 1993: 8–9). Since then considerable progress has been made in addressing shortcomings in unit cost information. A key step was the introduction of a nationally agreed standardised measure of outputs—casemix-adjusted separations.

The information on cost per casemix-adjusted separation in public acute-care hospitals (Table 17.3, p. 301) is not perfectly comparable, but still illustrates the benefits of information that allows comparisons across jurisdictions. An assessment that had data only on average annual growth in unit costs might conclude that Tasmania appeared to have made the most progress on cost containment. But casemix-based comparisons across jurisdictions suggest a more complex story, prompting a careful look at any caveats surrounding the data, and at variations in external factors that affect performance. For example, subsequent analysis by the Productivity Commission has revealed that Tasmania is the only state that levies payroll tax on its public hospitals, but this additional cost had not been excluded in the published data.

Table 17.3 Total recurrent cost per casemix-adjusted separation for selected public acute-care hospitals (1996/97 dollars)[a, b]

Year	Queensland	South Australia	Tasmania[c]
1993/94	$2389	$2361	$3004
1994/95	$2302	$2216	$2985
1995/96	$2349	$2306	$2941
1996/97	$2354	$2309	$2660
Apparent average annual change (%)	−0.5	−0.7	−4.0

a Cost changes over time may have been affected by changes in the set of hospitals covered by this data collection and other definitional changes.

b Total recurrent hospital cost per casemix-adjusted separation in public acute-care hospitals, deflated by the GDP-E deflator.

c Only Tasmanian public hospitals are liable for payroll tax, which is 6.6 per cent of payroll, including superannuation. Tasmania estimates that excluding payroll tax would lower reported costs by $133 per casemix-adjusted separation in 1996/97.

Sources: SCRCSSP (1995; 1997; 1998a; 1999) based on AIHW data

The Productivity Commission's report presents data that facilitate comparisons, but deliberately avoids making assessments of performance. Assessments are judgments that vary according to the importance placed on each of the often-competing objectives, and thus may vary by location. Moreover, local stakeholders have better knowledge of local conditions, and so are better able to explain or evaluate differences in measured performance than a national body, such as the commission. For example, with information on the cost per casemix-adjusted separation alone it is not possible to make a robust assessment of performance. Various factors, such as differences in geography, population density, or policy objectives may account for apparent variations in performance. The information can be perceived as a can-opener, which prompts the right questions about how to improve performance rather than providing the answers.

Timeliness—a variety of approaches to aged-care waiting lists
The lack of uniform indicators makes it difficult for jurisdictions to learn from one another, thereby restricting policy and implementation options. Indicators of timeliness of access to aged-care services, for instance, which account for $3.4 billion of total government health funding, are not

available at this time. Instead, access to nursing homes and hostel services has been measured in various jurisdictions by time on waiting lists for placement in residential accommodation. But different jurisdictions have used different approaches in their waiting process for nursing homes. Until recently, Victoria, Western Australia and Tasmania applied the following different methods for measuring waiting times:

- Victoria: overall placement rate at 30, 60, 90 and 120 days;
- Western Australia: mean waiting times in days; and
- Tasmania: weeks elapsing before placement into nursing homes and hostels.

By encouraging states and territories to adopt a standard measure of timeliness, the data become more valuable to all who use them.

An Iterative Approach

The fourth *Report on Government Services* was published in February 1999, and although there has been some improvement in the quality and range of data published, important gaps remain, as the previous section pointed out. The approach to filling these gaps has been to publish available (if imperfect) data and then address differences and shortcomings over time. Important policy decisions cannot be delayed, and imperfect data (appropriately acknowledged) are likely to lead to better decisions than no data. The data can signal to jurisdictions the extent to which different programs operating in different states and territories produce different results, at different costs, and thereby provoke consideration of these variations.

Developing better information is not an easy task for a number of reasons.

First, it can be difficult to develop a comprehensive framework that covers all aspects of performance. Some of the issues discussed above (such as developing indicators that reflect some aspects of quality of care) are recognised as areas requiring improvement. Moves are afoot by some governments to fill these gaps, with the support of experts, such as external consultants and the AIHW. By contrast, outcome indicators remain a challenge for all government services. In health, problems with developing outcome indicators in part reflect difficulties of isolating the effect of health care services on the general health of the population. Broad indicators of health (such as life expectancy, mortality rate, and cause of death) say as much about the income levels of the population, the level of education, and the standard of housing as they do about the performance of the health care system.

Second, there is a tension between the benefits of being able to compare performance across jurisdictions, and the cost of having indicators that may be less tailored to the particular needs of a specific agency or jurisdiction. Performance assessment should be cost-effective. Those undertaking measurement should avoid the temptation to reinvent the wheel when a methodology already exists and some indicators are available. But introducing indicators that were designed for another purpose, without considering the local environment, could also be counterproductive:

> Experience with administrative databases has demonstrated that some data is useless because those who collect the data have little investment, interest or training in supplying the data . . . To build data systems that people have confidence in, it is necessary to assure that those who supply the data get something useful from the system. (Poertner 1998: 97)

Measuring the quality of clinical care has proved to be a difficult task, as the support of practitioners is essential if good data are to be collected.

Third, there is a trade-off between comprehensive data and uniformly high-quality data. Given that cooperative processes are in their infancy, the Steering Committee that produces the *Report on Government Services* has placed greater importance on developing a comprehensive framework (that is, having performance information on as many key objectives as possible), than on uniformly high-quality or completely comparable data. Moreover, the Steering Committee's approach has been based on the premise that incomplete data are generally better than none. If data on a particular indicator are only available for some states and territories, they should still be published as soon as they become available. For example, data on elective surgery waiting times were only available for five of the eight states and territories for the 1999 report, and there were some differences in definitions and scope. These previously unpublished data were presented, with the appropriate caveats, rather than waiting in the hope that national data would be available for the 2000 report. This general approach reduces the likelihood of available data being confined to the lowest common denominator, which is a problem particularly when some agencies or jurisdictions are unable or unwilling to provide data, or adopt common definitions.

Providing a broader set of data, even if less uniform in quality, aids assessments of performance and minimises the likelihood of partial reporting or service providers focusing their efforts on achieving artificial service targets at the expense of fulfilling the needs of their clients (that is, goal displacement and indicator-chasing).

Moreover, reporting imperfect data or indicators can actually encourage efforts to develop better information. For example, reported capital costs per hospital separation differ across jurisdictions, but this could merely reflect differences in accounting treatment or, more importantly, in actual service delivery. Published comparisons using these imperfect data have prompted further work to understand the differences, as well as efforts to refine the underlying data.

However, not everyone agrees that more, albeit imperfect, information is likely to be better than less. The AIHW (1998b: 2), when comparing the reporting of its *Australian Hospital Statistics 1996–97* with that of the *Report on Government Services*, argued:

> For some performance indicators, not all the required data for reporting against the performance framework [of the Steering Committee] have been available from the [AIHW's] hospital data collections or other routinely compiled data sets. In some cases in the past, *ad hoc* requests for these data were made of states and territories, but the lack of quality and comparability of these data tended to reduce the overall quality of the performance indicator reports which incorporated them.

Fourth, it can be hard to ensure timely data in a cooperative process. A credible commitment to publish data on schedule, even if some data for some jurisdictions are not yet available, has strengthened incentives to deliver data in a timely manner—though this seems a bigger challenge for some data-providers in health and the community services than it does in other government services such as justice, public housing or vocational education and training. The national data on public acute hospitals, available for release in February 1999 in the *Report on Government Services 1999*, were for the year ending 30 June 1997. In contrast, most data for police, courts administration, corrections, emergency management, children's services, and housing, related to the year ending 30 June 1998. More widespread use of comparative performance information in determining state and territory budgets makes timely data even more important.

The approach in the *Report on Government Services* reflects, on the one hand, the preferences of policy-makers driving this project, and, on the other, the preference of particular central agency decision-makers (the report's prime audience) for a broad set of (possibly imperfect) indicators, rather than a smaller range of more uniformly high-quality data. Support for this approach has been reflected in positive feedback on the report. A survey of more than 200 users of the report found that it was seen as either 'important' or 'very important' by 80 per cent of users for strategic policy planning and policy evaluation; for assessing the resource needs of a department (63 per cent); for assessing resource performance (74 per cent); and for identifying other jurisdictions with whom to share information on services (65 per cent) (SRCSSP 1998).

Although both central and line agencies considered the information important for their key activities, central agency users rated the quality of the information more highly than line agency users (Table 17.4). This may be explained by the latter's greater familiarity with the data and their shortcomings, and their familiarity with alternative data sources.

Table 17.4   Rating of information in the *Report on Government Services 1998* (% of all central and line agency users surveyed)

In terms of:	Central agency users			Line agency users		
	Very good	Adequate	Poor	Very good	Adequate	Poor
credibility	36	56	8	29	59	12
relevance	51	47	3	34	58	8
objectivity	48	52	0	33	58	9
timeliness	22	74	0	23	69	8

Source: SRCSSP 1998

The differences in views about the information may also reflect different users' needs and expectations—the closer to the service provider, the greater the precision that may be required from data for decision-making purposes. For example, less precise and timely blood-test data may be more acceptable for monitoring blood stocks than for a decision on an individual's blood transfusion.

Conclusion

In this chapter we argue that more information, even though imperfect, is almost always going to be better than fewer data, particularly when the former is presented in a structured way with the appropriate caveats. Governments, like medical practitioners, must make timely decisions in a world where information is always going to be imperfect. As a result, the criteria for deciding whether information is useful should not be by reference to a 'gold standard', but by considering the value added by the information for the decision at hand.

However, while imperfect information is useful, better information is even more useful, so it is important to structure performance information processes to encourage cost-effective and rapid improvements in performance information, as well as timely reporting of the data. The process should

- have an explicit framework linking objectives to indicators, and highlighting current reporting gaps;
- publish on a regular (at least annual or more frequent) timetable;

- cover a range of services; and
- describe but not assess differences in performance.

In time, by working cooperatively, better performance information will be available. By enabling robust comparisons of service performance across jurisdictions, a process of learning from the diversity of experience in a federal system is facilitated, and governments are better able to assess the performance and resource needs of their own agencies.

18

Evidence–Based Health Care

Michael S. Frommer and George L. Rubin

Evidence-based health care refers to policy, public health practice, or clinical practice that makes use of knowledge derived from scientific research. The idea of evidence-based health care is not new. Since antiquity, practitioners have based treatments on evidence, or what they understood to be evidence (i.e. current knowledge). Thus concepts of evidence-based health care have varied according to the availability and nature of research-based knowledge, the individual and cumulative experience of policy-makers and practitioners, and the expectations of patients and communities.

For example, until as recently as about fifty years ago, the evidence base of medicine depended on the existence of an anatomical and pathophysiological rationale for treatments, tempered with the experience of clinicians who acquired their knowledge mainly from other clinicians. The cumulative experience of clinicians substituted for epidemiological information on the natural history of diseases and epidemiological evidence of the effectiveness of specific treatments. Patients and communities valued clinicians' experience (which often represented the epidemiology very accurately, even if it was unsystematic), their intuition, and their ability to apply pathophysiological principles to alleviate suffering.

Over the last fifty years, concepts of evidence-based health care have undergone a shift in emphasis. Intuition, unsystematic clinical experience, and the existence of a pathophysiological rationale have increasingly been seen as insufficient (Evidence-Based Medicine Working Group 1992). The contemporary concept of evidence-based health care demands an empirical demonstration of the benefit of health care interventions. Evidence of benefit comes either from the interpretation of individual studies that are judged to have used sound research methods, or from a systematic compilation of the results of two or more such studies. Rational decision-making based on rigorous and explicit methods is the hallmark: the empirical source of the evidence is explicit, the logic with which research findings are compiled into policy or practice recommendations is explicit, and the whole process is open to (and expected to withstand) critical scrutiny.

At an intellectual level, evidence-based health care has focused on the development of rules of evidence and rules for the evaluation of research and the synthesis of evidence from it. At a practical level, the challenge has been to integrate this rigorous empirical evidence with clinical or public health experience, to relate it to pathophysiological or public health principles, and to deliver effective health care that fulfils the needs and accords with the values of patients, practitioners and the community.

The term 'evidence-based health care' is often taken as meaning the practice of only those interventions for which there is empirical evidence of benefit. This restrictive usage is an implausible representation of the reality of health policy and practice. 'Evidence-based health care' must refer more broadly to the integration of science, experience, expectations and values, in a context of responsible resource usage.

Why Has Evidence-Based Health Care Emerged as a Major Theme?

This contemporary concept of evidence-based health care has been an increasingly prominent intellectual theme since Cochrane's monograph *Effectiveness and Efficiency* was published in 1972. Cochrane's analysis was confined to the clinical sector of the NHS in the United Kingdom, but the problems he identified have wide relevance and still apply strongly today. As the title of the monograph suggests, Cochrane highlighted two major deficiencies in health care. The first was effectiveness. Cochrane warned about the dangers of assuming 'that well-established therapies which have not been tested are always effective' (1972: 29). The second was efficiency. He pointed out that the clinical sector of the NHS was 'subject to a severe inflation with the output rising much less than would be expected from the input', and suggested that 'the inflation could be controlled by science, in particular the wide use of randomized controlled trials' (1972: 86).

Following on from Cochrane's analysis, it is not difficult to propose a web of interrelated reasons for the rise of evidence-based health care:

- Empirical evidence of benefit was (and still is) lacking for a large proportion of policy initiatives, public health programs and clinical interventions.

- Although these gaps remain, practitioners are confronted by an explosion of information. In medicine alone, over two million articles are published each year in an enormous number of journals (Mulrow 1995), and it is now impossible for any one clinician to read and appraise current publications, even in specialised fields. The imperative is to synthesise the expanding information base so that relevant, reliable evidence can be disseminated and implemented for the benefit of individual patients and populations.

- The cost of health care is increasing, with new technology undoubtedly contributing to the burden. The need to relate the cost to evidence of the benefit of new (and not-so-new) health care interventions is axiomatic.

- Aside from questions of cost, health care practitioners have an interest in knowing about the effectiveness of their work, and a culture of empirical measurement of processes and outcomes has suffused many health care disciplines. In general, practitioners aspire to improve the quality (i.e. effectiveness) of health care, and the use of evidence-based interventions is inevitably an important component of effectiveness.

- The professional interest in effectiveness is welcomed in political and managerial circles, due to widespread anxiety about the cost of health care.

- Those responsible for the management of health systems are acutely aware of wide variations in access to health services, rates of interventions, and health care outcomes. They are also aware that these variations do not necessarily have a simple relationship to the distribution of health care resources. They see evidence-based health care as having a potential to reduce these variations.

- Consumers of health care are increasingly well informed about the benefits and risks of health care, and their interest in empirical evidence of effectiveness is developing alongside cynicism about the value of professional intuition and unsystematic experience. Consumer interests are expressed in various forms, ranging from a quest for information about specific treatments to an inclination to pursue litigation. Inevitably there are instances where a patient comes to know more about a disease and its treatment than the doctor (Pemberton and Goldblatt 1998).

- Professional, consumer and managerial aspirations for information and for the analysis of complex empirical data are increasingly well served by information technology, and low-cost computers can analyse complex empirical data on a scale that Cochrane could not have imagined.

- Professional education increasingly teaches the importance of empirical evidence beyond the traditional wisdom of health care practice. Methods of accessing and appraising empirical evidence are strongly emphasised in modern graduate and postgraduate curricula.

If the rise of evidence-based health care can be attributed to these professional, social and economic forces, due recognition must be given to methodological innovations that have enabled the forces to find practical expression as part of the broader process of reform. These innovations have mainly been in epidemiology (originally a public health science) and its application across the spectrum of health endeavour, especially in the evaluation of clinical practice.

The pivotal step was development of the randomised controlled trial, which is now accepted as the most valid method of establishing a causal relationship between a health care intervention and its supposed outcome. The foundation stone in the history of the randomised controlled trial was Fibiger's study of the efficacy of anti-diphtheria serum in 1898 (Hrobjartsson et al. 1998). A landmark more relevant to the history of evidence-based medicine was the UK Medical Research Council's trial of streptomycin for pulmonary tuberculosis in 1948 (Medical Research Council 1948).

Randomised controlled trials have proliferated over the fifty years since the streptomycin trial, becoming an absolute requirement for the introduction of new drugs. Despite this proliferation, the evaluation and synthesis of research-based evidence, and its systematic linkage with clinical and public health activity, did not become part of the ethic and practice of mainstream health care until the 1990s. A tone of novelty is apparent in articles published as recently as 1992, advocating the systematic use of evidence from clinical research in clinical decision-making (Evidence-Based Medicine Working Group 1992).

The advent of the International Cochrane Collaboration in 1992 (Chalmers 1993) was a major impetus for the implementation of evidence-based health care. It has provided a forum that defined the rules for evaluating evidence, training in how to apply the rules, peer review mechanisms to scrutinise application of the rules, and a highly effective but simple infrastructure (enhanced by the growth of Internet e-mail) that brought together researchers and practitioners, often located on opposite sides of the globe, to formulate research-based recommendations on specific health care topics that attracted their interest. The Cochrane Collaboration has established methods for carrying out systematic reviews that grade and synthesise evidence from two or more research studies. It also publishes these reviews on CD-ROM and the Internet. Some 2000 systematic reviews have been published to date (Cochrane Library 1998).

The Cochrane Collaboration has been a major influence in the development of other focuses of systematic reviewing, such as the NHS Centre for Reviews and Dissemination in York (Sheldon and Melville 1996). Numerous generalist and specialist databases on evidence-based health care are easily accessible to anyone who has a computer linked to the Internet and fitted with a CD-ROM drive (Rubin and Frommer 1999). The organised information in these databases—the tools of evidence-based health care—can help practitioners to cope with the overwhelming production of research information.

How is Evidence-Based Health Care Implemented?

The implementation of evidence-based health care relies on the transfer of research-based knowledge into policy and practice. Research transfer is itself a knowledge-based process. Active steps are needed to disseminate the evidence, promote its uptake by decision-makers, change practice, and monitor and evaluate the consequences. Effective implementation involves the following four elements (Rubin et al. 1998):

- *good information:* research results that stand up to critical scrutiny and are synthesised and presented in forms that can be used to solve practical problems;
- *good access to information:* dissemination mechanisms and systems that make it easy for users (practitioners, managers, policy-makers, and consumers) to get the information;
- *supportive environments:* physical and intellectual environments in which research is valued and uptake of research-based knowledge supported and encouraged; and
- *promotion of knowledge uptake:* interventions that demonstrably promote the use of new (and existing) knowledge in decision-making for both policy and practice.

Good information

Evidence-based health care depends on the availability of good evidence obtained by rigorous and explicit methods, but what are the characteristics of good evidence? It is helpful to think of four dimensions of evidence: relevance, level, quality, and strength (National Health and Medical Research Council 1999).

The *relevance* of evidence refers to its usefulness: how close are the outcomes of the research studies to the information needed for policy, public health, or clinical decision-making? Does the research cover the outcomes that the decision-maker needs or wants to know about? Does it cover disadvantages of proposed interventions, as well as their benefits?

The *level* of evidence refers to the study design used in the research, or the method used to compile evidence from two or more studies. This determines the potential to eliminate or reduce systematic error, or bias, by design.

As noted above, randomised controlled trials give the best evidence about an intervention because they are less likely to be affected by biases than observational studies. However, there are many situations in which a randomised trial cannot be done, or has not been done. In such situations, decision-making may be based on the best evidence available, rather than the best evidence possible.

Evidence is often classified into five levels (Gray 1997), as shown in Table 18.1. Level I represents the best evidence; towards Level V, it is increasingly likely that bias will affect the results.

Table 18.1   Levels of evidence

Level	Type of evidence—description
I	Evidence from at least one systematic review of multiple well-designed randomised controlled trials.
II	Evidence from at least one properly designed randomised controlled trial of appropriate size.
III	Evidence from well-designed trials without randomisation, single group pre-post, cohort, time series, or matched case-control studies.
IV	Evidence from well-designed non-experimental studies from more than one centre or research group.
V	Opinions of respected authorities, based on clinical evidence, descriptive studies, or reports of expert committees.

Source: Gray 1997

The *quality* of evidence refers to methods used by researchers to minimise bias within a study design and in the conduct of the study. Level and quality of evidence must be considered together. A poor-quality randomised controlled trial may give less evidence than a high-quality observational study, though the observational study gives a lower level of evidence.

The *strength* of evidence depends on the magnitude of the effect of the intervention, that is, the magnitude of the relative risk, or the risk reduction, or other measure of change associated with the intervention. It also depends on the likely range of variation in the strength of evidence due to chance (the width of the confidence interval), and the reproducibility of the results in different studies.

The stock of research-based knowledge that has been rigorously appraised and summarised is expanding rapidly. But the application of this knowledge in practice depends on its expression in a usable form.

One form of expression of research-based knowledge is the clinical guideline. Clinical guidelines are 'systematically developed statements to assist practitioner and patient decisions about appropriate health care for specific clinical circumstances' (Institute of Medicine 1992: 2). Evidence-based guidelines explicitly qualify practice recommendations according to the research evidence available to support them, and guideline recommendations are graded accordingly (Grimshaw and Eccles 1998). Guidelines are intended to improve both the processes and the outcomes of clinical practice, and they have proliferated in recent years. Strong evidence exists to show that they do change practice (Grimshaw and Russell 1993), though it appears that guidelines alone do not produce large sustained improvements. Where there is general agreement about the approach to managing a clinical problem, guidelines may also reduce variations in practice, decrease costs, and map the approaches to the problem, which may be especially helpful for clinicians without experience of that particular problem (Margolis 1998).

In response to the rapid growth in the development and use of guidelines, the US Agency for Health Care Policy and Research has established an Internet-based National Guideline Clearinghouse (NGC), which gives access to a publicly available electronic repository for English-language clinical practice guidelines and related materials from all over the world (Agency for Health Care Policy and Research 1999). As it is available online, the NGC is a significant and influential international resource. It comprises both evidence-based and consensus guidelines, and includes comparisons of guidelines that cover similar topic areas.

Good access to information

Although the dissemination of research-based knowledge does not of itself lead to implementation, new knowledge will not be implemented unless it gets to the people who might want to (or ought to) use it. The dissemination process is often given insufficient attention in the implementation of evidence-based health care. It depends on four lines of deliberate action: target groups must be specified; decisions must be made as to the most appropriate media (e.g. print or electronic media); resources must be allocated for the design, production and distribution of materials; and the design, production and distribution process must be managed as a project, preferably with some evaluation and feedback (Rubin et al. 1998).

Supportive environments

The implementation of evidence-based practice is likely to be favoured in settings where research is valued, where there is critical debate of research methods and results, and where managerial commitment (both to effective information systems and to routines that facilitate their use) is expressed (Rubin et al. 1998). The existence of a close relationship between researchers and potential users of research-based knowledge is of great importance. Traditionally, researchers, practitioners and policy-makers have operated with very different imperatives, aspirations, methods, and time pressures from each other, and these differences are likely to have impeded the transition from research to policy and practice (Haines and Jones 1994; Lomas 1997).

Promotion of knowledge uptake

Many interventions to promote the implementation of research-based knowledge have been tried, underpinned by a variety of theoretical perspectives on factors that influence behaviour change. Systematic reviews suggest that the following types of interventions (which are more relevant to clinical than policy settings) are consistently effective (Bero et al. 1998):

- Educational outreach visits, which comprise visits by trained personnel to provide information to health care providers in their practice settings. This method, also known as academic detailing, appears to be effective when used alone or in combination with other interventions. It appears to be particularly effective when combined with a social marketing approach that identifies barriers to change.
- Decision-support systems and other reminders, which comprise manual or automated prompts for health care providers to take a specific action. Examples include reminders about screening, enhanced laboratory reports, follow-up appointment systems, and stickers on charts. The use of computerised decision-support systems has led to improvement in the performance of doctors in decisions on drug dosage, the provision of preventive care, and the general clinical management of patients, but not in diagnosis.
- Interactive educational meetings, which involve participation of health care providers in workshops that include discussion of practice, small-group interactive learning, and/or problem-based learning.
- Multifaceted interventions, consisting of two or more of the following: audit and feedback, reminders, local consensus processes, and marketing. These seem to be more effective than single interventions.

What are the Limitations of Evidence-Based Health Care?

The application of evidence-based health care is limited by several practical difficulties.

Gaps in research-based knowledge

On many health care topics, relevant research results are unavailable. Full-scale, systematic reviews typically take eighteen months to complete. A peer review process follows, after which there might be delays in publication of the conclusions. Consequently, by the time a systematic review appears in print, the intervention it assesses can be superseded by new technology.

In general, the rules of evidence that are used in evidence-based health care are more readily applicable to randomised controlled trials than to observational studies. Yet there are many situations where randomised trials have not been done or are not feasible. The potential for using the results of observational studies has not been fully exploited.

The fallibility of the evidence

The rigour and explicitness with which the evidence is assembled create an impression that evidence-based health care is an exact science, and that its practitioners can examine research with a high degree of objectivity. This is not the case. The methods of evidence-based health care depend significantly on the judgment of the practitioners and the vagaries of research publication. Studies with significant positive results are more likely to be published than those without such results, and studies reported in the English language are more likely to be published in international journals. Moreover, there is evidence that multiple publication occurs with surprising frequency. It is often difficult to determine in a meta-analysis whether two papers represent duplicate publications of a single trial or two separate trials. Biases such as these can seriously distort the results of meta-analyses which form the core of systematic reviews (Egger and Davey Smith 1998).

The challenge of implementation

The implementation of evidence-based health care often requires practitioners to change not only their practices but also their ways of thinking and working. Most health care practitioners are conscientious and knowledgeable, and it is difficult to induce change in people who see themselves (and are regarded by their peers) as doing a good job according to their training and professional norms. The practice of evidence-based medicine requires new skills and a new discipline on the part of practitioners who may already be overloaded: a capacity to crystallise clinical or other health care questions, search literature databases, and appraise research studies. These skills are well covered in the new professional curricula, but it will take a generation or two before the professional population is imbued with them and with the benefit of them. In the meantime, cynicism about evidence-based health care is likely to be prevalent among health professionals. The tendency to regard it as a 'movement' (which, like most other 'movements', has a high chance of being transient) reinforces the cynicism.

Moreover, even those who embrace evidence-based practice will often have difficulty applying research-based knowledge to specific problems, such as the clinical problems of individual patients. This difficulty is not insuperable, but considerable understanding of both human factors and epidemiological concepts is needed if, for example, the true benefit of a clinical intervention is to be assessed for an individual patient.

The Challenge of Evidence-Based Health Policy and Management

If the contents pages of the leading medical journals can be taken as a guide, evidence-based health care is an important aspect of present-day clinical practice, at least at an intellectual level. But it is much less clear that research evidence has influenced health policy and management. Although researchers and clinicians work independently of each other, the relationship between researchers and clinicians is closer than that between researchers and policy-makers, who often have little understanding of each other's work (Lomas 1997).

The Link between Effectiveness and Efficiency

Evidence-based health care holds (and is fulfilling) considerable promise for improving the health of individuals and communities. Numerous specific instances provide evidence for the effectiveness of the evidence-based approach, especially in clinical practice. But the evidence to support Cochrane's (1972: 86) ambitious assertion that 'the inflation [in health care costs at a health system level] could be controlled by science, in particular the wide use of randomized controlled trials' is much weaker. Even if ineffective health care interventions are weeded out by sanctions and disincentives, the economic benefit provided to a health *system* is likely to be hard to demonstrate. Any apparent saving will be diverted to underwrite the cost of other health care opportunities that may or may not have demonstrable benefit.

What is the Impact of Evidence-Based Health Care?

Impact on health care practice and health outcomes

The impact of evidence-based health care is difficult to separate from the impact of the clinical or health services research that generates the evidence. Instances in which research evidence has improved the performance and health outcomes of preventive and therapeutic health services are too numerous to list. Spectacular examples are the discovery of the central role of *Helicobacter pylori* in peptic ulcer (Marshall and Warren 1984), with the subsequent widespread adoption of antibiotic treatments for peptic ulcer, and the sustained reduction in the incidence of sudden infant death syndrome since the wide publication of information on risk factors in the early 1990s (Dwyer et al. 1995).

Research-based evidence has undoubtedly challenged medical claims about the value of specific interventions, ranging from laparoscopy to tonsillectomy (Black 1997), though the extent to which changes in practice have followed such challenges is not well documented. Common practices demonstrated to be ineffective tend to persist for long periods despite the evidence. For example, uterine dilatation and curettage continues to be used as a diagnostic and treatment intervention for dysfunctional uterine bleeding despite 1970s evidence of lack of effectiveness (Coulter 1993).

Impact on the organisation and funding of health care

Instances in which research evidence has influenced the organisation and funding of health care in Australia are harder to find than instances of improvements in health outcomes and the performance of health services. The volume of Australian health policy research and evaluation seems to be small, and it appears that policy decisions on the organisation and funding of health care are based more on assertion than rigorous evidence. Lomas (1997: 2) emphasises that 'whatever potential there is in greater use of evidence in decision-making cannot be realised until significant improvements occur in the linkage between current or future research and decisions on pressing or emerging issues'. The potential is illustrated by Australian research on consumer co-payments in medical care. This research was influential in ending the brief introduction (in 1991) of a compulsory co-payment under the national health insurance system (Medicare) for visits to a doctor. It probably also played a part in the retention of the Australian system of direct billing by doctors to Medicare, as the research suggested that abolishing direct billing would lead to increased medical fees and decreased services (Richardson 1991).

Impact on professional education

A challenge faced by all health professionals is the question of whether or not their practice is up to date. Traditionally the answer to this question has come from comparison with what colleagues do, or comparison with what funders, patients and the community expect. The rise of evidence-based medicine has provided a more structured frame of reference for continuing professional education: comparison with what the evidence suggests is best practice. The proliferation of evidence-based guidelines provides a very clear opportunity for continuing professional education.

The rise of evidence-based medicine has clearly influenced medical curricula in Australia. Modern curricula (such as the graduate-entry programs introduced in the 1990s at Flinders University and the Universities of Queensland and Sydney, and the pioneering medical curriculum at the University of Newcastle) emphasise problem-based learning and the development of critical appraisal skills (Lawson et al. 1998). These skills are the cornerstone of evidence-based health care. Some programs, such as that at the University of Sydney, contain teaching units dedicated to evidence-based medicine. Analogous developments are occurring in other Australian medical schools, in professional curricula for other health disciplines, and in postgraduate vocational education.

Recently the Commonwealth Department of Health and Aged Care has begun offering its managers and policy officers the opportunity to undertake recognised master of public health degree courses, which are offered on site. This educational opportunity will give departmental staff the critical appraisal skills needed to reorient policy thinking towards an evidence base.

Impact on consumer expectations and behaviour

It is likely that consumer expectations are helping to propel the rise of evidence-based health care, rather than the converse. People are becoming better informed about health and are receiving support from consumer organisations and governments for more and better information, and for greater involvement in decision-making. This inevitably (and desirably) exposes more of the uncertainties in health care practice, especially clinical medicine. Wennberg is quoted as saying:

We need more open acknowledgment that the scientific basis of many medical interventions is poor. Patients should know that wide variations in practice, especially in operative procedures, are not related to need but to the advocacy and skill mix of local doctors. When patients are fully informed about the risks of intervention and their preferences taken into account, operative rates for prostatectomy, for example, which vary tenfold in the US, fall to the lowest level and costs fall. (Richards 1998: 85)

Anecdotes suggest that doctors are increasingly encountering patients who have searched the literature and scanned the Internet on the diseases they think they have. Rather than threatening doctors who traditionally hold knowledge that their patients lack, this may provide opportunities for new, fruitful partnerships between doctors and patients (Pemberton and Goldblatt 1998). Of course, such relationships are likely to occur mainly with patients who are well off and well educated, with access to the knowledge sources, and the assertiveness to ask questions. Indeed, as Galbally notes in Chapter 15, the proliferation of health information has the potential to exacerbate existing variations in access to health services.

The ready access to information from a wide variety of sources, especially the Internet, has given rise to concerns about the quality of health information for consumers and has stimulated the development of evidence-based consumer information. The Cochrane Collaboration has established a Cochrane Review Group on Consumers and Communication, and a new government-funded Centre for Health Information Quality has been established in the United Kingdom to coordinate and support the development of materials for patients (Richards 1998).

Evidence-Based Health Care in Australia

Evidence-based health care is an international endeavour to which Australia has made a significant contribution. The development of evidence-based health care has been a model of international collaboration. It depends on the international exchange of research-based knowledge and collective experience in the implementation of research. The idea of evidence-based health care is becoming entrenched in practice in Australia as in all developed nations, driven by a combination of social, economic, professional, and consumer forces. In Australia (and elsewhere), its potential to improve the health of individuals and communities is beginning to be realised, but its potential impact on health policy has yet to be manifested.

Evidence-based health care and decision-making

Commonwealth, state and territory governments have endorsed evidence-based health care initiatives as means to improve the outcomes of health services, and since 1993 Commonwealth/state health funding agreements have incorporated a commitment to outcomes measurement. Although no formal evaluation has been undertaken, it is likely that these actions have had less of an impact on the development of evidence-based health care than the work of enthusiastic clinicians, public health practitioners, and consumer advocates who, by example and advocacy, have influenced their peers, their professional organisations, and their communities. Consumer organisations such as the Consumers' Health Forum and the Australian Consumers' Association have stimulated consumer involvement in evidence-based health care by encouraging people to seek health information and helping them to find it. A recent national review of health and medical research has encouraged the routine integration of research-based knowledge into health policy and practice, and has advocated an increase in funding and an expansion of capacity for research into health services (Wills and the Committee of the Health and Medical Research Strategic Review Committee 1999).

National concentration of effort on the health priority areas of cardiovascular disease, cancer, injury, mental health, and diabetes has helped to define key policy, public health, and clinical opportunities for the application of research-based knowledge in these fields. At a national level, the Commonwealth government has a significant opportunity to use the Medical Benefits Schedule to promote treatments and procedures of known effectiveness and to discourage interventions known to be ineffective. Steps have been taken to exploit this opportunity, but it is too early for the consequences to be known. The Pharmaceutical Benefits Schedule has been used in this way for many years. However, there is no formal evaluation of the consequences for health and health services of pricing policies, or policies that restrict or promote the availability of particular drugs.

Health system reforms at state and territory level have focused on questions of efficiency rather than effectiveness, seeking to meet increasing community demands for service delivery while controlling costs and dealing with concerns about resource allocation. In the pressurised environment of state health services, the pursuit of policies to link efficiency with effectiveness in the sense proposed by Cochrane (1972) has not been sustained as a priority. However, most states have invested significantly in institutional infrastructure to promote evidence-based health care. For example, the NSW Health Department has provided core funding to establish the Australian Centre for Effective Healthcare, a unit dedicated to the promotion of effectiveness, that is, people-centred, prevention-focused, safe, technically proficient, well-managed health care based on the best available evidence. The unit operates via a collaborative network throughout New South Wales and beyond. Several area health services in the New South Wales health system have established effectiveness units that link research with local practice, and analogous units have formed in other states.

The National Health and Medical Research Council (NH&MRC) has expressed an intention to turn to these units, singly or in collaborative networks, for evidence-based health advice. The NH&MRC itself has made a significant contribution to the development of evidence-based practice by developing and publishing evidence-based guidelines on such topics as the management of early breast cancer (NH&MRC 1995a) and pre-term birth (NH&MRC 1997), and the publication of guidance on the development of guidelines (NH&MRC 1995b). It has commissioned a publication on methods of disseminating and implementing research-based evidence, and has recently funded the Evidence Based Clinical Practice Program, providing competitive grants for projects designed to develop successful strategies for evidence-based clinical practice (Rubin et al. 1998). The NH&MRC also funds major centres that have an important influence in leading evidence-based practice, notably the NH&MRC Clinical Trials Centre and the National Breast Cancer Centre.

The Australian private health insurance sector has also expressed considerable interest in evidence-based health care. By Commonwealth government mandate, contracts between insurers and providers of acute care (hospitals) are required to include criteria that reflect quality of care, and insurers are tending to interpret quality as synonymous with effectiveness. This has stimulated some work on the specification of indicators of effectiveness. In a competitive environment, insurers are seeking to reaffirm the value of private insurance for their clients, and this includes providing information on the effectiveness of health services.

Current status and significance of evidence-based health care in Australia

Evidence-based health care in Australia is regarded with considerable enthusiasm. Policy commitment is apparent at Commonwealth and state/territory government and local health service levels through numerous separate activities. At the health system level, the impact of government policy on evidence-based health care has tended to be a by-product of programs mainly intended to control costs and promote rational resource distribution. Health service and institutional commitment to evidence-based health care is more direct and more immediate. Several new units in local health services and hospitals are, in the coming years, likely to make a major contribution, through research and advocacy, to the implementation of research-based knowledge. The promotion of evidence-based practice is a major preoccupation of peak professional organisations, notably the Royal Australasian College of Physicians and the Royal Australasian College of Surgeons (Barraclough 1998; Cameron 1998).

At a health system level it is too early to appraise the significance of evidence-based health care in Australia. With reference to Cochrane's analysis from 1972, its impact on the *effectiveness* of health care is likely to be realised sooner than its impact on *efficiency*. A key indicator of the former is the extent of its adoption, and first reports show that the adoption of evidence-based health care is patchy. A 1995 survey of all the 104 neonatologists and a random sample of 145 members of the Royal Australian College of Obstetricians and Gynaecologists practising in Australia showed that 72 per cent of neonatologists and 44 per cent of obstetricians used databases of systematic reviews regularly in clinical decisions. Of neonatologists who reported using systematic reviews, 58 per cent attributed some practice change to this use; the corresponding figure for obstetricians was 80 per cent (Jordens et al. 1998). A 1997 survey of randomly selected GPs in New South Wales showed that 43 per cent of respondents had access to the Internet (14 per cent were online at their workplaces); 22 per cent were aware of the Cochrane Library, 6 per cent had access to it, and 4 per cent had used it (Young and Ward 1999).

These studies suggest that, under the right conditions, evidence-based health care can become a part of ordinary practice. If the practice behaviour of Australian neonatologists were to become the norm in other fields of health practice, a profound change would be evident in the style and delivery of Australian health care. While this change is not yet widespread, evidence and the application of evidence have become very prominent themes in the written and spoken discourse of practitioners.

The significance of evidence-based health care for health service management and policy is less discernible. While clinical and public health policy-makers may look increasingly to research-based knowledge for their decisions, wider questions of health system organisation and funding policy in Australia tend to be informed more by demography, geography, and politics. The available empirical information on the effectiveness of these wider policy decisions is mainly financial. There is scant evidence to link changes in patterns of health service use, health status, or health outcomes with evidence-based initiatives.

Future of evidence-based health care in Australia

The factors that have promoted the rise of evidence-based health care are deeply entrenched in health systems everywhere, and they will inevitably sustain the development of evidence-based health care in Australia over the longer term.

In the short-to-medium term, it is likely that there will be substantial development in the infrastructure for evidence-based health care in Australia. This will be led by information technology. Current barriers for access to computerised databases (cost and the need for technical support in installation and operation) will be lowered, so access will become cheaper and easier. This will be especially important for the spread of evidence-based practice in community settings, notably general practice. Government incentive payments have already been proposed to encourage the adoption of information technology in general practice (Anon. 1999). The proliferating access to evidence databases in community practice will reinforce the use of evidence in hospital and managerial settings. Information technology will also lead consumer access to evidence databases.

In the short term, ease of access to the databases will outstrip the availability of evidence. Users will often be frustrated by easy access to evidence databases that do not contain the information they need. An acceleration of research and systematic reviewing will follow. It may be in the interests of purveyors of information technology and database systems to sponsor the research, which will inevitably be international. Australia is well placed to make a significant contribution to the international effort.

In the medium term, demand will increase for the empirical evaluation of initiatives intended to promote evidence-based health care. These demands are likely to come both from governments (which have invested on the promise of evidence-based health care), and professional groups (who identify with the rationale for evidence-based health care and find appeal in the availability of workable decision-support systems, but tend to be sceptical if new methods demand changes in professional behaviour).

The factors that have promoted the rise of evidence-based clinical and public health practice have not yet injected an expectation of empirical analysis into the Australian health policy process. In the short-to-medium term, demographic, geographic, and political imperatives are likely to remain the primary determinants of health policy at the system level. Australia has a track record of shrewd health policy decisions during the 1980s and 1990s (e.g. in the management of the threat from HIV), and these decisions were often made without the benefit of empirical evidence.

The strong capacity for policy analysis that exists in independent and government institutions in the United Kingdom, Europe, and North America has never formed in Australia. However, early signs of a growing capacity for independent health policy analysis are beginning to emerge from a few Australian universities, and in the medium-to-long term the existence of this capacity is likely to influence the style of policy thinking. Nevertheless, if the experience of other countries with heterogeneous populations and a diverse geography can be taken as a guide, empirical evidence is unlikely ever to dominate the other imperatives that influence the thoughts and actions of policy-makers in Australia.

Conclusion

Evidence-based health care has become embedded in the Australian health system. Its adoption is likely to be incremental, with information technology enhancing access to evidence derived from a rapidly expanding research base. Australian governments and health services have recognised that the rise of evidence-based health care is important and inevitable, and have made significant policy commitments and investments in infrastructure to support it. The implementation of evidence-based health care is the challenge for the present and the future, relying on the active transfer of research-based knowledge into policy and practice. Scientific evidence will contribute to the health of individuals and populations, but science will never be the sole determinant of health care. The effectiveness of health care depends not only on science but also on the experience, expectations, values, and resources of providers and communities.

19

Health in an Ageing Society: Cost Rhetoric Versus Service Reform

John McCallum

Australia and New Zealand are ageing in similar fashion. Currently the number of very old people aged 85+ is increasing more rapidly than any other population group and, in about 2010, large cohorts of health-conscious baby boomers will enter older age groups. Although the costs of pensions have been debated for some time, more recently the health costs of ageing have moved to the forefront of public debate. This chapter analyses this issue and assesses the nature of the challenge to the health system posed by an ageing society. It argues that a constructive debate over health and ageing should focus not on the health costs of population ageing, but rather on restructuring the health system to deal appropriately with the health and related needs of older people.

In 1998, Australian media were awash with stories of John Quinn, aged 79 (see Box 19.1, p. 326). His story deserves detailed discussion as it provides an actual example of the dilemmas of health care in an ageing society.

The Quinn case raises a number of issues about the health costs of ageing, and in particular about rationing, the ethics of decisions based on medical evidence, the relevance of quality of survival rather than just the fact of survival, and individual consumer rights in health care. Underlying the story is an explicit and an implicit concern about financing the growing health costs in ageing populations.

Many of the complex issues in the debate are yet to be resolved and go beyond the bounds of what can be incorporated in a short chapter. It is possible in this chapter to review the state of the public debate over the health care costs of ageing, and to outline emerging issues and some

---

Box 19.1   The John Quinn Case

John Quinn, aged 79, suffered a dissecting aneurysm, which caused a leaking aortic valve. This was extremely painful—'like a knife stabbed into the heart'. His family claimed that he was denied open-heart surgery by two major public hospitals but was operated on later at a private hospital. He was a war veteran and eligible for public or private treatment funded by the Department of Veterans' Affairs. Mr Quinn's son, Roger, says he is prepared to sign an affidavit that the family was told that open-heart surgery was not available because of his age. Dr Duncan Thompson of Royal Prince Alfred Hospital, Sydney, who made the decision to turn down surgery for Mr Quinn, said: 'The budget was not a consideration when I made the decision. I was trying to determine what would give him the best chance of survival. I estimated that his risk of not surviving surgery was 90 per cent.' Dr Peter Brady, head of cardiology at Royal North Shore Hospital, Sydney, a public hospital that refused treatment on the grounds of a lack of intensive-care beds, later operated on John Quinn at Sydney Adventist Hospital, a private hospital. Dr Brady says that he would operate on 80-year-olds if he believed that the result would be good. 'He would have died without the surgery', he said. Dr Bruce Barraclough, head of the [Royal] Australasian College of Physicians, said: 'It becomes a political decision as to how much of the public purse can be spent. Politicians will run a mile rather than speak of rationing. But it is not up to the doctor to be the advocate of the patient and the rationer of resources.' Professor Myles Little, head of the Centre for Value, Ethics and Law in Medicine at University of Sydney, said: 'the question of resource constraints will get worse and worse'. After surgery John Quinn spent the weekend with his wife Betty, children Roger, Tim and Jill, and two grandchildren. He walked a kilometre around the coastline near his home on Sydney's lower North Shore.

Source: Marion Downey, 'Life and Death: How Surgeons Make Decisions' and 'The Man who Went Shopping to Save His Life', *Sydney Morning Herald*, 5 November 1998.

---

practical options for health sector reform. The important area of costs will be examined at three levels: the national aggregates; by disease and health service sector; and, by way of illustration, for a specific disease over time.

Health Care Costs in an Ageing Society

The debate over health costs of ageing

The Australian debate about costs of health care in an ageing society rose to a crescendo in the 1990s. In 1994 the Australian Economic Planning and Advisory Council (EPAC) published population projections to 2051 and expressed particular concern about the implications for health costs of an ageing society. It projected an increase in aggregate health costs from $29 billion in 1990 to $126 billion in 2051, a rise from 8.4 per cent to 11.1 per cent of GDP. Whereas one-third of total health expenditure in Australia currently finances care for people aged 65 and older, by 2051 their share of expenditure would increase to more than 50 per cent (EPAC 1994).

The National Commission of Audit (1996) made a similar assessment of the high health costs of ageing. The headlines from this report, delivered in the first year of a new conservative national government, indicated that future health costs would be unsustainable unless health financing was restructured. In 1998 the Retirement Income Modelling (RIM) Unit in the Australian Treasury (Rothman 1998) projected a doubling of health costs to 2041 from 8.5 per cent in 1998 to 17 per cent of GDP (assuming a 2 per cent increase in annual growth costs above inflation). Reflecting these local and international debates, the OECD country report (1998a) on Australia highlighted health care costs and ageing. The OECD costings were higher than in the RIM work and assumed there would be less call on services because of expected delays in severe handicap for older people in the future.

These pessimistic predictions contrast markedly with Barer and colleagues' (1990) analysis of actual costs of hospitals, specialists in public hospitals, and GPs in Australia between 1976 and 1986. The costs of services per person, adjusted for increases in Medical Benefits Schedule fees, increased by 4 per cent per year, but only a tiny proportion of the increase was attributable to an ageing population. Another Australian study covering the period 1984/85 to 1989/90 (Deeble 1991) reached a similar conclusion. Further, Getzen's (1991) study of twenty countries, using WHO data, found cost increases were attributable not to ageing but to rising per capita income, technological changes, and other variables that affected the behaviour of people of all ages. More recently, Duckett and Jackson (1999), and Richardson (1999) demonstrated through analysis of hospital cost data (Duckett and Jackson) that older people cost no more to treat, and that conventional methodologies used to estimate future health care costs due to an ageing population are flawed (Richardson).

How is it possible that official predictions about the impact of ageing on health costs can so blatantly contradict the published historical evidence? The answer lies in the pessimists' use of methodologies which assume that rising health costs are caused by ageing simply because ageing and increased costs occur at the same time. In fact health costs have been increasing for people of all ages for many of the same reasons—there is no evidence that the elderly alone are the cause. Finally, it should be noted that Australia is already undergoing a rapid increase in its very-old population, a consequence of a baby boom around the First World War, so if ageing were a big factor we should be seeing it now. As well, countries such as Sweden already have the proportions of aged persons that Australia and New Zealand will experience in 2020 to 2030, and they have not fallen out of the league of developed nations because of high proportions of older people. The negative (even accusatory) tone of the debate, scapegoating the elderly, is unfortunate and unwarranted.

The crucial issue has been whether to project costs using historical costs from 'years from birth', or to project costs on a 'years to death' basis because the last years of life are most costly. For example, in the Dubbo longitudinal study (McCallum and Geiselhart 1996), we found that people 60 years of age and older who died during the first five years of the study used eight times more health services in cost terms than those who survived. The 'years to death' projection method is preferred because it is consistent with the historical and epidemiological evidence on costs that, since people live longer, the most expensive period of their health care is shifted to later in life. The 'years from birth' method, used in some projections, overestimates health expenditure per person by 4 to 8 per cent to the year 2030 in Australia (Eckerman 1992).

In an investigation of health care costs and ageing, the OECD (1996) modelled health costs associated with ageing in twenty countries. They applied the 'years from birth' scenario, which assumed that as people grew older they consumed more health care. Current health care expenditure per person was multiplied by the total number of older people. Under this model, health costs in Australia grew from 5.8 per cent of GDP in 1995 to 7.6 per cent in 2030, assuming cost increases at the same rate as GDP. In applying the 'years to death' scenario, the OECD multiplied current expenditure per person by the number of deaths in the elderly population; health costs were again assumed to grow at the same rate as GDP. This model took account of the high costs of health care in the period immediately before death. In this scenario, costs rose to 6.2 per cent of GDP in 2030, as opposed to 7.6 per cent under the previous method. The difference in projected costs by alternative methods is more than an academic spat. A smaller projected cost removes the appearance of fiscal crisis and puts the government under less pressure to cut services to the elderly.

Although the health costs of ageing are unlikely to be as high as official projections would indicate, it is undoubtedly true that most health costs in an individual's lifetime are accrued later in life. About a third of all costs are attributable to the tenth of the population aged over 65. Other factors that may lead to an increase in future costs include the possibility that healthy people with higher expectations may use more services, or that health professionals provide unnecessary services to enhance their incomes. Inappropriate use of services may be a greater concern for policy-makers and funders than the reasonable expectation of moderate cost increases in the last years of life. I argue that we need a better-informed debate about health service reform rather than concentrating on an alleged crisis in health costs of the aged.

This review of the costs-of-ageing debate has identified several issues:

- an unnecessarily negative tone about older people as a burden on society;
- a lack of consensus over appropriate methods of projection;
- potential cuts in health and related services to older people on the basis of flawed or at least disputed evidence; and
- distraction from the more fundamental issue of reforming the health system to respond more appropriately to the needs of older people.

The highest priority is to reform the health system so that it responds more appropriately to older people's needs. Once this is achieved, many cost issues will take care of themselves. In order to target health system reforms, however, specific cost information is required, including age-specific and disease-specific cost data.

Costs of diseases for older people

Although Australians 65 years and older constitute 11.8 per cent of the population (10.3 per cent of men and 13.3 per cent of women), in terms of health care expenditure they account for about three times their proportionate representation in the population. Thus Australian men aged 65 years and older account for 33.6 per cent of health costs, while older women in Australia account for 35.5 per cent of costs (Mathers et al. 1998). However, when disaggregated by type of disease, the pattern of health care costs attributable to older people is quite variable: they account for far less than their expected share of costs for some of the most costly diseases and higher than expected costs in others (Table 19.1, p. 330).

The detailed analysis shows costs associated with digestive and respiratory disease treatment in older people are lower than the overall proportion of total health costs attributable to older people. By contrast, the costs of health care for circulatory disease in older people are almost double the rates for all diseases combined (60 per cent for men and 71 per cent for women). To complicate the picture, the costs associated with treating

Table 19.1   Total health system costs, persons 65+ by sex, for diseases by health sector and ICD-9 Chapter 1993–94 ($million)

ICD9 Chapter	All hospital	Nursing homes	Medical services	Pharma-ceuticals	Dental & allied	Total costs	65+ % of all ages
All Diseases							
Men 65+	2351.6	646.1	598.8	486.4	178.8	4595.2	33.6
Women 65+	2532.4	1620.7	757.4	766.1	274.1	6340.8	35.5
Digestive							
Men	165.0	13.6	38.3	41.0	80.3	357.8	22.6
Women	175.4	17.7	40.2	53.8	119.7	430.3	20.2
Circulatory							
Men	553.8	189.1	123.8	158.4	12.0	1102.0	60.0
Women	481.7	318.0	147.5	155.9	13.1	1292.4	70.5
Musculoskeletal							
Men	170.6	78.7	59.9	6.0	28.8	394.3	31.3
Women	273.3	316.8	93.3	73.5	50.2	850.7	50.0
Mental							
Men	102.6	149.7	23.2	23.0	1.4	318.2	28.3
Women	147.5	453.3	47.2	50.5	2.7	743.4	49.3
Injury							
Men	185.5	33.2	18.4	6.9	9.7	268.8	18.8
Women	297.6	59.0	37.0	12.5	13.8	445.0	37.8
Respiratory							
Men	162.9	31.1	50.5	61.9	2.5	326.4	26.3
Women	134.6	58.8	50.0	65.8	4.3	331.4	26.1
Neoplasms							
Men	368.8	11.2	47.4	15.2	4.6	487.9	54.5
Women	265.0	18.1	34.1	17.9	3.4	376.9	37.3

Source: Mathers et al. 1998

musculoskeletal and mental diseases in older people are higher only for women (at about 50 per cent), whereas cancer treatment costs are higher only for men (at 55 per cent). Injury costs are lower for men but about on a par for all diseases for women.

Patterns of costs can be examined at different levels: costs attributable to a particular disease or condition, and to each health care 'sector'. The distribution of these costs across different health sectors varies considerably by type of disease. The potential for substitution of lower-cost services (e.g. community for hospital services) is evident in these patterns, and Australian Coordinated Care Trials are experimenting with this potential. As well, policy-makers need to analyse high-cost diseases and the high-cost contributions to them in order to target their interventions. The next section looks at the most expensive disease category in older people in Australia, circulatory disease, as a specific case where costs may be contained.

The case of circulatory disease

The decline in rates of coronary heart disease (CHD) illustrates the potential impact on health care (and health care costs) that can result from changes in the epidemiology of disease. If current downward trends continue, circulatory disease might be expected to become a low-prevalence condition by 2020. Australia would then find that funding for CHD, if unchanged, might be so excessive as to require massive reallocation of the medical and community workforce and reorientation of the health system. Will this type of decline in disease prevalence serve as a countervailing force, reducing the costs of ageing?

In Australia the prevalence of CHD increases with age from 9.4 per cent for ages 45 to 54 to 18.1 per cent for ages 75 and older. Reductions in CHD between 1950 to 1994 have been less pronounced among older groups than younger groups—65 per cent for people 45 to 54 but 40 per cent in the age group 75 years and older. Despite declining aggregate trends, approximately 80 per cent of coronary artery disease deaths now occur among older people, and it is estimated that the number of people requiring treatment for hypertension could double between 1996 and 2026 (Kelly 1997). Achieving continuing reductions in CHD at older ages will require greater expenditure on pharmaceuticals such as anti-hypertensives and cholesterol-lowering drugs, and on public programs to help people become more active and fit. The added costs of these measures may outweigh the marginal reductions in health costs. The emerging problem in an ageing society, in the prevention of cardiovascular disease as elsewhere, is that of competing risks and substitution.

Emerging Issues in an Ageing Society

Substitute morbidity and co-morbidity

It is argued elsewhere that we have reached a new phase in the history of population health—the age of substitute mortality and morbidity (McCallum 1997). Substitute morbidity is disease that results from the decrease in other diseases. For example, among people older than 85 we expect about 25 per cent to have dementia (Jorm et al. 1987), so preventing a CHD death at that age will leave a substantial risk of dementia and high costs of care. Substitution is evident in the declining death rate from CHD and the increase in cancer death rate in Australia and New Zealand. Co-morbidity is already the norm among patients seen in acute-care hospitals, though co-morbidity rates are much higher among older patients. For example, only 37 per cent of people admitted to Canberra hospitals in

1996 had a single condition, but the figure dropped to 19 per cent for people aged 70 and older. In total, about two-thirds of people had more than one diagnosis in the year they entered hospital (Figure 19.1).

The emerging challenge is calculating the health outcome and cost gains from treatment or prevention of diseases among older people, taking account of competing risks. This generally means lower benefit per unit cost of treatment than is currently claimed on a single disease assumption. The concepts of substitute morbidity and co-morbidity are beyond the current thinking in health policy and clinical decision-making around the world and, consequently, they are not reflected in planning and resource allocation. Substantial changes in health and costing models will be needed to deal with the new morbidity picture in an ageing population.

Quality of survival

Quality of life for older people, measured by ability to function well, is a more important health care focus than length of life (McCallum 1991). Using Australian Disability Survey evidence, it is possible to calculate the expected years that a person aged 65 is likely to spend in different disability

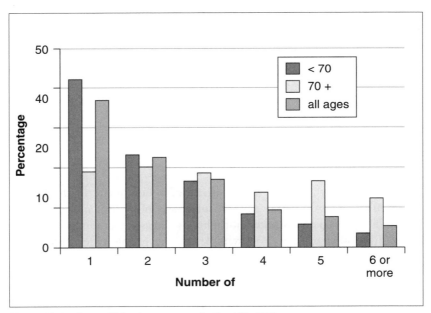

Figure 19.1 Co-morbidity by age group in the ACT, 1996

Source: Shadbolt et al. 1998 and unpublished data from the Continuum of Care and Health Outcomes Project

states (Table 19.2). Handicap is defined in Australian Bureau of Statistics (ABS) surveys as more severe than disability since handicap has associated social, economic and cultural costs accompanying loss of function, whereas disability is defined as loss of function alone.

Both men and women will spend more than half of their years remaining after age 65 free of handicap. On the negative side, of the sixteen years men have remaining at age 65 they will live almost two (or an eighth of their total livespan) with profound handicap; women will live almost four years, or a fifth of their remaining 19.5 years, with profound handicap.

The ABS disability surveys indicate that overall rates of severe handicap increased between 1981 and 1988, but returned to 1981 levels in 1993 (Table 19.3). Women's rates were almost double those for men.

Table 19.2 Health expectancies (HE) and proportions of life expectancy (LE) for men and women at age 65 in 1993

Expectations at age 65 with:	HE in years		HE/LE %	
	men	women	men	women
profound handicap	1.72	3.72	12.7	19.1
severe handicap	0.64	0.94	4.1	4.8
moderate handicap	1.62	1.64	10.3	8.4
mild handicap	3.34	2.90	21.2	14.9
disability only	1.90	1.19	12.1	6.1
disability free	6.51	9.09	41.4	46.7
Life expectancy at age 65	15.73	19.48	100	100

Source: Wen et al. (1995) and various ABS Disability Surveys

Table 19.3 Trends in rates of severe handicap (%) for persons aged 65+

Year	Severe handicap		
	Men	Women	Persons
1981	12.3	20.4	17.0
1988	13.1	22.6	18.6
1993	12.4	20.3	16.9

Source: Wen et al. (1995) and various ABS Disability Surveys

Analysis by Wen and colleagues (1995) shows that only a small proportion of the change observed is due to increased age-specific rates of severe handicap, that is, older people being 'sicker'. Most of the increase is simply due to increases in the absolute numbers of older people. Recent work conducted in the USA (Crimmins et al. 1997) is even more positive. Disability-free life expectancy in the USA increased from 1980 to 1990 for people aged 65 and older, while in the previous decade (1970–80) it decreased. To explain the turnaround, the authors point to improvements in education, the labour market and socio-economic circumstances, as well as health advances. These factors could well operate in Australia and New Zealand in the future to produce improvements in handicap-free life expectancy since any delay or decrease in overall handicap will reduce costs. This raises the practical question: what reforms in progress have most potential to reduce the costs of ageing?

Experiments and Innovations in Health Care for Older People

Healthy ageing strategies

The main response to the very dismal tone of the debate on the impact of ageing on health costs has been the development of a National Healthy Ageing Strategy, accepted by the Australian Health and Community Services Ministerial Council (AHMAC 1997). State governments have also developed cross-departmental Healthy Ageing Policies (NSW Ageing and Disability Department and NSW Health 1998). New Zealand has had a Prime Ministerial Task Force on Positive Ageing (1997) and has recommended a similar but broader public health approach to promote the well-being of older people (Public Health Group 1997). These policies have a broad focus on improving the health and well-being of older people but need to be developed in more specific directions. A number of strategies are aimed at preventing illness and disability and promoting well-being and participation.

Moreover, the evidence on the effectiveness of such interventions is, by the standards of evidence-based practice, rather limited. The most successful disease prevention programs, such as those aimed at CHD, are by no means simple in their impacts on potential health costs. Nor does the 'healthy ageing approach' deal explicitly with issues of substitute morbidity and co-morbidity. While excessive optimism is unwarranted, healthy ageing policy development is nevertheless a 'breath of fresh air' in the debate over improving health and controlling health care costs in an ageing society.

Coordinated Care Trials

Ineffective use of health services has also been addressed in both Australia and New Zealand through a series of Coordinated Care Trials (see Chapter 20). The Australian model involves pooling funds previously allocated to different service types, and providing a flexible set of services with the aim of achieving more cost-effective outcomes. Each older patient has a case manager. 'Care 21', based in South Australia, is one such Coordinated Care Trial (Care 21 1998). It involves consumers 65 and older, GPs, and a care planner, who together identify the client's needs and develop a care plan. Care 21 develops and uses clinical and community-care protocols based on best practice. Service coordination in both general practice and community agencies has been trialled, and mechanisms facilitating remote access follow. The jury is still out on the model's cost-effectiveness. The key issue to be evaluated is the degree to which substitution of lower-cost but more effective responses can be achieved through care coordination. Potential concerns are emerging about the extra costs of care planners and the increased costs associated with services previously not provided but recommended by care planners.

Development of sub-acute care

The Victorian state government has developed a new 'sub-acute' level in the service system, which has been funded by savings from the adoption of casemix in the acute-care hospitals. The system is aimed at providing more appropriate, sub-acute care for older people. Funding is based on treatment modality rather than diagnosis. Services are responsive to the Activity of Daily Living needs (ADLs) of older people, rather than around area, or historical, hospital funding. The system uses four categories identified by ADLs on admission: rehabilitation, geriatric evaluation and management, palliative care, and non-acute care. Payments are not determined by the standard casemix system but by one of a range of classification systems that have been developed for non-acute care, and that accommodate better the new realities of health for older people (see Johnson et al. 1997).

Advanced-care directives

The high cost of an individual's last year of life can also be approached from another angle: by allowing people to express their preferences for health care in advance, thus reducing care that is futile and unwanted. A range of experiments have been conducted with advanced-care directives (ACDs), which provide information about an individual's health and personal-care preferences in the event that they are unable to participate in decisions at a later date. ACDs contain instructions that restrict medical interventions but do not provide the opportunity for people to request medically assisted suicide. Most Australian states have legislation that allows advanced-care directives.

A series of studies shows that substituting hospice care for hospital care of the terminally ill saves between 31 and 64 per cent of health costs in the last month of life. Savings are even greater when care is provided in the community rather than in a hospital-based palliative-care facility. However, the longer the person receives palliative care, the less the savings (Emanuel and Emanuel 1994). ACDs and the palliative-care option demonstrate that even the health care costs associated with the highest-cost period of life can be addressed on a voluntary, 'win–win' basis.

Same-day surgery and day-of-surgery admission

Faster throughput of older people in hospitals is now the norm. At the shortest extreme, Australian day-only surgery rates increased 63 per cent in the late 1990s. Around 40 per cent of Australian, 70 per cent of US and 60 per cent of UK hospital procedures were done on the same day in the late 1990s, and the proportion was predicted to rise to around 80 per cent by the year 2000. Same-day surgery and day-of-surgery admission potentially generate cost savings by consolidating the treatment period into a shorter (though cost–intensive) hospital stay. However, the Australian experience is that 'freed' hospital bed-days are then assigned to another patient who otherwise might not have received treatment as quickly. This 'backfilling' adds to the total number of services provided (and the total cost), rather than substituting shorter (and cheaper) care for longer-stay hospital treatment.

Generally speaking, in Australia, the promise of more efficient, faster health care has not been reflected in lower expenditure. Moreover support available to older people in the community-care sector has not been expanded with the savings achieved from shorter hospital stays—the money has been retained in the hospital system. Although we may see gains in the future, it is possible that the increased supply of health services resulting from an increase in overall efficiency may again be blamed on older people. As doctors increase the total supply of services provided, older people may be blamed for absorbing those services, and hence for rising health costs. Ironically, in the process older people may in fact be the victims—recipients of inappropriate medical interventions that they do not want.

Conclusion

In this chapter I have argued that the issue of 'ageing and health' in Australia and New Zealand has been dominated by an alarmist and overstated debate about costs, and that the focus of the debate has distracted from the key issue of health sector reform. The case of John Quinn illustrates vividly the complexity of the issues. These arise from the very beginning, with the seemingly objective calculation of costs of health care for an ageing society, where the choice of methods and *a priori* assumptions determine the conclusions. In the process more urgent issues are neglected, notably the realities of substitute morbidity and co-morbidity and the need to focus on quality of life, not just survival.

The extreme positions taken in debate over the health costs of ageing have created an aura of pessimism about health and ageing that is clearly unwarranted. Survival of the majority of Australians and New Zealanders to older ages is an historic success. A range of promising experiments and innovations in progress needs further support, and the findings converted into changes in the provision and resourcing of health care for older people. The issues are clear and the reform options are available, though politically difficult. Health policy-makers would do well to shift from a narrow and negative concentration on costs to more serious consideration of the political strategies needed to deal with the reform of the health sector. Moreover, the debate must occur in the public arena if media reporting like the John Quinn case is not to become a regular and upsetting event.

20

A Model of Aged-Care Reform

Nigel Millar

The provision of health care is complicated, and its complexity and intricacies are often underestimated. Even the simplest procedure, such as an X-ray, can involve a prodigious number of health professionals and actions (Moss et al. 1998). The 'standard' discrete event in patient care will involve many such procedures. In the case of frail older people in hospitals, chronic problems and pathologies can multiply this complexity. In addition, hospital and health care for older people most often takes place in an emotionally charged environment with ethical overtones. As older and frail people increase both in number and as a proportion of the population, the use of health services by this group will rise as a proportion of all health services. The multiple health problems (co-morbidities) of the older population mean that modern health care as a whole will become more complex over the next two decades.

It is understandable, then, that health services and hospitals are struggling to come to terms with the problem of providing appropriate care to an ageing community. No wonder the purchaser–provider framework, with its seemingly facile descriptors of discrete and definable interventions, appears incompatible with the complex reality faced by health professionals.

The Elder Care Canterbury Project is a local initiative designed to resolve the evolving dilemmas of care generated by an ageing population. In essence, the project aims to demonstrate a means of focusing care on patient needs, resulting in more effective, appropriate, and efficient health services for older people in and around Christchurch, New Zealand.

The Care Environment

Christchurch is the major metropolitan area of the South Island of New Zealand. Its population is around 300 000, 50 000 of whom are over the age of 65. New Zealand's purchaser–provider restructure in the early 1990s (see Chapter 7) provided the impetus to clarify and define health care activities and costs. It also established a contractual basis for health care provision by the hospital and health services, originally known as CHEs. Two achievements of the first few years of reform were to clarify the services actually provided and to obtain better information on costs (see Chapter 10). But a substantial change in the pattern and effectiveness of service delivery had not emerged by the late 1990s (Ham 1998).

Health Services for the Frail Elderly

Effective provision of health care for older people is a major challenge for the New Zealand health system. Most structures and systems in acute-care hospitals in New Zealand, and elsewhere in the developed world, operate with the unstated assumption that each intervention is discrete and measurable, and can therefore be costed and contractually defined; an exception is some services focused specifically on areas of chronic disease and disability. Acute-care hospitals may consequently provide a technically excellent health intervention to a frail elderly person but find that it is ineffective due to previously unrecognised pathology, disability, psychological problems, or social difficulties.

Patients whose co-morbidities and complex needs do not respond quickly and completely to hospital treatment are stigmatised as 'bed-blockers', a term coined to describe patients who (wilfully, or so it is implied) overstay in hospital. The patient is thus seen as 'the problem', rather than as a person with multiple problems requiring thoughtful solutions. Nowhere is this more applicable than among older people.

Yet it has since been demonstrated that a proactive, specialised geriatric service can improve outcomes and shorten lengths of stay. This specialised approach also has a downside. It implies that older frail people cannot be suitably treated in mainstream services, thus providing the rationale to remove expertise in older people's health from those areas. It follows logically that unless new services for older people are comprehensive, and thereby duplicate all the mainstream functions, some frail older people will be stranded in regions where they are denied access to adequate health expertise and systems. Clearly, this alternative is wasteful as well as ineffectual. A practical alternative to health care for older people is needed.

The Origins of the Elder Care Canterbury Project

A number of parallel forces led to the creation of the Elder Care Canterbury Project in New Zealand. The initial impetus originated within the primary-care sector, where the grouping of many of the general practices into an independent practice association provided a forum for innovation (Malcolm 1997a). The IPA concluded that the needs of older people were not being addressed adequately. The local IPA then initiated discussions with specialist geriatricians and psychogeriatricians.

Simultaneously, the funding/purchasing agency, initially the Southern Regional Health Authority and now the Health Funding Agency (HFA), was looking for a means to address the health needs of older people and improve access to care in the area. The agency was struck by recurring 'winter bed crises': acute and rehabilitation services became overloaded each winter, creating a log-jam effect that resulted in cancellation of elective surgery and affected many other hospital services. The catalyst for Elder Care Canterbury was the regional health authority's request for proposal (RFP) in 1997 for the provision of health services for people over 75 years of age.

The prospect of reforming health services for older people stimulated much interest within a competitive climate, challenged the status quo, and triggered a redefinition of longstanding relationships. In this changing environment, the IPA was able to move from a disempowered 'referrer' and 'recipient' of services to play a significant role in service design and delivery. The Elder Care Canterbury project really began when the main parties, the two HHSs and the IPA (representing the majority of local GPs), sat at the same table with equal status and agreed to plan a response to the RFP. In the event, the response was not a formal business proposal but the Elder Care Canterbury project, designed 'to integrate and improve health services for older people in Canterbury'.

The Elder Care Canterbury Project

The Elder Care Canterbury project is not a defined corporate body and it has no formal business structure. It rests upon a written understanding by three main parties: Canterbury Health (the provider of acute health services), Healthlink South (the provider of the geriatric assessment treatment and rehabilitation service), and the Pegasus Medical Group (the provider of primary care). Canterbury Health and Healthlink South are the two local HHSs, whereas the Pegasus Medical Group is the local IPA, which includes most Christchurch GPs but also represents the remaining GPs in Christchurch and the surrounding rural area.

The agreed mission statement is to work cooperatively to develop a comprehensive health service for older people in Canterbury; to work with the community in an inclusive and collaborative way to develop the best possible service; and to focus the skills, knowledge, enthusiasm, and commitment of existing local providers and the wider community to design a service that meets the specific needs of the older people of Canterbury.

Early work on the project identified the major challenges facing health services for older people. These served as the drivers for change, confirming for the participants the reasons for their involvement and the benefits of their full commitment. The main drivers were predicted demand on health services, costs of provision, and, not least, quality of patient care.

Based on population predictions, local health services had expected a 20 per cent increase in demand for health services among the over-65 age group in the next fifteen years, but detailed analysis revealed a more startling prediction. Demand was expected to increase much faster in the higher age bands, a reflection of many factors, including the greater number of residents of older age (see Chapter 19). A 35 per cent increase in demand for health services was projected for the over-75s, but this climbed to 60 per cent for those over 80, and to 90 per cent for the very old, aged 85+.

A further factor considered by the group was the fact that morbidity rises exponentially in the older age ranges. Although this is mitigated to some degree by a lower uptake of service in the very old, lower utilisation rates might not persist as a more assertive older population grows to expect a higher degree of health intervention (Callahan 1996). Thus a massive increase in demand appeared inevitable, particularly in the acute service area, which was already experiencing a 10 per cent increase in acute admissions each year. It was clear that, should these predictions of demand materialise, the costs of health care provision would rise substantially.

The initial analysis of patient care revealed a number of systemic problems: blockages in gaining access to investigations, admission, transfer, and discharge; gaps in service; duplication of investigations; and uncertainty for patients and their carers. For instance, the *ad hoc* criteria governing patient access to investigation had led to anomalies, such as when a GP could not easily get an immediate X-ray, ultrasound examination, or echocardiogram. Yet these same investigations were readily available in the acute sector (hospitals). Thus on occasion an older person would be referred to a hospital emergency service when they required only an X-ray, only to be swept up in the acute-care process for what might have been an avoidable admission.

Delays encountered by older people in getting access to assessment and effective intervention resulted in increasing dependency and more severe illness, which led in turn to longer hospital stays and poorer outcomes. Although older patients undoubtedly received technically excellent speciality care, their care might not have been optimally coordinated and might have lacked other crucial interventions. Because the incentive structure was geared towards contractual obligations, providers understandably tended to focus on patient needs that fell within the boundaries of their service, and to underestimate the interdependence needed to obtain an effective outcome. These interventions might have been included in another provider's contract, but no incentive operated to facilitate coordination across providers. The care landscape was dotted with islands of excellence, with huge gaps in between. The contractual process seemed to reinforce the isolation, and it sometimes appeared that the islands were drifting further apart as the incentives for discrete services favoured an increasingly rigid adherence to contract specifications. This was a style of provision well suited to patients with single health problems requiring discrete and definable intervention. It was obviously unsuited to the wide-ranging and complex needs of the frail elderly.

Similar gaps were identified in the community and specialist aged-care arena. For example, an older person with a disabling upper limb fracture, unable to manage at home, could be admitted to an intensive assessment and rehabilitation ward but could not obtain temporary residential care without considerable personal expense. This was often beyond patients' means.

Duplication of effort and investigation was also clearly identified. Older people could undergo multiple assessments by a range of health professionals, only to have them repeated later when they were transferred to another service, or even when moving within a service. The project uncovered examples of stroke patients who had several physiotherapists during their care, and frail elderly people who had repeated assessments of cognitive status, the results of which were not shared between health professionals or health services. It appeared that patients were sometimes subjected to health services, rather than served by health care that responded to their need.

The combined picture—projected demand, anticipated cost escalation, and issues of quality—left no doubt about the need to restructure health care for older people in Canterbury. Solving only some of the problems would be a major improvement: primary-care providers would be able to access early, effective intervention; acute services would function more effectively and efficiently; and the specialist aged-care services would better achieve their goals of maintaining optimum independence for older people. More importantly, patients and their carers would benefit.

These early analyses cemented the relationships within the provider group and reconfirmed members' commitment to proceed. A key step in the process was the adoption of a patient focus, and problem analysis based on mapping the patient-care process. With this perspective, many of the issues of access and quality were clear.

Inclusion of stakeholders

A stakeholder analysis proved crucial in gaining support, both internally and among external stakeholders. As awareness of the project spread, suspicions and anxieties were aroused in those health services and professionals not directly involved, and within community action groups. The critical success factor in building cooperative alliances was adopting a principle of openness and inclusion.

The stakeholder analysis illuminated key groups with an important stake in health care for older persons:

- community-based organisations such as Grey Power and Age Concern;
- health care professionals and managers within the participating services;
- disability support providers in the community, such as home-care services, residential-care providers, and community rehabilitation services;
- non-aligned providers of clinical services, such as community pharmacies, radiology services, and laboratories; and
- Crown agencies such as the funder/purchaser Ministry of Health (the policy agency), and politicians.

Each of these diverse groups had a legitimate interest in health reform for older people. A defined structure was established to communicate with each group, to set the consultative process in motion, and to solicit their support and contribution.

On the many occasions when one group or another would raise concerns about the project, the most effective response was full sharing of information and an offer of inclusion. Groups and individuals who were expecting a well-developed, covert plan to restructure services (and potentially disadvantage them) were disarmed by inclusion and the expectation that they contribute to the development of service plans.

It was quite clear by the end of the project's first phase that success would require involvement of all stakeholders. The initial three participants—the two major hospital providers and the primary-care group—could not possibly have implemented significant change on their own; the expertise and support of all other stakeholders has been essential to the reform process.

Specific interventions

The second phase of the Elder Care Canterbury Project entailed the development of specific intervention projects. Building on the first phase, a range of project proposals was selected through a consultative process. These fell broadly into two areas: specific projects for a particular clinical scenario, and generic projects covering issues that cut across all clinical areas.

Clinically specific projects

The first projects were fractured neck of femur, stroke, and acute confusion (delirium). Each was seen as an area in which service improvement could be achieved; all were characterised by stakeholder commitment to quality and effective outcomes.

Two cooperative interventions in the care of older people with hip fracture had previously demonstrated significant benefits in length of stay and outcome (Sainsbury et al. 1986; Elliot et al. 1996). But there was no doubt among participants that further improvements were feasible. The project was renamed 'Broken Hip' on the advice of the community stakeholder group, who have continually reminded participants in all Elder Care Canterbury projects that specialist language and jargon should be avoided wherever possible.

Stroke was selected as a definable area with a wealth of international data. Stroke also involves significant input from a range of providers, including acute hospital services, specialist aged care, primary care, the voluntary sector, community support agencies, and providers of residential care.

Acute confusion, a common problem and distressing event for staff and carers, was in need of an organised and concerted approach. This project had perhaps the greatest potential to deliver benefits in clinical quality and cost, but because of the widespread and unpredictable occurrence of acute confusion, it posed the greatest challenge to the project.

Generic projects

The main generic projects in Elder Care Canterbury are contracts and funding, information, and 'positive ageing'.

The Contracts and Funding Project is a cooperative arrangement involving a range of providers. It aims to advise each of the clinical projects on the complex funding arrangements for older people's services. The project discerned that no one provider (person or agency) has a complete understanding of the processes by which services for older people are funded. Community support services can be provided by more than one source and can be funded from multiple sources. Criteria for obtaining community services are confusing: older people in the community may require several assessments of need because each service uses different diagnostic procedures. For example, an accident-related need requires assessment and funding from the Accident Compensation Corporation, personal health needs are the concern of the HFA, and age-related disability needs must be assessed and coordinated by the specialist aged-care service. Assessment procedures are documented for each agency; they are characterised by overlap, ambiguity, and artificial distinctions. Predictably, they cause confusion and disagreement among assessment services and providers. Patients and carers are left wondering why so many people and services must be involved in the simple process of needs assessment.

The project has obtained general consensus on diagnosing a patient's current status. The next step involved simplification of the assessment process, with attendant cost-savings and improved quality of service for older people requiring community support.

Access to clinical information is fundamental to improving health care for older people whose care cuts across traditional disciplinary and service boundaries. Each clinical project needs support to ensure that patients experience a smooth transition between services, and that accurate and timely information is always available at the point of patient care. The Information Project team, which includes health IT professionals from the three major sectors, ensures that the change process is reflected in the essential support infrastructure.

The Positive Ageing Project was the initiative of the community stakeholder group, who identified the importance of including a preventive and wellness focus in the Elder Care Canterbury project. This team supports the clinical projects. For example, it developed a hip fracture prevention initiative for the Broken Hip team. However, the Positive Ageing team also develops initiatives in its own right, such as a network connecting the many other services and agencies involved in preventive health care for older people, and it has identified many promising opportunities to improve service coordination and outcomes.

Methodology—an Emphasis on Process

The focus of the Elder Care approach is the redesign—or re-engineering—of care of older people, with a focus on the patient. Although service and support structures are important, the process adopted in Elder Care is central to its success. Each project involves the redesign of some aspect of health care for older people and follows established re-engineering methodology.

Team members are recruited first for their personal abilities, and second because of their professional relationships. Each team is balanced as far as possible to include the relevant health professions and organisations. Team sizes vary, but average between twelve and sixteen members. Clear briefings are given to the team to ensure that the care process focuses on the patient's needs. Team members are not expected to represent their organisation or profession but to contribute their expertise to further the patient's interests.

The start-up phase of the Elder Care Canterbury project has proved crucial to its smooth operation. The temptation to move too fast was wisely resisted. In the early stage of each project, substantial time is invested in establishing relationships and building trust. Practical matters, including funding and contracts, are initially set aside as the team describes as accurately as possible the current situation from the patient's perspective. The description is validated by ex-patients and relatives, and then discussed in detail with each of the stakeholder groups. Armed with a clear understanding of the issues, the team then considers ideas for redesign. Members are encouraged to be as radical as necessary and to challenge existing assumptions. Specific clinical projects use a 'patient care map'. Their aim is to develop a new and refined process aimed at the identified problems. Validation by the stakeholder groups occurs again, and a pilot design is implemented and measured with the assistance of the Information and Contracts and Funding teams. Major changes are finalised and approved by the senior executives of each of the contributing partners.

Progress to Date

Progress is never as fast as one would like in this type of ambitious undertaking. Experience has shown that the limiting factor is the time and effort required to gain the confidence and commitment of all who must be included in the reform process. Changing the current mindset has proved to be the greatest challenge. Health professionals who are still struggling with the consequences of health sector reform may resist change, and can be very effective in their resistance. Managers understandably feel threatened by change, and find ongoing re-engineering difficult to reconcile with their here-and-now accountability for financial outcomes. Culturally, people with years of experience working in health services are accustomed to being disempowered, rather than included in the decision-making process. They may therefore be cynical about the likelihood of meaningful progress through a participatory process.

Significant gains have been achieved despite these limitations. The first quantifiable success was exceeding a 70 per cent coverage rate for influenza vaccination in people over 65 years of age, which was accomplished by employing all the cooperative alliances built up in the early phase of the project. Qualitative indicators of progress and changing culture include the frequent acknowledgment of patient needs in many forums, within and outside the project.

Elder Care Canterbury is a compelling example of the delicate interplay of political, organisational and cultural forces inherent in reform of health services, which may threaten the established order. Project 'champions' must ensure that new ideas are not stifled and that challenges to accepted norms are not rejected out of hand.

The key success factors to date have been, first, the creation of an environment in which the accepted locus of control was no longer certain, yet participating stakeholders still felt sufficiently confident and committed. The second crucial success factor has been encouraging the health professions to lead change internally, through initiatives they generate, rather than waiting to have change forced upon them. Finally, the project has succeeded because of its inclusive approach in which criticism is actively sought and constructively answered, and potential conflict is exposed and diffused early, leaving energies to be channelled into improving health care for older people in Canterbury.

Conclusion

Abby Bloom

This volume has had an ambitious agenda. First, we have sought to familiarise students of comparative health systems and health reform with the
essential concepts, terminology, and points of debate in health reform. We
have also chronicled, analysed, and compared the experience of health
reform in two countries, each well advanced in the process. The third
purpose of the book has been to illuminate the shared and distinctive
features of health systems and the influence of crucial factors on their evolution, including reform, in order to give insight to students of reform and
guidance to decision-makers.

The book has intentionally selected those elements of Australia and
New Zealand's reform processes that are likely to be of most interest. It has
sought to reveal why certain results occurred, and the lessons to be drawn
from that experience. In choosing to highlight more innovative and
instructive aspects of the reform process, we have inevitably omitted other
interesting and potentially useful material. Each author has placed a different lens on the health reform process, and different values and philosophies
about health care have been evident in their approaches to topics.

Reform as a Response to Similar Pressures and Policies

We have seen that health reform in Australia and New Zealand responded
to the same factors experienced by many Western nations during the late
1980s and the 1990s: concerns with recurrent and investment funding,
efficiency, equity, and quality. At the heart of health reform everywhere is
a search for a better answer to essentially the same questions: how is a health

system best funded, how should provision be structured, how can equity be ensured and protected, and how can quality be monitored and maintained?

We have also seen that different participants in the reform process have different priorities and paradigms. Readers will also have noted repeated reference to some of the features of Australia and New Zealand that set them apart and distinguish their health reform models and processes, notably culture and values, history, and politics. In the present era of health reform each nation has found its own answers to the same dilemmas: infusing more capital into the health care system (often by enlisting the private sector), containing and/or shifting costs, and increasing efficiency. Both have attempted to deflect political controversy and focus more attention and effort on patients or consumers and on quality, and both have begun to introduce evidence-based practice. Both have also attempted to maintain 'social solidarity' by preserving universal tax-financed health care as the core of their health systems. As tensions persist, health care crises are frequently declared by different interest groups and fuelled by the media.

One of the major themes emerging from the experience of Australia and New Zealand is the striking similarity of the drivers of reform. Both nations were acutely aware that their health systems might not withstand the relentless cost and demand pressures imposed by technology, rising consumer expectations, and, to a lesser degree than commonly believed, an ageing population. Both nations undertook reform ostensibly as a means of charting a course through the next decades. In some cases, particularly New Zealand, the choices did not withstand a change in government. In Australia, with some exceptions, they did.

Both nations were influenced by convergent ideas and policies, that is, ideas that were in common currency internationally, notably the belief that a stronger market orientation would be an effective antidote to underperformance of the health sector as a whole (van de Ven 1996). In both nations health reform was distinguished by the same phases and policy instruments found elsewhere: an early focus on hospital management and budgeting, followed by a phase in which market-like mechanisms and budgetary incentives were introduced parallel with a focus on microefficiency and a stronger patient or customer focus (Ham 1998: 137). This included a distinction and separation among the different roles within the health system, a new generation of hospital managers, and intensive work on quality and patients' rights.

Both nations adopted the peculiar language of health reform, thereby lending credibility and an air of certainty to measures the efficacy and distributional effects of which were neither proved nor even evaluated locally or internationally. Who could argue against 'decentralisation'—placing authority in the hands of those whose actions determined outcomes? Or 'contestability'—government ensuring that it was, indeed, obtaining 'value for money' in its health care expenditure by 'testing' the market, pitting government-owned health services against the private sector? Or 'transparency', particularly as government attempted the unthinkable, involving the private sector increasingly in roles hitherto restricted to the public sector?

Lessons Learned

The health reform experience of Australia and New Zealand has generated important lessons, even if it has not produced a panacea.

First, the two nations have demonstrated how a universal insurance scheme, adequately funded through general revenue based on taxable income, and distributed according to need, can sustain an admirable level of access to an exceptionally high level of health care. However, events in Australia in the late 1990s are a reminder that social solidarity is never guaranteed, and must be vigorously protected.

Next, the experience in the two countries has shown that it is possible to make substantial progress on many important levels (clinical care, management, public health, distributional equity, and so on) even while the overall progress of reform is halting, fitful or even stalled at a national level.

An extremely important lesson from the antipodean experience of health reform is the fundamental influence of history, politics, and culture on the local interpretation and implementation of health reform.

The experience of the two nations has also shown that it is possible to instil a pervasive awareness of the contractual nature of health care funding and provision, and in particular the importance of the purchasing function. This has been achieved not only where the public integrated model has given way to a public contract model (e.g. New Zealand), but also at the state level in Australia (Victoria) and in some unexpected parts of the government health system, such as veterans' health care.

Linked with this is the lesson that the introduction of competition can generate enough incentives to increase efficiency, quality, and customer focus, even within a mixed market dominated by the public sector.

Both nations are excellent illustrations of how governments can introduce market-like mechanisms without abandoning a strong role for government in protecting and extending equity of access to health care, in regulation, and in providing incentives that foster better quality, cohesiveness of care, and responsiveness to epidemiological need. A related lesson is that it is possible to maintain a mixed public–private system, and to alter the mix, while essentially maintaining equilibrium, or at least a dynamic tension.

When comparing the current situation in the two nations, it appears that no particular advantage, or for that matter disadvantage, was caused by either the 'big bang' approach in New Zealand or the incrementalist approach in Australia. Some observers of the New Zealand scene may differ on this point, and suggest that the 'big bang' needlessly consumed efforts and productivity, and that the same results could have been achieved through gradual or incremental reform.

Both countries demonstrate that government must show strong resolve in the face of controversy and even opposition that inevitably springs from the interest-group dynamics involved in health care. In the end, the process has been intensive and wearing in both countries.

Next, the time-frame for health reform is longer than participants sometimes predict. It is hard to imagine health reform anywhere taking less than ten to fifteen years for the first phases alone. The reasons for this lengthy horizon include the multiple, diverse stakeholders with strong vested interests in the status quo, and the sensible hesitation about making profound changes to a system as complex, important, and politically charged as health care.

A further lesson is the difficulty of reversing many of the measures introduced in order to implement reform. Thus, in Australia, private hospital co-location contracts and the closure of government hospitals in favour of contractual purchase of services from the private sector have long-term implications. Indeed, it may be impossible ever to restore the pre-existing structures. In the former, private hospitals will be a feature on public hospital campuses for twenty years or more; in the latter, new patterns of supply will probably drive some historically dominant suppliers out of the market altogether. The Health Minister of one emerging economy recently confided that he would opt for corporatisation rather than privatisation as the first stage of reform for the logical reason that, if it failed, a partial measure would be more easily reversible than wholesale privatisation. If it worked, he could confidently recommend privatisation as the next step.

Another obvious lesson from the experience of Australia and New Zealand is the diversity of responses possible, even within a single country such as Australia, to the same questions about health reform. Different states have adopted different models and different implementation mechanisms, sequences, and timetables. Thus Victoria moved swiftly to introduce casemix, whereas New South Wales placed higher priority on other matters, notably more equitable distribution of health care funding according to socio-economic and epidemiological need. Different political ideologies and economic circumstances prompt different health reform strategies. Many countries will recognise that state-based reform rather than national reform may be inevitable and even preferable.

Like the USA, New Zealand and Australia have both been hampered by the dilemma of rationing in one form or another. In Australia, waiting lists have become a major electoral issue. In New Zealand, a considered, public process—compiling a list of priority treatment—became too controversial to implement as originally designed. Rationing, by whatever name, in any overt way, is unpalatable because, finally, individuals will be denied care.

Australia and New Zealand have made a further contribution to global health reform by adding new vocabulary and new interpretations. 'Coordinated care' and 'managed competition' are seeping into the Australian lexicon to denote managed care Australian-style.

Australia and New Zealand have a globally recognised reputation for public health and health promotion, and have illustrated, well in advance of other nations, how public health concerns can be incorporated into the reform process.

A final lesson from the experience of the two nations is the desperate need for evaluative research on health reform. The intensive evaluative component of Australia's Coordinated Care Trials is a rare and important exception. While the methodological difficulty of research into the impact of health reform is acknowledged, each country missed a valuable opportunity by failing to evaluate, particularly on larger issues. By failing to do so, they also limited the beneficial impact their experience might have had on other nations considering or undergoing reform.

The continuous redefinition of reform

As Ham (1998) has suggested, models and concepts of health reform itself are evolving continuously. By the time his edited collection of comparative studies of Western European and US health reform was published, Australia and New Zealand were already well advanced in grappling with the issues that he identified as part of 'the new reform agenda'. Australia and New Zealand are already well into, and pushing beyond, Ham's Phase Three of reform—the application of policy instruments such as public health, primary health care, managed care, health technology assessment, and evidence-based medicine (Ham 1998: 136). Davis (1999b: 135) has observed that governments in five major English-speaking nations— Britain, Canada, the USA, Australia and New Zealand—are entering a new stage of reform: 'regrouping—modifying reforms and strategies and reaching out to forge consensus and shape broader coalitions for change'.

In Australia, the outline of this next phase is already visible. As Galbally, and Lin and King, have described, the role of public health, including factors unrelated to health care, is already being addressed, though not formally as part of reform policy. Similarly, evidence-based health care is becoming mainstream, and the debate about rationing has been conducted in public view, at least in New Zealand.

The future: a sustainable, mixed health system affording universal coverage, or yet another phase in health reform?

Will the reforms stick? With health care providers 'change-weary and change-wary', and the public possibly sated with continuous media exposure of yet another alleged hospital privatisation, what lies ahead? Indeed, in late 1999, yet another health care crisis had been declared in Australia, and the state premiers, calling for the Commonwealth's Productivity Commission to undertake a review of the nation's health care system, had locked horns with the Prime Minister over whether or not there was in fact a crisis. In New Zealand a change in government in late 1999 suggested yet another policy direction would be soon evident. In Australia's most aggressively reform-oriented state, Victoria, the electorate, in late 1999, voted against the government that had led the reforms. Clearly the underlying structural tensions and the continuing increase in health care costs will not abate in the near future. What we can already see evolving is a new era, including the advent of new but obvious models that consolidate and extend the concepts that have evolved from the years of reform in the late 1980s and the 1990s.

Our bets are on consolidation and ongoing incremental change over the medium term. Why? Simply because there is no evidence of any real crisis that would seem to justify more radical and probably controversial systemic change. Although the Australian and New Zealand people have revealed some dissatisfaction with their health systems (Davis 1999a), it is doubtful that they are willing to abandon the essence and framework of Medicare at this time.

The scare stories about health care costs 'spiralling out of control' belong to another country, or perhaps another time. Nonetheless, at least in Australia, periodic suggestions of 'crisis' and claims that the system is fundamentally flawed and in urgent need of a fix make good headlines, and are an effective weapon in interest-group politics.

The lead theme for the next phase of reform may already be evident. Thus 'managed competition' (the Australian definition, preferably not what Uwe Reinhardt [1999: 94] calls 'sporadically attempted but badly mangled competition') appears to be emerging at the crest of the next wave of reform in Australia. 'Managed competition' is the locally acceptable term in Australia denoting what Ham (1998: 132) identifies as a combination of 'elements of the three strategies of reform ... the use of market-like mechanisms, policies to strengthen the management of health services and the development of budgetary incentives to improve performance—in an attempt to go beyond the scope of existing reform programs'. We see in 'managed competition' all the hallmarks of the 1980s expression 'primary health care'. It refers to a specific phenomenon in generic terms, and offers a widely accepted shorthand that means something valuable and desirable to everyone. Like primary health care, 'managed competition' can denote a model that lends itself to globalisation. It is also generic enough to require local interpretation: 'it comes in many forms, to meet the diverse needs of the various health care systems in which its operation has been proposed' (Scotton 1998: 214).

While the health systems of Australia and New Zealand were little known until recently, they have emerged among the leading models globally. In spite of entirely legitimate concerns raised by Hsiao and others about fundamental structural weaknesses, the level of access, equity and quality achieved in Australia and New Zealand is no mean feat. Ham (1998: 124) reminds Western European nations that having installed and maintained a system the funding of which is obtained largely through public sources is 'the correct approach'. It is at least an approach that has to date enabled the people of Australia and New Zealand, with the major exception of indigenous people, to enjoy a comparatively good level of health and health care.

Have the two countries found the 'holy grail'? Obviously not (Hsiao 1998: 13, 15–19). But the history of health reform in each suggests a continuing openness to reform, if not a rampant enthusiasm for it. The pattern of health needs will continue to develop, and the treatments available will be adopted as new technologies evolve. These two factors alone virtually guarantee that ongoing health reform will be necessary to maintain a balance among equity, access, and quality in health care, at an affordable cost, consistent with the strong premium that both Australia and New Zealand place on social solidarity.

References

Abel-Smith, B. 1967, 'An International Study of Health Expenditure', Public Health Papers no. 32, WHO, Geneva.

Agency for Health Care Policy and Research 1999, *Development and Implementation of the National Guideline Clearinghouse*, <http://www.ahcpr.gov/clinic/ngcfact.htm> 5 January.

Alford, R. R. 1975, Health Care Politics: Ideological and Interest Group Barriers to Reform, University of Chicago Press, Chicago.

American Hospitals Association 1994, *Transforming Health Care Delivery: Toward Community Care Networks*, American Hospitals Association, Chicago.

Anon. 1994, '"In 2010", Peering into 2010: A Survey of the Future of Medicine', *Economist*, 19 March.

Anon., [?] 1995, 'Medical Savings Accounts: Lessons from Singapore', *Health Affairs*, Summer: 260–6.

1999, 'Major Practice Incentive Payments Proposed for GP Information Technology', *GP Review*, 3(1): 1.

Ashton, T. 1996, 'Health Care Systems in Transition: New Zealand' Part I, *Journal of Public Health Medicine*, 18(3): 269–73.

1997a, 'Contracting for Health Services in New Zealand: A Transaction Cost Analysis', *Social Science and Medicine*, 46(3): 357–67.

1997b, 'The New Zealand Health System Three Years After Reform: How is the Patient Progressing?' *Health Economics Forum* (special supplement), 83 (February).

Ashton, T. and Press, D. 1997, 'Market Concentration in Secondary Health Services under a Purchaser–Provider Split: The New Zealand Experience', *Health Economics*, 6: 43–56.

Auditor-General of Victoria 1998, *Acute Health Services Under Casemix: A Case of Mixed Priorities*, Special report no. 56, Victorian Government Printer, Melbourne.

Australian Bureau of Statistics (ABS) 1996 Projections of the Populations of Australian States and Territories, AGPS, Canberra.

1997, *Private Hospitals Australia, 1996–97*, Cat. no. 4390.0, ABS, Canberra.

1999, Statistics Information Line, June 1999.

Australian Bureau of Statistics and Australian Institute of Health and Welfare 1997, *The Health and Welfare of Australia's Aboriginal and Torres Strait Islander Peoples*, AGPS, Canberra.

Australian Council on Hospital Standards (ACHS) 1996, *The Accreditation Guide for*

Australian Hospitals, 1st edn, ACHS, Sydney.

1998, The Equip Guide: Standards and Guidelines for the ACHS Evaluation and Quality Improvement Program, 2nd edn, ACHS, Sydney.

Australian Healthcare Association 1998, Redesigning the Future: An Australian Healthcare Association Discussion Paper on Health Policies for Australia, Australian Private Hospital Association, Canberra.

Australian Institute of Health and Welfare (AIHW).

1996, Australia's Health 1996: Fifth Biennial Report of the Australian Institute of Health and Welfare, AGPS, Canberra.

1997, Health Expenditure Bulletin no. 13, July.

1998a, Australia's Health 1998: Sixth Biennial Report of the Australian Institute of Health and Welfare, AGPS, Canberra.

1998b, *Hospital Statistics 1996–97*, AIHW, Canberra.

1998c, *International Health—How Australia Compares*, ISBN 0 642 24790 0, AIHW Cat. no. PHE 8 (ref. source: United Nations 1994).

1999, The Health and Welfare of Australia's Aboriginal and Torres Strait Islander Peoples, ABS, Canberra.

Australian Medical Association (AMA) 1995, 'Position Statement on Clinicians and Management', *Medical Journal of Australia*, 163, 18 September.

Badham, J. 1998, 'APHA Model Highlights Need for Reform', *Private Hospital. Australian Private Hospital Association Journal*, August–September: 8–9.

Barer, M., Nicoll, M., Diesendorf, M. and Harvey, R. 1990, 'From Medibank to Medicare: Trends in Australian Medical Care Costs and Use from 1976 to 1986', *Community Health Studies*, 14: 8–18.

Barnett, P. and Malcolm L. 1997, 'Beyond Ideology: The Emerging Roles of New Zealand's Crown Health Enterprises', *International Journal of Health Services*, 27(1): 89–108.

Barraclough, B. 1998, 'The Value of Surgical Practice Guidelines', *Australian and New Zealand Journal of Surgery*, 68: 6–9.

Bell, D. W., Ford, R. P. K., Slade, B. and McCormack, S. P. 1997, 'Immunisation Coverage in Christchurch in a Birth Cohort', *New Zealand Medical Journal*, 110: 440–2.

Berkman, L. and Syme, S. L. 1979, 'Social Networks, Host Resistance and Mortality: A Nine-year Follow up Study of Alameda County Residents', *American Journal of Epidemiology*, 109(2): 186–204.

Bero, L. A., Grilli, R. and Grimshaw, J. M., Harvey, E., Oxman, A. D. and Thomson, M. A. 1998, 'Closing the Gap Between Research and Practice: An Overview of Systematic Reviews of Interventions to Promote the Implementation of Research Findings', *British Medical Journal*, 317: 465–8.

Berwick, D. M. 1994, 'Eleven Worthy Aims for Clinical Leadership of Health System Reform', *JAMA*, 272(10): 797– 802.

Beuzenberg, A. 1997, 'New Zealand Health Reforms', *Health Estate Journal*, 51(2): 10–2.

Biener, L., Aseltine, R. H. Jr, Cohen, B. and Anderka, M. 1998, 'Reactions of Adult and Teenaged Smokers to the Massachusetts Tobacco Tax', *American Journal of Public Health*, 88(9): 1389–91.

Black, N. 1997, 'Health Services Research: Saviour or Chimera?' *Lancet*, 349: 1834–6.

Blair, S. 1998, Public Private Participation in Health: Recognising Future Income Streams Today—Will Competitive Purchasing be a Reality Today?, unpublished paper presented in Sydney, September.

Bloom, A. L. 1988, Where There Are No Data, unpublished PhD thesis, University of Sydney.

1995, Summary Findings: Quality Use of Paediatric Medicines, unpublished report to the Dept Health and Human Services.

1996, Education Strategies for Quality Use of Children's Medications, vol. 4 (unpublished), Health Innovations International, Sydney.

Bloom, A. L. and Schmiede, A. (forthcoming), 'Case Study: Planning a Public–Private Co-location in Queensland', in K. Eagar, P. Garrett and V. Lin (eds), *Health Planning in Australia* (publisher forthcoming).

The Book of Australia: Almanac 1991–92, Hodder & Stoughton, Sydney.

Braithwaite, J. and Hindle, D. 1998, 'Casemix Funding in Australia', *Medical Journal of Australia*, 168: 558–60.

Braithwaite, J., Vining, R. and Lazarus, L. 1994, 'The Boundaryless Hospital', *Australian and NZ Journal of Medicine*, [?] 24: 565–71.

Brand, I., Price, M., Newnham, P. and Newington, W. 1985, Final Report of the Review of the Repatriation Hospital System (Brand Committee Report), June, Canberra.

Brennan, G. 1999, 'Too Big a Gap Between Haves and Have Nots?' *Sydney Morning Herald*, 15 February: 13.

Brown, S. and Lumley, J. 1998, 'Are Cuts to Health Expenditure in Victoria Compromising Quality of Care?' *Australian and New Zealand Journal of Public Health*, 22(2): 279–81.

Burgoyne, J. and Lorbiecki, A. 1993, 'Clinicians into Management: the Experience in Context', *Health Services Management Research*, 6(4): 248–59.

Callahan, D. 1996, 'Controlling the Costs of Health Care for the Elderly—Fair Means and Foul', *New England Journal of Medicine*, 335(10): 744–6.

Cameron, D. 1998, 'President's letter', *Fellowship Affairs*, 17(3): 3.

Care 21 1998, *Partnerships for Wellness Proposal*, September, Adelaide.

Carter, M. 1998, 'Case Studies of Public Hospital Privatisation', *Health Issues*, 56.

Casemix Policy Unit 1998, *Draft Casemix Standards for NSW 1998/99*, NSW Health Department, Sydney.

Chalmers, I. 1993, 'The Cochrane Collaboration: Preparing, Maintaining and Disseminating Systematic Reviews of the Effects of Health Care', *Annals of the New York Academy of Sciences*, 703: 156–65.

Chandler, I. R., Fetter, R. B. and Newbold, R. C. 1991, 'Cost Accounting and Budgeting', in R. B. Fetter (ed.), *DRGs: Their Design and Development*, Health Administration Press, Ann Arbor, Michigan,

Chantler, C. 1990, 'Management Reform in a London Hospital', in Nan Carle (ed.), *Managing for Health Result, King's Fund*, pp. 74–85.

1994, 'How to Treat Doctors: The Role of Clinicians in Management', in National Association of Health Authorities and Trusts (NAHAT), *Speaking Up: Policy and Change in the NHS*, no. 3, December.

Cochrane, A. L. 1972, *Effectiveness and Efficiency: Random Reflections on Health Services*, Nuffield Provincial Hospitals Trust, London.

Cochrane, J. 1989, 'Influencing the Politics of Health Reform', in G. Gray and R. Pratt (eds), *Issues in Australian Nursing 2*, Churchill Livingstone, Melbourne.

Cochrane Library 1998, *CD-ROM, 4th Quarter 1998 Release*, Update Software, Vista, California.

Collins, P. 1990, 'Microeconomic Reform: The Achievements of the NSW Health System', address to the Royal Australian Institute of Public Administration, NSW Division.

Collyer, F. 1997, 'Privatisation and the Public Purse: The Port Macquarie Base Hospital', *Just Policy*, 10 (June): 27–39.

Committee of the Health and Community Services Ministerial Council 1997, *Draft National Healthy Ageing Strategy*, Commonwealth Dept Health and Family Services, Canberra.

Commonwealth Department of Finance 1995, *Clarifying the Exchange: A Review of Purchaser/Provider Arrangements*, Discussion Paper no. 2, Resource Management Improvement Branch, November.

Commonwealth Department of Health and Aged Care n.d., Australia's Health System (presentation), Canberra.

Commonwealth Department of Health and Community Services (DHCS) 1993, *Annual Report 1992–93*, Victorian Government, Melbourne.

Commonwealth Department of Health and Family Services 1997a, *Australian Casemix Report on Hospital Activity 1995–96*, AGPS, Canberra.

1997b, *General Practice in Australia, 1996*, Commonwealth Dept Health and Family Services, Canberra.

1998, General Practice: Report of the General Practice Strategy Review Group, Commonwealth Dept Health and Family Services, Canberra.

Commonwealth Department of Human Services 1995, *Call for Expressions of Interest in Conducting Trials of Co-ordinated Care*, September.

Commonwealth Department of Veterans' Affairs 1998a, Morbidity of Vietnam Veterans: A Study of the Health of Australia's Vietnam Veteran Community, vol. 1: Male Vietnam Veterans Survey and Community Comparison Outcomes, Commonwealth Dept Veterans' Affairs, Canberra.

1998b, Morbidity of Vietnam Veterans: A Study of the Health of Australia's Vietnam Veteran Community, vol. 2: Female Vietnam Veterans Survey and Community Comparison Outcomes, Commonwealth Dept Veterans' Affairs, Canberra.

Coney, S. 1996, 'The Relentless Unravelling of New Zealand's Health Care System', *Lancet*, 24 June, 347: 1825.

Considine, M. 1998, 'The Costs of Increased Control: Corporate Management and Australian Community Organisations', *Australian Social Work*, 41(3): 17–25.

Coulter, A. 1993, 'Diagnostic Dilatation and Curettage: Is it Used Appropriately?' *British Medical Journal*, 306: 236–9.

Council of Australian Governments (COAG) 1995, 'Task Force on Health and Community Services 1995, Health and Community Services: Meeting People's Needs Better', discussion paper, COAG, Canberra.

1996, Communiqué, June, Canberra.

Crane, P. J., Barnard, D. I., Horsley, K. D. and Adena, M. A. 1997, *Mortality of Vietnam Veterans—The Veteran Cohort Study*, A Report of the 1996 Retrospective Cohort Study of Australian Veterans, Dept Veterans' Affairs, Canberra.

Crichton, A. 1990, Slowly Taking Control? Australian Governments and Health Care Provision 1788–1988, Allen & Unwin, Sydney.

Crimmins E. M., Saito, Y. and Ingegneri, D. 1997, 'Trends in Disability-free Life Expectancy in the United States, 1970–1990', *Population and Development Review*, 23(3): 555–72.

Crown Company Monitoring Advisory Unit 1996, *Crown Health Enterprises: Briefing to the Incoming Minister*, Crown Company Monitoring Advisory Unit, Wellington.

Davies, P. 1998, 'A personal view of health reform in New Zealand: past, present and future', unpublished paper.

Davis, K. 1999a, 'Health insurance and income inequality: findings from a 1998 five nation survey of public health system views and healthcare experiences by income class', paper presented at Health Services Research Conference, AU.NZ Sydney, 10 August.

1999b, 'International Health Policy: Common Problems, Alternative Strategies', *Health Affairs*, 18(3): 135–43.

Deeble, J. 1991, *Medical Services through Medicare*, National Health Strategy Background Paper no. 2, February, Canberra.

Degeling, P., Kennedy, J., Hill, M., Carnegie, M. and Holt, J. 1998, *Professional Sub-Cultures and Hospital Reform*, Centre for Hospital Management and Information Systems Research, University of New South Wales, and Dept Sociology Policy, University of Newcastle-upon-Tyne.

Domberger, Simon 1998, The Contracting Organisation; A Strategic Guide to Outsourcing, Oxford University Press, New York.

Donaldson, C. and Gerard, K. 1993, *Economics of Health Care Financing: The Visible Hand*, Macmillan, London.

Dow, D. A. 1995, Safeguarding the Public Health: A History of the New Zealand Department of Health, Victoria University Press, Wellington.

Downey, M. 1999, 'Medicare—It Isn't Broken Yet', *Sydney Morning Herald*, 18 January.

Duckett, S. J. 1995, 'Hospital Payment Arrangements to Encourage Efficiency: The Case of Victoria, Australia', *Health Policy*, 34(2): 113–34.

1997, 'Doctors and Healthcare Reform', *Medical Journal of Australia*, 167: 184–5.

1998a, 'Casemix funding for Acute Hospital Inpatient Services in Australia', *Medical Journal of Australia*, 169 (supplement, 19 October): S17–21.

1998b, 'Making a Move on Medicare', *Australian Health Review*, 21(2): 22–7.

Duckett, S. J. and Jackson, T. J. 1999, 'Do the Elderly Cost More?', paper presented at Health Services Research AU.NZ 1999, Sydney, Australia, 10 August 1999.

Dwyer, T., Ponsonby, A. L., Blizzard, L., Newman, N. M. and Cochrane, J. A. 1995, 'The Contribution of Changes in the Prevalence of Prone Sleeping Position to the Decline in Sudden Infant Death Syndrome in Tasmania', *Journal of the American Medical Association*, 273: 783–9.

Eager, K. and Hindle, D. 1996, *The Australian Casemix Dictionary*, National Casemix Education Series no. 9, Dept Human Services and Health, Canberra.

Eastaugh, S. R. 1992, Health Care Finance: Economic Incentives and Productivity Enhancement, Auburn House, Westport.

Eckerman, S. 1992, 'Projected Health Expenditure and Ageing: Revised Methodologies,' paper presented at the Public Health Association conference, September, Canberra.

Economic and Budget Review Committee 1992, *Hospital Services in Victoria: Efficiency and Effectiveness of Health Service Agreements*, 35th Report, Parliament of Victoria, Melbourne.

Economic Planning and Advisory Council (EPAC) 1988, *Economic Effects of an Ageing Population*, Office of EPAC, Canberra.

1994, *Australia's Ageing Society*, Office of EPAC, Canberra.

Egger, M. and Davey Smith, G. 1998, 'Meta-analysis—Bias in Location and Selection of Studies', *British Medical Journal*, 316: 61–6.

Elliot, J. R. et al. 1996, 'The Added Effectiveness of Early Geriatrician Involvement on Acute Orthopaedic Wards to Orthogeriatric Rehabilitation', *New Zealand Medical Journal*, 109: 72–3.

Emanuel, E. J. and Emanuel, L. L. 1994, 'The Economics of Dying: The Illusions of Cost Savings at the End of Life', *New England Journal of Medicine*, 330(8): 540–4.

Evans, R. G. 1982, 'Health Care in Canada: Patterns of Funding and Regulation', in G. McLachlan and A. Maynard (eds), *The Public-Private Mix for Health*, Nuffield, London.

—— 1984, *Strained Mercy: The Economics of Canadian Health Care*, Butterworths, Toronto.

Evans, R., Barer, M. and Marmor, T. 1994, *Why Are Some People Healthy and Others Not?: Determinants of Health of Populations* (Institutions and Social Change), Aldine De Gruyter, New York.

Evidence-Based Medicine Working Group 1992, 'Evidence-based Medicine: A New Approach to Teaching the Practice of Medicine', *JAMA*, 268(17): 2420–5.

Feek, C. M., Barrow, G., Edgar, W., Henneveld, L., McKean, W., and Paterson, R.J. 1998, 'From Mr McKeown to Mr Williams: Clinicians Will Make Hard Decisions Over Rationing if They "Own" the Relationship Between Clinical Decision Making and Resource Allocation', paper presented at Second International Conference on Priorities in Health Care, London, 8–10 October.

Fougere, G., Marwick, J. and Scott C. 1986, *Choices for Health Care: Report of the Health Benefits Review*, Government Printer, Wellington.

Franks, P., Nutting, P. A. and Calancy, C. M. 1993, 'Health Care Reform, Primary Care and the Need for Research', *JAMA*, 270: 1449–53.

Fraser, D., Scott, J. and Gibbs, A. 1988, *Unshackling the Hospitals: Report of the Hospital and Related Services Taskforce*, Government Printing Office, Wellington.

Fuchs, V. R. 1974, Who Shall Live? Health, Economics, and Social Choice, Basic Books, New York.

Gardner, H. and McCoppin, B. 1989, 'Emerging Militancy? The Politicisation of Australian Allied Health Professionals', in H. Gardner (ed.), *The Politics of Health: The Australian Experience*, Churchill Livingstone, Melbourne, pp. 303–30.

Gauld, R. 1997, 'The Development and Implementation of Health Policy: New Zealand and Hong Kong Compared', *Journal of Health and Social Policy*, 8(3) 67–78.

Getzen, T. E. 1991, 'Population Ageing and the Growth of Health Expenditures', *Journal of Gerontology*, 47(3): S98–104.

Gibbs, A. 1998, 'Casemix in a Population/needs-based Funding Model: the NSW Application', *Healthcover*, 7(6): 38–39.

Gilbert, R. 1990, *A Resource Allocation Formula for the NSW Health System*, NSW Health Department, State Health Publication no. 90-36.

Gillies, P.1997, The Effectiveness of Alliances or Partnerships for Health Promotion: A Global Review of Progress and Potential Consideration of the Relationship to Building Social Capital for Health, Conference Working Paper, Fourth International Conference on Health Promotion, Jakarta, Indonesia.

Glennister, H. and Matsaganis, M. 1993, 'The UK Health Reforms: The Fundholding Experiment', *Health Policy*, 23: 179–91.

Grant, C., Forrest, C. and Starfield, B. 1997, 'Primary Care and Health Reform in New Zealand', *New England Medical Journal*, 110(1037): 35–9.

Gray, G. 1998, 'Access to Medical Care under Strain: New Pressures in Canada and Australia', *Journal of Health Politics, Policy and Law*, 23(6).

Gray, J. A. M. 1997, *Evidence-based Healthcare*, Churchill Livingstone, Edinburgh.

Grimshaw, J. and Eccles, M. 1998, 'Clinical Practice Guidelines', in C. Silagy and A. Haines (eds), *Evidence Based Practice in Primary Care*, BMJ Publishing Group, London.

Grimshaw, J. M. and Russell I. T. 1993, 'Effect of Clinical Guidelines on Medical Practice: A Systematic Review of Rigorous Evaluations', *Lancet*, 342: 1317–22.

Haines, A. and Jones, R. 1994, 'Implementing Findings of Research', *British Medical Journal*, 308: 1488–92.

Hall, J. 1998–99, 'Five Country Survey Shows Rising Public Dissatisfaction with Health Care Systems', *Healthcover*, 8(6): 11–15.

1999, 'Incremental Change in the Australian Health Care System', *Health Affairs*, 18(3): 95–110.

Hall, J. and Haas, M. 1992, 'The Rationing of Health Care: Should Oregon be Transported to Australia?' *Australian Journal of Public Health*, 16: 435–40.

Ham, C. 1995, *Management and Competition in the New NHS*, Radcliffe Medical Press, London.

1997a, Health Care Reform: Learning From International Experiences, Open University Press, Buckingham.

1997b, 'Reforming the New Zealand health reforms: Big bang gives way to incrementalism as competition is abandoned', *British Medical Journal*, 314: 1844–5.

1998, 'Lessons and Conclusions', in C. Ham (ed.), *Health Care Reform*, Open University Press, Philadelphia, pp. 119–40.

Ham, C. and J. Øvretveit (eds) 1998, *'The Background', Health Care Reform: Learning from International Experience*, Open University Press, Philadelphia.

Hannan, E. L. 1998, 'Measuring Hospital Outcomes: Don't Make the Perfect the Enemy of the Good!' *Journal of Health Services Research and Policy*, 3(2): 67–9.

Health Care of Australia 1996, Co-location of Public and Private Hospitals on a Shared Site—Will It Work?, unpublished speech, 19 November.

Health Department Victoria 1987, *Victorian Health Plan*, 1st edn, Health Department Victoria, Melbourne, 1987.

1989, *Annual Report 1988–89*, Health Department Victoria, Melbourne.

Health Department Victoria, Health Statistics Unit 1986, *DRGs 1982–83 and 1983–84*, Health Department Victoria, Melbourne.

Health Funding Authority 1998a, *The Next Five Years in General Practice*, Health

Funding Authority, Auckland.

1998b, Service Integration: Guidelines for the Development of Integration Demonstration Projects, Health Funding Authority, Wellington.

Healthcover 1998, 'Australia Scores Poorly on Harvard Experts' View of the Ideal Health System', *Healthcover*, October–November: 13–19.

Heggie, E. G. 1958, 'Organising for Health', in R. J. Latimer (ed.), *Health Administration in New Zealand*, New Zealand Institute of Public Administration, Wellington.

Heyssel, R. M., Gaintner, J. R., Kues, I. W. et al. 1984, 'Decentralized Management in a Teaching Hospital', *New England Journal of Medicine*, 310: 1477–80.

Hickie, J. B. 1994, 'Success of a New Health Administration Strategy: The Patient-focussed Institute with a Tripartite Management', *Medical Journal of Australia*, 161(5 September): 324–7.

Hindle, D. 1998, Book Review: R. Donato. and D. Scotton (eds), *Economics and Australian Health Policy, Australian Health Review*, 21(4): 277–82.

Hornblow A. 1997, 'New Zealand's Health Reforms: A Clash of Cultures', *British Medical Journal*, vol. 314, 28 June, 314: 1892–4.

Hospitals and Health Services Commission 1974, *A Report on Hospitals in Australia*, AGPS, Canberra.

Hrobjartsson, A., Gotzsche, P. C. and Gluud, C. 1998, 'The Controlled Clinical Trial Turns 100 Years: Fibiger's Trial of Serum Treatment of Diphtheria', *British Medical Journal*, 317: 1243–5.

Hsiao, W. C. 1992, 'Introduction: Comparing Health Care systems: What Nations Can Learn from One Another', *Journal of Health Politics, Policy and Law*, 17(4): 613–36.

1995, 'Medical Savings Accounts: Lessons from Singapore', *Health Affairs*, Summer: 260–6.

1998, 'Australia Scores Poorly on Harvard Expert's View of the Ideal Health System', *Healthcover*, 8(5):13–19.

Human Development Report 1998, Oxford University Press, New York.

Institute of Medicine 1990, *Medicare: A Strategy for Quality Assurance*, National Academy Press, Washington.

1992, *Guidelines for Clinical Practice: From Development to Use*, ed. M. J. Field and K. N. Lohr, Institute of Medicine, National Academy Press, Washington DC.

Jin, R. L., Shah, C. P. and Svoboda, T. J. 1995, 'The Impact of Unemployment on Health: A Review of the Evidence', *Canadian Medical Association Journal*, 153: 529–40.

Johnson, M., Grosvenor, J., Hguyen, Q., Chang, S. and McVernon, S. 1997, *Validation of the Community Home Nursing Groups and Cost Weights*, University of Western Sydney Centre for Applied Nursing Research, Campbelltown, NSW.

Johnston, C. and Stanford, M. 1996, 'Swapping Health Care Systems—Whose Grass is Really Greener?' *JAMA*, 276(24): 1986–7.

Jordens, C. F. C., Hawe, P., Irwig, L. M., Henderson-Smart, D. J., Ryan, M., Donoghue, D. A., Gabb, R. G. and Fraser, I. S. 1998, 'Use of Systematic Reviews of Randomised Trials by Australian Neonatologists and Obstetricians', *Medical Journal of Australia*, 168: 267–70.

Jorm, A. F., Korten, A. E. and Henderson, A. S. 1987, 'The Prevalence of Dementia: A Quantitative Integration of the Literature,' *Acta Psychiatrica Scandanavica*, 76: 465–79.

Kawachi, I. et al. 1997, 'Social Capital, Income Inequality and Mortality', *American Journal of Public Health*, 87(9).

Kelly, D. T. 1997, 'Our Future Society: A Global Challenge', *Circulation*, 95(11): 2459–64.

Kennedy, B. P., Kawachi, I., Lochner, K., Jones, C. and Prothrow-Stith, D. 1997, '(Dis)respect and Black Mortality', *Ethn Dis*,[??] Autumn, 7(3): 207–14.

Kerr, D., Malcolm, L., Schousboe, J. and Pimm, F. 1996, 'Successful Implementation of Laboratory Budget Holding by Pegasus Medical Group', *New Zealand Medical Journal*, 109: 354–7.

Klein, R. 1990, 'The State and the Profession: The Politics of the Double Bed', *British Medical Journal*, 301: 700–2.

Lang, H. G. 1987, 'Health Policy Formulation in New Zealand', in M. W. Raffel and N. K. Raffel (eds), *Perspectives on Health Policy: Australia*, Wiley, Chichester, NZ and USA.

Last, J. M. 1997, *Public Health and Human Ecology*, Appleton & Lange, Connecticut.

Laugeson, M. and Salmond, G. 1994, 'New Zealand Health Care: A Background', *Health Policy*, 29: 11–23.

Lawson, J., Reid, M. and Rotem, A. 1994, *Health System Reforms: Australia, Hong Kong, New Zealand, Singapore*, report of a symposium sponsored by the WHO Western Pacific Regional Office, in Wellington, NZ, May 1994, WHO Western Pacific Regional Office, Manila.

Lawson, K. A., Armstrong, R. M. and Van Der Weyden, M. B. 1998, 'A Sea Change in Australian Medical Education', *Medical Journal of Australia*, 169: 653–8.

Lewis, G. and Sloggett, A. 1998, 'Suicide, Deprivation, and Unemployment: Record Linkage Study', *British Medical Journal*, 317: 1283–6.

Light, D. W. 1997, 'From Managed Competition to Managed Cooperation: Theory and Lessons from the British experience', *Millbank Quarterly*, 75(3): 299.

Lin, V. and Duckett, S. J. 1997, 'Structural Interests and Organisational Dimensions of Health System Reform', in H. Gardner (ed.), *Health Policy in Australia*, Oxford University Press, Melbourne, pp. 64–80.

Lister, J. 1986, 'The Politics of Medicine in Britain and the United States', *New England Journal of Medicine*, 315(3): 168–73.

Logan, R. L. and Scott, P. J. 1996, 'Uncertainty in Clinical Practice: Implications for Quality and Costs of Health Care', *Lancet*, 347: 595–8.

Lomas, J. 1997, *Beyond the Sound of One Hand Clapping*, University of Sydney, Sydney.

MacIntyre, C. R., Brook, C. W., Chandraraj, E. and Plant, A. J. 1997, 'Changes in Bed Resources and Admission Patterns in Acute Public Hospitals in Victoria, 1987–1995', *Medical Journal of Australia*, 167(4): 186–9.

Macklin, J. 1990, The National Health Strategy: Setting the Agenda for Change, background paper no. 1, November.

McCaughan, B. C. and Piccone, D. M. 1994, 'Devolved Clinical Management and Casemix', *Medical Journal of Australia*, 161: S20–3.

Malcolm, L. 1993, 'Trends in Primary Medical Care Related Services and Expenditure in New Zealand 1983–1993', *New Zealand Medical Journal*, 106: 470–4.

—— 1996, 'Inequities in Access to and Utilisation of Primary Medical Care Services for Maori and Low Income New Zealanders', *New Zealand Medical Journal*, 109: 356–8.

—— 1997a, 'GP Budget Holding in New Zealand: Lessons for Britain and Elsewhere', *British Medical Journal*, 314: 1890–2.

—— 1997b, *An Evaluation of Pharmaceutical Management and Budget Holding in Independent Practice Associations and General Practices*, report prepared for the Transitional Health Authority and Pharmaceutical Health Funding Authority, Wellington.

—— 1998a, 'Capitated Primary Care: Policy, Problems and Prospects', *Health Manager*, 5: 7–9.

—— 1998b, 'Towards General Practice Led Integrated Health Care in New Zealand', *Medical Journal of Australia*, 169: 147–50.

Malcolm, L. and Barnett, P. 1994, 'New Zealand's Health Providers in an Emerging Market', *Health Policy*, 29: 85–90.

Malcolm, L., Wright, J., Barnet, P., in press, 'Emerging Clinical Governance: Developments in Independent Practitioner Associations in New Zealand', *New Zealand Medical Journal*.

—— 1997, 'Progress with the Development of Independent Practice Associations and Related Groups in New Zealand', *New Zealand GP Weekly*, February 12: 1–2.

Mant, A. 1997, *Intelligent Leadership*, Allen & Unwin, Sydney.

Mapa Highlights, *Greater Market Access: Tariff and Non-Tariff Measures* <http://www1.apecsec.org.sg/virtualib/history/mapa/vol1/nontarif.html>.

Margolis, C. Z. 1998, 'Developing and Constructing Practical Guidelines', in C. Z. Margolis and S. Cretin (eds), *Implementing Clinical Practice Guidelines*, American Hospital Association Press, Chicago.

Marmot, M. G., Bosma, H., Hemingway, H., Brunner, E. and Stansfeld, S. 1997, 'Contribution of Job Control and Other Risk Factors to Social Variations in Coronary Heart Disease Incidence', *Lancet*, 350(9073): 235–9.

Marmot, M. G., Fuhrer, R., Ettner, S. L., Marks, N. F., Bumpass, L. L and Ryff, C. D. 1998, 'Contribution of Psychosocial Factors to Socioeconomic Differences in Health', *Millbank Quarterly*, 76(3): 403–48, 305.

Marsh, A. and McKay, S. 1994, *Poor Smokers*, Policy Studies Institute, London.

Marshall, B. J. and Warren, J. R. 1984, 'Unidentified Curved Bacilli in the Stomach of Patients with Gastritis and Peptic Ulceration', *Lancet*, 1311–14.

Massaro, T. A. and Wong, Y. N. 1995, 'Positive Experience with Medical Savings Accounts in Singapore', *Health Affairs*, Summer: 267–72.

Mathers, C. 1994, 'Health differentials among adult Australians aged 25–64 years', Health Monitoring Series no. 1, AGPS, Canberra

1999, 'Gains in Health Expectancy from the Elimination of Diseases among Older People', *Disability and Rehabilitation*, 21: 211–21.

Mathers, C., Penm, R., Carter, R. and Stevenson, C. 1998, *Health System Costs of Diseases and Injury in Australia 1993–94*, AIHW, Canberra.

McCallum, J. 1991, 'Health: The Quality of Survival in Old Age,' in Australian Institute of Health, *Australia's Health 1990*, AGPS, Canberra.

1997, 'Ageing and Health: The Last Stage of the Epidemiological Transition', in A. Borowski, S. Encel and E. Ozanne (eds), *Ageing and Social Policy*, Cambridge University Press, Cambridge, pp. 54–73.

McCallum, J. and Geiselhart, K. 1996, *Australia's New Aged: Issues for Young and Old*, Allen & Unwin, Sydney.

McLaughlan, R. and Preston, M. 1998, *Repatriation Private Patient Scheme Review*, Commonwealth Dept Veterans' Affairs, Canberra.

Medical Research Council 1948, 'Streptomycin Treatment of Pulmonary Tuberculosis: A Medical Research Council Investigation', *British Medical Journal*, 2: 769–82.

Metropolitan Hospitals Planning Board (MHPB) 1995, *Developing Melbourne's Hospital Network: Interim Report*, MHPB, Melbourne.

Mills, A. 1998, 'To Contract or not to Contract? Issues for Low and Middle Income Countries', *Health Policy and Planning*, 13(1): 32–40.

Ministry of Health 1998a, *Health Expenditure Trends in New Zealand 1980–97*, Ministry of Health, Wellington.

1998b, *Purchasing for Your Health 1996/97*, Ministry of Health, Wellington.

Mooney, G. 1996, 'What Sort of Future Health Care System Do We Want?' *New Doctor*, 65, Winter: 21–3.

Mooney, J. G. and Scotton, R. (eds) 1998, *Economics and Australian Health Policy*, Allen & Unwin, Sydney.

Morgan, M., Calnan, M. and Manning, N. 1991, 'The Hospital as a Social Organization', in P. Worsley (ed.), *The New Modern Sociology Readings*, Penguin, Harmondsworth.

Moss, F., Garside, P. and Dawson, S. 1988, 'Organisational Change: The Key to Quality Improvement', *Quality in Health Care*, supplement, 7: S1–2.

Mulrow, C. D. 1995, 'Rationale for Systematic Reviews', *British Medical Journal* vol. 309, 1994: 597–9.

National Advisory Committee on Core Health and Disability Support Services 1992, *Core Health and Disability Support Services for 1993/94*, National Advisory Committee on Core Health and Disability Support Services, Wellington.

National Commission of Audit 1996, National Commission of Audit Report to the Commonwealth Government, AGPS, Canberra: 15–19.

National Expert Advisory Group on Safety and Quality in Australian Health Care 1998, *Commitment to Quality Enhancement: Interim Report*, Dept Health and Family Services, Canberra.

National Health and Medical Research Council (NH&MRC) 1995a, *Clinical Practice Guidelines for the Management of Early Breast Cancer*, AGPS, Canberra.

1995b, Guidelines for the Development and Implementation of Guidelines, AGPS, Canberra.

1997, Guidelines for Care Around Pre-Term Birth, AGPS, Canberra.

1999, A Guide to the Development, Implementation and Evaluation of Clinical Practice Guidelines, AusInfo, Canberra.

National Public Health Partnership (NPHP) 1997, *Public Health in Australia*, NPHP, Canberra.

1998, Memorandum of Understanding Between the Commonwealth and States and Territories to Establish the National Public Health Partnership, NPHP, Canberra.

Nicol, P., Balfour, H., Newton, N. and de Totth, A. 1998, *Purchase of Hospital Services from State Governments 97/98*, Australian National Audit Office, Commonwealth of Australia, Canberra.

Nord, E., Richardson, J., Street, A., Kuhse, H. and Singer, P. 1995, 'Maximizing Health Benefits vs Egalitarianism: An Australian Survey of Health Issues', *Social Science and Medicine*, 41(10): 1429–37.

NSW Ageing and Disability Department and NSW Health 1998, *NSW Healthy Ageing Framework 1998–2003*, Ageing and Disability Department, Sydney.

NSW Auditor-General 1996, Accounting for the Private Provision of Public Infrastructure: Water and Health Projects, vol. 1, Audit Office of NSW, Sydney.

NSW Department of the Auditor-General 1996, 'Port Macquarie Base Hospital Performance Evaluation Report: 1st January to 31 December 1995', draft, cited in O'Brien 1997, *The Litmus Test*.

NSW Health Department 1995, Caring for Health: Equity, Efficiency and Quality: The NSW Government's Economic Statement for Health, NSW Health Department, State Health Publication no. 96-73.

1988a, *Private Hospital Opportunities*, pamphlet distributed by NSW Health Department.

1998b, *Strategic Directions for Health, 1998–2003*, NSW Health Department, Sydney.

NSW Health n.d., Revision of the Program 2.3 Resource Allocation Formula, Sydney.

NZ Health Information Service n.d., *Fetal and Infant Deaths 1994*.

O'Brien, J. 1997, The Litmus Test: The Inside Story of the Port Macquarie Base Hospital Project, Wild & Woolley, Port Macquarie, NSW

Oceania Health Consulting 1997, *Purchaser Provider Separation and Public Health*, Dept Health and Family Services, Canberra.

Organisation for Economic Cooperation and Development (OECD) 1994, *The Reform of Health Care Systems: A Review of Seventeen OECD Countries*, Health Policy Studies no. 5, OECD, Paris.

1996, Ageing in OECD Countries: A Critical Policy Challenge, OECD, Paris.

1997, OECD Health Data 97: Software for the Comparative Analysis of 29 Health Systems, OECD, Paris.

Osborne, D. and Gaebler, T. 1992, Reinventing Government: How the Entrepreneurial Spirit is Transforming the Public Sector, Addison Wesley, Reading, Mass.

Øvretveit, J. 1995, Purchasing for Health: A Multidisciplinary Introduction to the Theory and Practice of Health Purchasing, Open University Press, London.

1998, Purchasing for Health: A Multidiscipinary Introduction to the Theory and Practice of Health Purchasing, Open University Press, Philadelphia.

Painter, M. 1998, 'After Managerialism—Rediscoveries and Redirections: The Case of Intergovernmental Relations', *Australian Journal of Public Administration*, 57(4): 44–53.

Palmer, G. and Wood, T. 1984, 'Diagnosis Related Groups: Recent Developments and their Adoption and Application in Australia', *Australian Health Review*, 7(2): 67–80.

Palmer, G. R. and Short, S. D. 1994, *Health Care and Public Policy: An Australian Analysis*, Macmillan, Melbourne.

Paterson, J. 1993, Address, Casemix Policy Launch, April, Melbourne.

Patton, G. C., Hibbert, M., Rosier, M. J., Carlin, J. B., Caust, J. and Bowes, G. 1996, 'Is Smoking Associated with Depression and Anxiety in Teenagers?' *American Journal of Public Health*, 86: 225-30.

Peabody, J., Bickel, W. S. and Lawson, J. 1996, 'The Australian Health Care System: Are the Incentives Down Under Right Side Up?' *JAMA*, 276(24): 1944–50.

Pemberton, P. J. and Goldblatt, J. 1998, 'The Internet and the Changing Roles of Doctors, Patients and Families', *Medical Journal of Australia*, 169: 594–5.

Perkins, R. J., Keith, J. P., Alley, P. G., Barnes, P. C., Fisher, M. M. and Hatfield, P. J. 1997, 'Health Service Reform: The Perceptions of Medical Specialists in

Australia (New South Wales), the United Kingdom and New Zealand', *Medical Journal of Australia*, 167: 201–4.

Philips Fox and Casemix Consulting 1999, *Health Services Policy Review*, discussion paper, Dept Human Services (Vic.), Melbourne.

Podger, A. 1997, 'Health Reform in Australia in an International Perspective', *Health Economics Forum* (special supplement), 83(February).

Poertner, J. 1998, *Future Directions in Outcome Measurement*, panel paper, Fifth Roundtable on Outcome Measures in Child Welfare Services: Summary of Proceedings, American Humane Society.

Powell Davies, P. G., Harris, M. F., Comino, E., Bolton, P., Fridgant, Y., Betbeder-Matibet, L., Mira, M. and MacDonald, J. 1997, *General Practice Integration: Summary Report*, General Practice Integration Research Program, School of Community Medicine, University of New South Wales, Sydney.

Prime Ministerial Task Force on Positive Ageing 1997, *Facing the Future: A Strategic Plan*, Dept Prime Minister and Cabinet, Wellington.

Private Health Insurance 1997, *Report No. 57*, 2 February, Industry Commission.

Private Health Insurance Administration Council (PHIAC) 1989, Quarterly Reports on Health Insurance Coverage since June 1989 (before that the Dept Health compiled this type of data).

Productivity Commission 1998, Implementing Reforms in Government Services (1998: Using Competitive Tendering for NSW Public Hospitals, Productivity Commission.

Public Health Group 1997, *The Health and Wellbeing of Older People and Kaumatua: Public Health Issues*, Ministry of Health/Manatu Hauora, Wellington.

Pusey, M. 1991, Economic Rationalism in Canberra: A Nation Building State Changes its Mind, Cambridge University Press, Cambridge.

Quality of Care and Health Outcomes Committee 1995, Guidelines for the Development and Implementation of Clinical Practice Guidelines, AGPS, Canberra.

Quiggan, J. 1995, 'Private Infrastructure: What Economic Theory Suggests', *Just Policy*, 4(September): 28–36.

Raffel, N. K. 1987, 'New Zealand's Health system: A Brief description', in M. W. Raffel and N. K. Raffel (eds), *Perspectives on Health Policy: Australia, New Zealand and USA*, Wiley, Chichester, pp. 133–7.

Read, P. 1991, 'Conference Buzz Words: Ambiguity, Flexibility and Joy', paper presented to the Area Health Service Conference, February 1991, NSW Health Department, State Health Publication no. 91-56.

Reeve, T. 1993, Coherent and Consistent Quality Assurance and Utilisation Review Activities in Public and Private Hospitals in Australia, Commonwealth Dept Health, Housing, Local Government and Community Services, Canberra.

Reinhardt, U. E. 1998, 'Abstracting from Distributional Effects, This Policy is

Efficient', in M. L. Barer, T. E. Getzen and G. L. Stoddart (eds), *Health, Health Care and Health Economics: Perspectives on Distribution*, John Wiley & Sons, Chichester, 1–52.

1999, '"Mangled Competition" and "Managed Whatever"', *Health Affairs*, 18(3): 92–4.

Renwick, M. and Sadkowsky, K. 1991, *Variations in Surgery Rates*, Health Services Series no. 2, AIHW, Canberra.

Rice, T. 1998, *The Economics of Health Reconsidered*, Health Administration Press, Chicago.

Richards, T. 1998, 'Partnerships with Patients', *British Medical Journal*, 316: 85–6.

Richardson, J. 1991, *The Effects of Consumer Co-payments in Medical Care*, National Health Strategy Background Paper no. 5, AGPS, Canberra.

1998, 'The Health Care Financing Debate', in G. Mooney and R. Scotton (eds), *Economics and Australian Health Policy*, Allen & Unwin, Sydney.

1999, 'The Effect of Ageing on the Cost of Health Services in Australia: Wrong Methods Give Wrong Answers', paper presented at Health Services Research, AU.NZ, 1999, Sydney, Australia, 10 August 1999.

Rothman, G. P. 1998, 'Projections of Key Aggregates for Australia's Aged— Government Outlays, Financial Assets and Incomes', paper delivered to the 6th Colloquium of Superannuation Researchers, July, University of Melbourne.

Rubin, G. L. and Frommer, M. S. 1999 (in press), 'Accessing Electronic Information for Effective Clinical Practice', in P. Harnett, P. Glare and J. Cartmill (eds), *Clinical Oncology: A Case Based Manual*, Oxford University Press, Oxford.

Rubin, G. L., Frommer, M. S., Vincent, N. and Phillips, P. 1998, 'Disseminating and Implementing the Evidence', in E. Wigglesworth (ed.), CD-ROM of papers prepared for the Workshop 'Evidence-Based Health Advice', November 1998, conducted by the Menzies Foundation and the Health Advisory Committee, NH&MRC, Menzies Foundation, Melbourne.

Saggers, S. and Gray, D. 1991, Aboriginal Health and Society: The Traditional and Contemporary Aboriginal Struggle for Better Health, Allen & Unwin, Sydney.

Sainsbury, R., Gillespie, W. J., Armour, P. C. and Newman, E. F. 1986, 'An Orthopaedic Geriatric Rehabilitation Unit: The First Two Years Experience', *New Zealand Medical Journal*, 99: 583–5.

Saltman, R. B. and von Otter, C. 1989, 'Public Competition vs Mixed Markets: An Analytic Comparison', *Health Policy*, 11: 43–55.

(eds) 1998, Implementing Planned Markets in Health Care: Balancing Social and Economic Responsibility, Open University Press, Philadelphia.

Saltman, R. B. and Figueras, J. 1998, 'Analyzing the Evidence on European Health Care Reforms', *Health Affairs*, March–April: 85–108.

Saltman, R. B., Figueras, J. and Salkellarides, C. 1998, *Critical Challenges for Health Care Reform in Europe*, Open University Press, Buckingham.

Sax, S. A. 1984, A Strife of Interests: Politics and Policies in Australian Health Services, Allen & Unwin, Sydney.

Scally, G. and Donaldson, L. 1998, 'Clinical Governance and the Drive for Quality Improvement in the New NHS in England', *British Medical Journal*, 317: 61–5.

Schick, A. 1996, The Spirit of Reform: Managing the New Zealand State Sector in a Time of Change, Crown Copyright, Wellington.

Schmiede, A. 1998, 'Collocation: Future Directions in Partnership', unpublished paper, 22 October.

Scott, C. 1996, 'Reform of the New Zealand Health Care System', *Leadership in Health Services*, 5(6): 32–9.

Scott, C., Fougere, G. and Marwick, J. 1986, *Choices for Health Care, Report of the Health Benefits Review*, Government Printer, Wellington.

Scotton, R. 1998, 'Managed Competition', in G. Mooney and R. Scotton (eds), *Economics and Australian Health Care Policy*, Allen & Unwin, Sydney.

Scotton, R. B. and Owens, H. J. 1990, *Case Payment in Australia: Issues and Options*, Public Sector Management Institute, Monash University, Melbourne.

Secretariat for the Review of Commonwealth/State Service Provision (SRCSSP) 1998, *Feedback on the Report on Government Services*, AusInfo, Canberra.

Segal, L. and Richardson, J. 1994, 'Economic Framework for Allocative Efficiency in the Health Sector', *Australian Economic Review*, 2nd Quarter: 89–98.

Sheldon, A. and Melville, A. 1996, 'Providing Intelligence for Rational Decision-making in the NHS: The NHS Centre for Reviews and Dissemination', *Journal of Clinical Effectiveness*, 1(2): 51–4.

Singer, P. 1997, 'Freedoms and Utilities in the Distribution of Health Care', in G. Dworkin and P. Brown (eds), *Markets and Morals*, Hemisphere, Washington.

Smallwood, R. A. and Lapsley, H. M. 1997, 'Clinical Practice Guidelines: to What End?' *Medical Journal of Australia*, 166: 592–5.

Smythe, T. 1998, 'Co-location of Public and Private Hospitals', speech to Australian College of Health Service Executives, Sydney, 14 October.

Stansfeld, S. A., Fuhrer, R., Head, J., Ferrie, J. and Shipley M. 1997, 'Work and Psychiatric Disorder in the Whitehall II Study', *Journal of Psychosomatic Research*, 43(1): 73–81.

Statistics New Zealand 1998, *Demographic Trends 1998*, SNZ and OECD database.

Steering Committee for the Review of Commonwealth/State Service Provision 1998, *Report on Government Services*, vol. 1: *Education, Health, Justice, Emergency Management*, Commonwealth of Australia, Canberra.

1995, Report on Government Service Provision 1995, AGPS, Canberra.

1997, Report on Government Services Provision 1997, AGPS, Canberra.

1998a, Report on Government Services 1998, AGPS, Canberra.

1998b, Superannuation in the Costing of Government Services, AusInfo, Canberra.

1999, Report on Government Services 1999, AusInfo, Canberra.

Steering Group Elder Care Canterbury 1998, *A Project to Integrate and Improve Health Services for Older People*, Elder Care Canterbury, Christchurch.

Stoelwinder, J. U. 1984, 'Commentary: A New Way to Fund Australia's Public Hospitals', *Australian Health Review*, 7(2): 118–20.

Street, A. and Duckett, S. J. 1996, 'Are Waiting Lists Inevitable?' *Health Policy*, 36: 1–15.

Swerissen, H. and Duckett, S. 1996, 'Specific Purpose Programs in Human Services and Health: Moving from an Input to an Output and Outcome Focus', *Australian Journal of Public Administration*, 55(3): 7–17.

1997, 'Health Policy and Financing', in H. Gardner (ed.), *Health Policy in Australia*, Oxford University Press, Melbourne, 13–45.

Sylva, K. 1997, 'Critical Periods in Childhood Learning', *British Medical Bulletin*, 53: 185–97.

Syme, L. 1986, 'Strategies for Health Promotion', *Preventative Medicine*, 15: 492–507.

1997, 'To Prevent Disease', in D. Blane, E. Brunner and R. Wilkinson (eds), *Health and Social Organisation*, Routledge, London.

Tehan, M. 1993, 'A Message from the Minister for Health', in *Casemix Funding for Public Hospitals: Victoria's Policy*, DHCS, Melbourne.

Tengs, T. O. and Meyer, G. et al. 1996, 'Oregon's Medicaid Ranking and Cost-Effectiveness', *Medical Decision Making*, 16(2): 99–107.

Titulaer, I., Tricket, P. and Bhatia, K. 1998, *Rural Public Health in Australia—1997*, AIHW, Canberra.

Turrell, G. 1995, 'Social Class and Health: A Summary of the Overseas and Australian Evidence', in G. Lupton and J. Najman (eds), *Sociology of Health and Illness: Australian Readings*, Macmillan, Melbourne.

UK Green Paper 1998, *Our Healthier Nation: A Contract for Health*, Cmd 3854, HMSO, <http://www.official −documents.co.uk/document/ohnation>.

Upton, Hon. S., Minister for Health 1991, *Your Health and the Public Health: A Statement of Government Policy*, GP Print Ltd, Wellington.

Van de Ven, W. P. M. M. 1996, 'Market-oriented Health Care Reforms: Trends and Future Options', *Social Science and Medicine*, 43(5): 655–66.

Victorian Commission of Audit 1993, *Report*, vol. 1, Government Printer, Melbourne.

Victorian Health System Review 1992, *Final Report*, vol. 1, Victorian Health System Review, Melbourne.

Victorian Hospitals' Association 1988, *Privatise Public Hospitals?* discussion paper, Victorian Hospitals' Association, Melbourne.

Viney, R. C., Keith, A., Williams, P. and Laffey, J. 1991, 'Case Payment: A New South Wales Perspective', *Australian Health Review*, 14(3), 235–44.

Wadsworth, M. 1997, 'Changing Social Factors and their Long Term Implications for Health', *British Medical Bulletin*, 53:198–209.

Ward, J. T. 1969, 'The Economics of Health services', in J. Latimer (ed.), *Health Administration in New Zealand*, NZ Institute of Public Administration, Wellington.

Wen, X., Madden, R. and Black, K. 1995, *Population Indicators of Needs for Disability Services: An Exploration*, Welfare Division Working Paper no. 9, AIHW, Canberra.

Whitehead, M. 1994, 'Is it Fair? Evaluating the Equity Implications of the NHS Reforms', in R. Robinson and J. Le Grand (eds), *Evaluating the NHS Reforms*, King's Fund Institute Policy Journals, Newbury.

Wilkinson, R. G. 1996, *Unhealthy Societies: The Afflictions of Inequality*, Routledge, London/New York.

Williams, A. 1988, 'Priority Setting in Public and Private Health Care: A Guide Through the Ideological Jungle', *Journal of Health Economics*, 7: 173–8

Williamson, O. E. 1975, Markets and Hierarchies: Analysis and Antitrust Implications, Free Press, New York.

Willis, E. 1989, *Medical Dominance: The Division of Labour in Australian Health Care*, Allen & Unwin, Sydney.

Wills, P. J. and the Committee of the Health and Medical Research Strategic Review 1999, *The Virtuous Cycle—Working Together for Health and Medical Research*, AusInfo, Commonwealth of Australia, Canberra.

Wilson, R. M., Runciman, W. R., Gibberd, R. W., Harrison, B. T., Newby, L. and Hamilton, J. D. 1995, 'The Quality in Australian Health Care Study', *Medical Journal of Australia*, 163: 469

World Bank 1993, *World Development Report 1993*, Oxford University Press, New York.
1997a, 'Expanding the Measure of Wealth: Indicators of Sustainable Development', CSD edn, Draft for Discussion, World Bank, Washington DC, pp. 5–15.
1997b, World Bank Report 1997: The State in a Changing World, Oxford University Press, New York.

World Health Organisation (WHO) 1978, *Primary Health Care: Report of the International Conference on Primary Health Care*, Alma-Ata, 'Health for All' Series, no. 1, WHO, Geneva.
1994, World Health Statistics: Annual 1993, WHO, Geneva.
1997, European Health Care Reform: Analysis of Current Strategies, WHO Regional Office for Europe, Copenhagen.

Wyke, A. 1997, 21st Century Miracle Medicine: Robosurgery, Wonder Cures and the Quest for Immortality, Plenum Press, New York.

Young, J. M. and Ward, J. E. W. 1999, 'General Practitioners' Use of Evidence Databases', *Medical Journal of Australia*, 170: 56–8.

Index

1. *Because nearly all entries in this index relate to health reform, only two entries are included under this specific head: health reform—conclusions, and health reform—definition. For other aspects of health reform, consult other heads.*
2. *Because nearly all entries relate to health reform in Australia and/or New Zealand, entries under Australia and New Zealand are restricted to matters that relate specifically to one or other nation. Please also refer to other major heads for information relating more generally to these nations.*
3. *For abbreviations used in this index, see pp. xx–xxii*